International Development Resource Books
Pradip K. Ghosh, editor

DISARMAMENT AND DEVELOPMENT
A Global Perspective

Pradip K. Ghosh, *Editor*

Foreword by Gamani Corea, Secretary-General of UNCTAD

Prepared under the auspices of the Center for International Development,
University of Maryland, College Park, and the World Academy of Development
and Cooperation, Washington, D.C.

International Development Resource Books, Number 17

Greenwood Press
Westport, Connecticut • London, England

Library of Congress Cataloging in Publication Data
Main entry under title:

Disarmament and development.

  (International development resource books, ISSN 0738-
1425; no. 17)
  Bibliography: p.
  Includes index.
  1. Disarmament. 2. Economic development.
  3. Developing countries. 4. Arms race. I. Ghosh,
Pradip K., 1947-   . II. Series.
JX1974.D512 1984   338.4'7355   83-26683
ISBN 0-313-24153-8 (lib. bdg.)

Library of Congress Catalog Card Number: 83-26683
ISBN: 0-313-24153-8
ISSN: 0738-1425

First published in 1984

Greenwood Press
A division of Congressional Information Service, Inc.
88 Post Road West, Westport, Connecticut 06881

Printed in the United States of America

10 9 8 7 6 5 4 3 2 1

PART II

STATISTICAL INFORMATION AND SOURCES

Contents

TO

ALVA MYRDAL

IN GRATEFUL RECOGNITION OF HER LEADERSHIP ROLE
IN DISARMAMENT RESEARCH

" Think what we could do if we were all
of us - to channel these vast sums of money
(for arms) into other fields ! we could
eliminate pockets of poverty. We could
improve health and education, If this
is true true for the United States how
much more must it apply to the developing
countries."

Eleanor Roosevelt, 1963

Copyright Acknowledgments

Reprinted with the permission of the Population Council from "The urban prospect: Reexamining the basic assumptions," by Lester R. Brown, *Population and Development Review* 2, no. 2 (June 1976): 267–277.

Reprinted with the permission of the Population Council from "Food for the future: A perspective," by D. Gale Johnson, *Population and Development Review* 2, no. 1 (March 1976): 1–19.

Reprinted with the permission of the Population Council from "Population, development, and planning in Brazil," by Thomas W. Merrick, *Population and Development Review* 2, no. 2 (June 1976): 181–199.

Reprinted with the permission of the Population Council from "Observations on population policy and population program in Bangladesh," by Paul Demeny, *Population and Development Review* 1, no. 2 (December 1975): 307–321.

Reprinted with the permission of the Population Council from "Population policy: The role of national governments," by Paul Demeny, *Population and Development Review* 1, no. 1 (September 1975): 147–161.

Reprinted with the permission of the Population Council from "Asia's cities: Problems and options," by Kingsley Davis, *Population and Development Review* 1, no. 1 (September 1975): 71–86.

Articles from *Impact of Science on Society,* Vol. XXIX, no. 3, © Unesco 1979. Reproduced by permission of Unesco.

Articles from *Impact of Science on Society,* Vol. XXIII, no. 4, © Unesco 1973. Reproduced by permission of Unesco.

Articles from *Impact of Science on Society,* Vol. XXV, no. 1, © Unesco 1975. Reproduced by permission of Unesco.

Articles from *Impact of Science on Society,* Vol. XX, no. 3, © Unesco 1972. Reproduced by permission of Unesco.

Articles from *Impact of Science on Society,* Vol. XXIII, no. 2, © Unesco 1973. Reproduced by permission of Unesco.

Articles from *Impact of Science on Society,* Vol. XXV, no. 3, © Unesco 1975. Reproduced by permission of Unesco.

Articles from *Impact of Science on Society,* Vol. XXIV, no. 2, © Unesco 1974. Reproduced by permission of Unesco.

Articles from *Scientists, the Arms Race and Disarmament,* © Unesco 1982. Reproduced by permission of Unesco.

Articles from *The Use of Socio-Economic Indicators in Development Planning,* © Unesco 1976. Reproduced by permission of Unesco.

Articles from *Methods for Development Planning: Scenarios, Models and Micro-Studies,* © Unesco 1981. Reproduced by permission of Unesco.

Article from *Socio-Economic Indicators for Planning: Methodological Aspects and Selected Examples,* © Unesco 1981. Reproduced by permission of Unesco.

PART II

STATISTICAL INFORMATION AND SOURCES

The Third World

Afghanistan
  Republic of Afghanistan
Algeria
  Democratic and Popular
  Republic of Algeria
Angola
  People's Republic of Angola
Argentina
  Argentine Republic
Bahamas
  Commonwealth of the Bahamas
Bahrain
  State of Bahrain
Bangladesh
  People's Republic of
  Bangladesh
Barbados
  People's Republic of
  Barbados
Benin
  People's Republic of Benin
Bhutan
  People's Republic of Bhutan
Bolivia
  Republic of Bolivia
Botswana
  Republic of Botswana
Brazil
  Federative Republic of Brazil
Burma
  Socialist Republic of the
  Union of Burma
Burundi
  Republic of Burundi

Cambodia
  Democratic Kampuchea

Cameroon
  United Republic of Cameroon
Cape Verde
  Republic of Cape Verde
Central African Empire
Chad
  Republic of Chad
Chile
  Republic of Chile
Colombia
  Republic of Colombia
Comoro Islands
  Republic of the Comoros
Congo
  People's Republic of the
  Congo
Costa Rica
  Republic of Costa Rica
Cuba
  Republic of Cuba
Dominican Republic
Ecuador
  Republic of Ecuador
Egypt
  Arab Republic of Egypt
El Salvador
  Republic of El Salvador
Equatorial Guinea
  Republic of Equatorial
  Guinea
Ethiopia
Fiji
  Dominion of Fiji
Gabon
  Gabonese Republic
Gambia
  Republic of the Gambia

Ghana
  Republic of Ghana
Grenada
  State of Grenada
Guatemala
  Republic of Guatemala
Guinea
  Republic of Guinea
Guinea-Bissau
  Republic of Guinea-Bissau
Guyana
  Cooperative Republic of
  Guyana
Haiti
  Republic of Haiti
Honduras
  Republic of Honduras
India
  Republic of India
Indonesia
  Republic of Indonesia
Iran
  Imperial Government of Iran
Iraq
  Republic of Iraq
Ivory Coast
  Republic of Ivory Coast
Jamaica
Jordan
  Hashemite Kingdom of Jordan
Kenya
  Republic of Kenya
Kuwait
  State of Kuwait
Laos
  Lao People's
  Democratic Republic
Lebanon
  Republic of Lebanon
Lesotho
  Kingdom of Lesotho
Liberia
  Republic of Liberia
Libya
  People's Socialist
  Libyan Arab Republic

Madagascar
  Democratic Republic
  of Madagascar
Malawi
  Republic of Malawi
Malaysia
Maldives
  Republic of Maldives
Mali
  Republic of Mali
Mauritania
  Islamic Republic
  of Mauritania
Mauritius
Mexico
  United Mexican States
Mongolia
  Mongolian People's Republic
Morocco
  Kingdom of Morocco
Mozambique
  People's Republic
  of Mozambique
Nepal
  Kingdom of Nepal
Nicaragua
  Republic of Nicaragua
Niger
  Republic of Niger
Nigeria
  Federal Republic of Nigeria
Oman
  Sultanate of Oman
Pakistan
  Islamic Republic of Pakistan
Panama
  Republic of Panama
Papua New Guinea
Paraguay
  Republic of Paraguay
Peru
  Republic of Peru
Philippines
  Republic of the Philippines
Qatar
  State of Qatar

Adopted from THE THIRD WORLD: PREMISES OF U.S. POLICY by W. Scott
Thompson, Institute for Contemporary Studies, San Francisco, 1978.

Abbreviations

ADC	Andean Development Corporation
AsDB	Asian Development Bank
ASEAN	Association of South-East Asian Nations
CARIFTA	Caribbean Free Trade Association
DAC	Development Assistance Committee (of OECD)
ECA	Economic Commission for Africa
ECE	Economic Commission for Europe
ECLA	Economic Commission for Latin America
ECOWAS	Economic Commission of West African States
EDF	European Development Fund
EEC	European Economic Community
EFTA	European Free Trade Association
ESCAP	Economic and Social Commission for Asia and the Pacific
FAO	Food and Agriculture Organization of the United Nations
GATT	General Agreement on Tariffs and Trade
GDP	gross domestic product
GNP	gross national product
IBRD	International Bank for Reconstruction and Development (World Bank)
IDA	International Development Association
IDB	Inter-American Development Bank
IFC	International Finance Corporation
IIEP	International Institute for Educational Planning
ILO	International Labour Office
IMF	International Monetary Fund
LAFTA	Latin American Free Trade Association
ODA	official development assistance
OECD	Organisation for Economic Co-operation and Development
OPEC	Organization of Petroleum Exporting Countries
UNDP	United Nations Development Programme
UNEP	United Nations Environment Programme
UNESCO	United Nations Educational, Scientific and Cultural Organization
UNHCR	Office of the United Nations High Commissioner for Refugees
UNITAR	United Nations Institute for Training and Research
UNICEF	United Nations Children's Fund
UNIDO	United Nations Industrial Development Organization
WFP	World Food Programme
WHO	World Health Organization

Rhodesia
Ruanda
  Republic of Ruanda
Samoa
Sao Tome and Principe
  Democratic Republic of
  Sao Tome and Principe
Saudi Arabia
  Kingdom of Saudi Arabia
Senegal
  Republic of Senegal
Seychelles
Sierra Leone
  Republic of Sierra Leone
Singapore
  Republic of Singapore
Somalia
  Somali Democratic Republic
Sri Lanka
  Republic of Sri Lanka
Sudan
  Democratic Republic of
  the Sudan
Surinam
Swaziland
  Kingdom of Swaziland
Syria
  Syrian Arab Republic
Tanzania
  United Republic of Tanzania

Thailand
  Kingdom of Thailand
Togo
  Republic of Togo
Trinidad and Tobago
Tunisia
  Republic of Tunisia
Uganda
  Republic of Uganda
United Arab Emirates
Upper Volta
  Republic of Upper Volta
Uruguay
  Oriental Republic of Uruguay
Venezuela
  Republic of Venezuela
Vietnam
  Socialist Republic of Vietnam
Western Sahara
Yemen
  People's Democratic Republic
  of Yemen
Yemen
  Yemen Arab Republic
Zaire
  Republic of Zaire
Zambia
  Republic of Zambia

Countries which have social and economic characteristics in
common with the Third World but, because of political
affiliations or regimes, are not associated with Third
World organizations:

China
  People's Republic of China
Cyprus
  Republic of Cyprus
Israel
  State of Israel
Kazakhstan
Kirghizia
Korea
  Democratic People's Republic
  of Korea
Romania
  Socialist Republic of Romania

South Africa
  Republic of South Africa
South West Africa
  Namibia
Tadzhikistan
Turkmenistan
Uzbekistan
Yugoslavia
  Socialist Federal Republic
  of Yugoslavia

Foreword

I am pleased to know of the International Development Resources Bock project. The 20 resource books which are published under this project, covering the whole spectrum of issues in the fields of development economics and international co-operation for development, and containing not only current reading materials but alsc up-to-date statistical data and bibliographical notes, will, I am sure, prove to be extremely useful to a wide public.

I would like to commend the author for having undertaken this very ambitious and serious project and, by so doing, rendered a most valuable service. I am confident that it will have a great success.

Gamani Corea

Secretary-General
United Nations Conference on Trade and Development

Preface

Stimulus for the publication of an international resource book series was developed in 1980, while teaching and researching various topics related to third world development. Since that time, I have built up a long list of related resource materials on different subjects, usually considered to be very important for researchers, educators, and public policy decision makers involved with developing country problems. This series of resource books makes an attempt for the first time to give the reader a comprehensive look at the current issues, methods, strategies and policies, statistical information and comprehensive resource bibliographies, and a directory of various information sources on the topic.

This topic is very important because within the framework of the current international economic order, developing an effective disarmament and development: global perspective policy is envisaged as a dynamic instrument of growth essential to the rapid economic and social development of the developing countries, in particular of the least developed countries of Asia, Africa and Latin America.

Much of this work was completed during my residency as a visiting scholar in the Center for Advanced Study of International Development at Michigan State University. Suzanne Wilson, Mary Ann Kozak, Kathy White and Susan Costello, students at the University, provided much needed assistance with the project. I am thankful to the M.S.U. Sociology department for providing necessary support services and Dr. James T. Sabin, Vice President, editorial of Greenwood Press who encouraged me in pursuing the work and finally agreeing to publish in book form.

I would also like to gratefully acknowledge the encouragement given to me by Dr. Denton Morrison to pursue this project and Dr. Mark Van de Vall who has been an inspiration to me since my graduate school days.

Finally, preparation of this book would not have been completed without the contributions from Robert McNamara, Inga Thorsson, Nicole Ball, Milton Leitenbert, Essam Galal, Christoph

Bertram, Peter Lock, Herbert Wulf, Alva Myrdal, Stephen Oluwole Awokoya, Barry M. Blechman, Edward R. Fried, Sam Cole, Olu Adeniji, Bernard Feld, Alfonso Garcia-Robles, Michel Rogalski, Carlos Yakubovich, Jan Oberg, Bert Rolig and many experts from the Stockholm Peace Research Institute and the UNEP and the Secretary General of the U.N. I am also gratefully indebted to Journal of Economic Literature, U.N. Documents and World Bank Publications for the much needed annotations, and a very special thanks to Tom and Jackie Minkel for their assistance in the preparation of this book in camera ready form.

PART I
CURRENT ISSUES, TRENDS, ANALYTICAL METHODS, STRATEGIES AND POLICIES, COUNTRY STUDIES

Introduction

This resource book has two multifaceted purposes. Firstly, to document and analyze the current trends in the global arms race and its impact on the third world countries--and to evaluate the progress made by them during the past decade in attaining long term objectives of a sustained economic growth and improvement in the quality of living future populations.

We are all very much familiar with the problems of Third World countries, usually described by Latin America (excluding Cuba) the whole of Africa, Asia (excluding its socialist countries, Japan and Israel) and Oceania (excluding Australia and New Zealand). They are plagued by poverty, very high rates of population growth, low growth rates of gross domestic product, low rates of industrialization, extremely high dependence on agriculture, rate of unemployment, and uneven income distribution. Although the expression "Third World countries" no longer has a clear meaning, majority of the international development experts would consider the poor developing countries to belong in the third world irrespective of their affiliation as aligned or non-aligned characteristic.[1]

Secondly, major purpose of this volume is to provide the researchers with the much needed knowledge about the different sources of information and available data related to arms race and development. Arms race in the developing countries have raised many complex issues. While these issues are largely dependent on national policies and priorities, their solution is of international concern.

It must be acknowledged that the arms race and development are in a competitive relationship, particularly in terms of resources but also in the vital dimension of attitudes and perceptions. The main conclusion of this report is that an effective relationship between disarmament and development can and must be established.

Economic growth and development would, of course, take place even with a continuing arms race but it would be relatively slow and highly uneven geographically. The cooperative management of interdependence, on the other hand, can be demonstrated to

be in the economic and security interests of all States.   But the adoption or rather the evolution of such an outlook is quite improbable if the arms race and failures to observe the principles of the United Nations Charter continue.

It would be virtually impossible to dispute the desirability of reversing the arms race in order to speed up the process of socio-economic development.   But the very disappointing history of disarmament efforts on the one hand, and the less than satisfactory results so far in establishing a new international economic order on the other, have underlain the regrettable reluctance   among   some   States   to   perceiving   a disarmament-development relationship.   Against this background, concrete   measures   within   the   framework   of   disarmament   for development   might   have   a   psychological   and   political   impact affecting positively the relations between developed and developing countries and thus international peace and security.

The third world countries are still in urgent need of greater allocations   to   meet   the   expanding   demands   of   their   growing populations.   But the developed world is also beginning to confront the   cumulative   results   of   its   past   patterns   of resource-utilization.   The marked economies are facing serious socio-economic   problems   like   unemployment   and   inflation.   The centrally   planned   economies   are   also   under   considerable   strain to make faster progress in achieving better consumer satisfaction and greater modernization in view of a slow-down in growth rates. For the world as a whole, the allocation of 5 to 6 percent of global   output   for   militray   purposes   is   becoming   a   questionable proposition in a climate of sluggish economic growth performance for   the   1980s,   as   compared   to   the   more   favourable   economic performance in earlier decades.[2]

The   imcompatibility   between   the   objectives   of   a   new international economic order and the recent trends in the arms race,   already   recognized   by   the   General   Assembly   at   its   Tenth Special   Session   of   the   United   Nations   (resolution   S-10/2),   has been confirmed by the Group's findings on the spill-over effects of the arms race into the area of international economic relations. Drawing upon empirical evidence to substantiate this point, the Group's   perception   of   the   disarmament-development   relationship suggests   that   its   political   recognition   would,   in   the   longer term,   significantly   expand   the   economic   and   social   horizons   of mankind.   Adoption of policies reflecting this relationship should be viewed positively rather than negatively, not as an unfortunate and   hazardous   necessity   but   as   one   of   those   all   too   rare opportunities   in   which   the   reallocation   of   resources   results in   a   substantial   increase   in   output   both   in   the   sector relinquishing the resources and in the sector that gains these resources.

The effect on the economic and social spheres in our societies of the arms race extend far beyond the fact that 5 to 6 percent of the world's resources are not available to help satisfy socially productive needs.   The very fact that these resources are spent on   armaments   accentuates   the   inefficient   allocation   of   the remaining 94 to 95 percent, within and between nations.   Three fundamental   characteristics   of   the   arms   race   reinforces   this disallocation: first,   the   sheer   magnitude   of   the   volume   of

resources;   second,   the   composition   of   expenditure,   most
particularly   the   stress   on   R   and   D,   affecting   investment   and
productivity   in   the   civilian   sector;   and   third,   the   fact   that
this massive effort has now been sustained for over thirty years.

As   an   illustration   of   the   contribution   which   can   be   made
by   disarmament   measures,   even   limited,   to   world   development,
one study submitted to the Group projects global economic prospects
under   three   types   of   hypothetical   scenarios,   viz.,   a   continued
arms   race,   and   modest   disarmament   measures   involving   the   release
of   some   resources   for   reallocation   to   the   developing   countries.
Utilizing   the   United   Nations   input-output   model   of   world   economy
it   is   calculated   that   an   acceleration   of   the   arms   race   would
adversely   affect   global   economic   well-being   in   all   but   one   of
the regions of the world.

In   contrast,   a   scenario   of   even   modest   disarmament   measures
is   shown   to   yield   higher   per   capita   consumption   for   different
regions   and   in   addition   bring   about   a   higher   world   GDP,   a   larger
capital   stock,   a   general   increase   in   the   agricultural   output,
to   mention   only   a   few   of   the   obvious   economic   gains.   Besides
these   global   economic   gains,   a   scenario   of   modest   disarmament
would   also   yield   significant   benefits   for   the   poorest   regions
of   the   world.   This   conclusion   is   by   itself   of   considerable
significance   when   it   is   remembered   that   in   many   cases,   increases
in   military   outlays   by   industrial   countries   have   been   accompanied
by   a   decline   in   their   aid   transfers,   despite   the   repeated   request
for   the   fulfilment   of   the   UN   targets   for   official   development
assistance   and   despite   the   fact   that   existing   volumes   of   assistance
are   grossly   inadequate   to   meet   the   basic   aid   requirements   for
the   poorer   countries.   The   report   shows   that   even   a   minor   part
of   savings   from   dramatically   enhancing   present   levels   of
assistance.

We   can   make   similar   calculations   for   the   past.   For   instance,
if   half   the   funds   spent   on   armaments   throughout   the   world   from
1970   to   1975   had   instead   been   invested   in   the   civilian   sector,
it   has   been   calculated   that   annual   output   at   the   end   of   that
period   would   have   been   200,000   million   dollars   higher   than   it
actually   was--a   figure   in   excess   of   the   aggregate   GNP   of   Southern
Asia   and   the   mid-African   regions.   And   mark   well,   this   growth
would   most   likely   have   been   achieved   without   any   extra   demand
for investible resources.[3]

This   book   focuses   attention   on   some   of   the   major   problems
faced   by   the   third   world   countries   and   the   policy   issues   posed
by   those   problems.   It's   aim   is   to   highlight   some   generalizations
that   serve   as   pointers   to   needed   disarmament   policies.   The   limited
extent   to   which   statistical   information   is   cited   in   this   book
is solely for illustrative purposes.

It   is   hoped   that   this   resource   book   will   be   of   use   not   only
to   those   directly   involved   in   the   formulation   and   implementation
of   development   policies   but   also   will   help   to   acquaint   a   wide
reading   audience   with   the   linkages   between   disarmament   and
development policies.

The   plan   of   the   reading   materials   in   Part   I   of   the   book
and   the   selection   of   the   seventeen   pieces   represents   a   specific

orientation, or bias. They present current international issues and trends affecting arms race in third world development, analytical methods, strategies and policies for disarmament.

Part II includes statistical information and a descriptive bibliography of information sources related to disarmament and development in the third world countries.

Part III is a select bibliography of books, documents and periodical articles published since 1970, relevant to disarmament and development. Annotations for the different titles have been compiled from The Journal of Economic Literature, International Social Sciences Index, U.N. Documents Index, World Bank Publications, Finance and Development, Book Publisher's promotion brochures and the IMF-IBRD Joint Library Publications.

Part IV consists of a directory of information sources. This section is in four parts, directory of United Nation information sources, listing of bibliographic sources, titles of selected periodicals published around the world and a directory of institutions involved in research relevant to disarmament and peace problems in the third world countries.

[1]Rodwin Lloyd, "Regional Planning Perspectives in Third World Countries," in TRAINING FOR REGIONAL DEVELOPMENT PLANNING: PERSPECTIVES FOR THE THIRD DEVELOPMENT DECADE, ed. by, Om Prakash Mathur, UNCRD, 1981.
Thompson, W. Scott, THE THIRD WORLD: PREMISES OF U.S. POLICY Institute for Contemporary Studies, San Francisco, 1978.

[2]"The Relationship Between Disarmament and Development", Report of the Secretary-General, DEVELOPMENT: SEEDS OF CHANGE, 1982: 1, pp. 16-20.

[3]Thorsson, Inga, "The Arms Race and Development: A Competitive Relationship", DEVELOPMENT: SEEDS OF CHANGE, 1982: 1, pp. 12-16.

The Relationship Between Disarmament and Development

SECRETARY-GENERAL OF THE UNITED NATIONS

I. SUMMARY, CONCLUSIONS AND RECOMMENDATIONS

This investigation suggests very strongly that the world can either continue to pursue the arms race with characteristic vigour or move consciously and with deliberate speed toward a more stable and balanced social and economic development within a more sustainable international economic and political order. It cannot do both. It must be acknowledged that the arms race and development are in a competitive relationship, particularly in terms of resources but also in the vital dimension of attitudes and perceptions. The main conclusion of this report is that an effective relationship between disarmament and development can and must be established.

Economic growth and development would, of course, take place even with a continuing arms race but it would be relatively slow and highly uneven geographically. The cooperative management of interdependence, on the other hand, can be demonstrated to be in the economic and security interests of all States. But the adoption or rather the evolution of such an outlook is quite improbable if the arms race and failures to observe the principles of the United Nations Charter continue.

It would be virtually impossible to dispute the desirability of reversing the arms race in order to speed up the process of socio-economic development. But the very disappointing history of disarmament efforts on the one hand, and the less than satisfactory results so far in establishing a new international economic order on the other, have underlain the regrettable reluctance among some States to perceiving a disarmement-development relationship.

From **DEVELOPMENT: SEEDS OF CHANGE**, 1982:1, reprinted by permission of the publisher.

Against this background, concrete measures within the framework of
disarmament for development might have a psychological and
political impact affecting positively the relations between
developed and developing countries and thus international peace and
security.

Several past studies on the relationship between disarmament
and development, including a United Nations report on the subject
in 1972[1] reflect a note of caution in projecting too close an
association between them. In most cases, this cautious attitude
reflects goals contingent upon each other which could somehow be
seen to detract from the urgency of achieving fast progress in each
separately. Most of these studies, therefore, were content with
projecting the enormous contrasts between the magnitude of
resources claimed by the world-wide military activities and the
relatively modest outlays required to provide for the basic unmet
needs of the poorer sections of society, particularly in the
developing countries. The relationship between disarmament and
development thus acquired a strong normative content on the basis
of its desirability.

The developing countries are still in urgent need of greater
allocations to meet the expanding demands of their growing
populations. But the developed world is also beginning to confront
the cumulative results of its past patterns of
resource-utilization. The marked economies are facing serious
socio-economic problems like unemployment and inflation. The
centrally planned economies are also under considerable strain to
make faster progress in achieving better consumer satisfaction and
greater modernization in view of a slow-down in growth rates. For
the world as a whole, the allocation of 5 to 6 percent of global
output for military purposes is becoming a questionable proposition
in a climate of sluggish economic growth performance for the 1980s,
as compared to the more favourable economic performance in earlier
decades.

Another worrisome development in the changed socio-economic
context for this study, however, is the growing uncertainty in
East-West relations spilling into the entire field of international
economic relations. The danger of politico-strategic
considerations influencing these relations is more real than ever
before. It seems likely that progress in establishing a new
international economic order will be adversely affected by the arms
race, which not only claims resources but also influences the scope
and content of international economic cooperation. To the extent
that achievements in the international economic order are affected
by the dynamics of the arms race, the relationship between
disarmament and development involves more than a contrast between
the resources claimed by military activities and the basic unmet
needs of the poorer sections of society. Also the normative appeal
to direct some of the armament-related resources into the
developmental field acquires an element of self-interest if it can
be demonstrated that the need for such a reallocation is shared by
all social systems irrespective of their current levels of
development.

A major objective of the present study, therefore, was to look
beyond the strong normative and logical arguments to examine how

the disarmament-development relationship might influence viable policy-options of States, firmly rooted in their own enlightened national interest. The moral and rational appeal of the relationship is not questioned, but is reiterated. Moreover, the Group has been able to assemble substantial historical and empirical evidence for viewing it as an economic imperative.

The conceptual basis for this study is described in chapter II, which defines the framework and scope of the relationship between disarmament and development. After examining the conventional exposition of the subject, in the light of recent development, the Group has placed the disarmament-development relationship in the context of a triangular interaction between disarmament, development and security.

As with the concept of security, the Group has also adopted a broad definition of development which, besides the need for sustained economic growth, would involve the opportunity and responsibility for full participation in the economic and social processes and a universal share in its benefits as a result of profound economic and social changes in society. In projecting development as a global requirement, the Group has outlined the dimensions of economic interdependence and contrasted the benefits of cooperative management with the potential threats inherent in continuing an attitude of preserving the status quo. Relying upon recent experiences to demonstrate that the economic fortunes -- and thus the security -- of all nations are interdependent and destined to become more so, the Group has argued that failure to bring the arms race under control is likely to be associated with a vicious circle of confrontation and mutual denial, with declining prospects for mutually advantageous economic cooperation and shrinking options for all nations. Developments in East-West detente and in the North-South dialogue in recent years illustrate this possibility.

The incompatibility between the objectives of a new international economic order and the recent trends in the arms race, already recognized by the General Assembly at its Tenth Special Session of the United Nations (resolution S-10/2), has been confirmed by the Group's findings on the spill-over effects of the arms race into the area of international economic relations. Drawing upon empirical evidence to substantiate this point, the Group's perception of the disarmament-development relationship suggests that its political recognition would, in the longer term, significantly expand the economic and social horizons of mankind. Adoption of policies reflecting this relationship should be viewed positively rather than negatively, not as an unfortunate and hazardous necessity but as one of those all too rare opportunities in which the reallocation of resources results in a substantial increase in "output" both in the sector relinquishing the resources and in the sector that gains these resources. The appalling dimensions of poverty, the threatening scarcities, the destruction of the environment and the resultant global economic malaise are problems largely of our own making. It is, in principle, well within our collective technological and intellectual capabilities and within the earth's carrying capacity to provide for the basic needs of the world's entire population and to make progress toward

a more equitable economic order at a pace politically acceptable to all.

In sum, the Group's study has confirmed that the sustained arms race represents a critical, and still intensifying, challenge for mankind. The danger of war is currently growing, owing to the new dimensions assumed by armaments competition -- quantitative and qualitative, conventional and nuclear -- and to the use or threat of use of force by States in non-conformity with the principles of the United Nations Charter. The greatest danger to all mankind, and one that would put its very existence in jeopardy, is the risk of any conflict leading to the use of nuclear weapons. The need to prevent this risk is becoming all the more urgent. At the same time -- and this is an aspect that the Group's investigation have led it to emphasize very strongly -- the protracted arms race has entailed serious economic and social consequences for the people of all nations. Taken together, these considerations underline the extreme urgency of abandoning the use of force in international relations and taking concrete measures toward disarmament, under effective international control.

The magnitude of resources claimed by world-wide military activities are described in chapter III. In it, the prevailing use for military purposes of labour, industrial capacity, raw materials and land is documented as comprehensively as possible.

The Group's calculations and projections about the use of raw materials for military purposes are made against the background of serious concern over the availability of adequate supplies of oil and minerals, that is, non-renewable raw materials. While visualizing no immediate exhaustion of supplies till the end of the century, the Group foresees some difficulties in terms of dependable access to supplies of raw materials. Realizing that current projections of demand vis-a-vis known reserves are based largely on the historical pattern and growth of consumption, the Group feels that accelerated growth and industrialization in the developing countries could have a significant impact on their general validity. Very rough extrapolations based upon published estimates of the United States share in the consumption of a selected group of non-energy minerals for military purposes, suggest that anything between 3 to 11 percent of 14 such minerals are utilized world-wide for military purposes. The use of petroleum for military purposes, including indirect consumption in military industry, has been estimated at 5 to 6 percent of total global consumption.

The available data on the land area used for military purposes is far too sketchy to permit reliable global estimates. While it is negligible as an absolute share of world-wide land utilization and vast areas of land in the world are of no more interest to the military than to other land users, the military use of land is not without consequence. Moreover, as an indication of trends, military requirements for land have risen steadily over the course of this century owing to increases in the size of standing armed forces and, more particularly, the rapid pace of technological advances in weaponry. Despite its small relative share in the use of land, the military can and often does compete directly with civilian demands, be they urban, industrial, agricultural,

recreational or based on environmental concerns.

The world military R and D effort also has some characteristics which cannot be reflected in a statistical portrayal. In the first place, the technological arms race has complicated the process of political assessment and efforts to control the race through negotiation. Secondly, military R and D expenditure is even more highly concentrated than total R and D. While six countries account for about 85 percent of total R and D, just two countries account for a similar share of military R and D.

Since international trade in arms is not officially recorded in world trade statistics, no comprehensive and official body of data is available. Rough estimates, however, indicate that almost $26 billion is annually traded in the international traffic in arms. Besides the transfer of military hardware, arms transactions also involve large-scale training programmes and, for an extended interim period, technical personnel as part of a weapons deal. Crudely estimated, these "services" constitute approximately 15 percent of the current global value of the arms trade.

In chapter IV, the Group examined a series of questions: Can a world faced with a universal slow-down of economic performance afford to continue the use of real resources for military purposes on the scale just summarized? Is it possible to demonstrate that the present socio-economic problems are, to some extent, a cumulative result of the past patterns of military consumption? Will the multiplicity of costs conventionally associated with military outlays be less tolerable in the future than those perceived in the past? What are the direct and indirect benefits likely to follow a reversal of the present trends in the arms race? These and other related issues are addressed in that chapter, which analyses the socio-economic consequences of the arms race and implementation of disarmament measures.

The historical and empirical evidence analysed by the Group has made it take a position that military outlays, by definition, fall into the category of consumption and not investment. Consequently, steadily high or increasing military outlays are likely to have a depressing effect on economic growth, directly through displacement of investment and indirectly through constraints on productivity which itself depends to a considerable degree on the R and D effort currently biased in favour of military technology. The co-existence of high levels of military spending and high rates of economic growth in the past cannot be taken as evidence of a causal relationship between the two. The availability of unutilized and under-utilized resources among the less developed economies may produce short-term results suggesting a parallelism between high rates of growth and significant military spending. But in the long term, the totality of adverse socio-economic consequences of sizeable military outlays outweigh any immediate spin-offs.

In accordance with the explicit directive from the General Assembly, the Group has given special attention to the burden-measurement and opportunity costs of the arms race for the developing countries. Military outlays put unequal burdens on economies at different levels of national income, working thereby to the detriment of less developed economies. Also, their urgent

need for an uninterrupted flow of external inputs like capital, finance, trade and technology makes the less developed economies susceptible to the effects of military outlays in the developed world, in addition to the burden of their own military spending. The developing countries are, thus, the worst affected victims of an adverse strategic environment dominated by the seemingly endless arms race among its major participants.

But policies pursued in implementing the disarmament-development relationship to the benefit of the developing countries will also improve the universal economic prospects. The catalytic effect of strengthening the economic content of detent will by itself be a major dividend for East-West relations. Besides, an improved economic performance by the South will stimulate demand in the North and significantly improve its employment opportunities. Rough estimates about the global consequences of gradual reductions in military spending, proportionate to the magnitude of current military outlays among different countries, suggest that the diversion of a part of released resources to developing countries will (a) substantially improve the per capita GDP, industrial employment and capital stock for the developing countries; and (b) provide significant economic gains for all the regions in the world including the most developed.

The need to view the disarmament-development relationship in a dynamic economic environment has been further elaborated in chapter V, which examines the technological feasibility and economic potentials of the process of conversion from military to civilian purposes. While recognizing the importance of the post-war conversion or reconversion experience, the Group has argued that the problem is now so influential and ingrained that preparing for its solution cannot be defferred until disarmament measures are agreed upon. The character of the military sector has changed dramatically over the post-war period and conversion of resources now used for military purposes will be qualitatively different from the demobilization exercises following past world conflagrations and military conflicts.

The world-wide defence industry is characterized by a high degree of geographical and sectoral concentration. It also involves a considerable degree of specialization in its work-force and a very pronounced emphasis on research and development, particularly in economies with sophisticated military sectors. This apparent exclusiveness of the defence industry should not, however, prove to be an insurmountable problem because:

-- Conversion and redeployment is not a phenomenon uniquely associated with disarmament. Any form of economic and social change represents a continuous process of conversion. Particularly in modern industrial economies, the factors of production must respond continuously to the development of new products and the phasing-out of old ones and to the introduction of new production techniques;

-- A significant part of military demand is directed at goods and services that are essentially identical to those consumed in the civilian sector. In this case, the problem is a relatively minor one of ensuring that civilian demand fills the gap left by

cutbacks in military spending. Primary responsibility for conversion, in an over-all sense, will inevitably fall on the central government, particularly in regard to initiating preparations for such a process. The nature and extent of government involvement, following disarmament measures, in the process of conversion itself will vary from country to country, depending in large part on the type of economic system but also on many other factors.

A relatively major problem in preparing for conversion, however, pertains to resources unsuited for the production of civilian goods such as those involved in combat aircraft, missiles, warships, tanks and so on. The primary need here would be for advance consideration of how their capabilities can be altered to permit the smoothest possible transition to the production of socially useful goods and services. A commitment to preparing for conversion will be an investment in minimizing the problems of transition. Such a commitment would entail thinking through the problems likely to be encountered by workers, industries and communities in the event of reductions in military business and devising measures and arrangements to overcome or minimize them.

While advance preparations for conversion will go a long way in mitigating the displacement effects on personnel and industries, a diversion of the converted human and material resources into the less developed economies could provide an additional cushioning effect against any major economic disruption in the economies with high military spending. In this respect, prevailing and prospective economic conditions throughout the industrialized world are clearly not favourable. Their economic difficulties are to some extent symptoms, not merely of a temporary cyclical downturn, but of a more profound economic malaise. The saturation of major consumer markets and the emergency of serious supply-side constraints on economic growth -- energy, raw materials, pollution and so on -- all suggest the need for significant changes in the structure of industry, in the direction of future investment and in the pattern of consumer demand. The Group's argument about the transitional difficulties associated with conversion being lessened, if cast in a framework of international cooperation, is based upon growing evidence suggesting that the pattern of imports of capital goods by developing countries would coincide significantly with the productive capacities released by disarmament measures in the industrialised countries. More than one of the Group's case studies of disarmament and conversion have indicated that, when increased resource transfers to developing countries were factored in as one of the options for conversion, it was found that the transfer policy least disruptive for the converting economies involved goods and services closely matching the new emphasis in developing countries on providing basic needs and promoting self-reliance, that is, agricultural machinery, fishing technology, machinery for mining, manufacturing, construction and hydropower plants and equipment and personnel for education and health programmes.

Possible institutional arrangements for the transfer of additional resources released through disarmament measures to the developing countries are considered in <u>chapter VI</u> which examines

the various proposals made in the United Nations to that effect. In doing so, and in accordance with the mandate of the General Assembly, the Group gave particular consideration to the French proposal, made at the Tenth Special Session, for the establishment of an international disarmament fund for development. It is realized that the Second Disarmament Decade and the Third United Nations Development Decade are passing by without concrete achievements on either front, thus giving little scope for optimism. But in its examination of the technical feasibility and political realism of a fund-type institutional link between disarmament and development, the Group's view was influenced by its general position that resources involve more than finances.

Three basic contributory principles are found in the various proposals for promoting the reallocation of financial resources from armaments to development:

-- The armaments levy approach, in which national assessments for development contributions are based on some measure of States' allocation of resources for military purposes;

-- Voluntary contributions on the model of numerous other United Nations organizations and specialized agencies;

-- The disarmament dividend approach, in which the savings resulting from disarmament measures, or a portion thereof, are allocated to development needs.

In the context of a disarmament-development relationship, the Group considered a disarmament dividend approach as the most attractive among the three examined. This approach was also found implicit in the second phase of the French proposal, although the initial stage of its implementation relies mostly on an armament-levy type of approach. This attempt to combine a levy with a dividend certainly constitutes an important political initiative, but its full technical implications remain to be examined both on grounds of feasibility and acceptance by the major military spenders.

On the basis of its findings and conclusions, implicit in this entire report and more explicitly summarized above, the Group makes the following recommendations:

1. That all Governments, but particularly those of the major military Powers, should prepare assessments of the nature and magnitude of the short and long-term economic and social costs attributable to their military preparations so that their general public be informed of them.

2. That Governments urgently undertake studies to identify and to publicize the benefits that would be derived from the reallocation of military resources in a balanced and verifiable manner, to address economic and social problems at the national level and to contribute towards reducing the gap in income that currently divides the industrialized nations from the developing world and establishing a new international economic order.

3. A fuller and more systematic compilation and dissemination by Governments of data on the military use of human and material

resources and military transfers.

4. That the disarmament-development perspective elaborated in this report be incorporated in a concrete and practical way in the ongoing activities of the United Nations systems.

5. That Governments create the necessary prerequisites, including preparations and, where appropriate, planning, to facilitate the conversion of resources freed by disarmament measures to civilian purposes, especially to meet urgent economic and social needs, in particular, in the developing countries.

6. That Governments consider making the results of experiences and preparations in their respective countries available by submitting reports from time to time to the General Assembly on possible solutions to conversion problems.

7. That further consideration be given to establishing an international disarmament fund for development and that the administrative and technical modalities of such a fund be further investigated by the United Nations with due regard to the capabilities of the agencies and institutions currently responsible for the international transfer of resources.

8. That the Secretary-General take appropriate action, through the existing inter-agency consultative mechanism of the Administrative Committee on Coordination, to foster and coordinate the incorporation of the disarmament and development perspective in the programmes and activities of the United Nations systems.

9. That the Department of Public Information and other relevant United Nations organs and agencies, while continuing to emphasize the danger of war -- particularly nuclear war -- should give increased emphasis in their disarmament-related public information and education activities to the social and economic consequences of the arms race and to the corresponding benefits of disarmament.

NOTES

[1]Disarmament and Development, ST/ECA/174 (United Nations publication, Sales No. E.73.IX.1).

Development and the Arms Race

ROBERT MCNAMARA

The old order is certainly passing. Perhaps the beginning of
its breakdown can be dated from that cold December day in 1942 when
a few hundred yards from where we are now sitting the first nuclear
chain reaction began. The consequences of that even were to
transform our whole concept of international security because now
man had the capacity not merely to wage war, but to destroy
civilisation itself.

If I may on this occasion speak quite personally, I had of
course to wrestle with the problem of the fundamental nature of
international security during my tenure as U.S. Secretary of
Defense, and in 1966 I spoke publicly about it in a speech to the
American Society of Newspaper Editors in Montreal.

My central point was that the concept of security itself had
become dangerously over-simplified. There had long been an almost
universal tendency to think of the security problem as being
exclusively a military problem, and to think of the military
problem as being primarily a weapons-system or hardware problem.

"We tend to conceive of national security", I noted, "almost
solely as a state of armed readiness: vast, awesome arsenal of
weaponry". But, I pointed out, if one reflects on the problem more
deeply it is clear that force alone does not guarantee security
and that a nation can reach a point at which it does not buy more
security for itself simply by buying more military hardware.

That was my view then. It remains my view now.

No nation can avoid the responsibility of providing an
appropriate and reasonable level of defense for its society. In an
imperfect world that is necessary. But what is just as necessary
is to understand that the concept of security encompasses far more
than merely military force, and that a society can reach a point at
which additional military expenditure no longer provides additional

From **DEVELOPMENT: SEEDS OF CHANGE**, 1982:1, reprinted by permission
of the publisher.

security.

Indeed, to the extent that such expenditure severely reduces the resources available for other essential sectors and social services -- and fuels a futile and reactive arms race -- excessive military spending can erode security rather than enhance it.

Many societies today are facing that situation. Certainly the world as a whole is. Any sensible way out of the problem must begin with the realisation of the dangers and disproportionate costs that extravagant military spending imposes on human welfare and social progress.

Global defense expenditures have grown so large that it is difficult to grasp their full dimensions.

The overall total is now in excess of $400 billion a year.

An estimated 36 million men are under arms in the world's active regular and paramilitary forces, with another 25 million in the reserves, and some 30 million civilians in military-related occupations.

Public expenditures on weapons research and development now approach $30 billion a year, and mobilise the talents of half a million scientists and engineers throughout the world. That is a greater research effort than is devoted to any other activity on earth, and it consumes more public research money than is spent on the problems of energy, health, education, and food combined.

The United States and the Soviet Union together account for more than half of the world's total defense bill, and for some two-thirds of the world's arms trade.

And yet it is not in the industrialised nations, but in the developing countries that military budgets are rising fastest.

On average around the world, one tax dollar in six is devoted to military expenditure, and that means that at the present levels of spending the average taxpayer can expect over his lifetime to give up three or four years of his income to the arms race.

And what will he have bought with that? Greater security? No. At these exaggerated levels, only greater risk, greater danger, and greater delay in getting on with life's real purposes.

Is there any way, then, to moderate the mad momentum of a global arms race?

No very easy way, given the degree of suspicion and distrust involved. But, as one who participated in the initial nuclear test ban arrangements, and other arms limitation discussions, I am absolutely convinced that sound workable agreements are attainable. These matters clearly call for realism. But realism is not a hardened, inflexible, unimaginative attitude. On the contrary, the realistic mind should be a restlessly creative mind -- free of naive delusions, but full of practical alternatives.

Eleven years in the Bank, combined with visits to some 100 of the developing countries, have contributed immeasurably to my international understanding. They have permitted me to explore the whole new world that has come to political independence -- in large part over the past quarter century.

I have met the leaders of this new world -- their Jeffersons Washingtons and Franklins -- and have sensed their pride and their peoples' pride in their new national independence, and their frustrations at their economic dependence.

I have shared their sense of achievement at the remarkable rate of economic growth which many of them attained, largely by their own efforts. But I have been appalled by the desperate plight of those who did not share in this growth, and whose numbers rose relentlessly with the great tide of population expansion.

There are today more than one billion human beings in the developing countries whose incomes per head have nearly stagnated over the past decade. In statistical terms, and in constant prices, they have risen only about two dollars a year: from $130 in 1965 to $150 in 1975. But what is beyond the power of any set of statistics to illustrate is the inhuman degraduation the vast majority of these individuals are condemned to because of poverty. Malnutrition saps their energy, stunts their bodies, and shortens their lives. Illiteracy darkens their minds, and forecloses their futures. Preventable diseases maim and kill their children. Squalor and ugliness pollute and poison their surroundings. The miraculous gift of life itself, and all its intrinsic potential -- so promising and rewarding for us -- is eroded and reduced for them to a desperate effort to survive.

The self-perpetuating plight of the absolute poor tends to cut them off from the economic progress that takes place elsewhere in their own societies. They remain largely outside the entire development effort, neither able to contribute much to it, nor benefit fairly from it.

And when we reflect on this profile of poverty in the developing world we have to remind ourselves that we are not talking about merely a tiny minority of unfortunates. On the contrary, we are talking of about 40 percent of the total population of over 100 countries.

Is the problem of absolute poverty in these nations solvable at all? It is. And unless there is visible progress towards a solution we shall not have a peaceful world. We cannot build a secure world upon a foundation of human misery.

Now how can we help lift this burden of absolute poverty from off the backs of a billion people? It is clear that we in the richer countries cannot do it by our own efforts. Nor can they, the masses in the poorest countries; do it by their own efforts alone. There must be a partnership between a comparatively small contribution in money and skills from the developed world, and the developing world's determination both to increase its rate of economic growth, and to channel more of the benefits of that growth to the absolute poor. Most of the effort must come from the developing countries' own governments. By and large they are making that effort.

In the past decade, the poor nations have financed over 80 percent of their development investments, out of their own meager incomes. But it is true they must make even greater efforts. They have invested too little in agriculture, too little in population planning, and too little in essential public services. And too much of what they have invested has benefitted only a priviledged few.

That calls for policy reforms, and that is, of course, always politically difficult. But when the distribution of land, income, and opportunity becomes distorted to the point of desperation,

political leaders must weigh the risk of social reform against social rebellion. "Too little too late" is history's universal epitaph for political regimes that have lost their mandate to the demands of landless, jobless, disenfranchised, and desperate men.

In any event, whatever the degree of neglect the governments in the poor countries have been responsible for, it has been more than matched by the failure of the developed nations to assist them adequately in the development task.

Today, Germany, Japan, and the United States are particularly deficient in the level of their assistance. The case of the United States is illustrative. It enjoys the largest gross national product in the world. And yet it is currently one of the poorest performers in the matter of Official Development Assistance. Among the developed nations, Sweden, the Netherlands, Norway, Australia, France, Belgium, Denmark, Canada, New Zealand, and even -- with all its economic problems -- the United Kingdom: all of these nations devote a greater percentage of their GNP to Official Development Assistance than does the U.S. In 1949, at the beginning of the Marshall Plan, U.S. Official Development Assistance amounted to 2.79 percent of GNP. Today, it is less than one-tenth of that, 0.22 percent of GNP. And this after a quarter century during which the income of the average American, adjusted for inflation, has more than doubled.

There are, of course, many sound reasons for development assistance. But the fundamental case is, I believe, the moral one. The whole of human history has recognised the principle that the rich and powerful have a moral obligation to assist the poor and the weak. That is what the sense of community is all about -- any community: the community of the family, the community of the nation, the community of nations itself.

Moral principles, if they are really sound -- and this one clearly is -- are also practical ways to proceed. Social justice is not simply an abstract ideal. It is a sensible way of making life more livable for everyone. Now it is true that the moral argument does not persuade everyone. For those who prefer arguments that appeal to self-interest, there are some very strong ones.

Exports provide one out of every eight jobs in U.S. manufacturing, and they take the output of one of every three acres of U.S. farm land -- and roughly one-third of these exports are now going to the developing countries. Indeed, the U.S. now exports more to the developing countries that it does to Western Europe, Eastern Europe, China, and the Soviet Union combined. Further, the U.S. now gets increasing quantities of its raw materials from the developing world -- more than 50 percent of its tin, rubber, and manganese plus very substantial amounts of tungsten and cobalt, to say nothing of its oil. The U.S. economy, then, increasingly depends on the ability of the developing nations both to purchase its exports, and to supply it with important raw materials. And the same sort of relationship of mutual interdependence exists between the other industrialised countries -- the Common Market, and Japan -- and the developing world.

Thus, for the developed nations to do more to assist the developing countries is not merely the right thing to do, it is

also increasingly the economically advantageous thing to do. What will it cost the United States and the other industrialised countries to do more? Far less than most of us imagine.

The truth is that the developed nations would not have to reduce their already immensely high standard of living in the slightest, but only devote a miniscule proportion of the additional per capita income they will earn over the coming decade. It is not a question of the rich nations diminishing their present wealth in order to help the poor nations. It is only a question of their being willing to share a tiny percentage -- perhaps 3 percent -- of their incremental income.

It is true that the developed nations, understandably preoccupied with controlling inflation, and searching for structural solutions to their own economic imbalances, may be tempted to conclude that until these problems are solved, aid considerations must simply be put aside. But support for development is not a luxury -- something desirable when times are easy, and superfluous when times become temporarily troublesome. It is precisely the opposite. Assistance to the developing countries is a continuing social and moral responsibility, and its need now is greater than ever.

Will we live up to that responsibility? As I look back over my own generation -- a generation that in its university years thought of itself as liberal -- I am astonished at the insensitivity that all of us had during those years to the injustice of racial discrimination in our own society. Will it now take another 50 years before we fully recognise the injustice of massive poverty in the international community? We cannot let that happen. Nor will it happen -- if we but turn out minds seriously to the fundamental issues involved. Increasingly the old priorities and the old value judgments are being reexamined in the light of the growing interdependence between nations -- and it is right that they should be. Once they are thought through, it will be evident that international development is one of the most important movements underway in this century. It may ultimately turn out to be the most important.

Our task, then, is to explore -- a turbulent world that is shifting uneasily beneath our feet even as we try to understand it. And to explore our own values and beliefs about what kind of a world we really want it to become.

The Arms Race and Development: A Competitive Relationship

INGA THORSSON

Common sense alone tells us that military preparations are an economic burden. The arms race and development are to be viewed in a competitive relationship, particularly in terms of resources. Or to put it another way: the arms race and underdevelopment are not two problems; they are one. they must be solved together, or neither will ever by solved.

It is a historical fact that governments have, over the past 30 years, spent vast resources on armaments, resources which -- on grounds of morality, on grounds of equal human justice, on grounds of enlightened self interest -- ought to have been directed to ending world poverty and building for human and material development. In this way world armaments are among the causes of poverty and underdevelopment.

The 1972 U.N. study on this same theme concluded that disarmament and development "stand fundamentally apart". Taking their point of departure, this statement is still true. Ten years ago and, as duties of the industrialized countries went, development was simply equated with development assistance. But since then, the development discussion has been broadened to involve basic structural changes in all societies, within states and among states, including more equitable distribution of income, access to the means of production and greater participation by all groups in decision making, and progress towards the establishment of a New International Economic Order.

In the present study we have introduced a new conceptual framework, defined in a dynamic triangular interrelation between disarmament, development and security. We have taken a broader approach to the problem of security. In our era, national security can no longer be equated with military might. Even less can international security, i.e. security for all, do so. Also, we

From **DEVELOPMENT: SEEDS OF CHANGE**, 1982:1, reprinted by permission of the publisher.

demonstrate that threats to security may be made and aggravated in many ways, including those that go far beyond purely military threats. It was recognized by the first Special Session on Disarmament that the arms race itself has become a threat to the security of nations. Thus, disarmament, particularly nuclear disarmament, would directly enhance security, and, therefore, prospects for development.

National security is not a goal in itself. Its ultimate purpose must be to secure the independence and sovereignty of the national state, the freedom of its citizens -- freedom and the means to develop economically, socially and culturally, which defines exactly what we mean by "development". In today's world this can never be achieved by any state at the expense of others. In a world of interdependence, only through global, or international security, will it be possible to reach the objective of national security for the ultimate goal of freedom, well-being and human dignity for people throughout the world.

Today there is an array of intensifying non-military threats which aggravate the security problems of states. Such non-military threats can be described as:

-- widespread reductions in prospects for economic growth;
-- existing or impending ecological stresses, resource scarcities -- notably in the field of energy and certain non-renewable raw materials -- and a growing world population. Today's stresses and constraints may translate into tomorrow's economic stresses and political conflicts;
-- the morally unacceptable and politically hazardous polarization of wealth and poverty.

The appalling dimensions of poverty, the destruction of the environment, the accelerating race for arms and the resulting global economic malaise are largely problems of our own making. The Group states that it is well within our collective capabilities and within the earth's carrying capacity to provide for basic needs for the world's entire population, and to make progress towards a more equitable economic order, at a pace politically acceptable to all. The Group reaffirms that the arms race is incompatible with the objectives of a New International Economic Order. Of course, also in the future, economic growth is possible even with a continuing arms race, but it would be relatively slow, and very unevenly distributed both among and within regions of the world. We show, on the other hand, that a co-operative management of interdependence can be in the economic and security interests of all states. But the adoption or rather the evolution of such an outlook is quite improbable if the arms race continues.

It is imperative that non-military challenges to security are treated as non-military. If this is not recognized, if states fail to accept and persevere in tackling these challenges through voluntary measures and co-operation, there is a grave risk that the situation will deteriorate to the point of crisis where, even with a low probability of success, the use of military force could be seen as a way to produce results sufficiently quickly. This is far from being a remote possibility. In recent time there has been a

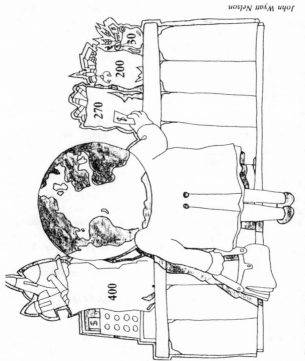

John Wyatt Nelson

Global military expenditure has increased 30-fold since 1900. It now absorbs well over $ 400 billion a year - approaching $ 1 million per minute - and if the current trend continues, could reach $ 1,000 billion a year in current prices by year 2000. - UNEP 1980.

marked and increasing tendency in international relations actually to use or threaten to use military force in response to non-military challenges, not only to "security", but also to the secure supply of goods and the well-being of the nations which face these challenges.

The study has documented that at least 50 million people are directly or indirectly engaged in military activities world-wide. This figure includes, inter alia, an estimated 500,000 qualified scientists and engineers engaged in research and development for military purposes.

Military research and development remains by far the largest single objective of scientific enquiry and technological development. Approximately 20 per cent of the world's qualified scientists and engineers were engaged in military work at a cost of around 35,000 million dollars in 1980, or approximately one-quarter of all expenditure on research and development. Virtually all this R and D takes place in the industrialized countries, 85 per cent in the USA and the USSR alone. Adding France and Britain would push this share above 90 per cent.

It stands to reason that even a modest reallocation to development objectives of the current capacity for military R and D could be expected to produce dramatic results in fields like resource conservation and the promotion of new patterns of development, better adapted to meeting the basic needs of ordinary people. This is, inter alia evident from the fact, which is also among our findings, that, on an average, a military product requires 20 times as much R and D resources as a civilian product.

The 1972 report on the subject identified more than 70 possible alternative uses. Our present investigations suggest, in more elaborated and detailed ways, for instance, that production workers in the military sector could quite easily transfer their skills to the development, production and installation of solar energy devices. Environment, housing and urban renewal are other areas likely to gain from the possible rechanneling of military R and D. New transport systems, particularly in urban areas, are sorely needed and have long been regarded as a major civilian alternative for the high technology industries in the military sector.

In purely financial terms, world-wide military expenditures by 1981 exceed, as we all know, the astounding level of 520,000 million dollars, representing 6 per cent of world output. Member States certainly realize that this amount is roughly equivalent to the value of all investible capital in all developing countries combined.

The effect on the economic and social spheres in our societies of the arms race extend far beyond the fact that 5 to 6 per cent of the world's resources are not available to help satisfy socially productive needs. The very fact that these resources are spent on armaments accentuates the inefficient allocation of the remaining 94 to 95 per cent, within and between nations. Three fundamental characteristics of the arms race reinforces this disallocation: first, the sheer magnitude of the volume of resources; second, the composition of expenditure, most particularly the stress on R and D, affecting investment and productivity in the civilian sector;

and <u>third</u>, the fact that this massive effort has now been sustained for over thirty years.

As an illustration of the contribution which can be made by disarmament measures, even limited, to world development, one study submitted to the Group projects global economic prospects under three types of hypothetical scenarios, <u>viz</u>., a continued arms race, an accelerated arms race, and modest disarmament measures involving the release of some resources for reallocation to the developing countries. Utilizing the United Nations input-output model of world economy it is calculated that an acceleration of the arms race would adversely affect global economic well-being in all but one of the regions of the world. A wealth of numerical data is presented in <u>chapter III</u> of the report. I will here highlight some general results. Besides the negative impact on per capita consumption, an accelerated arms race will also result in a decline of the world's stock of capital, reduce the value of non-military, exports, and entail reductions in industrial employment in the poorest regions of the world.

In contrast, a scenario of even modest disarmament measures is shown to yield higher per capital consumption for different regions and in addition bring about a higher world GDP, a larger capital stock, a general increase in the agricultural output, to mention only a few of the obvious economic gains. Besides these global economic gains, a scenario of modest disarmament would also yield significant benefits for the poorest regions of the world. This conclusion is by itself of considerable significance when it is remembered that in many cases, increases in military outlays by industrial countries have been accompanied by a decline in their aid transfers, despite the repeated request for the fulfilment of the UN targets for official development assistance and despite the fact that existing volumes of assistance are grossly inadequate to meet the basic aid requirements for the poorer countries. The report shows that even a minor part of savings from modest disarmament has the potential of dramatically enhancing present levels of assistance.

We can make similar calculations for the past. For instance, if half the funds spent on armaments throughout the world from 1970 to 1975 had instead been invested in the civilian sector, it has been calculated[1] that annual output at the end of that period would have been 200,000 million dollars higher than it actually was -- a figure in excess of the aggregate GNP of Southern Asia and the mid-African regions. And mark well, this growth would most likely have been achieved without any extra demand for investible resources.

Military outlays fall by definition into the category of consumption and not investment. As a consequence, steadily high or increasing military outlays tend to depress economic growth. This effect may be direct through displacement of investment, and indirect through constraints on productivity.

A study conducted in the late 1960s by Emile Benoit is much cited as showing that military outlays do not have negative effects on economic growth for developing countries. In reality Benoit's own conclusion was more modest.[2] He said:

Thus we have been unable to establish whether the net growth effects of defence expenditures have been positive or not. On the basis of all the evidence we suspect that it has been positive for the countries in our sample, and at past levels of defence burden, but we have not been able to prove this.

This suspected positive relationship of Benoit's has been contested as spurious, since it was simultaneously correlated with other important socio-economic factors in the economies of those developing countries, particularly a high net inflow of foreign assistance. Based on today's level of research, it can now be confidently refuted. In our study we do recognize that the availability of unutilized and underutilized resources in developing countries may produce short-term results, suggesting a parallelism between high rates of growth and significant military spending, a situation which is, by the way, frequently associated with foreign dependence. In the long run, however, the totality of the socio-economic consequences of sizeable military outlays outweigh any immediate economic spinoffs into the civilian sector.

On the basis of the present report, and the research commissioned for it, we can confidently conclude that military budgets are deadend expenditures in all kinds of economies, be they market, centrally planned, or mixed; be they industrialized or developing. Military expenditures do <u>not</u> foster growth. Through their inflationary effects -- thoroughly analysed in the study -- and the general economic and political malaise to which they contribute, military spending <u>inhibits</u> the capital investment required for development. Through the drain on the most valuable research talents and funds, it <u>restrains</u> productivity gains and <u>distorts</u> growth in science and technology. The military sector is not a great provider of jobs. On the contrary it is shown that military spending is one of the least efficient kinds of public spending. It drains away funds that could relieve poverty and distress. The very nature of military spending heightens tensions, reduces security and underpins the system which makes even more arms necessary.

This study has in my view strengthened the economic and social case for the disarmament-development relationship by identifying military spending as an impediment to economic growth and social development and the arms race as an obstacle to the establishment of a New International Economic Order.

The Group has indicated the political and economic potentials of rationally imperative alternatives in suggesting that policies aimed at implementing the disarmament-development relationship are likely to broaden the base of East-West detente and put the North-South dialogue in a mutually advantageous frame of reference.

Its report should not be considered an individual project. I should like to express a hope for an effective follow-up process, to the benefit, first of all, of the billions of human beings inhabiting this world of ours.

NOTES

[1]United Nations Disarmament Fact Sheet, No. 9, "Cost of the Arms Race", 1979.

[2]Emile Benoit, Defence and Economic Growth in Developing Countries, Lexington Books, 1973, p. 4.

Disarmament and Development: Their Interrelationship

NICOLE BALL
MILTON LEITENBERG

I. THE INDUSTRIALIZED AND DEVELOPING COUNTRIES

Since 1960, the United Nations has been concerned with identifying the links which exist between disarmament and social and economic development, especially for developing nations. While a recent UN report stated that 'disarmament and development are closely related in material fact', most other UN resolutions and reports have stressed the need to 'establish' such a link.[1] Ordinarily, it is assumed that the 'disarmers' will be the industrialized nations -- especially the United States and the Soviet Union -- while the 'developers' will be the developing countries. Because the industrialized nations account for some 80% of world military expenditures -- with the US and the USSR alone spending between 50 and 60% of the world total, depending on the accounting methodology used -- this is not an unreasonable distinction to make. Therefore, it is clear that substantial reduction in the military outlays of this group of countries -- and particularly of the US and the USSR -- is essential if meaningful disarmament is to occur. However, it cannot be said that such reductions would <u>automatically</u> result in social or economic development for either the industrialized or the developing countries.

It is increasingly argued that military expenditures in the industrialized countries act as a brake on developed-nation economic growth. This effect is said to occur primarily because military expenditures divert capital for investment and manpower for scientific research and development from the civilian sector. More specifically, it has been suggested that military industries

From **BULLETIN OF PEACE PROPOSALS**, Vol. 10, No. 3, 1979, (247-259), reprinted by permission of the publisher.

in industrialized countries absorb much of the capacity of
precisely those sectors -- transport machinery, machinery,
chemicals, electronics -- which are most dynamic in terms of
exports. Where economic growth is 'export-led' such absorption of
export capacity by military expenditure reduces the potential for
economic growth.[2] Inflation has also been linked to high levels of
military expenditure in industrialized countries. (To the extent
that inflation is 'exported' to developing nations through higher
prices for the import of technology or of manufactured goods and so
on, this is also a development-related problem.) Though this claim
of a link is often made, there is rather surprisingly virtually no
body of empirical research demonstrating a causal relationship
between military expenditures and inflation. The claim derives
from the classical economic statement that military spending tends
to be inflationary because it adds to the purchasing power of the
work force without producing goods that they can buy. First, this
would theoretically obtain only in a situation of full employment.
Second, this situation can -- in equally classical economic
terms -- be modulated by taxation policies. Another major
mechanism by which it is suggested that military expenditure
contributes to inflation in peacetime is by driving up the prices
of resources and skilled labor, which are not under the same
competitive restraints in the defense production sector as they are
in other commercial sectors, producing an effect which then spreads
to the rest of the economy.[3]

II. REALLOCATION OF RESOURCES: WORDS AND DEEDS

Even if military expenditure of industrialized countries does
reduce their growth rate, lower military spending may not result in
economic and social development for either developed or developing
nations. The reallocation of resources is a political matter which
depends on the political priorities of governments. The fate of
two attempts at reduction is illustrative.
In 1973, the Soviet Union proposed that the permanent members
of the UN Security Council cut their defense expenditures by 10% on
one occasion, and that they donate 10% of the money thus saved to
economic development of developing nations. The United States,
Great Britain, and France underlined the difficulties involved in
reaching mutually agreeable military expenditure figures for each
country, while the US termed as 'impractical' any attempt to link
defense expenditure reduction with development. China saw the
Soviet proposal as no more than an attempt to disguise an expansion
of the Soviet military. Once the UN Secretariat attempted to
create a mechanism for arriving at mutually agreeable estimates of
military expenditures, the Soviet Union announced that such an
effort 'would lead to unnecessary difficulties in the practical
solution of the question,'[4] when it was precisely the only
practical solution to the question. It is unimaginable that the US
and its Western allies would, in the present political climate,

agree to a proposal in which the 10% cut from Soviet military expenditures would be deducted from the announced Soviet figure for its own military expenditure. The Soviet figure is 25-30% of what the actual Soviet military expenditure is estimated to be by Western defense ministries. For its part, the USSR refuses, and has always refused, any bilateral or multinational exercise to determine just what its military expenditure is, using indices analagous to those used by Western nations in calculating military expenditure. The USSR proposals have been put forward in a way that most observers would even assume were calculated to assure Western refusal. In turn, the Soviet Union flatly rejects the Western attempts to set a context in which they would consider such proposals.

It is clear that political questions relating to comparative military balances and military forces were paramount for the permanent members of the Security Council in determining their response to the 10% military expenditure reduction proposals. Their reactions serve to underline, particularly at the present moment, their overwhelming involvement in the politics of East-West military competition, rather than a primary concern for development. The reality in 1978 and in recent years is reflected in the announcement by a number of countries of increases in military expenditures, in several cases quite sharp increases.

In 1976, France announced a 14.2% increase in its defense budget from the 1975 level; in 1977, a 16.8% increase over 1976 spending; for 1979, a 14% increase over 1978.[5] At the same time, France's Foreign Minister expressed the following sentiments:

> Another important concern of the international community results from the build-up of nuclear and conventional weapons, a senseless waste of resources -- $350 billion a year -- that could surely be put to better use for development. So arms reduction is clearly one of the priorities today.[6]

It is pertinent, particularly in regard to the 10% military expenditure reduction proposals just discussed, to indicate the degree of political cliche capable of being spoken by everyone, irrespective of their actions. There are virtually dozens of similar statements by Soviet spokesmen. Such statements, most often made at the UN, reflect the priorities of almost no one.

Between 1971 and 1976, Japan's real annual increase in defense spending was 4.6%. The Japanese defense budget for FY 1977 contained a 13.7% increase over that of 1976; for FY 1978, there was an additional 12.4% increase.[7] Military expenditures of the Warsaw Treaty Organization nations have risen constantly at least since 1966, with particularly sharp increases in 1972-73, 1973-74, and 1975-76. Further increases were requested this year, which apparently produced a minor diplomatic crisis upon Romania's refusal to accede to the request.[8] USSR military expenditure has been rising by a nearly constant percentage of 3-5% since 1964. The constant increase and the absence of severe resource constraints on military spending since 1964, despite apparent difficulties with various sectors of the Soviet economy during the

same period, underline the degree to which Soviet military expenditure is politically determined. The announced USSR defense budget for FY 1979 is approximately one-third the amount estimated by US and British government agencies.[9]

In the United States, President Carter has forsaken his Presidential campaign pledge to reduce military spending, and his Administration has effected two successive increases in military expenditure, after accounting for inflation, of around 2.7%. Increases in US military expenditure at the same rate have been projected for the next four years as well.[10] These increases are part of a NATO effort to increase military expenditure by 3% in each member country for several years. The 1978 legislative experience of a transfer amendment in this US Congress -- a measure that would have cut the defense budget by $4.8 billion and transferred the funds to social programs -- was disastrous. The Senate bill was voted down by a 77-14 margin on April 25. A more modest reduction of $1.4 billion in military spending was killed on a 70-21 vote. In the House of Representatives, despite a substantial debate dominated by pro-transfer amendment forces, the amendment failed on a 313-98 count on May 3. The only bright spot in the US budget battle over defense expenditures was the general failure of advocates of increased military spending to add more for military expenditure above the increases requested by the Administration.

As for the developing nations themselves, SIPRI data have indicated the relatively sharper rise -- from very much lower absolute levels -- of the rate of increase of military expenditure. The basic trend over the past twenty years has been the relatively rapid rate at which military spending has increased in the Third World, compared with military spending in Europe and North America. In 1957, the two major alliances of industrialized countries -- NATO and the WTO -- accounted for 85% of total military expenditure. In 1976, this figure had fallen to 70%. The Third World share rose over this period from about 5% in 1957 to 15% in 1976. Over these two decades, military spending in the Third World increased at an average annual rate of nearly 10%, compared with a world increase of about 3%. However, military expenditure in developing nations varies considerably. Twelve nations -- five of them in the Middle East -- account for 70% of Third World military expenditure.[11]

Finally, even assuming that 1% of the military expenditure of the five permanent members of the Security Council had been turned over to developing nations in, say, 1976, this would have amounted to only about $2.8 billion.[12] While this amount is approximately 40% of the annual official economic aid given to developing countries in recent years, it is not a very considerable sum of money.

A second important example of this nature is the US-Soviet 'mutual example' reduction exercise of 1963-64. Not only was this exercise shrouded in much secrecy -- a good deal of the material relating to it remains classified -- but there apparently was absolutely no consideration given to using any money saved in any way for economic development of the developing nations. The exercise was part of a US-USSR effort to ease political tension

after the Cuban missile crisis, and other purposes it served also
pertained to US-USSR relations. Further, for domestic political
reasons, the US Administration was particularly anxious to keep the
mutual effort secret, in order not to produce domestic and
legislative political opposition, as well as opposition from the
NATO allies of the United States. However, insofar as the
reduction of US and Soviet military expenditures increases global
security and stability and provides an example for all other
countries, a continuation -- especially with a public
acknowledgement of the situation which the US government refused to
make -- of such an exercise might have had at least indirect
benefits for economic development throughout the world. However,
the exercise may already have been approaching the limits to which
the US Administration was willing to carry it when rising US
involvement in Vietnam put an end to it entirely.

III. USE OF SAVINGS FROM DISARMAMENT

    Rhetoric in favor of creating a link between disarmament and
development notwithstanding, it is clear that there are numerous
political impediments that must be recognized and overcome if,
first of all, disarmament is to take place and, then, such a link
is to be established. However, were the industrialized nations
seriously to seek reductions in arms expenditure and to use such
savings for economic growth, there are a number of ways in which
this goal might be approached.
    At least some of any military expenditure reductions will have
to be allocated to the conversion of defense industries in the
industrialized nations to forestall pressure to maintain defense
production at current levels so as not to produce new unemployment.
This has been implicitly recognized in at least two UN reports.[13]
Ideally, such conversion would be undertaken in a manner consistent
with the promotion of economic development in the developing
nations. However, the question of development-related conversion
is no longer as simple as it may have once seemed. This is
precisely because of the recognition of the need for a New
International Economic Order. Whereas in 1972, a group of UN
experts headed by Alva Myrdal could apparently argue in favor of
expanding exports from industrialized to developing nations as a
means both of compensating for reductions in defense expenditure in
the former and of encouraging development in the latter,*[14] there
is concern among developing nations to reduce their dependence on
imported manufactures, to equalize the terms of trade between
developing and industrialized countries, and to obtain more
favorable access for their manufactured goods in the industrialized
countries. Such ideas were extant in the 1950s but more attention
is being paid to them since 1975. Therefore, simply to convert
tank factories to tractor production or chemical warfare
establishments to fertilizer production -- in the hope of exporting
the output to developing nations -- will not promote social and

economic development in the Third World. In fact, based on past experience, it may positively hinder such development.**

A second repository of money saved through reductions in defense expenditures would be the developing countries themselves. Funds could either be made directly available to individual countries through some mutually agreeable distribution scheme[15] or could be donated to some international program of benefit to all developing nations, such as a commodity support scheme or research and eradication programs for a particular tropical disease. Even here there are problems. Simply to give individual developing nations money does not ensure that the money would be used to further the development process. That depends on political decisions within each country. Donor attempts to dictate the uses to which such funds were to be put might produce disagreement over what constitutes 'the development process' and over the right of individual developing nations to control that process as they see fit. Furthermore, not all international programs designed to increase the quality of life in developing nations actually succeed in doing that -- at least for the large majority of Third World populations.[16]

IV. CURBING MILITARY EXPENDITURES IN DEVELOPING COUNTRIES

There has been rather little attention given -- at least at the intergovernmental level -- to the possibility of disarmament in the developing nations as a contribution to Third World development. In part, this is because developing nations -- particularly non-oil-producing countries -- spend considerably smaller absolute amounts on defense than the industrialized nations, despite recent rises in the percentage of world military expenditure accounted for by Third World countries.[17] At the same time, Third World countries resist any consideration of curbs on their own arms expenditure in a context in which industrialized nations refuse to reduce their military spending, although the possibility remains that even with developed country arms spending reductions, Third World countries would continue to increase their military expenditures.

Following the impasse which developed in the 1973-75 period with the 10% military expenditure reduction proposal, a number of other proposals for military expenditure reductions were made, largely in the past two years in anticipation of the UN Special Session on Disarmament. Many of these have focused on reductions in Third World expenditures. One study published in 1977 under UN auspices argued that if Third World countries reduced their arms expenditures -- and used the savings either for investment or for welfare purposes -- the developmental impact would be much greater than if the industrialized countries provided Third World countries with 1% of their military expenditures on one occasion.[18] While that may be true, this study downplays the importance of developed country arms expenditures to the continuance of the arms race -- as

discussed below. It also does not question the wisdom of continuing export-oriented, foreign capital and technology-dominated development strategies which have in the past not proven highly successful for the majority of the world's population.

In fact, the relationship between military expenditure, economic growth, and social development in the Third World is not yet well understood. An increasing amount of research is only now being directed at just this relationship. As noted above, evidence does exist which demonstrates certain negative effects of military spending on economic growth in developed countries. A very large number of studies have been done on the effects of disarmament on industrialized-country economies, primarily that of the United States.[19] For the developing nations, research has centered around the impact of armament on [under]development. Virtually nothing has been written on the likely impact of disarmament on developing-nation economies, although, by implication, certain broad outlines might be discerned from those studies dealing with armament and [under]development.

V. TWO SCHOOLS OF THOUGHT: GROWTH PROPONENTS AND STRUCTURALISTS

Two broad schools of thought concerning the relationship between armament and [under]development exist. The first is primarily concerned with discovering the impact of defense expenditure on economic growth, generally regarded in terms of GNP expansion. The second school focuses on the relationship between defense expenditure, self-sustaining economic growth, and social development.[20]

The central message of the first school is that there are some growth-inducing (i.e. GNP-expanding) aspects of military expenditure in developing nations. Some analysts discuss primarily the unquantifiable characteristics which they attribute to Third World armed forces: their organizational capabilities; their discipline; their incorruptibility; their technical training; their rejection of status quo maintenance by previous political elites; their nation-building ideology.***[21] Others attempt to relate military expenditure data to GNP increases or decreases. The best-known of this latter group is the study undertaken for the US Arms Control and Disarmament Agency by Emile Benoit.[22] The Benoit study is the most ambitious statistical survey undertaken into the relationship between Third World defense expenditure and economic growth. For this reason, its conclusion -- that military expenditure does not have an identifiable negative impact and may have some positive impact on Third World economic growth -- is widely quoted. Unfortunately, there are serious problems with Benoit's analysis.

First of all, there are drastic shortcomings to the data available and to the statistical methods employed. Much of this is acknowledged by Benoit. Perhaps more seriously, there are a set of

judgmental problems which strongly bias the results of Benoit's statistical analysis and which call into question his conclusions. For example, the external aid component used in the regression analysis is composed solely of bilateral, government-to-government economic aid. Foreign private investment and multilateral economic aid is not included because they 'were not provided in order to help the recipients maintain high defense levels and would presumably have been provided without regard to the level of the defense program'.[23] Yet, omitting these financial inflows presumably understates the effect of economic aid on economic growth and allows the importance of military expenditure to be inflated.

Furthermore, Benoit shows a curious tendency to reach conclusions exactly the opposite of what his data would seem to indicate. For example, Benoit used two time-series of data: one for 1950–65 and one for 1960–65. Although the longer series is considered more reliable in statistical terms, Benoit rejected the multiple regression analysis results from that series which seemed to show that high growth rates are _not_ linked to high defense expenditures in favor of the results from the shorter time-series showing that some sort of link does exist.

For such reasons, the results of Benoit's analysis should be treated with considerable circumspection. Another statistical analysis undertaken more recently discusses the methodological shortcomings of Benoit's statistical work and proposes an alternative methodology. This study concludes that military expenditure has not significantly increased industrial development in five Latin American countries.[24] In addition, such statistical analyses are not helpful in ascribing causality -- which is, of course, precisely what Benoit was interested in doing. Nor should high rates of GNP growth be equated with the creation of self-sustaining economic growth or with social development.

The second broad school of thought on the armament-[under]development relationship is particularly concerned with the negative impact of military expenditure on the creation of self-sustaining economic growth and social development. For some, notably the UN, the misallocation of resources resulting from defense expenditure plus the low level of resource transfers to the Third World is the primary block confronting development. Other groups and individuals which recognize that at least some types of military expenditure may result in a net diversion of resources from economic development include parts of the US government and even some of those who argue in favor of the growth-inducing effects of military expenditure.[25] For others, mainly a small but growing number of academic researchers, the problem is a structural one. While this latter group agrees that misallocations of resources for military purposes can distort the development process, they argue that fundamental social and economic change within and between nations is vitally necessary if either disarmament or development is to take place.

One characteristic of the writings of most of the 'growth-inducing' school is that very general propositions are set forward which are meant to apply to all developing countries but which are at best backed by a few anecdotal observations. These

are open to counter-observations -- none of which explain much
about the actual role of military establishments and military
expenditures in the development process. The researchers concerned
with structural imbalances are, therefore, particularly interested
in investigating the ways in which military expenditures interact
in reality with different economic systems.

Over the last five years or so, several theoretical papers
have been written about the allocation of resources for military
purposes in Third World countries. While it is recognized that
in-depth studies are urgently needed to understand how the process
works in specific countries, some general propositions have been
elaborated. It is argued that it is of first importance to
understand the role played by the military (and police and/or
paramilitary force) in maintaining a status quo beneficial to the
country's leaders.****[26] It is interesting to note that this
function is the precise inverse of the interpretation offered by
the military-as-growth-inducing school. It points out that the
military as national rulers have in fact not aided development.
Both schools agree that the military serves to maintain the
'internal stability' of Third World countries. The
'growth-inducers' have thought that this was fine. In addition,
their ideological position maintained that this was necessary to
oppose the spread of communist governments. The structural critics
point out that the military elites have suppressed social change
and have not produced development. This maintenance of the
status quo directly works against the establishment of a New
International Economic Order and the adoption of 'basic human
needs' development strategies.[28]

VI. THE IMPACT OF WEAPON TRANSFERS

It is argued that equally important in maintaining an
inequitable economic and social status quo is the increased
dependence of Third World countries on industrialized ones due to
weapons imports and/or domestic arms production. One way this
occurs is by contributing to a capital-intensive industrialization
pattern -- either to produce spare parts for imported weapons or
the weapons themselves -- which makes it difficult to channel
resources into more labor-intensive enterprises. A second aspect
of this process is the transformation of social relations which
results from the transfer of military technology, a product -- like
other forms of technology -- of the society in which it has been
developed. The technological dependence on industrialized
countries is intensified by the high rate of obsolecense of
imported advanced-technology weapons.[29] The domestic production of
weapons by Third World countries does not reduce the foreign
exchange burden of military expenditures but, because no developing
country has yet become completely independent of the major weapons
producers, it may actually increase the outflow of scarce financial
resources.[30] The external dependence of Third World weapons

importers or producers is increased by the need to obtain foreign exchange for the purchase of weapons, production facilities, licenses etc. (generally accomplished by expanding exports or by obtaining foreign loans) and by the need for foreign manpower, technical and/or financial assistance in producing the infrastructure necessary if advanced-technology weapons are to be used at all. Also of relevance to the dependency issue is the desirability of exporting the finished armament to make production more economical.[31]

None of this may be incompatible with increased economic growth, especially as measured by expanding GNP:

> Armaments may facilitate growth <u>within</u> the constraints established by [structural] patterns [common to peripheral countries], though at the same time typing up resources that could be put to much better use under alternative structural arrangements.[32]

Yet, it is increasingly clear that existing structural relations between and within countries have in most cases not produced either self-sustaining economic growth or social development for the majority of Third World populations.

Almost every researcher currently studying the relationship between armament and [under]development points to the need for additional research based on the situation actually obtaining in individual countries. Both the theories set forward by those who concentrate on the 'growth-inducing' effects of military expenditure and by the structural critics can be seen as indications of the direction which future research must take. For example, the 'growth-inducers' place much importance on the 'nation-building' or 'unifying' aspect of the military. However, upon closer examination, many Third World militaries are dominated by one or another ethnic group which, far from working in the interests of the entire nation, can facilitate divisiveness and even national disintegration.[33] On the other side, the argument is made that domestically produced weapons can be more costly for Third World countries in terms of foreign exchange and R&D resources than imported weapons would be. However, much more data are needed to substantiate this thesis.

VII. THE 'PROBLEM AREAS' APPROACH

Additional pointers might be found in looking at the armament-[under]development relationship in terms of 'problem areas', such as those identified by RIO.[34] While this kind of division would be useful in ensuring that all aspects of the relationship were considered, there is a danger inherent in overcompartmentalization: the failure to analyze as a whole all the relevant pieces of a problem.

The relationship between armament and [under]development is a

complex one, any aspect of which is likely to touch on several 'problem areas' simultaneously. Take, for example, the question of the impact of military expenditure on Third World industrialization. It has been suggested that military expenditure -- particularly the import or domestic production of sophisticated weaponry -- drains capital and skills from other economically more productive uses. There is also the evidence discussed previously that attempts to reduce external dependence by expanding domestic arms production only <u>increases</u> a country's dependence on foreign technology and capital and expands its foreign exchange expenditures. Thus, at a minimum, a consideration of the relationship between military expenditure and Third World industrialization would need to touch upon questions of industrialization, trade, the international division of labor, Third World debt, multinational corporations, technology transfer (or the lack thereof), scientific R&D, and manpower resources. Focusing on one 'problem area' without reference to others would obscure the ways in which all these elements interact.

VIII. THE UNDERLYING POLITICAL CONDITIONS AND THEORIES

Both disarmament and development are political problems not amenable to the technical solutions so often proposed for them. Rather, the political conditions which serve to perpetuate both the arms race and the process of underdevelopment must be addressed. It is increasingly widely accepted that the development strategy of the 1950s and 1960s has failed to improve the conditions of life for the majority of people in the Third World. Yet, the writings of the 'growth-inducing' school are clearly rooted in the 1950s/1960s development strategy. What is not widely recognized or understood is the role which military establishments, military expenditures, arms trade and production, and military aid have played in undermining social and economic development.

For the past 25 years, the dominant development theory has focused on methods of increasing GNP, primarily through industrialization, on the benefits of foreign aid and investment, and on the expectation that resources invested in 'modernizing' elites would 'trickle down' to the rest of the population. A modern industrial sector -- created through foreign aid, investment and the transfer of technology -- was to increase the demand for agricultural products. The resultant increase in rural incomes was to expand the market for the products of industrialization. The 'communist challenge' made it imperative that development occur rapidly to forestall rebellion on the part of 'discontented' Third World populations. Because many civilian governments appeared too weak to face this challenge adequately, US academics (sometimes financed by government contracts) began to advise strengthening Third World militaries, identified as the new elite. Third World armed forces were seen as ". . . adept at creating and leading mass organizations, having the habits of discipline, hierarchical

organization, and responsible command . . .".[35]

The kinds of 'growth-inducing' benefits ascribed to military expenditure are precisely those elements required for the establishment of externally-oriented market economies. By arguing that military expenditure is not incompatible with economic growth (taken as synonymous with 'development') but may actually increase it by attracting foreign aid and investment, by training recruits in modern skills and civil applications, by providing dual-use infrastructure and services, by increasing industrialization and exports, and so on, the 'growth-inducers' both demonstrated their belief in and helped to establish more firmly the industrialization-/and growth-oriented 'trickle-down' development strategy.

In the 1960s, high economic growth rates in a number of developing countries gave the impression that 'development' was occurring. Now, however, it is evident that expanded GNP is not synonymous with economic and social development.[36] One reason for this is that the 'trickle-down' development theory has not produced the anticipated results. It has been estimated recently that under the existing development strategy more than half the world's population would not meet RIO's 'basic needs' goals by the year 2000, even with an annual GNP growth rate of 5%.[37] What has happened, after two decades 'dedicated' to international development, is that the rich have gotten richer and the poor have gotten poorer. This conclusion which, until fairly recently, was the preserve of left-wing critics of the current development strategy has now been documented in such places as the Indian government's Draft Five Year Plan 1978-1983 and the Asian Development Bank's Second Asian Agricultural Survey.[38]

What is more, for countries continuing to rely on an industrialization-/and export-oriented development strategy, conditions are likely to deteriorate over the next few years. The ILO reports that 'the flow of real resources on concessionary terms has been stagnant and, indeed, moving progressively away from the established targets'. Nor do they expect the aid situation to improve in the next few years.[39] Trade liberalization is a distinctly unpopular topic with industrialized countries facing their own economic problems. Nor is it expected that the terms of trade for primary commodities will improve significantly.[40] While by some reports the debt situation of Third World countries is improving, at least marginally, and despite some debt rescheduling and write-offs, developing country debt continues to increase. It reached $220 billion in 1978. It has been estimated that by 1980, the six largest Third World borrowers from private Western banks -- South Korea, Mexico, Brazil, Argentina, the Philippines, and Peru -- will be using 50% of all their new loans for debt servicing. A number of countries, such as Zaire, Zambia, Guyana, and Peru, have recently been in serious trouble with their debts. In Peru's case, it is now widely acknowledged that a large part of the problem has been caused by excessive arms imports.[41]

IX. ALTERNATIVE STRATEGIES—ALTERNATIVE PRIORITIES

While excess military expenditure is part of the problem for many developing nations, it is the total allocation of resources within military-led or military-dominated societies that is of greatest importance. Considerable research is necessary to understand the precise ways in which militaries have influenced a pattern of allocating resources which has either promoted or facilitated the continuation of a situation in which strategies ostensibly designed to promote 'development' have ended by enriching a minority at the expense of the majority of the world's population. Such research is vitally necessary if the new development strategies now being promoted -- New International Economic Order (NIEO) and basic human needs -- are to be pursued successfully. These new strategies are directed at equalizing relations both between and within nations. They are concerned with self-reliant economic development in which industrialization as promoted in the past will play a more peripheral role and rural/agricultural development will move more toward center stage. There is considerable interest in developing indigenous technologies and in identifying technologies with fairly high labor components.

In view of this search for an alternative development strategy, research which has concentrated on identifying the beneficial impact of military establishments and military expenditure on the expansion of GNP now seems particularly inadequate. A focus on GNP has allowed the distributional aspect of economic growth to be ignored and has helped to obscure the contribution of the rural -- largely non-monetary -- sector to the economy. Furthermore, the use of percentage of GNP devoted to different kinds of government expenditure as an indicator of a government's priorities can be quite misleading. In particular, it can grossly understate the amount of financial resources a government is devoting directly to military purposes. A fairly small (2.0-2.5%) military expenditure/GNP figure can mask a much larger (15-25%) military expenditure/national budget figure.[42]

The calls for an NIEO and a basic human needs approach to development have intensified the search for alternative measures of government priorities. One focus has been on producing 'quality of life' indices, using literacy rates, infant mortality, life expectancy, and so on. Other suggestions have included targeting different economic strata of society for different economic growth rates; targeting a certain percentage of total population for receiving a minimum standard of housing, health care, sanitation and water services, and so on by a specific date; or combining 'quality of life' indices with such targets.[43]

The table in Appendix 1 shows that there is some evidence linking higher national budget expenditures for military purposes (in percentages) with lower rankings in literacy rates, life expectancy, and infant mortality. It also shows that there are exceptions and that generalizations based on such data are difficult to make. Detailed, country analyses are required to

understand the links that do exist between the prevailing allocation of resources based on existing military relations and the prevailing structure of social and economic relations, both among and within states. For example, even 'growth-inducers' recognize that the large-scale importation of sophisticated, advanced-technology weaponry may prove more costly to developing nations -- in terms of foreign exchange, skilled labor, capital investment -- than the import of less-sophisticated arms. In addition, it has been posited that the import and/or production of such weapons affects a country's industrialization pattern and its societal organization and can increase its reliance on an export-oriented development strategy. All of these elements will militate against the self-reliant, basic human needs oriented development strategy that is increasingly being identified as essential for improvement in the conditions of life for the majority of the world's population.

At the same time, if the NIEO and the basic human needs strategies cannot succeed under existing international and domestic military relations, this does not imply a rejection of all security arrangements. What is necessary is to discover new forms of security relations compatible with NIEO and basic human needs development strategies and consistent with a less-armed world.[44] To the degree that military elites are instrumental in maintaining the status quo and in thwarting reforms through military coups, structural changes in social and economic relations probably require structural changes in military relations, both domestically and internationally.

NOTES

1. United Nations, Economic and Social Consequences of the Arms Race and of Military Expenditures, Updated Report of the Secretary-General, E.78.IX.1. New York: 1978, p. 66. The establishment of a link is called for in UN Resolution 2685 (XXV) 1970; UN Resolution 3281 (XXIX), December 1974; Section A, Paragraph 5, International Development Strategy for the Second Development Decade; United Nations, Department of Economic and Social Affairs, Disarmament and Development, E.73.IX.1, New York: 1973; United Nations, Reduction of Military Budgets of States Permanent Members of the Security Council by 10 Per Cent and Utilization of Part of the Funds Saved to Provide Assistance to Developing Countries, E.75.I.10, New York; 1975.

2. Kurt W. Rothschild, 'Military Expenditure, Exports and Growth', _Kyklos_ 26 (1973): 804-815; Ruth Leger Sivard, _World Military and Social Expenditure_, 1977, Leesburg, Va.: WMSE Publications, 1977, p. 13; Seymour Melman, _The Permanent War Economy_, New York: Touchstone, Simon & Schuster, 1974; Seymour Melman, testimony before the House Committee on Armed Services, _Overall National Security Programs and Related Budget Requirements_, Washington, DC: US Govt. Printing Office, December 1975, pp. 280-363; Michael Boretsky, 'Trends in U.S. Technology: A Political Economist's View, _American Scientist_ 63 (January-February 1975): 70-82; R. H. Bezdek, 'The 1980 Economic Impact -- Regional and Occupational -- of Compensated Shifts in Defense Spending', _Journal of Regional Science_ 15:2 (August 1975): 183-198; United Nations, _Economic and Social Consequences_ (see note 1), pp. 39-57; Bernard Udis, ed., _Adjustments of the US Economy to Reduction in Military Spending_, ACDA/E 156, Boulder, Colo.: University of Colorado, December 1970.

3. Ann Crittenden, 'Guns Over Butter Equals Inflation', _New York Times_, 19 November 1978; Lloyd J. Dumas, 'Payment Functions and the Productive Efficiency of Military Industrial Firms', _Journal of Economic Issues_ 10:2 (June 1976): 454-474.

4. United Nations, Department of Political and Security Council Affairs, UN Centre for Disarmament, _The United Nations Disarmament Yearbook. Volume I: 1976_, New York: 1977, p. 237. All of Chapter XX (pp. 233-245) is concerned with this proposal and its aftermath.

5. R. R. Ropelewski, 'French Defense Budget Up, But Inflation's Impact Felt', _Aviation Week & Space Technology_ 103:19 (10 November 1975): 17; R. Mauthner, 'France Plans Big Increase in Its Military Spending', _Financial Times_, 29 January 1976; 'French Seek Sixth Nuclear Missile Submarine', _Aviation Week & Space Technology_ 109:14 (2 october 1978): 22.

6. 'Address by Louis de Guiringuad, French Minister of Foreign Affairs, at the Presentation of the Foreign Affairs Budget Before the National Assembly, November 8, 1977 (Excerpts)', 77/148. New York: Press & Information Division, French Embassy, mimeo.

7. 'Japan Defense Asks Record Budget', _New York Times_, 29 August 1976; Drew Middleton, 'Japan Sets 12% Rise in Defense Budget', _New York Times_, 12 February 1978; S. Jameson, 'Japan Taking on Bigger Defense Role', _Los Angeles Times_, 14 June 1978.

8. US Arms Control and Disarmament Agency, _Arms Control, 1977_, Washington, DC, p. 36; D. Binder, 'US Aides See a Possible Bloc Crisis Over Rumania', _New York Times_, 29 November 1978.

9. 'Soviet Defense Budget is 26.4 Billion' (Associated Press), 29 November 1978; US Central Intelligence Agency, _A Dollar Cost_

Comparison of Soviet and US Defense Activities 1967-1977, SR 78-10002, Washington, DC: Janaury 1978.

10. B. Weinraub, 'Pentagon is Seeking 56 Billion Increase Over Next Five Years', New York Times, 3 February 1978; G. C. Wilson, 'US Committed to Record Peacetime Arms Spending', Washington Post, 15 October 1978.

11. Press Release, 'World Armaments and Disarmament, SIPRI Yearbook, 1977', Stockholm International Peace Research Institute.

12. Figure derived from US Arms Control and Disarmament Agency, World Military Expenditures and Arms Transfers, 1967-1976, Washington, DC: July 1978, Table II.

13. UN Department of Economic and Social Affairs, Disarmament and Development, (see note 1 above), p. 14; UN General Assembly, Report of the Ad Hoc Group on the Relationship Between Disarmament and Development. Note by the Secretary-General, A/S-10/9, Annex 3, 5 April 1978, pp. 8-9.

14. UN Department of Economic and Social Affairs, Disarmament and Development, Table 3, pp. 30-31.

15. See, for example, Barry M. Blechman & Edward R. Fried, Disarmament and Development: An Analytical Survey and Pointers for Action, C/AC.54/L.90. New York: Committee for Development Planning, Economic and Social Council, United Nations, 26 January 1977; Lincoln Bloomfield & Harlan Cleveland, Disarmament and the UN: Strategy for the United States, A Policy Paper, Princeton, NJ: Program in International Affairs, Aspen Institute for Humanistic Studies, 1978 [also appears as 'A Strategy for the United States'. International Security 2:4 (Spring 1078): 32-55]; Valery Giscard d'Estang, 'Interview, 9 February 1978', New York: Press & Information Division, French Embassy, mimeo.

16. On problems associated with health care, for example, see the special section entitled 'Health and Medicine' in Far Eastern Economic Review, 25 November 1977, pp. 33-52.

17. The US Arms Control and Disarmament Agency, op. cit. (see note 12 above), pp. 33-71, has just begun to express military expenditure as a percent of national budget expenditure as a percent of gross national product. From these figures, it is evident that many Third World governments are spending large amounts of their income on defense. An argument in favor of measuring defense expenditure in terms of budget expenditures and not GNP is found in Milton Leitenberg & Nicole Ball, 'The Military Expenditures of Less Developed Nations as a Proportion of their State Budgets. A Research Note', Bulletin of Peace Proposals 8:4 (1977): 310-315. It has heretofore been a drawback that the most widely consulted sources have

relied on the military expenditure as a percent of GNP measurement. For example, US Arms Control and Disarmament Agency, World Military Expenditures and Arms Transfers series; Stockholm International Peace Research Institute, Yearbooks; and the annual Agenda volumes produced by the Overseas Development Council.

18. Blechman & Fried, op. cit. (see note 15 above).

19. Three surveys of the literature on this topic have recently been undertaken: Ulrich Albrecht, et al., 'Rustungskonversionsforschung. Eine Literaturstudie mit forschungsempfehlungen', sponsored by the Deutsche Gesellschaft fur Friedens- und Konfliktforschung, Bonn. This version is in printed in German; a short summary in English appears in Ulrich Albrecht, 'Researching Conversion. A Review of the State of the Art', in Experiences in Disarmament, ed. Peter Wallensteen, Uppsala: Uppsala University, Report No. 19, June 1978, pp. 11-43; M. Waengborg, B. Ljung, et al., Nedrustning och Utveckling, Synpunkter pa FN-Studiens problemstallningar och forskningslaget inom omradet, Stockholm: FOA-1, 28 February 1978, mimeo; Milton Leitenberg & Nicole Ball, 'Materials Prepared in Analysis and in Support of the Proposal, Disarmament and Development [United Nations, A/AC.187/80, August 31, 1977]', Report to the Ministry of Foreign Affairs, Sweden, Ithaca, NY: February 1978, mimeo.

20. A good summary of the literature on these topics is found in Mary Kaldor, 'The Military in Development', World Development 4:6 (1976): 459-482. [Reprinted as 'The Military in Third World Development', in Disarmament and World Development, ed. Richard Jolly, Oxford: Pergamon Pres, 1978, pp. 57-82. The bibliographic section of the original article is reproduced in a slightly expanded version on pp. 161-170 of the book.]

21. For example, see Guy J. Pauker, 'Southeast Asia as a Problem Area in the Next Decade', World Politics 11:3 (April 1959): 352-345; Lucien W. Pye, 'Armies in the Process of Political Modernization', in The Role of the Military in Underdeveloped Countries, pp. 69-89, ed. John J. Johnson, Princeton, NJ: Princeton University Press, 1962; Morris Janowitz, The Military in the Political Development of New Nations, Chicago and London: Phoenix Books, The University of Chicago Press, 1964.

22. Emile Benoit, Defense and Economic Growth in Developing countries, Lexington, Mass.: Lexington Books, 1973 [a summary is found in Emile Benoit, 'Growth and Defense in Developing Countries', Economic Development & Cultural Change 26:2 (Janaury 1978): 271-280]; Gavin Kennedy, The Military in the Third World, London: Duckworth, 1974; Thomas A. Brown, Statistical Indications of the Effect of Military Programs on Latin America, 1960-1965, P-4144, Santa Monica, Calif.: Rand Corporation, July 1969, mimeo.

23. Benoit, <u>Defense and Economic Growth in Developing Countries</u>, pp. 35-36, 92.

24. Vlademar F. Marcha, 'The Impact of Military Expenditures on the Process of Industrialization in Latin America: Evaluation of Statistical Analyses', School of Engineering and Applied Science, Columbia University, New York, 1975.

25. See, for example, US Congres, Senate Committee on Foreign Relations, Report: <u>Arms Transfer Policy,</u> 95th Cong., 1st Sess., Washington, DC: US Govt. Printing Office, 1977, pp. 25-26, 95-99; US Congress, House Committee on Foreign Affairs, Report: <u>The International Transfer of Convention Arms,</u> Prepared by US ACDA, 93rd Cong., 2nd Sess., Washington, DC: US Govt. Printing Office, 1974, pp. 77-82; Emile Benoit, 'International Defense Planning: The Economic Setting', in <u>International Defense Planning: A Study of Methods for Sharing Skills and Concepts in Defense Policy Planning</u>, pp. 43-56, Browne & Shaw Research Corporation, Waltham, Mass.: November 1967.

26. For example, Ulrich Albrecht, Dieter Ernst, Peter Lock & Herbert Wulf, 'Armaments and Underdevelopment', <u>Bulletin of Peace Proposals,</u> No. 2 (1974): 173-185.

27. Maurice Odle, 'Guyana -- Caught in an IMF Trap', <u>Caribbean Contact,</u> October 1978, pp. 10-11.

28. For example, Jan Oberg, 'The New International Economic and Military Orders as Problems to Peace Research', <u>Bulletin of Peace Proposals</u> 8:2 (1977): 142-149.

29. Mary Kaldro, 'Military Technology and Social Structure', <u>Bulletin of the Atomic Scientists,</u> 33:6 (June 1977): 49-53; Mary Kaldor, 'Arms and Dependence', 'Preview' of the 1978 UN Special Session on Disarmament, The Arms Control Association and the Carnegie Endowment for International Peace, Talloires, France, 2-4 September 1977, mimeo; Peter Lock & Herbert Wulf, <u>Register of Arms Production in Developing Countries,</u> Hamburg: Study Group on Armament and Underdevelopment, IFSH, mimeo, 1977, pp. iv-xxxvi.

30. Stockholm International Peace Research Institute, 'Chapter 22: Domestic Defence Production in Third World Countries', <u>The Arms Trade with the Third World</u>, Stockholm: Almqvist & Wiksell, 1971, pp. 737-740; Signe Landgren-Backstrom, '10: Domestic Defence Production in Third World Countries', in <u>World Armaments and Disarmament</u>. SIPRI Yearbook 1973, Stockholm International Peace Research Institute, Stockholm: Almqvist & Wiksell, 1973, pp. 354-356.

31. Herbert Wulf, 'Dependent Militarism in the Periphery and Possible Alternative Concepts', Hamburg: Study Group on Armament and Underdevelopment, IFSH, mimeo, 1978; Robin

Luckham, 'Militarism and International Dependence', in Disarmament and World Development, pp. 35-56, ed. Richard Jolly, Oxford: Pergamon Press, 1978; SIPRI, The Arms Trade with the Third World, pp. 723-782.

32. Luckham, op. cit., p. 44.

33. For example, Cynthia H. Enloe, 'The Issue Saliency of the Military-Ethnic Connection. Some Thoughts on Malaysia', Comparative Politics 10:2 (January 1978): 267-285; Cynthia H. Enloe, The Ethnic Soldier (forthcoming in 1979 by Penguin); Mary Kaldor, 'The Arms Trade and Society', Economic and Political Weekly 11:5, 6, 7 [Annual Number] (February 1976): 293-301.

34. Jan Tinberger, Coordinator, RIO: Reshaping the International Order. A Report to the Club of Rome, New York: E. P. Dutton & Co., 1976. This suggestion is also put forward in Oberg, op. cit., (see note 28 above), p. 147.

35. Pauker, op. cit. (see note 21 above), p. 340.

36. International Labour Office, Time for Tansition. A Mid-Term Review of the Second United Nations Development Decade. Geneva: 1975, pp. 82-83; Morris D. Morris, Measuring the Condition of the World's Poor: The Physical Quality of Life Index, Washington, DC: Overseas Development Council, mimeo, 31 August 1978, pp. 45-46; C. T. Kurien, 'The New Development Strategy: An Appraisal', Economic and Political Weekly 13: 31-33 [Special Number] (1978): 1257; Robert S. McNamara, 'Address to the Board of Governors', Nairobi, 24 September 1973, Washington, DC: World Bank, pp. 10-12.

37. Morris, op. cit., p. 96. For a discussion of the failure of the 'trickle down' strategy in India see Kurien, op. cit., pp. 1257-1264. See also, International Labour Office, op. cit., pp. 72-73; Ho Kwon Ping, 'Asian Agriculture's Decade in the Wrong Direction', Far Eastern Economic Review, 15 September 1978, p. 48.

38. Kurien, op. cit., and Ho Kwon Ping, op. cit., pp. 48-50. the ADB-sponsored survey has recently been published as Asian Development Bank, Rural Asia: Challenge and Opportunity, New York: Praeger, 1978.

39. International Labour Office, op. cit., p. 71.

40. Clyde H. Farnsworth, 'U.S. Toughens Stand on Third-World Aid', New York Times, 6 February 1978; Mary Campbell, 'Less Debt Than Supposed', Financial Times, 30 May 1978; Ho Kwon Ping, op. cit., p. 48.

41. Ann Crittenden, 'Imbalanced Payments and World Capital Flow', New York Times, 18 February 1978; Juan de Onis, 'Latin Curse:

Inflation and Staggering Foreign Debt', The New York Times
International Economic Survey, 5 February 1978, p. 89;
Campbell, op. cit.

42. Leitenberg & Ball, 'The Military Expenditures of Less
Developed Nations as a Proportion of Their State
Budgets . . .', (see note 17 above).

43. Morris, op. cit.; International Labour Office, op. cit., pp.
82-83.

44. Wulf, op. cit., (see note 31 above).

*There is some ambiguity in the original report on the phrasing
of this question; presumably the developing countries were to
be given increased aid in the form of credits to purchase
materials from the industrialized countries.

**The failure of the development strategies of the 1950s and
1960s to generate self-sustaining economic growth and to
promote social development is further discussed below.

***We suspect, in fact, that there is no body of knowledge
supporting claims to any special organizational or managerial
ability on the part of military elites in developing
countries. The notion of the military as 'national-builders'
or 'unifiers' in particular was by and large a theoretical
construct which flourished for a short period in the late
1950s and early 1960s when the large proportion of military
governments was a relatively new phenomenon. Now, several
more years have passed and there is some record of the
performance and operation of military governments. The degree
of rationalization that this construct contained as support
for the US foreign policy position of backing such military
governments also is now far more apparent.

****This occurs with non-military governments -- as any regular
reader of the Indian journal Economic and Political Weekly can
attest -- as well as military governments. However, India is
not the only example of a non-military government relying on
force to suppress discontent. Nor are supposedly 'socialist'
countries exempt.[27]

Dynamics of the Arms Race:
A Third World View

ESSAM GALAL

I. INTRODUCTION

More and more of the developing countries, often referred to as the Third World, are inclined to view themselves as the victims of an escalating arms race, led by a handful of industrialized countries. However it may be described, the global armament phenomenon remains heavily concentrated. For over three and a half decades since the Second World War, the two major military powers the United States and the U.S.S.R. together with their allies in NATO and the Warsaw Pact have continued to account for virtually all the global expenditure on the military R & D, almost 85 per cent of the global military spending, more than 90 per cent of the world-wide military production and roughly 95 per cent of the international exports of military hardware.

By contrast, in 1981 between 14 to 16 per cent of global military spending and not more than 7 to 8 per cent of world-wide military production was spread among over 130 developing countries, their total number having increased three-fold since the Second World War. Almost every newly independent country has incurred some form of military spending and for most of them, making some military allocations became a reflex act after gaining a sovereign status. The reciprocal compulsions it has generated between those developing countries which have some historically rooted animosities, or some outstanding geographical frontier disputes, and the military competition which has resulted from it have by now become a familiar feature of the tension-ridden Third World.

The military competition among several of the developing countries and the arms race among a few industrialized powers do

From **THE ARMS RACE AND DISARMAMENT**, UNESCO Press, 1982, (57-67), reprinted by permission of the publisher.

not, however, belong to the same category of inherent dynamics which govern the world-wide arms race. Nowhere is the difference between them more striking than in the relative shares of each in the global military R & D and military production. Collectively all the Third World countries combined do not incur even a barely calculable fraction of the world-wide military R & D expenditures; individually, not more than 12 to 16 out of the over 130 developing countries possess any significant armament production facilities. Their procurement of military hardware, almost entirely from the industrialized world, however, has continued to increase both in volume and sophistication. This factor, more than any other, has inextricably linked the military competition among the developing countries with the dynamics of the arms race of the industrialized world.

II. INVOLVEMENT OF THE THIRD WORLD IN THE ARMS RACE

Virtually all the military conflicts in the developing countries have been fought with imported weaponry and in more than two-thirds of the over 120 conflicts, either one or the other industrialized exporters of military hardware has been reported to have viewed its eventual outcome as of some relevance to the geopolitical dimensions of its strategic rivalry with its own global adversary. An intricate chain of listening posts, naval facilities, military bases, and implicit or explicit understandings for direct and indirect military support by the exporting to the importing country have produced a complicated set of changing supplier-client relationships in the area of international arms transfers. Clients left in political or economic orphanage by one supplier have been readily picked up by another; even in regions where the origins of several of the conflict situations had little to do with the strategic rivalry of the major adversaries in the global arms race ,the subsequent military build-ups have conformed more to the assessments of the military needs of the supplier than of the client. A most striking example of this is the Middle East, which as a region alone accounts for more weapon imports than all the other developing countries put together. A detailed description of the geo-strategic importance of the Middle East, besides its obvious feature as the largest known reserve base of oil which, incidentally, is an almost irreplaceable source of petroleum for the military industry, falls outside the scope of this paper. What is relevant in the present context is its illustrative significance to demonstrate the inherent dangers of a global situation whereby the dynamics of a heavily concentrated arms race is increasingly spread over the developing countries.

The dynamics of the arms race involves much more than a sum total of the military spending of the individual countries and an up-dated list of its numerical participants. The purposes it serves, the forces which drive it, and the forms in which it manifests itself, have been widely analysed in such a way as to

allow each of the major participants in the arms race to present a benign image of its own military build-up while attributing aggressive intentions to its adversary. In this broad sense, the arms race has increasingly become a world-wide phenomenon; and although its intensity differs markedly between regions, no major region and few countries have stayed out of the arms race. As pointed out by some of the United Nations studies on the subject, the term arms race is not appropriate to describe the gathering momentum for the process of expanding and improving military forces. This process may intensify the wider arms race, particularly in regions where countries are exposed to political, military and other kinds of pressures, where the rivalries of the other states lead to involvement or interference, where territories are under foreign occupation and where countries feel their sovereignty and independence to be directly threatened.[1] Essentially, however, the phenomenon of the arms race involves simultaneous increases in military outlays of two or more nations whose foreign and defence policies are heavily interdependent; the military outlays of countries having little contact or no salient interest in each other cannot be appropriately described as an arms race.

> The primary engine of the world-wide arms race is constituted by the qualitative arms race among the largest military Powers. This is due chiefly to the virtual monopoly of these powers in the development of advanced military technology, to their overwhelmingly large share of world production and world exports of advanced weaponry, and to the global character of their interests, politically and militarily. . . . All significant developments in armaments originate here and spread from here to the rest of the world, with greater or lesser time lags. For many types of conventional weaponry these time lags seem to have diminished in recent years. Meanwhile, as these weapons are being assimilated in the countries at the periphery of the arms race, new generations are under development at the centre to supersede them, preparing the ground for a new round of transfer and emulation. Outside of this small number of producing countries, arms races or competitions are substantially and often wholly dependent on external supplies of arms, technicians and instructors[2].

III. MILITARY POWER AND NATIONAL SECURITY

For the developing countries, the dynamics of the arms race, as described above, implies a close relationship between military power and national security. The familiar dilemma about whether the major arms participants are insecure because they are armed, or armed because they are insecure, continues to persist. The fact is

that the heavy concentration of military power among the industrialized countries has so far been paralleled by the absence of open military confrontation among them. The notion that military power deters conflict cannot be easily dismissed as long as the major arms race participants do not bring about some meaningful reductions of their military power, particularly in the field of nuclear arsenals. The risk of horizontal nuclear proliferation among the developing countries will continue unabated as long as there is no nuclear disarmament among the major military powers. As pointed out by the United Nations Study on Nuclear Weapons:[3]

> If there is no progress towards nuclear disarmament the nuclear arms race will go on. Some States may then claim it justifiable to try to acquire a nuclear capability to deter massive attacks against their civilian populations as well as to defend themselves in a conventional military conflict.
>
> It is considered likely by many that the system of security which is inherent in the strategic relationship between the super-Powers based as it is on a nuclear "balance of terror", has discouraged them for over three decades from initiating military conflict directly with each other. It is also assumed that it has prevented regional conflicts in which either might be involved to escalate to global nuclear conflict. This has not, however, prevented either super-Power from major involvement in large-scale conventional military conflicts on a sub-global level. It is even suggested that confidence in the efficacy of the mutual strategic deterrence at the global level may have had the effect of diminishing inhibitions about super-Power involvement in certain regional conflicts.
>
> To live in a world with nuclear weapons also means that certain innate elements of the nuclear arms race endanger international peace and security. Periods may come when one or the other, and sometimes both, of the super-Powers become less confident about their state of national security. This could occur when one considers that the other has acquired a competitive edge in strategic nuclear capability. It is almost axiomatic that the level of international security is adversely affected when a super-Power becomes uncertain about its own security. In general, the state of international security would thus come to vary with the ups and downs of the nuclear arms race. It is indeed a fact that the dynamic of the nuclear arms race has caused an increase in the level of nuclear capability at which the deterrence balance is perceived to be established by the two super-Powers.
>
> The super-Powers' reliance on nuclear weapons for their security confers legitimacy on these weapons as instruments of power. The efforts to encourage states to accept binding multilateral commitments to forgo nuclear

weapons will therefore be hindered unless the
nuclear-weapon States themselves demonstrate a readiness
to take meaningful measures towards the elimination of
nuclear weapons. Acquisition of nuclear weapons by more
states is, however, likely to undermine international
security.

In their anxiety to contain nuclear proliferation among the
developing countries, some of the major nuclear powers have
followed a policy of encouraging nuclear abstinence by supporting
conventional military build-ups of a potential nuclear power. In
some cases, this has actually resulted in improving the military
power of a developing country involved in an adversary relationship
with a hostile neighbour; this situation comes close to either
putting a premium on the announcement of an intention to acquire
the nuclear capability or superimposing a higher level of military
build-up between both adversaries. Neither conforms to the clearly
defined position taken in the First Special Session on Disarmament
(UNSSOD I) which in its final document had clearly stated:
"Enduring international peace and security cannot be built on the
accumulation of weaponry by military alliances nor be sustained by
a precarious balance of deterrence or doctrines of strategic
superiority."[4]
A super-imposition of a higher level of military build-up
among the developing countries involved in conflict situations will
not promote the cause of either international security or
disarmament. Unless, of course, the pursuit of international
security continues to be preoccupied, as it has been since the two
World Wards, with the prevention of another war in the European
theatre, and the search for disarmament remains obsessed, as it is
now, with the American-Soviet arms control negotiations, which also
serve the purpose of communicating politico-economic threats,
assessing military capabilities and adjusting strategic priorities.
The either/or proposition between international security and
disarmament does not preclude the desirability of making the two
contingent upon each other. From a purely strategic viewpoint,
however, the proposition that international security will promote
disarmament, and the other way around, has not been proven by the
experience of the industrialized countries. The East-West
negotiations on European security, culminating in the Helsinki
Accords of 1975, were neither preceded nor followed by European
disarmament. If anything, these negotiations -- and their eventual
outcome -- have been accompanied by a constant build-up of
East-West military strength of mutually recognized deterrent
capabilities, notably in the nuclear field. The acquisition of
some level of nuclear conventional deterrence between and among the
various adversaries in the Third World may or may not result in a
series of accords similar to that of Helsinki outside Europe. In
any case these would not further the prospects for disarmament in
the Third World any more than has been the case so far in Europe.
A fundamental difference between the security concerns of
Europe and the Third World lies in the specificity and urgency of
their respective threat perceptions. The East-West threat
perceptions related to each other reflect security concerns about

avoiding or fighting a war which has never been actually fought in the past. Such a war is also highly unlikely to occur in the near future, unless both the East and West enter a joint pact for simultaneous suicide and murder. The threat perceptions of the Third World, which came to be identified and described as such only after the two World Wars, emanate from specific security crises actually experienced or directly witnessed. Virtually all the local wars fought since the Second World War have actually occurred in Asia, Africa and Latin America. Even when an industrialized power was militarily involved in a local war, as in the Congo, Vietnam or Chad, the actual fighting took place on the territories of the Third World. Europe has seldom been a theatre of war since the Second World War and the strategic doctrines accompanying this phenomenon do not provide a viable option to bring about a similar no-war situation in the Third World.

IV. STRATEGIC DOCTRINES AND THE THIRD WORLD

European notions of strategy have not changed substantially since Clausewitz defined it as "an approach to war which links the outcome of a number of military engagements" and described its object as "the achievement of a favourable overall position in which your opponent has no remaining courses of action open to him reasonably likely to reverse the course of war". The notions of a grand strategy, developed since Clausewitz's time, have expanded the original concept to include factors other than military strategy and a time span covering both war and peace. Paul Nitze's analysis of the European strategy for the 1980's, for example, starts with a definition of ground strategy in which "all factors bearing on the evolving situation — including economic, political and psychological factors as well as military — are taken into account over long periods of time, including times both of peace and war". Both the East and the West have evolved strategic doctrines based upon this grand strategy which determines their respective views of the security issues in the Third World. The establishment of a politico-military detente in Europe has not changed their strategic objectives in the rest of the world.

The achievement of an overall favourable position, the knowledge of an identifiable and constant opponent, and the capability to employ a whole range of political, economic and military power constitute the key elements of the prevailing strategic doctrines which the Third World has not endorsed in order to overcome its security concerns. The Third World has not yet reached a favourable overall position comparable to the politico-territorial status quo cemented in Europe by the Helsinki Accord; both the political order and the territorial frontiers are still the subject of unsettled claims within and among the Third World countries. The Third World also has no identifiable single opponent comparable to the chief adversary perceived in the East-West framework; most of the Third World countries have their

own adversaries and few among them are inclined to delegate their
strategic responsibilities to the overall leadership of a single
power comparable to the United States and the Soviet Union in their
respective alliance systems. The experience of the Organization of
American States in the Inter-American alliance system does not
provide an exception, because even in Latin America the latest
indications are of intra-regional fragmentation challenging the
hemispheric reliance on the United States.

Above all, few among the Third World countries have the
economic and military resources comparable to those employed by
East and West in pursuit of their grand strategies. Even those who
possess such resources are constantly under pressure from the
competing claims of national security and developmental concerns.
The challenge of providing socio-economic content to political
freedom, in the initial stages of nation-building, has been
exacerbated by the series of security crises faced by most of the
Third World countries. As the euphoria of national independence
has given way to a rising discontent of unfulfilled socio-economic
expectations, under-development or mal-development by itself has
become a source of insecurity. Ethnic, tribal or communal
frictions within nation-states have been aggravated by real or
perceived denial in the process of economic development and the
resulting political instability within these countries has largely
obliterated the thin line dividing the internal from external
threats to national security.

The only strategic objective shared by the Third World is
national survival as independent nation-states. The only strategy
endorsed by them in the pursuit of this objective is an attempt to
gain maximum advantage from resources that are insufficient to
provide for meeting the twin challenges of national security and
development. Their national security concerns, by and large,
revolve around their territorial frontiers except in cases where
these frontiers still conform to a colonial or racial pattern.
Their developmental needs reflect a clear distinction between
economic growth and development: the former describing goods and
services, and the latter pertaining to the quality of life in
general. The sheer abundance of human or natural resources in a
particular Third World country does not detract from the overall
resource insufficiency, particularly when the competing claims of
national security and development are taken into account.

The irrelevance of the prevailing strategic doctrines among
the industrialized world for the Third World security issues is
reflected in the conspicuous absence of a strategic component in
the non-aligned movement which, by definition, stipulates a
judgement of East-West issues on the merits of a specific
situation. Operating at different levels of economic development,
enjoying varied degrees of social homogeneity and political
legitimacy, having military power and capability, and confronting
different adversaries in their respective threat perceptions, the
major element of commonality binding the increasing membership of
the non-aligned movement is the stated aspiration to stay outside
the arena of East-West differences.

Many of the East-West dominated security arrangements with the
Third World countries were clearly entered into with different sets

of strategic objectives. The East-West framework viewed these arrangements as a co-optation of junior partners outside Europe: the Third World countries joined them in the expectation of receiving additional leverage in their conflicts with actual or perceived adversaries. Since the threats perceived by the Third World not only materialized earlier but also originated in situations different from those dominating the East-West issues, most of these arrangements proved either inadequate or irrelevant to deal with the crises in the Third World. Iran opted out of the United States security umbrella after discovering that its role as a junior partner, to be the Eastern bulwark of the Western alliance system, did not equip it to deal with the phenomenon of Islamic fundamentalism which to a certain degree was also a reaction to the Shah's preponderant reliance upon a massive military build-up to demonstrate his national and regional ambitions. The strategic objectives assigned to CENTO did not converge with those of its individual members: neither Pakistan, nor Iran, nor Turkey got out of it the expected politico-strategic advantages and the alliance withered away. SEATO had another quit burial as one after another of its members realized that the alliance was either unwilling or incapable of putting its collective weight behind the crises actually confronting its individual members.

A growing tendency among the developing countries to set up domestic armament production centres can in part be seen as a demonstration of extreme reluctance to get involved in the politico-military competition of their arms suppliers. Even if the purely financial costs of importing weaponry appear lower than those of producing them domestically, the overall terms of transfer may involve politico-military costs which few developing countries can afford to sustain without serious consequences. These imply dependence on supportive equipment and personnel, and the risk of becoming an actual theatre of war in a possible confrontation over threats which may be alien and even irrelevant to the importing country's own security. In this context, it is extremely important that the conflict-situations among the developing countries be urgently resolved in accordance with the principle of "undiminished security of all States" stated unequivocally in the final document of UNSSOD I.

The urgency of this task cannot be overstated because these conflict situations not only constitute a major factor in the military spending of the developing countries, but also provide easy targets for the principal arms exporters from the industrialized world in pursuit of their politico-military rivalry. It is here that a basic difference of approach can be seen between the security concerns of a majority of the states and those of the major military powers, particularly the two described as "Super Powers". The former overwhelmingly share a rather narrow definition of national security; a direct or indirect threat to their national frontiers or their right to self-determination and national independence. On the other hand, the two major military powers continue to define their national security in terms that project their perceived interests far beyond their borders, leading to measures of intervention, neocolonialism and the risk of the division of the world into spheres of interest which is at wide

variance with the principles of equality of sovereign states and non-interference in the affairs of others. The Third World interest in a narrower definition of national security is more in consonance with both the letter and the spirit of the Final Document of the UNSSOD I which in more than thirty references to national security broadly used the term in relation to direct threats of aggression across the geographical frontiers of sovereign states.

V. IMPLICATIONS OF THE DYNAMICS OF THE ARMS RACE

While differing from the major military powers in their respective national security concerns and, hence, the enormity of the military effort needed to meet them, the developing countries share the near universal concern about two of the most serious implications of the dynamics of the arms race: its unimaginably deadly, destructive potential and its incalculably colossal wastage and misallocation of the world's far from infinite resources. Irrespective of whether they are actually used or not, the continuous production, stockpiling, and deployment of nuclear arsenals is irreversibly affecting the global human and natural environment. The human (labour), natural (fuel and non-fuel minerals), and material (capital and technology) resources consumed by the world-wide military activities are severely narrowing the socio-economic options both at the national and international levels.

There is no target strong enough to resist the intense effects of nuclear weapons nor a meaningful defence against a determined nuclear attack. Figures and rough estimates of the human and physical devastation likely to result from a limited or partial use of these weapons may be given, but there exists a virtually comprehensible limit beyond which such figures have no meaning except a categorical imperative that a nuclear war must never happen:

-- the total number of existing nuclear warhead may well be in excess of 40,000. The explosive yield of an average warhead ranges from 100 tons to more than 20 million tons of TNT and in principle there is no upper limit to the explosive yield which may be attained;

-- a single Poseidon submarine with its 16 MIRVed missiles can deliver warheads to 160 separate targets; these warheads have a total explosive yield of 6.4 Mt., a larger explosive power than that of all the munitions fired in the Second World War; still this megatonnage is of the order of one or a few thousandths of the megatonnage in either the United States or the Soviet strategic arsenal;

-- the largest nuclear warhead ever tested released an energy approximately 4000 times that of the bomb used over Hiroshima.[5]

A total nuclear war or an all-out nuclear exchange would be tantamount to the highest level of human madness because those

surviving it would be envying the dead in terms of the socio-economic and political climate they would inherit. Even the most medically advanced among the industrialized countries do not have the facilities to treat more than 200 patients of a nuclear attack in a day during normal conditions. The situation can only be imagined if along with human beings, the physical and material equipment, including hospitals, is destroyed during a nuclear attack. For the developing countries, the effects of a nuclear war would be incalculably more disastrous because few among them possess even the rudimentary elements of civil defence, for a conventional war, let alone facilities to treat any survivors of a nuclear holocaust.

In purely financial terms, the global military expenditure in 1981:

-- amounted to roughly $120 for every man, woman and child on earth;

-- was comparable to the combined GNP of all the countries in Africa and Latin America;

-- exceeded the annual income of roughly two billion people in the world's poorest countries;

-- was more than twenty-five times larger than the developmental assistance provided by the industrialized to the developing countries.[6]

Approximately $110 billion, or roughly one-fifth of the total global military expenditure in 1981, was going into improving the existing stockpiles of nuclear weapons. Less than one tenth of this would have been ample to finance a world-wide programme of research and development to discover new and renewable sources of energy, e.g. wind energy, oil shale, tar sands, ocean energy, draught animal power, peat, biomass, solar energy, etc.

-- a mere $1 billion would go a long way in initiating global efforts on nuclear waste disposal;

-- only $5 billion would be adequate to meet the costs of a world-wide programme for overcoming pollution;

-- only $4 billion would suffice to eradicate hunger through direct food aid to the world's poorest children;

-- a bare $1 billion additional allocation to the WHO's budget would enable it to provide world-wide child immunization whooping cough and tetanus. At present only 10 per cent of the 80 million children born per year in the developing countries are immunized against these and 10 may die every minute in the absence of immunization.[7]

As compared to $13 billion in 1960, the world expenditure on military R & D was estimated to be well over $35 billion in 1981:

-- the world expenditure in military R & D accounted for roughly one-fourth of the entire world investment in R & D for all other purposes;

-- military R & D alone claimed expenditures roughly equal to the combined R & D investments for energy, transportation, communication, health, agriculture, and pollution control;

-- the average expenditure differential between civilian and military R & D is growing wider: R & D programmes for some of the most sophisticated weapons systems are sometimes twenty times more research intensive as compared with investments in the civilian

sector. One single weapons programme, the MX missile system, was
allocated $1.5 billion in R & D in 1981;

    -- it is estimated that not more than 20 per cent of the
results of the military R & D can be used in any notable way for
civilian purposes.[7]

    Much too often in the past, the developing countries have been
viewed as the major beneficiaries of disarmament because it was
hoped that the diversion of even a fraction of the resources
currently claimed by world-wide military activities would go a long
way in providing for a bulk of the basic unmet needs of the poorest
sections in these countries. A recent United Nations study on the
relationship between disarmament and development has virtually
overturned this argument by suggesting that any additional resource
diversions to developmental channels will be an indirect investment
in detente and, therefore, to the confidence-building measures
urgently required to halt and reverse the arms race.

    From the point of view of the Third World, this line of
reasoning not only merits being quoted as the conclusion of this
chapter, but also needs to be taken up as a possible means of
follow-up action by the UNSSOD II:[6]

> The development of a more stable South capable of
> sustaining its independence through a better economic
> performance is likely to reduce the areas of political
> conflicts among the East and West and put detente on a
> more stable basis than it has been during the last few
> years of its constant re-examination. Viewed in this
> context, any direct additional investments in the
> development of developing countries may become an
> indirect contribution to detente. Greater flows of
> external assistance to the developing countries will
> further the prospects for development but relating this
> process to military restraint among the major military
> spenders is likely to create a new political climate
> which by itself may become a catalyst for military
> restraint. The amount of financial resources released
> for development through disarmament measures will be a
> major benefit for development but the awareness that it
> is a conscious attempt at viewing development as an
> integral part of detente will be a major bonus for
> East-West relations.[8]

NOTES

1. <u>Economic and Social Consequences of the Arms Race and of Military Expenditures</u>. United Nations Publication. Sales No. E.78.IX.1, paragraph 15.

2. <u>Ibid</u>. paragraph 17.

3. <u>Comprehensive Study on Nuclear Weapons,</u> Report of the U.N. Secretary General A/35/392, September 1980, Paras 398–401.

4. <u>Final Document, Special Session of the General Assembly on Disarmament, 1978</u>. United Nations, Department of Public Information, DPI/679, February 1981, paragraph 13.

5. <u>Comprehensive Study on Nuclear Weapons, op. cit</u>., paragraph 9.

6. <u>Study on the Relationship between Disarmament and Development</u>, United Nations, 1981, A/36/356. paras 102–104.

7. Estimates provided by the Centre for Disarmament, United Nations, New York, 1982.

8. <u>Study on the Relationship between Disarmament and Development</u>, <u>op. cit</u>. paragraph 241.

Arms Race Indicators

STOCKHOLM INTERNATIONAL PEACE RESEARCH INSTITUTE

I. WORLD MILITARY EXPENDITURE

Increased military spending is one major indicator of the growing use of resources in the world for military purposes. Throughout the 1970s world military expenditure continued to increase steadily in real terms. By 1979, estimates by the Stockholm International Peace Research Institute (SIPRI) of world military expenditure had reached the figure of some $480,000 million[1] at current prices -- and the 1980 figure will certainly go above $500,000 million. In real terms this represents an almost fourfold increase during the thirty years since 1948. Current budget figures indicate strongly that the rise in world military spending is accelerating. In this respect the first United Nations 'Decade for Disarmament' (the 1970s) has ended in total failure.

The waste of resources is not the only cause for concern. There are also some ominous implications in the rise in military spending. There were upswings in world military expenditure before the First World War and before the Second World War. And in the post-war period the big upswings were at the times of the Korean and the Viet Nam wars.

It is the impending figures for the two great power blocs which are especially disturbing, as experience has shown that increases by either side are often used as justification for increases by the other side. On the NATO side, we have the decision of 1978 to set a target of a 3 per cent annual rise, in real terms, in military spending. The United States has even gone beyond this figure. The United States five-year plan for military spending envisages a 4 per cent annual increase in volume from fiscal year

From **ARMAMENTS, ARMS CONTROL AND DISARMAMENT**, UNESCO Press, 1981, (15-34), reprinted by permission of the publisher.

Stockholm International Peace Research Institute

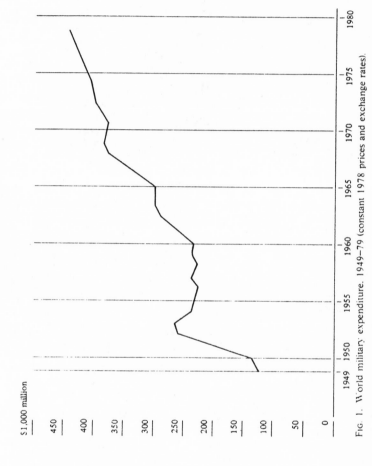

$1,000 million

FIG. 1. World military expenditure. 1949–79 (constant 1978 prices and exchange rates).

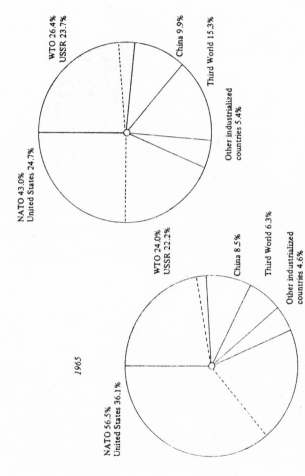

1979

NATO 43.0%
United States 24.7%

WTO 26.4%
USSR 23.7%

China 9.9%

Third World 15.3%

Other industrialized
countries 5.4%

1965

NATO 56.5%
United States 36.1%

WTO 24.0%
USSR 22.2%

China 8.5%

Third World 6.3%

Other industrialized
countries 4.6%

FIG. 2. Distribution of world military expenditure, 1965 and 1979.

1980 to 1985. Over those five years, the total additional spending over and above the present level of military expenditure will be about $80,000 million (at 1980 prices). The level and trend of military spending in the Soviet Union are a matter of great argument -- not helped by the incredibility of official figures released by the USSR. The United States has estimated that Soviet military spending had risen at a rate of 3-5 per cent annual in the 1970s. This estimate was given as one of the reasons for increased NATO spending.

As far as the rest of the world is concerned, the general picture is one of fairly rapid rates of growth in military expenditure over the decade. The general upward trend outside NATO, the Warsaw Treaty Organization (WTO) and China has been of the order of 7-8 per cent a year from 1970 to 1979.

There have been some groups of states where military expenditure has risen even more rapidly. For example, the members of the Organization of the Petroleum Exporting Countries (OPEC) have spent a significant part of their increased income on weapons. Their rate of increase of military expenditure, as a group, has for the past decade been 15 per cent a year in real terms. Another area where military spending has been rising rapidly is southern Africa -- South Africa and the adjoining states -- with an annual real growth rate in military spending of 16 per cent a year. In the Far East, Japan, although devoting less than 1 per cent of its gross domestic product to military purposes, has none the less moved up to seventh place in the world rank order of military expenditure. In South America military spending has risen to about 5 per cent a year (in real terms) on the continent as a whole.

The only area of the world where military spending (in real terms) was not much higher in 1979 than in 1970 was Oceania.

II. NUCLEAR ARMAMENTS

Although the bulk of military spending goes towards the upkeep of conventional weapons and forces, nuclear weapons are by far the greatest threat to the survival of mankind.

In 1945 two nuclear bombs with a total explosive power of about 30 thousand tonnes of high explosive destroyed the cities of Hiroshima and Nagasaki, killing about 300,000 people. Since that time, the world's nuclear arsenals have grown to the equivalent of over a million Hiroshima bombs.

The nuclear arsenals of the world contain more than 60,000 nuclear weapons -- an equivalent of about four tonnes of explosive per person. If even a fraction of these weapons were to be used, this would result in a catastrophe of unimaginable proportions.

Utterly catastrophic though a nuclear world war would be, many scientists believe it to be increasingly likely. The nuclear arsenals themselves have for so long been so huge as to make any further quantitative increases meaningless, at least from the military and strategic points of view. A major reason for

pessimism, however, is that improvements are constantly being made in the quality, particularly as regards accuracy and reliability, of strategic weapons. New warheads for the United States Minuteman intercontinental ballistic missile, for example, are so accurate that 50 per cent should fall within 200 metres of the intended target at intercontinental ranges. The next generation of these missiles will be accurate to within a few tens of metres. All military targets would be vulnerable to such weapons.

Such precision, together with other advances, may give military decision-makers misplaced confidence that they can actually fight and win nuclear wars, rather than simple deter them. Deterrence based on mutually assured destruction will then no longer be regarded as the main role of the strategic nuclear force, the temptation to strike first will increase dangerously, and the risk of nuclear war by miscalculation, accident or madness will increase correspondingly. This is probably not due to the deliberate decisions of political leaders, but rather to the sheer momentum of military technology. Nuclear war fighting weapons are being made available, pressures build up for their deployment and nuclear strategies are rationalized accordingly.

Planned deployments of nuclear weapons by the United States and the USSR are not significantly affected by the Strategic Arms Limitation Treaty (SALT II), which establishes equal limits for these powers on the total numbers of strategic delivery systems. Within the numerical limits set, each side is free to determine the structure of its strategic nuclear forces.

More ominous than any other weapon development is the continuing emergence of weapons with distinct nuclear warfighting capabilities.

Among such weapons being developed in the United States is the MX missile system (ICBM), with a related mobile basing scheme to reduce vulnerability. The MX will carry ten warheads, the maximum allowed by the SALT II treaty. Each warhead will have substantially greater accuracy and explosive yield than warheads on current United States Minuteman III ICBMs. Furthermore, a laser or radar system may be introduced to guide the warhead on to its target, giving it hitherto unattained accuracy. The first MX is expected to become operational in 1986, and the full force of 200 MX missiles by 1989. From then on, the MX will significantly increase the capability of the United States to threaten the Soviet fixed ICBM force.

While current submarine-launched ballistic missiles (SLBMs) do not possess the necessary combination of accuracy and explosive yield to pose a real threat to hardened targets such as missile silos, the United States is developing a new type of SLBM, the Trident II, which will probably have a definite capability against hardened targets. This new missile will eventually be deployed on new Trident submarines. A variety of sophisticated guidance mechanisms are under consideration for use on Trident II; thus Trident II may be more accurate than any strategic missile in operation today.

The United States is not alone in developing new generations of strategic nuclear weapons. The USSR has in operation, and under continued production, a series of multiple-warhead ICBMs capable of

destroying a high percentage of United States fixed ICBMs. The new
Soviet ICBMs -- the SS-17, SS-18 and SS-19 missiles -- are
ostensibly a response to the new Soviet ICBMs, and the USSR is
likely to react to the deployment of the MX. Thus, the strategic
nuclear arms race continues.

III. NUCLEAR-WEAPON ACCIDENTS

There are many thousands of nuclear weapons and their delivery
systems in the world's arsenal, a significant portion of which are
on alert. It is, therefore, hardly surprising that nuclear-weapon
accidents occur. But few realize just how frequently they do
occur. Data on accidents of nuclear-weapon systems given in the
SIPRI Yearbook 1977 suggest that there have been at least 125
nuclear-weapon accidents in the past thirty years -- a frequency of
one every three months.
Thirty-two accidents are listed, involving Untied States
weapon systems, in which nuclear weapons were believed to have been
destroyed or seriously damaged. In fifty-nine other United States
accidents, nuclear weapons may have been in danger of destruction
or serious damage. Also listed are twenty-two Soviet nuclear-
weapon accidents, eight British and four French. And the lists
relying as they do on open sources, are certainly incomplete.
Some of the nuclear-weapon accidents are bizarre. A United
States Corporal missile with a nuclear warhead is recorded as
'rolling off a truck into the Tennessee River'. On 9 April 1968
the United States strategic nuclear submarine Robert E. Lee 'became
snagged in the nets of a French trawler' in the Irish Sea. Among
the Soviet incidents is one in which 'American personnel recovered
a nuclear weapon from a Russian airplane that crashed in the Sea of
Japan'. And in September 1974 a Soviet guided-missile destroyer
allegedly exploded and sank in the Black Sea. A number of Soviet
nuclear-powered submarines have been snagged by Norwegian or
Japanese fishing boats. Some have collided with United States
submarines.
On at least nine occasions United States submarines, some of
them armed with nuclear weapons, have collided with other,
apparently Soviet, vessels within or close to Soviet territorial
waters while on intelligence-gathering missions. There are probably
similar incidents involving Soviet nuclear-armed submarines on
intelligence missions. Such events vividly recall President
Kennedy's warning of the danger of a nuclear world war being
started by accident.
One incontestable fact is that nuclear-weapon accidents do
occur, are quite frequent worldwide, and occur with probably all
the different nuclear-weapon systems containing nuclear warheads,
and in probably every kind of activity in which these weapon-
delivery systems take part: in silos, in the air, in harbours,
under the sea-surface, on land and so on.
It is true that in the 100 or more nuclear-weapon accidents

Salt II limits

			United States	USSR
		MIRVed ICBM launchers	550	608
	820	MIRVed SLBM launchers	496	144
(MIRV) 1 320	1 200	Heavy bombers equipped for long-range ALCMs	3	0
2 250		Non-MIRVed ICBM launchers	504	790
		Non-MIRVed SLBM launchers	160	806
		Heavy bombers not equipped for long-range ALCMs	570	156
		Total	2 283	2 504

Total systems by deployment category

	United States	USSR
ICBM launchers	1 054	1 398
SLBM launchers	656	950
Heavy bombers	573	156
Total	2 283	2 504

FIG. 3. SALT II limits and United States and Soviet strategic nuclear forces as of 18 June 1979 (Key: ALCM (air-launched cruise missile): ICBM (intercontinental ballistic missile): MIRV (multiple independently targetable re-entry vehicle): SLBM (submarine-launched ballistic missile).)

and incidents that have occurred in the post-war years, there has been no nuclear-weapon detonation, but there has been very extensive radioactive contamination in several instances. A new aspect, the possibility of weapon capture and terrorism, is receiving increasingly serious attention in several government and international agencies. The presence of a nuclear-weapon storage site close to a civilian population centre is questionable on at least several grounds of prudence. It would seem that preventive measures of caution, care and security -- such as remote locations of sites -- should be of equal interest to both military and civilian administrators.

IV. STRATEGIC AND EUROSTRATEGIC NUCLEAR WEAPONS

In Vienna, on 18 June 1979, after almost seven years of negotiation, President Carter and President Brezhnev signed the SALT II agreements for the limitation of strategic nuclear arms.

The treaty sets an overall limit on the number of strategic nuclear delivery vehicles and sub-limits on certain categories of these weapons. Ensuring equal numbers of strategic weapons cannot in itself create nuclear parity, because the two powers place different emphasis on various force components. However, the numerical symmetry may provide an equal basis for future reductions. Furthermore, for the first time an arms-control treaty requires the dismantling of nuclear weapons.

The aggregate ceiling, which covers intercontinental ballistic missile (ICBM) launchers, submarine-launched ballistic-missile (SLBM) launchers, heavy bombers and long-range air-to-surface ballistic missiles (ASBMs), has been set at 2,400 until the end of 1982, when the ceiling will be lowered to 2,250. Under the 2,250 limit, the United States will have to dismantle thirty-three vehicles -- probably mothballed bombers and/or outdated ballistic missile launchers will be chosen for this purpose. The USSR will have to dismantle 254 operational strategic nuclear delivery vehicles, and will also probably choose obsolete weapons.

However, the sub-limits on systems able to deliver multiple independently targetable re-entry vehicles (MIRVs.) are disappointingly high. Far from causing a reduction, they will in effect allow an increase in the number of missiles with multiple warheads, each warhead capable of being aimed at a separate target. A sub-limit of 1,200 on launchers of MIRVed ballistic missiles permits the United States 154 and the USSR 448 additional launchers of these sophisticated missiles. Furthermore, a sub-limit allowing 820 launchers of MIRVed ICBMs will allow this most threatening element of the strategic nuclear forces to increase in number.

With the high number of warheads permitted on ballistic missiles, plus the high number of cruise missiles permitted on current heavy bombers, the total number of deliverable warheads in the United States and Soviet strategic nuclear arsenals is expected to rise by 50 to 70 per cent between now and 1985. Thus, the

strategic nuclear firepower of both sides will augment considerably, notwithstanding the SALT II treaty. In 1980 the United States had 10,154 strategic nuclear warheads, of which 6,610 were on MIRVed launchers, while the estimates for the USSR were 7,078 strategic nuclear warheads with 4,752 on MIRVed launchers.

Furthermore, the parties will be able to improve the accuracy and explosive yield of warheads on current ICBMs, thereby increasing their lethality. The side will also be able to introduce one new type of ICBM, while there are no restrictions on new types of SLBMs. Certainly, the strategic nuclear forces -- especially the fixed ICBMs -- of both sides will be more vulnerable to a first-strike attack in 1985 than they are today. Consequently, pressures may mount to prepare for launching vulnerable missiles on very short notice -- perhaps less than half an hour -- to avoid their being destroyed. This compression of the time available for the evaluation of information and of options in a crisis heightens the chance of nuclear war by accident or miscalculation.

The treaty also contains some qualitative limitations, such as restrictions on the modernization of existing types of ICBMs. However, these limitations are minor and will not prevent certain important improvements to missiles on both sides. Nevertheless any limitations imposed on ICBMs must be welcomed.

Among the limits imposed by the short-term protocol is a ban on the deployment of ground- and sea-launched long-range cruise missiles as well as on the deployment of mobile ICBM launchers and on the flight testing of mobile ICBMs. The restrictions in the protocol may turn out to be pointless, however, as neither party will be ready to deploy the weapons in question by the end of 1981, when the protocol is to expire.

SALT II represents a definite step forward in that the two powers have pledged to maintain an agreed data base for weapon systems included in the various categories limited by the treaty. This regular exchange of information on the most powerful weapons possessed by the parties could serve as an important confidence-building measure.

The spotlight has recently fallen on so-called Eurostrategic weapons. Defining these weapons is extremely difficult. By and large, Eurostrategic weapons could be defined as nuclear weapons located in or targeted on Europe and having a range longer than that of the existing short-range tactical nuclear weapons, but shorter than that of the intercontinental strategic nuclear weapons. A heterogeneous array of missiles and aircraft is contained under the rubric 'Eurostrategic weapons'. Often referred to as 'grey area systems' these weapons are not covered by any of the current international arms-control negotiations.

The debate on Eurostrategic weapons is focused on the newest generation of United States and Soviet medium- and intermediate-range nuclear-weapon delivery systems. The Soviet SS-20 missile, which can carry three independently targetable nuclear warheads to ranges of up to 4,000 km, substantially increases the Soviet Union's nuclear potential in Europe. This missile has been deployed and is still under production, as is the other controversial Soviet Eurostrategic weapon, the Tu-22M Backfire

bomber. It should be noted that under certain conditions the Backfire bomber is capable of carrying out intercontinental missions. This bomber was therefore a contentious issue during the SALT II negotiations, but was finally excluded from the treaty limitations. However, the USSR pledged not to produce more than thirty Backfires a year and not to upgrade the Backfire so as to carry out intercontinental missions.

Two new United States Eurostrategic systems, under development, are planned to be deployed in a number of NATO countries. These will be ground-launched cruise missiles and the Pershing II ballistic missile (replacing the Pershing I of shorter range). In December 1979, NATO decided to base 464 ground-launched United States cruise missiles and 108 United States Pershing II missiles in Western Europe. The reason given for this decision was that the Soviet SS-20 missiles and Backfire bombers posed a new threat to NATO. Both types of NATO missile will be capable of penetrating a significant distance into the Soviet Union and will possess exceptional accuracies. Furthermore, the flight-times of Pershing II missiles from their bases in the Federal Republic of Germany to targets in the Soviet Union will be extremely short -- only a few minutes -- affording virtually no warning of attack. The cruise missiles, although considerably slower, will be able to fly zigzag flight paths at 'tree-top' altitudes to avoid air defences. Although the protocol to the SALT II treaty prohibits the deployment of ground and sea-launched cruise missiles with a range exceeding 600 kilometres, it does not prohibit their development. In any event, the protocol is due to expire at the end of 1981, that is, before these missiles are ready to be deployed.

These new Eurostrategic weapons, on both sides, must be seen as increasing the risk of nuclear war in Europe, which would amount, in fact, to the destruction of Europe.

V. COMPREHENSIVE TEST BAN

Since August 1945, when the first bombs were dropped on Hiroshima and Nagasaki, there have been over 1,200 nuclear explosions, carried out mainly to test and improve the efficiency of nuclear weapons.

In 1963 the Partial Test-Ban Treaty (PTBT), prohibiting atmospheric tests, was signed and contained a clear commitment to seek a comprehensive ban on all nuclear testing. No such ban has been achieved. In fact, the rate of testing has gone up: an average of forty-five explosions a year after the treaty as against only twenty-seven a year before the treaty. The USSR, the United Kingdom and the United States are responsible for over 90 per cent of all nuclear explosions.

In 1979 there were fifty-three nuclear explosions, all underground, France and the USSR conducting more tests than in any year since 1963-1969 -- nine and twenty-eight tests, respectively.

Arms race indicators

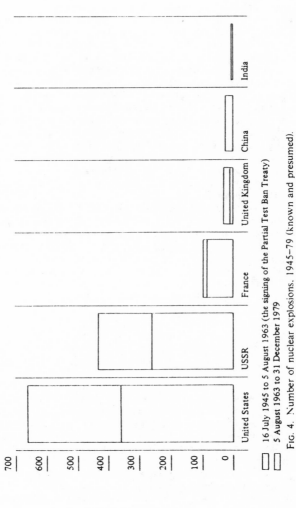

□ 16 July 1945 to 5 August 1963 (the signing of the Partial Test Ban Treaty)
□ 5 August 1963 to 31 December 1979

FIG. 4. Number of nuclear explosions. 1945–79 (known and presumed).

The United States was responsible for fifteen explosions in 1979, the United Kingdom only one, and China none at all for the first time since it started testing in 1964. According to United States sources, a low-yield nuclear explosion may have taken place on 22 September 1979 in the southern hemisphere, somewhere in a vast area including parts of the Indian and Atlantic oceans as well as southern Africa and Antarctica.

Intensive testing in recent years has coincided with tripartite United Kingdom/United States/Soviet talks on a treaty prohibiting nuclear-weapon tests in all environments. But these talks, which started in 1977, have, as yet, produced no result. Multilateral talks on a test-ban treaty have not even been initiated. More intensive negotiations are needed -- verification of compliance is no longer an obstacle to reaching an agreement.

A comprehensive test-ban treaty would make it difficult, if not impossible, for the nuclear-weapon powers to develop new designs of nuclear weapons or to improve the existing designs. Such a treaty would also reinforce the Non-Proliferation Treaty by demonstrating the awareness of the major nuclear powers of their obligation to halt the nuclear arms race. To be of real value, a comprehensive test-ban must be of permanent duration.

VI. NUCLEAR PROLIFERATION

It is clear that the nuclear-weapon powers have a potential for massive destruction unparalleled in history, and the risk of horizontal proliferation needs to be emphasized. A by-product of the nuclear-power generation industry is plutonium-239, which can be used as an explosive in nuclear weapons. Materials that can be used for nuclear weapons are being produced in an increasing number of countries.

The technology of nuclear weapons is now widely known. To make a number of reliable, efficient and lightweight fission weapons for a national military programme is a complicated business. To construct a crude nuclear device, of unpredictable yield, however, is not beyond the capacity of small groups of people. The fear thus arises that not only governments, but also criminal and terrorist groups, could conceivably manufacture nuclear explosives.

To prevent the spread of nuclear weapons the world community relies mainly on the Treaty on the Non-Proliferation of Nuclear Weapons (NPT), which entered into force in 1970. By 1 March 1980 the number of parties to the NPT had reached 112, evidence that the non-proliferation idea had been accepted by most nations, including many highly developed states. Under the NPT, the nuclear-weapon states are committed not to transfer, while the non-nuclear-weapon states are under an obligation not to receive, manufacture or otherwise acquire, nuclear weapons or other nuclear explosive devices, nor to control them.

The non-nuclear-weapon states are obliged to conclude

safeguard agreements with the International Atomic Energy °Agency (IAEA) covering all their peaceful activities to ensure that there is no diversion of nuclear material to the manufacture of nuclear explosives. All parties to the treaty have the right to exploit nuclear energy for peaceful purposes, and those in a position to do so must co-operate with other countries in developing peaceful nuclear technology. All parties are committed to pursuing negotiations in good faith on effective measures contributing to the cessation of the nuclear-arms race at an early date and to nuclear disarmament, including a treaty on general and complete disarmament.

However, the NPT sets no limits as to how close a country may come to nuclear-weapon assembly. A number of countries well able to construct nuclear weapons once they decide politically to do so and which have access to fissile material are not parties to the treaty.

A treaty that denies a powerful weapon to most signatories in order to preserve a firebreak between the 'haves' and 'have-nots' has obvious limitations in its appeal. In the case of the NPT, the situation is aggravated because the 'haves' are continuing to build up their already formidable nuclear-weapon strength. To redress the glaring imbalance in NPT obligations, the United States and the USSR must now undertake specific obligations to reduce significantly their strategic and tactical armaments.

The most immediate threat to the non-proliferation regime is posed by the spread of reactor-grade plutonium, a few kilos of which are readily convertible into an explosive device. Just one reactor with an electrical energy output of 1 GW(e) can produce about 250 kg of plutonium annually -- enough for about fifty Nagasaki-type bombs. So far a total of 100,000 kg of plutonium, in an unprocessed state, has been accumulated from nuclear reactors. There are at present about 230 nuclear-power reactors generating about 120,000 megawatts of electricity (MW(e)) in twenty-two countries, but another 230 or so power reactors are under construction. It has been predicted that by the year 2000, reactors generating about 600,000 MW(e) will be operational and about 250,000 kg of plutonium will be produced annually -- enough to make roughly 50,000 bombs of the Nagasaki type.

With pressures towards the recycling of plutonium and a fast-breeder regime, in which large quantities of plutonium would be used, the proliferation danger could increase dramatically: in a plutonium economy, such large amounts of plutonium would need to be reprocessed that it would be almost impossible for safeguards to detect diversion. And there is certainly no feasible technical means of preventing plutonium from being diverted. The International Nuclear Fuel Cycle Evaluation (INFCE), initiated by the United States in 1977, has made it crystal clear that, if there is to be any real solution to the proliferation problem, it must be a political one.

Internationalization of the nuclear fuel cycle would be an important element in such a solution. The sensitive parts of the cycle, that is, uranium enrichment, fuel fabrication and reprocessing, should be managed on an international scale and operated only under the authority of an international agency, with

TABLE 1. Power reactors as of 31 December 1979[1]

| Country | Operating reactors | | Reactors under construction | |
	Number of units	Total MW(e)	Number of units	Total MW(e)
Argentina	1	345	1	600
Belgium	4	1 676	4	3 811
Brazil	—	—	3	3 116
Bulgaria	2	816	2	828
Canada	10	5 245	14	9 751
Cuba	—	—	1	408
Czechoslovakia	2	491	3	1 142
Finland	2	1 080	2	1 080
France	16	8 163	21	20 290
German Democratic Republic	4	1 287	5	2 040
Germany. Federal Republic of	15	8 782	10	10 638
Hungary	—	—	2	816
India	3	602	5	1 087
Italy	4	1 382	3	1 996
Japan	21	13 249	11	9 408
Mexico	—	—	2	1 308
Netherlands	2	499	—	—
Pakistan	1	125	—	—
Philippines	—	—	1	621
Republic of Korea	1	564	6	5 137
South Africa	—	—	2	1 843
Spain	3	1 073	7	6 302
Sweden	6	3 700	6	5 682
Switzerland	4	1 926	1	942
Taiwan	2	1 208	2	1 902
USSR	30	10 616	18	15 200
United Kingdom	32	6 890	6	3 714
United States	69	50 644	88	96 408
Yugoslavia	—	—	1	632
TOTAL	234	120 363	227	206 702

1. Construction in Austria and in Iran has been interrupted. so the plants are not included.
Source: Based on Power Reactors in Member States (IAEA. Vienna. 1979).

full responsibility for the security of plants. An international repository of spent fuel and a bank of fresh fuels should be established and could form a starting-point to the internationalization process. Under a scheme for internationalization, diversion risks could be reduced significantly. Also, if we do eventually enter the dangerous arena of a fast-breeder economy, it would happen under international guidance.

All efforts should be put into strengthening the nonproliferation regime, and especially the NPT -- the main legal and political barrier against the spread of nuclear weapons. However, a longer-term solution must include the resolution of regional security problems, so that states do not perceive the need to develop nuclear weapons for security reasons. Also, the belief that nuclear weapons bring prestige must be disproved. So long as the nuclear-weapons powers imply, by continuously expanding and improving their nuclear arsenals, that nuclear weapons have high political and military utility, other countries may come to share this belief.

VII. THE TRADE IN ARMS

The international arms trade is one of the most alarming factors contributing to the growing militarization of the world. The arms trade with Third World countries has caused the most attention and concern, both because to a large extent it represents an extension of the conflict between East and West and because the weapons supplied to these countries have been extensively used. It remains a fact that practically all wars since 1945 have been fought in the Third World and with conventional weapons supplied by the main industrialized arms-producing countries.

While the arms-manufacturing countries once supplied primarily second-hand or obsolete weapons to underdeveloped countries, they have during recent years transferred many of the most advanced conventional weapons to the Third World. Very sophisticated weapons can often be purchased on the arms market even before they enter the arsenals of the producer countries.

The trade in arms has, for many years, been increasing at an alarming rate. In 1979, for example, the value of global arms exports was five times greater than it was in 1969, and twelve times what it was in 1959. In the 1970s -- the Decade for Disarmament -- the total value of major arms imports[2] was about $61,000 million -- three and a half times as much as that of the previous decade and seven times greater than that of the 1950s. Nor are there any signs that the average yearly rate of increase (25 per cent for the period 1975-1979) will slow down. On the contrary, the early 1980s will see increased investment in conventional weaponry, which sooner or later will enter the arms market.

Not only was there a growth in the volume of the arms trade in the 1970s. There was also an increase in the number of importing

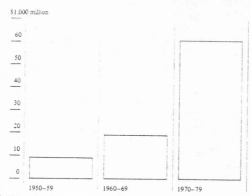

$1,000 million

60

50

40

30

20

10

0

1950–59   1960–69   1970–79

FIG. 5. Value of major weapons exports (in constant 1975 prices).

Third World importing regions

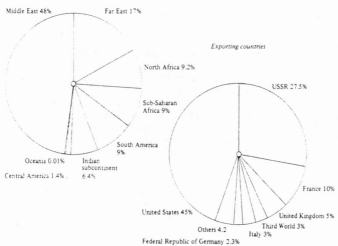

Middle East 48%   Far East 17%

Exporting countries

North Africa 9.2%

USSR 27.5%

Sub-Saharan
Africa 9%

South America
9%

Oceania 0.01%   Indian
subcontinent
Central America 1.4%   6.4%

France 10%

United States 45%   United Kingdom 5%

Others 4.2   Third World 3%
Italy 3%

Federal Republic of Germany 2.3%

FIG. 6. The importers' and exporters' shares of major-weapon supplies to the Third World, 1970–79.

countries and a demand for more sophisticated weapon systems. Furthermore, owing to the transfer of knowhow, the number of countries producing weapons domestically is growing rapidly. Today some fifty-six countries produce major weapons and twenty-four of these are in the Third World. If small arms are included then the number of weapon-producing countries is much greater.

Two-thirds of the global arms trade involves transfer of weapons to the Third World, a good part of which suffers from underdevelopment, starvation and disease. In the 1970s the United States was the biggest supplier of arms to the Third World, accounting for 45 per cent of exports. The Soviet Union was the second largest arms supplier, with a share of 27 per cent. Much further behind were the next two big arms suppliers -- France and the United Kingdom. After that came the new exporters of the 1970s -- Italy and the Federal Republic of Germany, followed by the Third World countries as a group. The largest Third World exporters of major arms were Israel, Brazil, Iran, Jordan, South Africa, Libyan Arab Jamahiriya, Singapore and Argentina.

The Middle East was throughout the 1970s the largest arms-importing region in the world, followed by the Far East and by Africa, which only started its big military buildup after 1970.

The United States was the biggest arms exporter to the Middle East, the Far East and South America, while the Soviet Union was the biggest supplier to Africa, the Indian subcontinent and Central America. The international arms trade is very much a Western affair, with NATO countries responsible for 66 per cent of exports while the members of the Warsaw Treaty Organization account for 28 per cent.

Transfers of conventional arms have on several occasions been the subject of discussions in the United Nations, but no measure of control has so far been successfully negotiated. Many Third World countries view with suspicion proposals for limiting the international flow of arms, regarding such proposals as attempts to impose unilateral arms limitation on them. However, the traffic in arms is encouraged by the suppliers of these weapons. The great powers export arms to gain political or economic influence, or military bases, in Third World regions. Moreover, certain governments believe that selling weapons helps their economies, especially during economic recession. And commercial firms use their considerable political influence to obtain export licences.

There is always a danger that both the United States and the USSR could be drawn into a regional conflict, which could thus escalate into a world war. And this is more likely if these powers are the main suppliers of the weapons used in the original conflict.

VIII. NAVAL ARMS RACE AND SUBMARINE WARFARE

New trends, both in the quantities of warships being procured and in the pace of their technological advancement, indicate that

TABLE 2. Rank order of Third World major arms importers. 1975–79

Importing region	Percentage of Third World total	Largest recipient countries	Percentage of region's total	Largest supplier to each country	Largest suppliers per region
Middle East	48	Iran	31	United States	United States
		Saudi Arabia	14	United States	USSR
		Jordan	13	United States	France
		Iraq	12	USSR	United Kingdom
		Israel	10	United States	
		Syria	6	USSR	
Far East	16	Republic of Korea	38	United States	United States
		Viet Nam	16	USSR	USSR
		Taiwan	13	United States	France
		Malaysia	5	United States	China
		Philippines	5	United States	
		Indonesia	5	United States	
North Africa	11	Libya	65	USSR	USSR
		Morocco	20	France	France
		Algeria	14	USSR	United States
		Tunisia	1	Italy	United Kingdom
Sub-Saharan Africa	10	South Africa	24	France	USSR
		Ethiopia	13	USSR	France
		Angola	9	USSR	United States
		Mozambique	9	USSR	United Kingdom
		Sudan	6	France	
		Nigeria	5	United Kingdom	
South America	9	Brazil	24	United States	United States
		Peru	20	USSR	United Kingdom
		Argentina	17	United Kingdom	France
		Chile	14	France	Italy
		Venezuela	13	Italy	
		Ecuador	8	France	
Indian subcontinent	5	India	52	USSR	USSR
		Pakistan	28	France	France
		Afghanistan	13	USSR	United Kingdom
		Bangladesh	3	China	China
		Nepal	0.3	France	
		Sri Lanka	0.2	France	
Central America	1.5	Cuba	45	USSR	USSR
		Mexico	28	United Kingdom	United Kingdom
		Bahamas	6	United States	United States
		Honduras	5	United States	France
		El Salvador	5	Israel	
		Guatemala	4	Israel	
Oceania	0.02	Papua New Guinea	63	Australia	Australia
					United States
		Fiji	37	United States	

the naval arms race is now more intensive than ever before.

Developments in naval weapon systems provide a good example of the evolutionary character of the present qualitative arms race. New types of naval weapons do not differ much in external characteristics from their predecessors. Where they do differ is in the greater efficiency of their elementary components: more energy-rich fuel composition; greater engine efficiency; more accurate guidance systems; greater resistance to electronic, optical and other counter-measures; increased adaptability to various firing platforms; and smaller size and lower weight. In addition to these features of weapons per se, several technological improvements have taken place in entire weapon systems, where the weapons are only links in a whole chain -- from remote surveillance, discovery and location of a target, through quick and accurate delivery of the weapon in order to execute the attack and the destruction of the target, to the assessment of the post-attack damage and to possible re-attack.

Available figures clearly show that in the past decade a steep rise has occurred in the numerical and qualitative characteristics of the world's light naval forces. The number of missile-armed fast patrol boats (FPBs) in the world grew in so short a time-span as 1975-78 from 398 to 811 (outstanding orders included), that is, more than doubled; the number of all types of FPBs grew in the same time from 1,972 to 2,483; and the number of other patrol craft (including missile-armed corvettes) grew from 1,899 to 2,475. There is now only one region in the world where FPB forces do not exist, namely Australia and Oceania. The numbers of missile-armed FPBs, that is, vessels most suitable in a combat role, grew most rapidly in Europe, the Middle East and Far East Asia. Whereas in 1960 only one state possessed FPBs, in 1970 seventeen countries, and in 1978 more than one-third of the countries (122) having direct access to the sea -- forty-five to be precise -- were already operating FPB forces.

Ballistic missiles carried aboard nuclear submarines are relied upon by both the United States and the USSR to provide the most secure form of deterrent retaliatory capability. This reliance is based on the assumed invulnerability conferred by the enormous difficulty of the task of locating and destroying all the missile submarines of an opponent in the opening stages of a nuclear attack.

Because of advances in geodetic knowledge of the earth's shape, in navigation systems for submarines, and in guidance systems for the missiles, SLBMs are now acquiring the degree of accuracy that is necessary for hitting missiles buried in hardened silos. Previously each side could feel reasonably assured that SLBMs were indeed only deterrent weapons, because they were only accurate enough for such soft and extensive targets as cities.

An enormous amount of effort is being put into new command, control and communication (C3) systems for missile submarines. There is still considerable doubt as to whether C3 links to submarines can function in a nuclear-war environment. If they cannot, then the viability of the deterrent concept is endangered.

However, the biggest threat to the deterrence concept is the increasing ability of anti-submarine warfare (ASW) systems to

detect and destroy missile submarines. Although there is no single breakthrough imminent which will make the oceans militarily transparent, there are a number of lines of technological progress coming to fruition which will, taken together, offer a high probability of detecting missile submarines anywhere in the ocean. If the location of the submarines is known, then their destruction becomes relatively easy.

If the invulnerability of both the submarines and their C3 systems cannot be guaranteed, then there will in turn be an increased temptation to further adapt the missile submarines to first-strike counterforce roles.

IX. MILITARY USE OF OUTER SPACE

Considerable qualitative advances are being made in almost all fields of military technology. An excellent example is the military use of outer space.

Military satellites are able to navigate weapons to their targets with a high degree of accuracy; they can be used to pinpoint geographical positions with great precision so that no target can remain invulnerable; and they increase the possibility of fighting wars by remote control.

With the development of reconnaissance and early-warning satellites more emphasis seems to be placed on a strategic doctrine of flexible response and limited nuclear war. Early-warning satellites can detect almost immediately the launching of an enemy missile, while reconnaissance satellites can give precise target information and also quickly assess the damage. This allows the prompt response essential in a limited exchange of nuclear weapons.

Military satellites are used for reconnaissance, early warning of attack, communications, navigation, and for meteorological and geodetic measurement. They have also been used to observe conflict areas on earth. Over 50 per cent of all military satellites have been launched for reconnaissance purposes. They provide photographic and electronic reconnaissance, early-warning systems and a means of ocean surveillance.

The surface movements of naval forces can be closely monitored by ocean-surveillance satellites. Oceanographic satellites provide information about ocean conditions over the entire globe in real time. Such information is vital to the functioning of long-range submarine-detection systems and is also used by submarines to avoid detection.

Early-warning satellites are launched to give notice of the launching of enemy missiles. They also carry sensors to detect nuclear explosions both on the surface of the earth and in the atmosphere so as to check treaty violations.

Military communications satellites are replacing other systems for global strategic networks, for command and control of nuclear forces and for tactical battlefield and naval networks. The increasing complexity of modern means of warfare, involving a host

of mobile weapon systems such as aircraft, missiles and ships, places enormous demands on new military navigation systems. Navigation satellites will play an increasing role. By means of a satellite-based system, it will be possible to guide a weapon anywhere on earth to within ten metres of its target. In addition, the detailed maps made possible by geodetic and reconnaissance satellites allow the military forces to achieve greater accuracy for some of the most advanced weapons, such as cruise missiles.

A more recent military activity in space is the development of ways of destroying hostile satellites. In addition to some conventional techniques, high-energy laser and particle-beam weapons are also envisaged for this purpose. This is a dangerous activity because early-warning satellites and reconnaissance satellites provide reassurance against nuclear attack. The threat of their destruction would cause considerable anxiety.

Another dangerous development would be systems based in space for destroying ballistic missiles in flight. Currently, high-energy lasers and heavy-particle beams are being considered for this purpose. Effective ballistic-missile defence would actively encourage thinking in terms of nuclear-war fighting.

On the positive side, military satellites play a useful role in verifying arms-control agreements. But only two nations possess the technology for such extensive data gathering. Therefore, broad international participation in verification of multilateral arms-control agreements by satellites has been demanded for many years.

X. ECOLOGICAL WARFARE

There is a discernible trend for modern warfare to become ever more destructive of the environment. Moreover, the weapons of mass destruction available today could be employed so as to have a catastrophic environmental impact. There is the further suggestion that man will soon attain the technological sophistication to permit the manipulation of certain forces of nature such as hurricanes, tsunamis, or earthquakes. If these abilities were to be employed for hostile purposes, their environmental impact could be truly widespread, long lasting and severe.

Hostile environmental disruption is open to a priori criticism since its effect, although more or less subtle, is unavoidably indiscriminate, uncontainable, and long lasting. The impact is thus felt not only by the enemy military forces, but probably as well by the civil sector, by third parties, and by future generations. Moreover, all living things on earth deserve at least some measure of respect and protection in their own right. Humans must think of themselves less as owners of the land and lords of the birds and beasts, and more as temporary residents and guardians of the land and what it supports. A concern over the ecological consequences of war does not preclude direct traditional anthropocentric concerns. It may, in fact, enhance such concerns via a civilizing influence and also perhaps by awakening a new

ominous, particularly the development of small, low-yield nuclear weapons, of enhanced radiation weapons and of tactical concepts for their use in battle. Delivered with higher accuracy and causing less collateral damage per warhead, their use on the battlefield may seem more acceptable, so that the step from non-nuclear to nuclear war may be more readily taken. Once they are used on the battlefield, escalation towards full-scale nuclear war becomes a dangerous possibility.

The importance of the changes now under way in the field of nuclear armaments and their carriers is not that their performance in missions traditionally assigned to them is improving year by year, but that essentially new types of missions are becoming possible. New technologies open the way for new doctrines. These in turn give an appearance of rationality to the deployment of weaponry embodying these technologies. At the same time they increase the dangers of war and alter the terms of the disarmament equation, rendering it more complex and more intractable.

The proliferation of nuclear technologies continues at an accelerating pace. France and China acquired a nuclear weapons capability in the 1960s. In 1974, India, which is not a party to the Non-Proliferation Treaty, conducted a nuclear explosion experiment underground. It was officially termed a peaceful nuclear explosion experiment. This explosion demonstrated how readily and cheaply a small nuclear weapons capability could be derived from a major civilian nuclear programme. In other cases a nuclear weapons capability could have been acquired without being demonstrated in a nuclear explosion. Civilian nuclear programmes, and with them, to a variable degree, the technical expertise and the fissile material required for military programmes, have spread all over the world during the 1970s. In 1975, nineteen countries had nuclear power plants in operation, and another ten countries will have them by 1980. Experimental reactors are now in operation in well over fifty countries. As far as most industrialized and several developing countries are concerned, there are no longer serious technological or economic barriers against initiating a nuclear weapons programme.

Also, as regards conventional weapons, developments have been far-reaching. Throughout the 1960s conventional weapons systems underwent continual and rapid refinement in terms of size, speed, propulsion, fire-power, accuracy and so forth. Unit costs for major weapons systems typically doubled in real terms during this period. For aircraft it was noted they doubled about twice as fast. Sophisticated weaponry, including supersonic aircraft, became commonplace in the armouries of industrialized as well as less developed countries.

New precision-guided munition (PGMs), remotely piloted vehicles (RPVs) and other devices have been developed to carry a conventional warhead to its target with hit probabilities close to '1', or, in the case of RPVs, for reconnaissance and similar missions. This group of weapons is a whole family of devices using the latest developments in such fields as laser technology, micro-electronics, electromagnetic sensors in the radar, infra-red and optical ranges and wide-band data links for a variety of remote automatic guidance and/or homing devices. A first generation of

characterized some earlier developments, such as the advent of the atom bomb or of space technology, there is a danger that it may seem as though military technology has remained relatively unchanged. Such complacency would be entirely unjustified. Recent developments have profoundly influenced military capabilities, worldwide destructive potentials and strategic conditions, possibilities and doctrines.

The most important and spectacular aspect of the arms race in the 1960s was the development and the full-scale deployment of intercontinental ballistic missiles (ICBMs) and of submarine-launched missiles (SLBMs), and the associated deployment of satellite surveillance and communication systems. By the end of that decade there was widespread concern that a new arms-race spiral might result from the development of anti-ballistic missile systems (ABMs) and from counter-measures in the form of increasing numbers of launchers and, more particularly, of increasing numbers of warheads per launcher to saturate ABM systems. The technical form for the latter development of multiple and independently targetable re-entry vehicles (MIRVs).

Moreover, a major post-MIRV innovation is already at an advanced stage of development. This is a manoeuvrable re-entry vehicle (MARV) which can change direction in the terminal stages of its trajectory. This could make defence against ballistic missile attack more difficult, but in particular, if combined with developments now taking place in terminal guidance systems, it can provide MARVed missiles with pinpoint accuracies of a few tens of metres instead of current accuracies of somewhat less than one kilometre. With such accuracies, the silos now protecting the land-based ICBMs can be destroyed with near certainty with a single warhead at the first attempt. As a result it becomes possible to consider using 'strategic' nuclear weapons in new ways. In addition to being a means of massive reprisals against centres of population and industry to serve as a basic deterrent, it becomes possible to think of using ballistic missiles in 'counter-force' roles to gain military advantage at the outset of a war by striking at the weapons and military installations of the opponent, or to use them to conduct supposedly 'limited' nuclear war. The adoption of doctrines of this kind could greatly enhance the probability of nuclear war.

No less significant are the implications of the deployment of long-range cruise missiles. These weapons, now under development, are best described as small, highly manoeuvrable, low-flying pilotless aircraft. They can be equipped with a nuclear as well as a conventional warhead. Current models have ranges of several thousand kilometres and accurate guidance systems, which readjust the trajectory at intervals by comparing terrain features with a map. The accuracy is therefore independent of the range. It will be impossible to determine from its geometry alone whether a cruise missile carries a nuclear or a conventional warhead and, within wide limits, what range it may have. Moreover, it is a small and easily concealed vehicle. Future agreements on strategic weapons may thus become very difficult to negotiate because they would be difficult to verify.

Developments in nuclear weapons technology proper are equally

Economic and Social Consequences of the Arms Race

UNITED NATIONS GROUP OF CONSULTANT EXPERTS

I. DYNAMICS OF THE ARMS RACE

The arms race is increasingly a worldwide phenomenon and, although its intensity varies markedly between regions, few countries and no major region has stayed out of it. The competition in armaments between the largest military powers is by far the most important. It involves the greatest diversion of resources, the greatest inherent dangers and constitutes the principal driving force of the worldwide arms race. The competition is even more intense than is suggested by the immense size and the rapid expansion of their arsenals, because it takes place primarily in a qualitative rather than a quantitative dimension, each new generation of weapons being more complex and more destructive than the systems it replaces.

The primary engine of this worldwide arms race is constituted by the qualitative arms race among the largest military powers. This is due chiefly to the virtual monopoly of these powers in development of advanced military technology, to their overwhelmingly large share of world production and world exports of advanced weaponry, and to the global character of their interest, politically and militarily. The six main military spenders not only account for three-quarters of world military spending, but for practically all military research and development (R&D) and for practically all exports of weapons and military equipment.[1]

The past decade has seen a continuous stream of new developments in the sphere of nuclear and conventional means of warfare. Because these technological and qualitative changes have not displayed the spectacular, eye-catching qualities which

From **ARMAMENTS, ARMS CONTROL AND DISARMAMENT**, UNESCO Press, 1981, (40-57), reprinted by permission of the publisher.

NOTES

1. Unless otherwise indicated, throughout the work the sign
    $ = United States dollars.

2. The SIPRI data on transfers of major weapons include aircraft,
    armoured vehicles, missiles and warships. According to SIPRI
    statistics, major weapons account for about 40 per cent of
    total arms sales. The remaining 60 per cent consists mostly of
    related equipment, electronics, support, training, spares, guns
    and small arms.

3. SIPRI has dealt with the problems of war and the environment in
    two books, namely, The Ecological Consequences of the Second
    Indochina War, Stockholm, Almqvist & Wiksell, 1976, and Weapons
    of Mass Destruction and the Environment, London, Taylor &
    Francis, 1977.

purposes would diminish the capacity for waging chemical warfare, at short notice at any rate.

Complete and effective prohibition of all chemical weapons and their destruction is one of the most urgent disarmament measures.

XII. MILITARY RESEARCH AND DEVELOPMENT (R & D)

Apart from the huge increase in the volume of resources devoted to military uses the other distinguishing feature of the post-war period has been the extraordinary emphasis given to technological advances. The intensity of the drive -- though not the drive itself -- to develop and produce better machines is basically military in origin. A major conclusion drawn from events during the Second World War was that failure to have on hand the most technologically advanced weapons would have disastrous consequences. As a result, military research and development (R&D) was given the highest priority. In the major countries the quantity and quality of the scientific and engineering workforce were deliberately maximized (through changes in the educational system and by modifying relative wage and salary rates) to meet the enormously increased military demand.

Since these developments occurred in parallel in both East and West, the anticipated dangers of lagging technologically became a self-fulfilling prophecy. For the last thirty years new and improved weapons have emerged at an unmanageably rapid rate with no signs of any relaxation.

About 10 per cent of military spending is for military R&D. This activity -- which also absorbs more than one-half of the world's most highly qualified physical and engineering scientists -- is the one which makes possible the arms race. Without military R&D, the production of weapons for replacement may continue, the size of the world's arsenals may increase, and the weapons of the small and medium powers may (because of the arms trade) eventually approach in quality those of the great powers. But, in terms of the development of new, more sophisticated, more destructive and increasingly expensive weapons, the arms race would cease. In practice, however, military R&D is the hardest of all military activities to restrain. In fact, since the Second World War the only significant limits to developments in military technology have been the innovative capabilities of the Soviet and United States societies.

constituency to war-related concerns. That is to say, a respect for the environment should reinforce the incentive to attain a disarmed world.

The Second Indo-China War was the first in modern history in which environmental disruption was an intentional and sustained component of the strategy of one of the belligerent powers. In an attempt to subdue a largely guerrilla opponent, the United States pioneered a variety of hostile techniques causing widespread environmental disruption which were aimed at denying its enemy concealment, freedom of movement, and local sources of food and other supplies.

The three ecologically most destructive techniques of the Second Indo-China War were; (a) the massive and sustained expenditure of high-explosive munitions (about 14 million tons of bombs, shells and the like); (b) the profligate dissemination of chemical anti-plant agents (about 55,000 tons of herbicides); and (c) the large-scale employment of heavy land-clearing tractors (about 200 so-called Rome ploughs).

Among the ecological lessons to be learned from the military tactics employed during the Second Indo-China War are: (a) that the vegetation can be severely damaged or even destroyed with relative ease over extensive areas -- and, of course, with it the ecosystems for which it provides the basis; (b) that natural, agricultural and industrial-crop plant communities are all similarly vulnerable; and (c) that the ecological impact of such actions is likely to be of long duration.

XI. CHEMICAL WEAPONS

Chemical weapons increasingly seem to be regarded as useful tactical weapons in specific situations. The question of eliminating chemical weapons has been on the agenda of international disarmament bodies for the past twelve years. Progress towards a ban on chemical weapons is extremely slow, mainly because of perceived problems with verification.

A major issue in discussions on chemical disarmament is how to eliminate the large existing stocks of chemical warfare (CW) agents and the facilities for their production, and how to verify that this has been done. For example, a difficult verification problem is how the existence of allegedly concealed or undeclared chemical munition stockpiles can be confirmed or refuted in situations were trust is lacking.

The maintenance of aging stockpiles of chemical weapons in the vicinity of densely populated and heavily trafficked areas is associated with environmental hazards. Further hazards are associated with the handling and transportation of chemical weapons.

Although some highly toxic chemicals are manufactured for ordinary industrial processes, strict limitations on these chemicals as well as destruction of those suitable only for warfare

characterized some earlier developments, such as the advent of the
atom bomb or of space technology, there is a danger that it may
seem as though military technology has remained relatively
unchanged. Such complacency would be entirely unjustified. Recent
developments have profoundly influenced military capabilities,
worldwide destructive potentials and strategic conditions,
possibilities and doctrines.

The most important and spectacular aspect of the arms race in
the 1960s was the development and the full-scale deployment of
intercontinental ballistic missiles (ICBMs) and of submarine-
launched missiles (SLBMs), and the associated deployment of
satellite surveillance and communication systems. By the end of
that decade there was widespread concern that a new arms-race
spiral might result from the development of anti-ballistic missile
systems (ABMs) and from counter-measures in the form of increasing
numbers of launchers and, more particularly, of increasing numbers
of warheads per launcher to saturate ABM systems. The technical
form for the latter development of multiple and independently
targetable re-entry vehicles (MIRVs).

Moreover, a major post-MIRV innovation is already at an
advanced stage of development. This is a manoeuvrable re-entry
vehicle (MARV) which can change direction in the terminal stages of
its trajectory. This could make defence against ballistic missile
attack more difficult, but in particular, if combined with
developments now taking place in terminal guidance systems, it can
provide MARVed missiles with pinpoint accuracies of a few tens of
metres instead of current accuracies of somewhat less than one
kilometre. With such accuracies, the silos now protecting the land-
based ICBMs can be destroyed with near certainty with a single
warhead at the first attempt. As a result it becomes possible to
consider using 'strategic' nuclear weapons in new ways. In
addition to being a means of massive reprisals against centres of
population and industry to serve as a basic deterrent, it becomes
possible to think of using ballistic missiles in 'counter-force'
roles to gain military advantage at the outset of a war by striking
at the weapons and military installations of the opponent, or to
use them to conduct supposedly 'limited' nuclear war. The adoption
of doctrines of this kind could greatly enhance the probability of
nuclear war.

No less significant are the implications of the deployment of
long-range cruise missiles. These weapons, now under development,
are best described as small, highly manoeuvrable, low-flying
pilotless aircraft. They can be equipped with a nuclear as well as
a conventional warhead. Current models have ranges of several
thousand kilometres and accurate guidance systems, which readjust
the trajectory at intervals by comparing terrain features with a
map. The accuracy is therefore independent of the range. It will
be impossible to determine from its geometry alone whether a cruise
missile carries a nuclear or a conventional warhead and, within
wide limits, what range it may have. Moreover, it is a small and
easily concealed vehicle. Future agreements on strategic weapons
may thus become very difficult to negotiate because they would be
difficult to verify.

Developments in nuclear weapons technology proper are equally

ominous, particularly the development of small, low-yield nuclear weapons, of enhanced radiation weapons and of tactical concepts for their use in battle. Delivered with higher accuracy and causing less collateral damage per warhead, their use on the battlefield may seem more acceptable, so that the step from non-nuclear to nuclear war may be more readily taken. Once they are used on the battlefield, escalation towards full-scale nuclear war becomes a dangerous possibility.

The importance of the changes now under way in the field of nuclear armaments and their carriers is not that their performance in missions traditionally assigned to them is improving year by year, but that essentially new types of missions are becoming possible. New technologies open the way for new doctrines. These in turn give an appearance of rationality to the deployment of weaponry embodying these technologies. At the same time they increase the dangers of war and alter the terms of the disarmament equation, rendering it more complex and more intractable.

The proliferation of nuclear technologies continues at an accelerating pace. France and China acquired a nuclear weapons capability in the 1960s. In 1974, India, which is not a party to the Non-Proliferation Treaty, conducted a nuclear explosion experiment underground. It was officially termed a peaceful nuclear explosion experiment. This explosion demonstrated how readily and cheaply a small nuclear weapons capability could be derived from a major civilian nuclear programme. In other cases a nuclear weapons capability could have been acquired without being demonstrated in a nuclear explosion. Civilian nuclear programmes, and with them, to a variable degree, the technical expertise and the fissile material required for military programmes, have spread all over the world during the 1970s. In 1975, nineteen countries had nuclear power plants in operation, and another ten countries will have them by 1980. Experimental reactors are now in operation in well over fifty countries. As far as most industrialized and several developing countries are concerned, there are no longer serious technological or economic barriers against initiating a nuclear weapons programme.

Also, as regards conventional weapons, developments have been far-reaching. Throughout the 1960s conventional weapons systems underwent continual and rapid refinement in terms of size, speed, propulsion, fire-power, accuracy and so forth. Unit costs for major weapons systems typically doubled in real terms during this period. For aircraft it was noted they doubled about twice as fast. Sophisticated weaponry, including supersonic aircraft, became commonplace in the armouries of industrialized as well as less developed countries.

New precision-guided munition (PGMs), remotely piloted vehicles (RPVs) and other devices have been developed to carry a conventional warhead to its target with hit probabilities close to '1', or, in the case of RPVs, for reconnaissance and similar missions. This group of weapons is a whole family of devices using the latest developments in such fields as laser technology, micro-electronics, electromagnetic sensors in the radar, infra-red and optical ranges and wide-band data links for a variety of remote automatic guidance and/or homing devices. A first generation of

PGMs made their appearance in the Indo-China war. In the Middle East in 1973, the enormous potential of such weapons against tanks and aircraft was demonstrated. Both the type of technology involved and their cost make PGMs accessible to many countries, and, indeed, many have them now in their inventories.

The new weapons, together with developments in such areas as night-vision devices, battlefield surveillance and communications, are likely to accelerate the pace of modern warfare and to place a still higher premium on standing military forces. Last but not least, with dramatic improvements in accuracy, the yield of the explosive charge becomes a less important parameter in performance. There have been suggestions, for example, that some of the missions now assigned to 'tactical' nuclear weapons could be performed by precision-delivered weapons with a conventional warhead. In principle this could mean that military planners would be more willing to dispense with the use of nuclear weapons in a limited conflict, but in practice it could equally well have the effect of blurring the distinction between the use of nuclear and non-nuclear weapons, thus enhancing the risk of an armed conflict developing into nuclear war.

A range of new weapons and munitions based on blast, fragmentation and incendiary effects has been developed, and was used, notably during the Indo-China war, for saturation bombing over large areas. Such carpet-bombing techniques approach nuclear weapons as regards the blind, indiscriminate destruction they cause, the long-term ecological effects to which they give rise, and the high proportion of wounded and maimed among casualties. Other weapons of massive and indiscriminate destruction have not lagged behind. The effectiveness of incendiary weapons has been considerably increased, and the development of binary nerve gases and their munitions (which are relatively innocuous to handle as the nerve gas is only assembled in flight) could seriously weaken the remaining technical and operational constraints on the deployment of chemical weapons.

Significant developments have also taken place in a number of other fields such as radar technology, anti-submarine warfare techniques, low-altitude interceptor aircraft, laser-guided cannon and many more.

The strong qualitative momentum of the current arms race has a number of important consequences for the way it develops, the insecurity it generates and in terms of the possibilities for disarmament. In an arms race where the emphasis is on quantity, where technological development is slow and of little consequence, countries may be expected to match their armament efforts to the stocks or the growth rates of the military forces of their opponents. There is room for saturation levels or for mutually agreed ceilings and reductions. Under conditions of rapid military innovation, on the other hand, the decisive factor in the military procurement plans of countries at the forefront of the technological arms race is not so much the actual military strength of their opponents but rather those technological advances which opponents might be able to achieve over the next decade or so (ten years being the typical gestation period for a major technological advance). Inevitably, as the apprehensions of military planners

shift from the force levels towards the R&D efforts of their opponents, it is increasingly on the R&D efforts of their own country, which are known, that they will have to base their plans.

In an arms race where the stress is on technological advances the process of weapon and counter-weapon development therefore tends to become in some measure an <u>intra</u>-national process, in some cases only marginally related to the stages actually reached by other countries. Each country is actively seeking means of defeating its own most advanced weapons and of neutralizing its own most recent defences, thus conferring on the development of military technology a momentum and a rate of obsolescence much greater than in comparable civilian applications. A qualitative arms race with its long lead time and its emphasis on future possibilities rather than current realities tends to move in one direction only: one country's advances in weaponry will be emulated by others, but its self-restraint need not be. Similarly an increase in international tension may accelerate the arms race, but an improvement of the international climate will not necessarily suffice to slow down.

The arms race is not only becoming more dangerous; it is also becoming more complex and more firmly entrenched. It is sustained by a variety of forces acting together, and it must be expected that to remove one of them is not sufficient to reverse its course. In fact, it may be assumed that it is not one or a few single factors but precisely their multiplicity which confers upon the arms race its great inertia and which has rendered it so intractable from the point of view of disarmament, any limited successes in one field tending to be offset very quickly by developments in other sectors of the arms race.

The commitment to incessant qualitative change is deeply embedded in the inner logic of the arms race. Agreements on qualitative and technological restrictions are not easily reached, not least because of difficult verification problems. But if the difficulties of securing some measure of control over this dimension of the arms race are particularly great, so too is the urgency of the need to take determined steps in this direction. Each passing year sees the initiation of a spate of new weapons, and existing programmes become more deeply entrenched in the military and political systems of countries and thus more difficult to stop.

In light of the developments described above, it is necessary to expound openly the dangers of the continuation of the arms race, and to dispel illusions that lasting peace and security can coexist with huge accumulations of means of destruction. The adoption and implementation of resolute measures in the field of disarmament and particularly nuclear disarmament, ultimately leading to general and complete disarmament, has become imperative. At the same time it is necessary to intensify efforts for the adoption of partial measures of military disengagement and disarmament that can contribute to the achievement of that goal.

II. THE ARMS RACE IN TERMS OF RESOURCES

The arms race, with its economic costs and social and political effects, nationally and internationally, constitutes an important obstacle to effective progress in establishing a new international economic order. Resources now being absorbed by the arms race are scarce and needed for socially constructive ends. Every year military activities throughout the world absorb a volume of resources equivalent to about two-thirds of the aggregate gross national product of those countries which together comprise the poorest half of the world's population.

Since the Second World War none of the major military powers have been at war with one another, but world military expenditure has been rising steadily. Over the past half century it has increased in real terms by a factor of 10, corresponding to an annual increase of nearly 5 per cent. Since the Second World War the direct costs of the arms race have exceeded $6,000 billion (in 1975 prices) or about as much as the aggregate GNP of the entire world in 1975.

Public expenditures for health services have expanded rapidly in recent years. Nevertheless, public health expenditures (to which privately financed medical care should be added to complete the picture) only amount to about 60 per cent of military expenditure on a world basis. Again differences between countries are very large. Even greater imbalances exist in the critical field of research funding. The resources devoted to medical research worldwide are only one-fifth of those devoted to military research and development. In all cases the resources consumed in the military sector are very large compared with the social expenditures of governments, even in such important fields as education and health, indicating the unfortunate priorities that govern the allocation of public funds throughout the world. In the world as a whole there are almost as many soldiers as there are teachers.

Such comparisons of gross expenditure for wholly incommensurate ends are, however, relatively meaningless as they stand. They give only a crude indication of the sacrifices in terms of social and economic progress that the arms race entails. A more adequate assessment would require a survey of the needs for increased resources for social and other non-military purposes, and a comparison of the costs of meeting those needs with the costs of military programmes.

The most alarming situation of all is in the area of nutrition. Half a billion people throughout the world are severely malnourished and millions more subsist on diets that are far below minimal needs. A large proportion of young children in developing countries are blocked in their physical and mental development because of diet deficiencies, which entails incalculable consequences for the next generation. In recent years famine has struck entire regions of the world, and on a per capita basis food production in the developing countries as a whole has been declining. Yet the poorest countries, those with per capita

incomes below $200, generally countries whose military expenditures are modest in relation to GNP, nevertheless spend (on average) about as much for military activities as they spend on agricultural investment.

The vast benefits which could result from even trifling cuts in military expenditures, and the reallocation of the funds thus saved, are particularly obvious in the field of health. The World Health Organization (WHO) spent around $83 million over ten years to eradicate smallpox in the world. That amount would not even suffice to buy a single modern strategic bomber. The WHO programme to eradicate malaria in the world, estimated at a cost of some $450 million, is dragging on owing to lack of funds. Yet its total cost over the years is only half of what is spent every day for military purposes, and only a third of what will be spent, strictly for procurement, for each of the new Trident nuclear-missile submarines.

Moreover, the potential benefits of a transfer of resources from the military to the health sector reach far beyond the immediate humanitarian aspect. The implementation of such eradication programmes would by itself release important resources in the medical sector for new tasks, and, improving the general health standard in affected areas, would enhance the ability of people to improve their social and economic conditions in other respects. Such cumulative benefits are indeed a general feature of many development programmes, particularly of those which are directed towards the most destitute sectors of the population. In this respect as well expenditures for development purposes stand in stark contrast to military expenditures, which are a waste in themselves, which induce other countries to similar wastage, and which undermine the potential for future growth.

It is in the field of scientific and technological capability that the diversion of resources to military ends is most massive. It is estimated that at the present time some 25 per cent of the world's scientific manpower is engaged in military-related pursuits. In the past the fraction has been even higher. Indeed, it has been estimated that of total cumulative R&D spending since the Second World War some 40 per cent has been directed at achieving military ends. By far the largest part is spent on the development of equipment which has no conceivable civilian use.

As already noted, military research and development is overwhelmingly concentrated in the six main military spenders. Together they are reported to account for 96 to 97 per cent of world military R&D. As only a small percentage of the world's scientific and technical manpower is found in the developing countries, it follows that military research and development in the world absorbs perhaps ten times the entire scientific and technological capabilities available in developing countries. Moreover, technological innovation has been very rapid in the military field. One important consequence is that as high-technology weaponry spreads from the technologically leading countries to countries where the technical and industrial base is narrower, and as these countries engage in the production of advanced weapons themselves, military requirements take an increasing toll of already scarce technical skills and equipment.

The civilian spinoffs from military research, if not in all cases negligible, have been trifling in comparison with the resources with which they were brought and with the results that could have been achieved if the efforts had been aimed directly at the civilian application.

Manpower is another one of the very large drains on resources which the arms race entails. The armed forces around the world total approximately 22 million people. The total manpower absorption by the military, direct and indirect, can only be guessed at. For the United States there is for every three persons in the armed forces another four in military-related employment. Military and military-related activities everywhere absorb a much higher proportion of the most qualified categories of persons than the share of the military budget in the gross national product might lead one to expect. This is obviously true of research personnel, engineers and technicians. It is also true in the field of administrative and managerial skills. In some cases the proportion of industrial employment directly or indirectly engaged in military-related production seems to be much higher than the proportion of GNP diverted to military ends. In any case it is evident that the overall drain on highly qualified manpower resources is often larger than either military budget figures or overall figures for military-related employment suggest.

The protection of the environment is an important part of the resource problem. Military activities impact in several ways on the task of repairing the environmental damages of the past and preventing or minimizing further degradation. One fact, perhaps in the long term the most important of all, is simply the diversion of financial and scientific resources involved in the arms race. Effective solutions to environmental problems will in many cases require large research and development efforts and considerable investments for reprocessing, for air and water purification and for many other tasks. Effective action in this field, not least where large-scale international co-operation is required, would be greatly facilitated by the abatement of the arms race and, not least, by the release of important scientific and technical resources which this would bring about.

The world's armed forces are also major consumers of a wide range of nonrenewable resources, both energy and raw-material reserves, though statistical information on this is fragmentary or non-existent. Extrapolating from United States figures, world military consumption of liquid hydrocarbons (excluding petroleum products used in the production of weapons and equipment) has been estimated to be about 700 to 750 million barrels annually. This is twice the annual consumption for the whole of Africa and corresponds to approximately 3.5 per cent of world consumption. For jet fuel, on the other hand, military consumption (in peacetime) is reportedly one-third of total consumption for the United States. Even though information is mostly lacking, it is evident that the military contribution to the depletion of natural resources is substantial in many cases.

Judging by the figures for the latest years, the share of output wasted on armaments is rising again for the world as a whole and for a majority of countries. This reflects the slower rate of

growth of world output in recent years and the continued rise of military expenditure in most countries. Moreover, there has not been, of course, any long-term redeployment of resources away from the military at all. The long-term transfer has been entirely the other way: from the civilian economy where growth is generated, to the military sector which has appropriated a substantial part of that growth, increasing in absolute terms (and in constant 1973 prices) by almost 80 per cent from $150,000–$160,000 million in 1960 to $270,000–$280,000 million in 1977.

III. THE ARMS RACE AND ECONOMIC AND SOCIAL DEVELOPMENT

One aspect of the economic and social impact of the arms race is the constraining effect on consumption, private and public, and on growth.

In this period under review, the economic outlook for the world has darkened considerably. This has underlined the intolerable character of the waste of resources and has added to the urgency of the many social and economic problems facing the world, problems whose effective alleviation would be greatly facilitated by the reallocation to socially constructive ends of the resources now spent on the arms race. In the 1970s inflation of a magnitude unprecedented in post-war history hit many countries.

The high level of military spending in the world not only diverts resources that are urgently needed for dealing effectively with these problems, but also helps to exacerbate these problems. Large military expenditures contribute to the depletion of natural resources, tend to aggravate inflationary tendencies and add to existing balance-of-payments problems. In this way, they have contributed to economic disruption and political instability in some countries. Even so, the implications of an arms race and of military expenditures on the scale typical of the post-war period are much more pervasive than mere economic considerations would suggest. Being one of the main factors shaping the international context, the arms race exerts a profound influence on the politics, economy and society of many countries.

So far, the high levels of military expenditure have not been noticeably affected by the economic recession which hit many countries after 1973. In some countries there is a marked contrast between a still buoyant military sector on the one hand and a depressed civilian economy and tightening or downright austere government budgets on the other. In some limited aspects of the arms race, one can even register a new impetus directly related to features of the present economic crisis: some countries have been able to improve their balance-of-payments position by increased arms exports.

One of the main economic problems of the first half of this decade was the accelerating inflationary process in many countries of the world. Theory and data are not at the point where the role

of military expenditure in stimulating inflation can be qualified, but consideration of the various ways in which it can have an effect suggests that its contribution is not inconsequential. High military expenditures sustained over a long period of time are likely to aggravate upward pressures on the price level in several ways. First, military expenditures are inherently inflationary in that purchasing power and effective demand is created without an offsetting increase in immediately consumable output or in productive capacity to meet future consumption requirements. This excess demand creates an upward pressure on prices throughout the economy.

Second, there are reasons to believe that the arms industry offers less resistance to increases in the costs of labour and of the other factors of production than do most other industries, partly because of its highly capital- and technology-intensive character, and partly because cost increases in this sector can more readily be passed on to the customer. These increases in the cost of the other factors of production then spread to other sectors of the economy, including sectors where the rate of growth of productivity is lower, forcing up their prices as well. Finally, and more generally, the diversion of substantial capital and R&D resources away from the civilian sector impedes the long-term growth of productivity and thereby renders the economy more vulnerable to inflationary pressures. Inflationary trends, whatever their origin, tend to be exported, affecting other countries in the form of price increases, scarcities or in other ways, depending on the circumstances. The inflationary impact of military expenditure on the prices of exported military goods to developing countries results in a deterioration of their terms of trade.

As regards economic development and growth in particular, the maintenance and arming of large standing military forces absorbs a volume of resources substantial enough to affect all the basic parameters involved: the volume and structure of investment, the size and composition of the work force and the rate of technological change. Some 20 per cent of total world output is devoted to fixed capital formation, world military expenditures being equivalent to 25 to 30 per cent of this.

In most countries, therefore, there is scope for significant rises in investment if military budgets are reduced. Even crude calculations indicate that the potential effects of this on growth could be substantial. If the greater part of world military expenditure could, instead, be allocated to investment, growth rates might be expected to increase by 1 or 2 per cent. This is in fact very large.

If half the funds spent on armaments throughout the world in the period 1970-75 had instead been invested in the civilian sector, annual output at the end of the period could have been perhaps $200,000 million larger than it was. The sum of $200,000 million is somewhat more than the aggregate GNP of southern Asia and the mid-African region, the two large regions of acute poverty and slow growth in the world, with a total population of over 1,000 million people. Over a longer period the effects on world output of the reallocation of part of world military expenditures to

investment purposes would be even more spectacular.

The glaring investment needs throughout the world in housing, urban renewal, health, education, agriculture, energy, environment and many other fields need no further emphasis. Continued economic growth presupposes increasing investments in energy and raw materials extraction, both from traditional sources and from new ones. Estimates of the costs of combating pollution indicate requirements of the order of 1.4 to 1.9 per cent of GNP under moderate assumptions and of the order of 2.5 to 4 per cent in a more maximalist version. To eliminate extreme poverty and to diminish the gap between developing and developed countries, developing countries need to increase investments very considerably. To reduce by half before the end of the century the gap in per capita incomes between rich and poor countries, currently of the order of 13:1, the same calculations indicate among other things that the rate of investment in poor countries would have to be raised to 30 to 35 per cent of GNP, and in some cases 40 per cent. World agricultural production would have to increase three or fourfold as compared with 1970. This would require substantial investment in opening up new land, in irrigation and in the institution of high-yield techniques. It is hard to imagine that such programmes would be at all possible without radical cuts in military budgets.

Manpower is another major factor in the growth equation where a massive diversion to military ends is taking place. It is still a widespread belief today that disarmament or discontinuation of some specific weapons programme would swell the ranks of the jobless, particularly when unemployment is already high. It should be stressed that such conceptions are wrong. Military outlays are not unique in their ability to generate employment. In fact, whereas military expenditures obviously create jobs in the industries supplying the armed forces, the growing high-technology component in military expenditures has eroded their direct and their overall job-creating potential. Today there is rapidly accumulating evidence that high military budgets instead of alleviating overall unemployment contribute substantially to it. According to the United States Government estimates (and only for this country do figures seem to be available) $1,000 million of military expenditure creates 76,000 jobs. But if the same amount is spent for civilian programmes of the federal government it creates an average of over 100,000 jobs, and many more than this if channelled into activities that are particularly labour-consuming. Calculations indicate that if the same $1,000 million were released for private consumption by means of tax cuts it would create 112,000 new jobs. In other words, a 10 per cent cut in the military budget, that is to say a cut of $8,000-9,000 million and a corresponding tax reduction, could diminish unemployment by 0.3 million, and more than this if cuts and alternative programmes were selected with a view to maximizing the effect on employment. Thus, the proposition that military expenditure generates employment at least effectively as, if not more than, non-military expenditure is demonstrably false.

The third major factor in the growth equation is technological change. Throughout the world an estimated 400,000 engineers and

scientists are working on military projects. The opportunity cost of this diversion of resources is impossible to quantify. Its magnitude is suggested by recalling that, while scientific and technological advances have yielded enormous benefits for mankind, some 40 per cent of the financial resources devoted to R&D since the Second World War have been used in the military field. Military technology is moving further and further away from any conceivable civilian use, and is anyway focusing on fields which are mostly irrelevant for the solution of the more important present and future problems of the world. There can be no doubt that, in the final analysis, technological innovation in the civilian sector and, with it, growth are not futhered by military research and development but are greatly impaired by it.

It has often been pointed out that in some developing countries the military sector has contributed substantially to technological training and has helped to raise the level of technical skills, providing partial compensation for the resources spent on military activities. It is clear, however, that programmes of industrial development, civilian community projects and the like can achieve those results in a more direct, pertinent and cost-effective way.

The international sale of arms, or, more precisely, of military goods and services, today by far the most important part of arms transfers, is an aspect of the arms race which also has direct and indirect implications for the economies of the countries involved. For all those countries which are not major weapons producers themselves, an increase in military expenditures will normally mean increased imports and will result in a deterioration of the balance of trade. The fact that imports for military purposes generate no income and no exports with which to service the added debt further aggravates the longer-term effect on the balance of payments. For some developing countries facing acute debt-servicing problems, the balance of payments aspect of the costs which the worldwide character of the arms race imposes on all countries is particularly salient.

The trade in arms has opposite effects on the economies of importing and exporting countries. What is involved is a highly unequal exchange, detrimental in particular to efforts to bridge the gap between poor and rich countries. For the importer of arms it is in economic terms a pure waste of surplus which could have been used productively. Even when weapons are provided as gifts there are maintenance, operations and infrastructure costs to be included on the debit side. In contrast to the import of civilian goods these outlays raise neither consumption nor production and generate no future output from which to pay for them. Not so for the exporting country. That part of its arms production which is destined for its own armed forces again figures at a first approximation simply as an economic loss. But its production of weapons for export is no different in economic terms from any other export production. Importing countries are subsidizing military R&D in the arms-exporting countries. This also applies when, instead of importing weapons, countries produce them under licence. In a very real, although often marginal, way importing countries are thus helping to perpetuate the lead in military technology of

the main arms-exporting countries and to sustain the rate of innovation and obsolescence in weaponry.

In the countries with a centrally planned economy the negative consequences of military expenditures are in principle of the same character as in other economic systems, but they make themselves felt in a different socio-economic context. Also for these countries military expenditures represent lost opportunities for economic and social development. Military expenditures are a drain on resources which could have been used for civilian purposes, either to accelerate growth and modernization in such fields as industry, agriculture and transport or to raise the standard of living and improve the quality of life.

Certain additional comments can be made with respect to the developing countries. In many of these countries, economic and social development programmes are largely determined and financed by the government. Military expenditure and development programmes appear as direct alternatives for the allocation of government resources. In recent years military expenditure in many of these countries has been growing faster than the civilian economy, thus narrowing the scope for effective development programmes. More specifically, the general negative effects of resource diversion to military uses tend to be aggravated in developing countries because modern armed forces make heavy demands on many of the resources which are most needed for development and which constitute severe bottle-necks in many cases: foreign exchange, skilled technical and managerial manpower and maintenance, repair and industrial production capacity.

The continuation of the arms race tends to draw all countries along with greater or lesser delays. In the process the limited strength of smaller countries and of countries with a limited industrial and technological base is undermined. These countries find themselves in a situation where the rate of innovation in military technology is set by countries with much greater resources. Under these conditions, merely keeping abreast in the arms race will require ever greater sacrifices. An ongoing arms race with its inherent tendency to spread and intensify in geographical, technological and economic terms will constitute an ever greater obstacle to social and economic progress in all countries and to the urgent development tasks of developing countries in particular. No task is more urgent than to stop this technological spiral at the centre of the world arms race where it originates, and through substantial disarmament in the leading military powers to pave the way for major reductions in arms expenditures throughout the world.

The domestic consequences of involvement in the arms race cannot be reduced to the economic costs and to the direct social consequences of diminished civilian production and growth. To regard it thus is to miss one side of the picture altogether. Contemporary military institutions are often such powerful and pervasive parts of society that they can have a considerable impact on political and social conditions and perceptions and can place important constraints on the evolution of societies. In this sense they can represent a major social force, influencing the social, political and ideological development of a country. It should be

recognized that the military institution in the wide sense
(including such institutions as paramilitary forces or secret
services which may be formally independent of it) enjoys a unique
position of strength in many societies. This is due to a variety
of factors. First, there is its sheer mass combined with a
centralized organization. Second, there are the privileged
relations which the armed forces may entertain with key sectors of
industry, being at once a customer and a link to government.
Third, there is a privileged relation to the state and many areas
of government policy (foreign, industrial, infrastructural,
regional and others, depending on the circumstances). Fourth, the
military institution can, to a varying degree, protect its
operations from public scrutiny, and conduct a variety of
activities under the label of national security. These may range
from the establishment of a full-fledged covert foreign service or
the covert conduct of foreign wars to moderate or more
comprehensive surveillance of categories of political opponents.
Last, but of course not least, the armed forces enjoy a monopoly of
physical force and a position of instrument of ultimate recourse,
vis-a-vis other states and internally.

It is the integration of this social force with industry and
government which has been described as the 'military-industrial
complex', whose 'total influence -- economic, political, even
spiritual -- is felt in every city, every statehouse, every office
of the Federal Government'.[2]

Such interpenetration is in no sense an exclusively American
phenomenon. Wherever they occur, military-industrial or military-
economic-political complexes have a self-preserving and self-reinforcing character. They are powerful, resourceful and pervasive
coalitions that have developed around one common purpose: the
continued expansion of the military sector, irrespective of actual
military needs. In those countries where their influence is
strong, such complexes are obviously an important factor in the
perpetuation of the arms race. Many studies of the
military-industrial complex in the United States (but their results
can to a greater or lesser degree be generalized to other
countries) have shown its ability to keep fears alive, to stimulate
them when needed, and to initiate compensating activities to offset
the effects of more marginal types of arms-control measures.
Disarmament efforts, if they are to be successful, will have to
take account of this.

In most cases one may assume that the military institution and
the armed forces have a double role. They are at once an ultimate
recourse in external affairs and an ultimate arbiter in internal
affairs. These roles are not always unrelated. In an environment
of external confrontation the limits of tolerated dissension get
narrowed down, and when means for satisfying basic needs and
aspirations are scarce, there could be a temptation to seek
temporary refuge in domestic repression or in the escalation of
foreign confrontation. Here governments can get trapped in an
impossible situation where an increasing burden of military
expenditures further delays economic and social progress, freezes
social structures and exacerbates social tension, while other
policies seem to be precluded by the context of confrontation and

arms race with neighbouring countries. The conjunction of external and domestic confrontation, both of them temporarily stabilized through military buildup but ultimately exacerbated by it, can give rise to a particularly precarious situation.

The arms race not only entails heavy economic sacrifices. It also threatens and perverts democratic processes, and weakens those processes of social evolution which provide the only real hope for the future of mankind.

IV. INTERNATIONAL IMPLICATIONS OF THE ARMS RACE

The arms race represents a waste of resources, a diversion of the economy away from its humanitarian purposes, a hindrance to national development efforts and a threat to democratic processes. But its most important feature is that in effect it undermines national, regional and international security. It involves the constant risk of war engaging the largest powers, including nuclear war, and it is accompanied by an endless series of wars at lower levels. It raises an ever-greater barrier against the development of an atmosphere in which the role of force in between countries, affecting the volume and direction of exchanges, diminishing the role of co-operation among states and obstructing efforts towards establishing a new international economic order on a more equitable basis.

The international consequences of the arms race may be grouped under three headings, even though in practice these effects are in many ways interrelated. First and foremost, there is the strictly military aspect: on the one hand, a long series of wars, some of them of extreme destructiveness, seldom caused in any strict sense by the arms race, but very often inflamed by it; on the other hand, an ever-present possibility of nuclear conflagration.

Second, there are the economic effects (and, by implication, social effects) in the widest sense: the effects of the arms race and military expenditures on trade, on aid, on technological and scientific co-operation and on other kinds of exchange between countries. By diverting vast resources away from production and growth, and by contributing to inflation and the economic crisis which have affected many countries, the arms race directly and indirectly impedes the full development of international exchanges.

Third, there is the impact of the arms race on international political conditions. In an environment characterized by high military preparedness on all sides, conflicts, even minor ones, tend to be exacerbated and security considerations become salient in the policies of countries. This is an environment conducive to the creation of spheres of influence, in which local conflicts tend to become linked to regional or global confrontations and in which social and political developments are likely to be resisted if they seem to call existing alignments into question. The frictions arising from this rigidity at a time when the relative economic, political and military weight of countries changes more rapidly

than ever are themselves possible sources of conflict.

One point most persistently stressed in documents and analyses pertaining to the new international economic order is the need for increasing development assistance in all its forms, not only in the form of official grants and loans on concessional terms, but also in the form of development-promoting measures with a concessionary component in such fields as trade in food and industrial goods, transfer of technology and many more. The arms race has not only diminished the priority given to aid in the policies of donor countries, it has also distorted the flow of bilateral assistance, in some cases to a marked degree.

Present levels of development assistance are clearly inadequate measured against the needs, and they even fall far short of the targets, not overly ambitious, set in the International Development Strategy for the Second Development Decade. During the first half of the decade, from 1971 to 1975, official development assistance from the developed market economies amounted to 0.32 per cent of their combined gross national product, reaching not even half of the strategy target, 0.7 per cent. Transfer to development assistance of funds equivalent to a mere 5 per cent of their current military expenditures would have been sufficient to meet the target fully.

Disarmament and development are by far the most urgent problems facing the world. It is therefore with good reason that the General Assembly and other United Nations bodies have repeatedly stressed the connection between them: the fact that these two tasks are likely to succeed together, or else fail together.

A major aspect of the arms race in terms of the international system is its political effects in general, and its effect in fostering and exacerbating conflict in particular. In an international environment dominated by an arms race on the scale of the last decades, military-strategic considerations tend to shape the overall relations between states, affecting to a greater or lesser extent all other relations and transactions. Foreign policy and international exchanges generally tend to become subordinated to 'security' considerations in the widest sense. But there is no natural limit to the precautions that may seem necessary. In this way, the creation of spheres of influence, local, regional or global, and sometimes interference, direct or roundabout, in the domestic affairs of other states becomes a natural corollary of a worldwide arms race.

While it is probably not true to say that the arms race causes conflicts in any strict sense -- the causes of conflicts are ultimately political, economic, etc. -- a context of intense military preparedness can, of course, greatly enhance them, cause them to erupt into war, to spill over into neighbouring countries and block their peaceful settlement. The arms race produces a political climate in which minor incidents can be blown up to international crisis proportions and in which even insignificant disputes which under other circumstances could have been easily settled by negotiation become matters of great principle and the object of armed clashes.

The arms race tends to render the international political

environment more rigid and more resistant to change. It fosters concern for the political and social options chosen by other countries, in particular by those countries that are deemed to have strategic importance, and it promotes a pattern of alliances and alignments that may reinforce confrontation and, in some cases, domination. Under such conditions processes of social transformation or emancipation are likely in many cases to be resisted. They become painful processes, postponed for too long, and they may end in protracted and destructive conflict, as several of the longest and most painful wars of the recent past have shown.

The preparation and implementation by all countries of a comprehensive programme of disarmament, and first of all nuclear disarmament, is an urgent necessity to avert the danger of nuclear war, foreclose use of force or the threat of the use of force, establish a lasting peace, eliminate the factors opposing the democratization of international relations and build step by step a new international economic, political and social order.

V. CONCLUSIONS

The main task of this report has been to analyse the social and economic consequences of the arms race. What emerges with particular force is the multiplicity of those consequences, not only in the field of security proper, but in all aspects of civil life. The social, political, technological and industrial options of countries are affected by their participation in the arms race. International policies, not only in the military field, but also in the fields of international trade and of co-operation and exchanges generally, are influenced by the climate of confrontation and apprehension engendered by the arms race. Many of the major problems faced by the world community, problems of development, economic imbalance and inflation, pollution, energy and raw materials, trade relations and technology, and so forth, are enhanced and exacerbated by the arms race. Progress in other areas such as health, education, housing and many more is delayed owing to lack of resources.

Discussion of the consequences of the arms race -- social, economic and military-political -- presupposes some conceptual view of the phenomenon itself. Likewise, effective progress towards disarmament presupposes some understanding of the forces and processes that drive the arms race along. There is a growing body of literature on this question, but it is mainly confined to consideration of one or a few countries and to exposition of the one or the other particular model of the armaments process. The impact on disarmament efforts has therefore been virtually non-existent. What seems to be needed is not only an elaboration or integration of these several approaches to obtain a clearer understanding of the interplay of forces that sustain the arms race, but the gathering together of these separate strands in a way that could inform and guide action. What is needed even more is a

clear outline of the views of different countries and groups of countries as to what constitutes the fundamental mechanisms of the arms race. Effective action to reverse it would seem to presuppose some agreement as to where the problem lies and what it consists of.

It has been stressed throughout this report that the two most important goals of the international community, disarmament, on the one hand, and development, on the other, which the States Members of the United Nations are committed to pursue vigorously, each in its own right, are in fact intimately linked. Development at an acceptable rate would be hard if not impossible to reconcile with a continuation of the arms race. Research and development is one area where the misdirection of efforts is glaring. In this as in other respects, vast resources, badly needed for development, are being consumed as countries make ever-greater sacrifices for military purposes.

Substantial progress in the field of disarmament would represent a decisive turning point as regards development, imparting new momentum to efforts in this direction and greatly facilitating progress in this field. Progress towards disarmament would release internal material, financial and human resources both in developed and in developing countries and would permit their redeployment to purposes of development. In fact, disarmament should be so designed that this close connexion between disarmament and development gets full recognition. Provisions to ensure the transfer to development purposes of part of the resources released, provisions to ensure that measures of armaments limitation are so designed that they do not impede the transfer of technology for peaceful ends and other similar provisions must be an integral part of disarmament measures.

Effective progress towards disarmament presupposes the elaboration of an overall plan, persuasive in concept and workable in application, a 'Strategy for Disarmament' as it were. This must be based on a thorough assessment of the problems involved, the forces propelling the arms race and the experience of the past. It should involve specification of priorities, decision on targets and adoption of programmes and, where appropriate, timetables. This strategy must be comprehensive enough to ensure a fair and equitable response to the concerns of every country, and flexible enough to permit taking realistic and concrete steps in the immediate future, in intermediate stages and in the final stage. In short, a framework is needed within which endeavours can be co-ordinated and against which progress can be measured. This is no less essential in the field of disarmament than it is in the field of development, or in any other field where a multiplicity of efforts is to lead effectively to a common goal.

To impart a new momentum to disarmament efforts it seems necessary not only to engage all countries in these endeavours on a basis of equality, but also to involve the peoples of all countries more actively and in a more coherent and organized fashion than has been the case hitherto. A variety of movements and organizations -- political, professional, religious and others -- can play an important role in this respect, and have in fact done so in the past. The negative consequences of the arms

race, in terms of endangering their existence and in terms of social and economic sacrifices, affect all peoples of the world. They have an obvious right to information about the military policies and programmes of governments and their implications. Much of the secrecy in this field is not justified by military requirements. In some cases it results from mere tradition, in others it serves such purposes as shielding questionable or unnecessary armaments programmes from public scrutiny and public criticism. Without endangering the security of any country much greater openness of information could and should be applied in this field.

Given the character of the present arms race, effective disarmament will presuppose progress in two directions simultaneously: curtailment of the qualitative arms race, and reductions of military budgets. The first involves the erection of boundaries against further developments in weaponry. The agreements on biological weapons and on anti-ballistic missile systems are steps in this direction. Responsibility for continued and more rapid progress in this respect overwhelmingly rests with the main military powers and with the two largest powers in particular, which are alone in producing the full range of modern weapons and where most innovations in military technology and all innovation in nuclear weapons and their means of delivery originate.

Progress towards disarmament, it has been indicated, will require systematic co-ordination and planning with the participation of all states. This points, on the one hand, to the need for more effective means at the international level for information, research and evaluation on questions of disarmament to enable all Member States, not only the largest ones, to obtain effective insight and to take initiatives in questions of disarmament. On the other hand, the United Nations, and first of all its plenary organ, the General Assembly, whose task it is to harmonize the efforts of states in the attainment of their common goals, should be able to fulfil its role of overall guidance in the field of disarmament more effectively than it has been able to do in the past.

NOTES

1. Reference here and elsewhere to the 'six main military spenders' -- the United States of America, the Union of Soviet Socialist Republics, China, France, the United Kingdom of Great Britain and Northern Ireland and the Federal Republic of Germany -- should not be allowed to conceal the very large differences within this group. Not all of these countries are leading in the process of arms innovation or in the production and export of arms: military expenditure (even more so military expenditure per capital) differs widely within this group of countries; and not all of them have military capabilities that give them a global military-strategic importance.

2. President Eisenhower, Farewell Speech to the Nation.

Consequences of the Transfer of Military-Oriented Technology on the Development Process

PETER LOCK
HERBERT WULF

I. THE HISTORICAL CONTEXT

It is part of history that the military as an institution has always been involved in the process of subjugation, dominance, exploitation, and dependence of some social formation by others. Some observers maintain that the present unprecedented process of the militarization in most parts of the Third World carries distinct far-reaching features, classifiable as part of an evolving New International Military World Order. This paper hopes to contribute evidence to the hypothesis that qualitative changes, or at least changes of extraordinary quantity, are finally surfacing. Against the prospects that social and economic inequalities are bound to increase at the international level as well as within the nations of the Third World, the control of the means of violence becomes a key variable in political systems of the Third World.

The changes in the role of the military and its impact on the formation of the society can best be delineated within a historical context. Intensified militarization in the underdeveloped world can partly be explained by crisis situations in the capitalist world. During World War I the colonized people of Africa and Asia witnessed their active integration into the fighting units of the British and French armies in Europe. The incipient industrial base of India was expanded in order to support British war production, raw materials and food were shipped to Europe backing up the war economy. More than one hundred thousand soldiers from African and Asian colonies, particularly from India, lost their lives in combat.

Politically independent countries of Latin America, China,

From **BULLETIN OF PEACE PROPOSALS**, Vol 8, No. 2, 1977, (127-136), reprinted by permission of the publisher.

Turkey, and a few more states were drawn into furious competition between the industrial powers of Europe and the USA and Japan over political and economic influence. Sending military missions for training and the supply of arms and equipment were considered to enhance the political influence of the supplier nations. In this situation, the role of the government in the politically independent states in the periphery expanded considerably; and, due to metropolitan rivalry, the military was particularly able to expand its role and participation in political and economic affairs. And even in India the officer corps of the Indian Army started successfully an Indianization program.[1]

During World War II Third World territories witnessed their full integration into the Allied war production. Particularly with US military assistance, arms production facilities and maintenance work shops were set up in India and other areas of British influence. These were later to become the bases of all national programs for arms production in newly independent states. The territories occupied by Japanese imperialism were likewise characterized by the installation of industrial facilities for war production. The Japanese built aircraft in Manchuria and Korea, as did the Allies in India. The Latin American nations faced a virtual embargo of industrial equipment, with the partial exception of Brazil, after sending an expeditionary corps to Italy. In consequence, ideas to pursue a self-reliant supply strategy for the armed forces won ground.

After World War II, the colonial powers tried to re-establish rapidly the status quo ante, since there were no realistic chances within the existing system to convert the wartime production potential into a contribution to industrialization and development strategies. In India, the dismantling of existing facilities was resisted to some extent; much was maintained as a basis for the Indian arms industry, which employs today more than 200,000 people. Argentina, on the other hand, initiated a vigorous attempt under Peron to industrialize the country within the context of a capitalist latecomer national development strategy, placing heavy emphasis on military technology and national arms production. The strategy met stiff opposition from the United States, and failed.

In Latin America and wherever colonial control was lifted, the United States moved in, generously providing military 'aid', training the armies and establishing a worldwide bilateral and multilateral system of military alliances, formal and informal agreements. The relative position of the military within the local political system was stepped up.

The position of the military in the political system of peripheral states was further reinforced when the political stability and alliance with the western world were challenged as a consequence of continued economic crises, increased inequalities, liberation movements in the colonies, and rural guerillas in independent states. Based on British expediency developed in Malaya, the United States established huge training centers for all aspects of counter-insurgency warfare.[2] Preemptive control of social conflicts became the central element of military doctrine as taught and supported by US military 'aid' and economic policy. At the same time, concepts of development were proposed, assigning to

the military a key role for a temporary period. Particularly in US literature it was argued that the military was the only modern, rational, and bureaucratically organized body in traditional underdeveloped societies; thus the army was, according to these concepts, particularly prepared to speed up the development process and guide the political system accordingly.

While the United Nations declared the 1970s as second development decade, a new unprecedented flow of modern arms was pouring into a large number of developing countries. Military 'aid' from the United States was cut drastically. Shipments of sophisticated weapons increased and reached the level of $20 billion in 1975. The expansion ('tous azimuts') of the military within the political systems of developing countries is escalating, and no indication of limits seems to exist.

II. ABSORPTION OF IMPORT CAPACITIES

The capacity of developing countries to import what is needed for development and industrialization is often drastically reduced by the importation of military technologies.

On a global scale, armaments constitute less than 2% of commodities entering the world market. The recorded volumes of arms transfers, however, represent but a part of all imports originating from military activities. But as evidenced in Table 1, the import statistics of developing countries conceal a large proportion representing armaments. The magnitudes involved in some cases reach one third of total imports (Turkey 1969) or one fourth (Korea 1965, Egypt 1969).

A yet more appropriate parameter for measuring the arms import burden would be the volume of those commodities essential for large-scale industrialization as represented in category No. 7 of the Standard International Trade classification ('machinery and transport equipment'). These imported capital goods can be taken as an index for the proportion of imported technology in total imports.[3] In many cases a substantial portion of imported technology is directly related to military activities,[4] as can be seen in column 5 of Table 1. The proportion of arms imports exceeds in all of the major recipient countries one third and often one half of foreign technology imports -- at least for one year during the period observed. The significance of these figures reveals itself fully if one considers the specific economic properties of armaments: namely, not contributing to the expansion of the productive capacity[5] of an economy other than supposedly in political terms. A case in point is Iran. Despite considerable revenue from oil exports, the country's budget was not balanced in 1976: a deficit of course related to huge weaponry deliveries especially from the US.[6]

The figures in Table 1 should be read with caution. Since regular international statistics do not account for armaments, weapons enter possibly as transport equipment and the like.

TABLE 1. Imports of Goods and Import of Arms of the Major Third World Arms Importers

Country	Year	1 Total Imports Cif in Mio U.S.$	2 Imports of S.I.T.C. No.7c) in Mio U.S.$	3 Military Imp. in Mio U.S.$	4 Military Imp. as % of Total Imp.	5 Military Imp. as % of S.I.T.C. No. 7
Egypt a) (UAR)	1965	933	218	92	9.9	42.4
	1968	666	162	156	23.4	96.3
	1969	638	153	160	25.1	104.6
	1974	2949	565	583	19.8	103.2
India	1968	2507	704	168	6.7	23.9
	1970	2097	490	100	4.8	20.4
	1972	2230	604	205	9.2	33.9
	1973	3146	754	180	5.7	23.9
Iran	1964	669	221	26	3.9	11.8
	1968b	1407	580	135	9.6	23.3
	1972b	2593	1111	415	16.0	37.4
	1974b	6544	2072	870	13.3	42.0
Israel	1965	835	232	46	5.5	19.8
	1968	1089	278	55	5.1	19.8
	1970	1451	442	232	16.0	52.5
	1974	4237	1025	636	15.0	62.0

TABLE 1. (continued)

South Korea (Rep. of)	1965	450	60	104	23.1	173.3
	1968	1468	533	323	22.0	60.6
	1972	2522	762	510	20.2	66.9
	1974	6844	1849	114	1.7	6.2
Saudi Arabia	1968	652	189	79	14.1	41.8
	1971	806	248	19	2.4	47.7
	1974	3473	n.a.	393	11.3	
Turkey	1965	572	214	83	14.5	38.7
	1969	747	301	241	32.3	80.1
	1972	1508	677	327	21.7	48.3
	1973	2099	864	205	9.8	23.7

Source: United Nations, Commodity, Trade Statistics, *Statistical Papers*, Series D; US Arms Control and Disarmament Agency, *World Military Expenditures and Arms Transfers, 1964–1973*, Washington; UNCTAD, *Handbook of International Trade and Development Statistics*, New York, 1976.

Notes:

a) Figures in Column 1 and 2 represent the imports of the former United Arab Republic. Military Imports in Column 3 are the combined figures for Egypt and Syria.

b) Figures in Column 1 and 2 for financial year (March till March).

c) SITC No. 7 – Machinery, Transport Equipment.

Furthermore, available sources on arms transfer differ substantially, or account for only a certain part of the arms trade, as SIPRI does for example.[7] Often, however, it is virtually impossible to distinguish between 'civilian' and 'military' technology. West German companies have delivered to the apartheid regime in South Africa such 'civilian' items as computers and teleprinters, which have been of utmost importance in making the South African communications headquarters operational.

Once a modern weapon system of advanced technology has been purchased for the armed services, a chain of supplementary import demands is induced. To remain operational, modern fighter aircraft, tanks or naval units require an extensive network of support facilities. A logistical system for the timely provision of spare parts is indispensable. For an extended period foreign specialists are required, and adequate residential areas for them must be provided. The chain of demands, generally with a high import content, seems endless.

From the scattered evidence available, we may assume that the militarily-induced chain of supplementary imports incorporates predominantly advanced, capital-intensive technologies. Given the volume and the political priority of military activities in many developing countries, the complex and expensive properties of these imported commodities cannot but have profound repercussions on the general pattern of industrialization. Not only do military imports absorb the import capacity at the time the transfer takes place: they also constitute a claim on future and potential import capacity since they do not contribute to the expansion of the productive capacity and since they have high opportunity costs. Furthermore, large proportions of future imports bills are claimed to keep the military imports operational, since military technologies reflect the confrontation of highly industrialized countries and thus cannot be serviced from the limited industrial base of a developing country without large imports of hardware as well as of software.

III. DOMESTIC ARMS PRODUCTION AND INDUSTRIAL PATTERN

A 1976 survey of arms production reveals 46 developing countries engaged in domestic arms production or preparing for the manufacture of arms.[8] This figure includes 5 countries belonging to the 'periphery' of Europe, as well as 8 Latin American, 12 African, 5 Near and Middle Eastern, and 16 Asian countries. The level of domestic arms production attained so far in the respective countries differs by a wide margin. Most industries are restricted to the manufacture of small arms or ammunition, in relatively small quantities; others specialize in the construction of small naval craft only. In some countries, however, domestic arms production has attained a considerable level and a relatively high degree of diversification, including even production for export. Argentina, Brazil, India, Israel, South Africa, Spain, possibly Taiwan and

Yugoslavia are to be mentioned, while other nations like Egypt, Iran, Pakistan, and Turkey are about to expand their domestic arms industry.

From Table 2 we note that a total of 36 countries engage in small-arms production of some kind, while only a few have actually achieved self-sufficiency in the supply of light infantry weapons. Modern fighter aircraft, jet trainer or aeroengines are built in 12 developing countries, generally under license, while light aircraft are manufactured in 14 nations of the Third World. Eight aircraft manufacturers throughout the Third World produce or assemble helicopters; for missiles and rockets the corresponding figure is 11; for military electronics and avionics 9. The construction of hulls for small naval craft and fighting ships takes place in more than 30 developing countries, while engines, armament and electronic equipment are normally imported. About 10 developing nations have constructed warships for their navies above 500 ts or plan to do so, while 8 countries produce armored personnel carriers or even tanks.

At present more new projects than ever are still in the pipeline, some of them quite demanding. Eight more countries are pursuing plans to take up the production of modern fighter aircraft or jet trainers. Additional countries are certain to enter the register of domestic arms production soon. Other countries will expand and diversify their present productive capacity. As can be seen from Table 2, in most of the projects and probably in all countries a licensor from an industrialized country is involved in domestic arms production. Quite often the share of locally added value in the production of weapon systems is minimal. All this clearly indicates that the present boom in the arms trade with the Third World is associated with an equally mushrooming proliferation of industrial installations for the domestic manufacture of arms.

Possibly due to a highly competitive situation, European and US producers are prepared to join national production schemes in developing countries. Such participation allows them to enter markets otherwise inaccessible; low labor costs may attract a metropolitian producer to manufacture certain labor-intensive components in developing countries and by re-exporting them increase the total sales to the country concerned. The existence of export restrictions may also lead to the transfer of production or assembly lines, but sometimes merely the subsidies (often in the form of tax exemptions) suffice to induce a metropolitan arms manufacturer to establish military production in a developing country.

The transfer of the necessary technology usually takes place step by step and follows a pattern well known in other sectors as well. Facilities for maintenance and overhaul are followed by assembly lines. Some components are ordered from local industry, stepping up the percentage of locally produced components and finally entering into license production. The last stage is the production of locally designed weapon systems, if possible without dependence on imported components -- no 'latecomer', however, having arrived at this stage so far. The heavy expenditure on military research and development in the leading industrial nations suggests that even the most pretentious arms production strategy

TABLE 2. Domestic Arms Production in Developing Countries

	1 Fighter Aircrafts, Jet Trainers, Aeroengines	2 Light Aircrafts	3 Helicopters	4 Missiles, Rockets	5 Large Fighting Ships	6 Medium Fighting Ships (up to 500 ts)	7 Small Fighting Ships and others (below 100 ts)	8 Submarines	9 Tanks and APC	10 Small weapons, ammunition, guns etc.	11 Electronics and Avionic
Europe											
Greece	1	1			1	1	n		1^2	1	1^1
Spain	1	1	1	1	n 1	1	1	1	1	1	n
Portugal	1^1	1 1			1	1	n		1^1	1	
Turkey	i 1^1	i 1				1	n	1 n	n	1	
Yugoslavia	i 1	i 1	1	1	1	1	n			1	
Latin America											
Argentina	i 1	i 1	1	1	1	i 1	i	1	1	1	n 1
Brazil	i 1	i 1		i 1	1	n		n	1	1	
Chile	1					n			i	i	
Colombia		1				n			i	i	
Dominican Rep.						1					
Mexico	1^1	1			n 1					i	
Peru	1^1	1				i	1			1^1	
Venezuela	n^2						1			n	
Africa											
Algeria										n	
Congo										n	
Gabon										1	
Ghana						1	n			1	
Guinea											
Ivory Coast							n				

TABLE 2. (continued)

Malagasy Rep.		1[1]					1	1				1	1	n[1]
Nigeria		1	1			n	n	1				1	1
South Africa													1
Sudan													?
Zaire													1
Morocco													

Near/Middle East

Egypt	1	1[2]	1	1	1[1]	4[1]	n	1	1	1[1]	1	1	1
Iran													
Israel	i	1[1]	i	1[1]	1[1]		i	1	i	i	i	1	i
Saudi Arabia													1
Yemen (Aden)								?			?		

Asia

Bangla Desh	i	1	i1	1	1	1	1	n[1]	n	1	1	1	1
Burma		1	1	1			n	n	n	i	i	i	
Hong Kong		1		1				n	n[1]				1
India		1[1]		1[1]			n	n	n		n	n	n
Indonesia		1[1]	1		1[1]		1	n[1]		1	1	1	1
Korea (North)													
Korea (South)							1	n[1]			1	1	1
Malaysia										n[1]		1	
Nepal	1[1]	i1[1]	1[1]	1[1]	1	1		1				
Pakistan		1	1			n						
Philippines									1			
Singapore											1	1	1
Sri Lanka		1	1	1	n[2]	n	1	n[1]			n	n	n
Taiwan											1	1	1
Thailand	1	1										
Vietnam	1									n		n

will always remain outpaced by technological advances of the leading manufacturers. Thus it might be concluded that developing nations can arrive at a self-reliant position in military technology only if they abstain from imitating military doctrines and weapon systems developed in the context of confrontation between industrialized nations.

Even the installation of relatively simple arms manufacture -- e.g. automatic guns and machines guns -- requires a high percentage of imported inputs. Figures recently published by the US government indicate that between 53% and well over 80% of total costs of several programs to install factories for the production of US guns (M 16) are accounted for by imports. These figures include installation and production over a period of five years or more. All countries concerned, like Taiwan, South Korea, the Philippines, had at least an incipient industrial base when arms manufacture was taken up.[9]

Apart from imports, other scarce factors of production are absorbed as well, qualified technical labor, modern infrastructure, electricity, etc. at present technological levels, the import of advanced military equipment and/or the necessary means of production operates as a pull-sector directing industrialization towards capital-intensive technology and preparing for a pattern that tends to exclude alternative labor-intensive strategies for national development.

IV. IMPACT OF MILITARY TECHNOLOGY

Design and techniques of production of advanced weapon systems reflect the economic conditions and the political situation in industrialized countries. Their operational capability in the pursuit of legitimate defense by a recipient Third World country has still to be proven. Alternative military strategies implying less complex military technology which could be provided from the national industrial base at reasonable cost are conceivable, but these would require the evolution of new doctrines.

The armaments dynamics in the industrial metropoles are characterized by constantly increasing procurement costs. On the basis of statistical extrapolation of present trends, a study prepared by the rand Corporation concludes that by the year 2036 the US air force will be able to afford only one fighter aircraft, due to price escalation. Heavy outlays in research and development constantly produce technological obsolescence of military equipment, thus constantly accelerating the demand for replacement schemes. Complex weapon systems call for highly qualified military personnel, which in turn leads to drastically increased wage bills in modern armies. The high proportion of 'labor costs' in military budgets further reinforces the technological 'escalation' because a deliberate strategy is being developed to replace combatants whenever possible by 'capital'. The vision of an automated battlefield is but a logical extension of present trends in

armaments dynamics.

In the Third World, however, conditions differ from the industrialized nations particularly with respect to labor costs: soldiers receive low wages. Qualified personnel is scarce and training is expensive and cannot be carried out quickly. Thus, for the operation of advanced equipment, foreigners must be hired in large numbers and at high costs.

Recently it has been argued that various new cheap technologies are in the offing, particularly appropriate to enhance the military capability of developing nations at low cost. Missiles and the so-called precision guided munitions are often mentioned in this connection. This view neglects the likelihood of effective though expensive electronic countermeasures becoming operational very soon. Consequently the successful application of 'cheap' technologies will require a complex and henceforth expensive electronic 'environment', including target-acquisition, countermeasures, command-and-control equipment.[10] There are few chances that the distribution of military power between industrialized nations and the Third World will change significantly as a result of technological 'innovations' originating from the armaments dynamics in industrialized countries. This could be achieved only by a fundamentally different military doctrine, one based on the resources available and directed towards self-reliance.

V. INTERFERENCE WITH DEVELOPMENT PROCESSES

The import of military technology is associated with changes in infrastructures, in consumption of energy and raw materials of aggregate demand and supply, and in the labor market. The imposition of a sophisticated military infrastructure frequently disturbs traditional sectors like subsistence agriculture.

The transfer of military technology requires the installation of sophisticated infrastructures such as harbors, airports, bases, transportation and communications systems. Such installations are suboptimal for development processes and often negative for existing traditional infrastructures. A few examples suffice to illustrate this point. Strategic roads and bridges, for example, can certainly be used also for civil purposes, and isolated regions can be integrated into a communication and transportation network. The stability of a bridge, however, has to be much higher to carry a tank than to carry a bullock cart. Thus larger amounts of construction material are spent for military purposes and are unavailable for development. This example is quite realistic, since in many developing countries the infrastructure at the end of World War II was so underdeveloped that tanks and airplanes could not even reach the border of neighboring countries, due to lack of roads, bridges, and airports. In the meantime, in a great number of developing countries, construction programs have been undertaken for strategic reasons. Some of the major arms importers are also

main importers of cement (Iran, Saudi Arabia, Turkey, Nigeria, Kuwait, Egypt, Bahrein, Indonesia) and are planning big cement industry projects to enable further construction of military infrastructure. Similar examples can be quoted for the installation of telecommunication systems.

Besides the uneconomic investment of resources, the installation of militarily-motivated infrastructures has effects on already existing infrastructures and modes of production. In colonial India or in Vietnam, for instance, the construction of railways, respectively roads, had devastating effects on the existing canal system. Suddenly, the canal systems were no longer competitive for transportation because in the cost calculations for roads and railways the military inputs had not to be taken into account: these were simply overheads to be borne by the whole society. The effects were lasting. The canal systems deteriorated, traditional employment opportunities were destroyed, agricultural production suffered, and instead of locally produced means of transportation, expensive foreign-made equipment was imported. Similarly, the construction of a marine base can have devastating effects on the local fish industry. In Thailand it can be observed at the moment that most modern runways or hospitals for example are too expensive to be maintained for civilian purposes after US withdrawal.

In extreme cases, the military might even occupy land to such an extreme that scarcity is aggravated. Singapore is a case in point: the military occupies approximately 10% of the tiny 226 square mile island. Lack of space has forced the military to look elsewhere for training, in Taiwan for example. For civilian purposes, land has to be reclaimed now from the sea. As can be seen in the case of Thailand, installation of military bases and especially the US war expenditures had an impact on growth in aggregated demand and the structure of supply. The injection of foreign funds into a local economy might result in higher growth rates, but at the same time the structure of supply has 'biased' development towards secondary and tertiary activities, which are not self-supporting in a long run. Especially in a few South-East-Asian countries US military spending was a contributing factor in the stagnation of traditional exports and stimulation for luxury imports. Such a development cannot easily be reversed. It was not only US money which has been spent (or wasted): the effects on the local economy are long lasting.

The transfer of military technology also leads to an absorption of scarce qualified local personnel (especially in research and development); it further leads to the transfer of highly specialized personnel from metropolitan countries, since the technical capacities of an underdeveloped country are too weak to service, maintain, use or produce sophisticated weapons. In India, the Defence Research and Development Organization and related military research projects employ more scientists, engineers, and technicians than private industry as a whole employs for research and development. Arms production employs more than 200,000 people, most of them highly qualified.

It is often argued the arms industry creates new employment opportunities and has positive effects on the qualification

profiles of the labor force. Most of the work-places created, however, require a high amount of scarce capital; and it is legitimate to ask how many jobs could have been created if the scarce funds had been invested elsewhere. It is doubtful that the acquired qualifications in the arms industry are of particular value for other civilian activities. While a truck driver can most likely use his skill acquired during army service afterwards, this is normally not the case with special knowledge, aerodynamics or missile propulsion technology for example.

The mobility of labor has always been an important means for transferring military technology and know-how. The transfer of qualified personnel in the arms production sector has been limited in the past mainly to small design teams of a few scientists and engineers only. A new dimension has been reached now in Iran. By 1980, some 50-60,000 US specialists are expected to be working in arms production and maintenance in Iran. The growing demand for technical services which can no longer be provided by the US forces has spurred the formation of a new corps of 'white collar mercenaries'.[11]

VI. CONCLUDING REMARKS

Obviously the transfer of military technology and the militarization process in the Third World are closely related to the armaments dynamic in industrialized countries. Perceived conflict formations on the East-West level have been projected into the Third World; and as a result of economic crises (balance of payment problems, unemployment, idle capacities) in some industrialized countries arms export has been dramatically increased. Besides economic and technological determinants, the intensification of the military transfer process is primarily a political decision, taken in supplier and recipient countries. While existing relations between the industrialized and the underdeveloped world might be modified, the dominance and dependence pattern is not changed basically by the increased transfer of arms.

The import of sophisticated capital-intensive technology and especially the installation of complex arms production programs enhance the dependence on suppliers from industrialized countries and prove to be negative for adequate development. Thus, armaments have to be considered as a determining factor for the continuation of uneven development and underdevelopment. Arms, their application or the threat to apply them, may be necessary for the functioning of the production and accumulation process, but at the same time they represent a reduction of the available social surplus.[12] The cost of maintaining a certain mode of production and of controlling social frictions by force might rise to a level higher than the total amount of distributable surplus -- a status some Third World countries are already approaching.

This is no surprise, since the increase of inequality marks

the development processes in almost every peripheral country. The affluence of the few becomes ever more provocative in the face of the poverty-stricken masses. In order to maintain the convenient status quo, the elites virtually have to establish different forms of apartheid. The number of the military, paramilitary, and police forces is increased continuously in order to secure the existing order. Official and private institutions from metropolitan countries are only too willing to transfer the necessary expertise, equipment, and strategies for the military and police forces. But in many cases the booming public security forces do not suffice to maintain the law and order of the few. Many private institutions are being set up in order to guarantee the uneven distribution of income and property. In this respect the trends in the metropolitan countries and the Third World are very much alike.

An alternative to the present prevalent trend of armament and underdevelopment would be to concentrate on an entirely different development model, i.e. on the production of goods to meet the basic needs of the majority. Instead of relying on the import of sophisticated labor-saving technology and the production of goods for the world market (such unnutritious crops as coffee) to earn the foreign exchange required to pay for imports, in the alternative model of development the production of simple goods for mass consumption and nutritious food would be stressed. Instead of adapting the production structure to the supply and demand in industrialized countries, self-reliance would be favored and the economy would be dissociated from the world market and its criteria of profitability as far as possible. Optimal resource allocation and equal distribution would be emphasized, instead of concentrating on the growth of isolated and specialized industrial sectors.

In order not to create any misunderstanding, we should emphasize that we do not accept the notion Third World countries should be kept disarmed while the industrialized countries monopolize the means of coercion. On the contrary, we personally believe the developing countries have the legitimate right to defend themselves against external aggression. But this right can at present be exercised -- if at all -- only with the consent or at least tolerance of the major arms suppliers. As long as Third World countries rely on military technology designed and produced in industrialized countries, as long as a military doctrine for the Third World is accepted which has been prescribed for them and taught by strategists from industrialized countries, political independence and military self-reliance cannot be achieved in the Third World. To reduce possible political pressures, along with the acceptance of an alternative development model, a <u>military doctrine</u> capitalizing on available resources and know-how would have to be introduced.

NOTES

[1] S. P. Cohen, The Indian Army. Its Contribution to Development of a Nation, Berkeley 1971.

[2] M. D. Wolpin, Military Aid and Counter Revolution in the Third World, Lexington 1972.

[3] Such an index is chosen for example by E. K. Y. Chen, 'The Empirical Relevance of the Endogenous Technical Progress Function,' in Kyklos, Vol. 29, 2/1976, pp. 256-271, to measure the import of foreign technology.

[4] The transfer of technology involved in civil and military imports of developing countries is a function of the level and complexity of the existing structure of production and the infrastructure in general. It appears safe to assume that technology transfer contributing to an expansion of the productive capacity of the receiving country is trifling in military imports. The figures recorded include many ordinary 'non-technology' items, but can still serve as an approximation of military technology imported, because military technologies are extremely demanding upon the existing level of production and infrastructure and are therefore associated with forward linkages of considerable volume and high import content of equally sophisticated technologies. Statistics of military transfers do not account for these additional military imports. The juxtaposition of military transfers and important groups of investment goods in import statistics in Table 1 should thus serve as a meaningful indication of the military drain on the investive capacity of developing countries.

[5] See M. Kidron, Western Capitalism Since the War, (London 1968), especially chapter 3, or P. Baran and P. M. Sweezy, Monopoly Capital, New York 1966.

[6] According to fiscal year 1977 Congressional presentation by the Pentagon, over US $8 billion in arms and services remain to be delivered through the 1982 time frame.

[7] See the registers in the SIPRI Yearbooks and the corresponding methodological remarks.

[8] P. Lock & H. Wulf, Register of Arms Production in Developing Countries, Hamburg 1977, mimeo. It is likely that a few more countries engage in some kind of domestic arms production without being recorded in the survey.

[9] For details see P. Lock & H. Wulf, Deutsche Rustungsexporte und Sicherheitspolitik, in Studiengruppe Militarpolitik, Materialian fur eine alternative Militarpolitik, forthcoming.

[10] See R. Burt, 'New Weapons Technologies', Adelphi Papers No. 126, Sumemr 1976, pp. 9 and 18.

[11] M. T. Klare, 'Hoist with our own Pahlavi', The Nation, 31 Jan. 1976, Vol. 222, No. 4, p. 113.

[12]M. Kaldor, 'The Arms Trade and Society', <u>Economic and Political Weekly</u>, Vol. XI. Nos 5, 6, & U, 1976, pp. 293-301.

Arms Control and Technological Change

CHRISTOPH BERTRAM

For the past two decades, the control of arms through mutual agreement has seemed one of the most promising ways to pursue stability and rational accommodation between East and West in the nuclear age. The concepts of arms control, articulated and refined in the late 1950s and early 1960s, were soon tried out in practice. In 1969 the Soviet-American talks on the limitation of strategic arms (SALT) got under way, leading to a series of treaties and agreements in 1972 and 1974. Since 1973, delegations from member states of the two East-West military alliances, the Warsaw Pact and NATO, have met regularly to seek agreement on the reduction of theatre forces in Europe, so far without result. However slow the process, advocacy of arms control remains the symbol with which politicians in East and West seek to demonstrate the sincerity of their desire for peace.

After almost four years of negotiation, the Soviet Union and the United States now seem on the threshold of a SALT II agreement. Yet one should be careful not to hail the new agreement too enthusiastically as evidence of successful arms control. It is more the result of the determination of both sides to overcome that major obstacle to agreement that has, in recent years, increasingly tended to render compromise more and more difficult: the dynamics of technological change in modern arms competition.

At first glance, this is no more than a banality. After all, there has rarely been a period in which the characteristics of weapons have remained and even defined those of civilian industrial technology: they have never stood still. Arms-controllers have always been familiar with this problem, and when they have negotiated quantitative restrictions on weapon systems, they have defined them not just in terms of numbers but in qualitative terms as well: battleships, ICBMs, MIRV launchers, etc. This measure is

From **ARMAMENTS, ARMS CONTROL AND DISARMAMENT**, UNESCO Press, 1981, (144-156), reprinted by permission of the publisher.

adequate at times when the dynamics of technological change are relatively restrained, but it ceases to be sufficient when military technology undergoes major qualitative changes, when the performance of weapon systems alters so drastically that the categories of agreement can no longer embrace them and when all consensus on quantities of weapons inherent in a mutual arms-limitation accord is jeopardized by performance improvements on one side which are not matched by equivalent advances on the other.

I. THE DILEMMA

Technological change has characterized much of the competition in arms between East and West over the past three decades. Sometimes new technologies were the result of major breakthroughs, in concept at least, if not always in implementation; reliable intercontinental delivery systems carrying nuclear weapons against far-distant targets; multiple and independently targetable warheads which increased the destructive capability of each missile launcher; antiballistic missile technology; sea-based missile launchers; satellite reconnaissance -- to name a few in the strategic nuclear field. Others were the result of a cumulation of evolutionary improvements; much of the technology of precision guidance and target acquisition which will considerably affect the performance of both strategic and conventional weapons belongs in this category. Yet the problem of technological change, while always present, did not seem to worry arms controllers unduly until very recently. They felt that priority had to be given to restricting the numbers of specific weapon systems and that this would also restrict the weapon technologies that went with them. Qualitative arms control was, in this sense, a by-product of quantitative arms control.

This approach was never satisfactory, though perhaps the best available. Today it is in danger of becoming inadequate for three reasons, one political, the other two technical.

Political Strains

Politically, arms control has been seen as a symbol of East-West detente, perhaps the most tangible and unambiguous of all such symbols. If East and West are able to agree on limiting or reducing the forces they have available to pit against each other, this will indeed be one token of their sincere commitment to peace and accommodation. But arms-control agreements will only acquire this politically important symbolic significance if they are regarded both in East and West as fair and equitable: if not -- if

public or official opinion on one side feels 'we have been had' -- an agreement will not be interpreted as a genuine gesture towards detente but as a confirmation of long-held suspicions.

The trouble is that, because of technological change and the difficulty of incorporating it in an agreement, it has become almost impossible for arms-control negotiators to produce treaties which will be unequivocally fair and equitable. A bargain struck on the basis of the technological characteristics of specific weapons existing at the time of agreement will become inequitable as one side or the other introduced qualitative improvements which have not been ruled out, or deploys alternative weapon systems which bypass the restrictions agreed upon. Theoretically, it might be possible to resolve this problem by entering into new negotiations once the base of the old agreement shows signs of erosion. However, given both the inherent speed of technological innovation and the widespread tendency of politicians, analysts and the media to speed it up further in their minds by assuming that a known technology is already a deployed one, the intervals between agreements would have to be very brief indeed. The complexity of negotiating new, or renegotiating old, quantitative restrictions would undermine the hope that new and more durable results could be achieved in time. As a result, arms-control treaties and agreements which consist of striking numerical balances are drawn into inevitable political controversy, generating doubts over, rather than promoting confidence in, detente and increasing the political risk for the leaders on both sides.

The fate of the Soviet-American Interim Agreement on the Limitation of Offensive Strategic Weapons of 1972 is a case in point. The numerical balance struck in the agreement soon appeared, rightly or wrongly, to many in the United States to give a one-sided advantage to the Soviet Union, as Soviet weapons developments were catching up with American qualitative superiority. Rapid renegotiation became necessary, not least for domestic political reasons, which gave rise to the Vladivostok Accord only thirty months later. But even this compromise, which granted MIRV parity to the Soviet Union in exchange for an equal ceiling of total strategic forces, did not remove SALT from political controversy in the American debate. The dynamics of technological change eroded not only the basis of the original agreement, but also -- and more importantly -- eroded much of the desired political effect which both sides had sought to achieve. Rather than being a promoter of detente and political trust, inadequate arms control has become a consumer of trust.

Limits to Verification

The second reason why technological change is rendering inadequate the current practice of negotiating quantitative restraints is the increasing difficulty of verification. That agreements on arms limitation must be adequately verifiable has been accepted wisdom

for a long time, and technological inventiveness has indeed made this a realistic and unobtrusive principle in permitting the detailed observation of the military effort of another country through satellite reconnaissance. But verification depends on what is observable. Today, significant improvements in military forces and weapons are becoming less and less assured, then fewer and fewer arms can be covered by agreement, and arms control becomes more and more irrelevant. But, without adequate verification, how can even the most promising arms-control agreement provide both sides with the trust in compliance by the other?

Neither of the two techniques for solving this dilemma suggested in recent arms-control negotiations justify much optimism. The first is to verify compliance to qualitative arms restrictions -- for example, which missiles are equipped with MIRV -- through the observation of weapons tests. This is based on two questionable assumptions: first, that responsible governments and cautious generals will not entertain the idea of deploying new weapons technology without thorough testing; second, that all test will be adequately observable. While adequate testing is desirable, it would scarcely be undertaken if camouflage were to be of higher importance, particularly since military planners are used to living with a high degree of uncertainty anyway. In addition, many of the more important new weapons technologies in command, control and communications, guidance and target acquisition elude observation altogether.

The other technique for rendering accountable the unobservable characteristics of weapons is the 'counting as if' method: a weapon system (say, an intercontinental missile of uncertain performance) is regarded, for assessment's sake as if its performance were certain. The SALT II negotiations have already provided one such example: since the Soviet ICBM SS-18 had been tested both with MIRV and with a single warhead, the United States declared that within the Vladivostok limit of 1,320 MIRV launchers, it would count each Soviet SS-18 as if it carried more than one independent warhead. This may be helpful in specific cases, but as a general device its efficacy is more than doubtful. Elevated to a standard measure for assessing qualitative, non-observable weapons improvements, 'counting as if' is a positive stimulus to maximum exploitation of qualitative advanced and hence to qualitative arms competition: why should either side maintain a single warhead on a missile if it counted as a multi-warhead missile anyway? Moreover, it only makes sense if the weapons characteristics are known and the form the subject of agreed numerical limitations. 'Counting as if' is at best an auxiliary device, but it is not a satisfactory answer to the verification problem at a time of technological change.

Multi-Mission Weapons

It might still be possible to make do with a less than satisfactory

answer if it were not for another, and probably the most important, feature of current weapons technology: the defiance of traditional categories of weapons definition. Not only does technology improve performance within existing and defined weapons categories: it also makes possible multi-category and multi-mission weapons. The distinction between nuclear and non-nuclear systems, or strategic and theatre weapons was never absolutely clear-cut but it was sufficiently precise to allow arms-control negotiators to operate with it, incorporate it in treaty language and provide governments with a relatively unambiguous notion of their mutual obligations. It was possible, by restricting certain weapon systems, to restrict certain military missions: a limit on battleships limited also the amount of fire-power a navy could project beyond the shores; a ceiling on offensive intercontinental missiles also restricted the ability to launch a first strike against the other side; a freeze on theatre nuclear delivery vehicles also curtailed the destruction of specific theatre targets beyond the range and yield of conventional systems.

The trend towards multi-category and multi-mission systems is rapidly eroding this link between restrictions by category and curtailment of military performance. Limitation of the numbers of a particular category of weapons system no longer restricts the military mission the system used to support, since that mission can be allocated, albeit sometimes less effectively, to other, unrestricted systems. The particular feature of technology that makes this possible is the interchangeability of those factors which define weapon performance: range, yield and accuracy. In the past, a weapon of intercontinental range had to have a warhead which was both nuclear and high-yield, in order to make up for the inaccuracy caused by distance, and both features were more or less rigid requirements: there was no way of replacing the nuclear by a conventional explosive, since the weight differential would significantly reduce the range of the delivery system, and no way of substituting the high nuclear yield by a lower one, since this would drastically reduce destructive efficiency. But increasingly over the past years these absolute thresholds for performance requirements have become relative, largely as a result of the dramatic improvement in missile accuracy. Accuracy is no longer a function of range, as inter-continental delivery systems can attain Circular Error Probability (CEPS) as low as 100 metres over thousands of kilometres. Low accuracy no longer has to be offset by high explosive yields, and conventional explosives, guided to the heart of a point target, can sometimes produce destructive effects of a kind previously reserved for certain nuclear missions.

The initial motivation for these performance improvements was to render delivery systems more effective, i.e., to produce better strategic or better theatre weapons. Their real and long-term significance, however, lies elsewhere: the visible size and configuration of a weapon system are no longer reliable indicators of its performance and mission, as performance elements within the same shell can be allocated differently and can even be changed rapidly to produce a wide range of mission capabilities.

The most obvious example of this development is the modern cruise missile: it can be a tactical or a theatre weapon, but with

a smaller warhead load and the resulting increase in range, the same system can also be turned into a long-range weapon, capable of reaching strategic targets deep inside enemy territory. It can, at least theoretically, carry a nuclear or a conventional warhead. Cruise missile ranges can be as high as 4,000 kilometres and as low as desired, and their mode of launch __ from the air, from sea-based launchers or from the ground -- is equally variable.

Variability is also the feature of another weapon system, the Soviet SS-20 IRBM. Its booster consists of the last two rocket stages of the three-stage ICBM SS-16. By adding the third stage, an intermediate-range ballistic missile targeted on Europe or China can be turned into an ICBM targeted on the United States. The time required for conversion is estimated by some to be no more than a few hours.

It would, of course, be an exaggeration to claim that this trend towards multi-category, multi-mission weapons is entirely new. Theatre arms, like artillery, air-defence systems or tactical aircraft, have for long been 'dual-capable', i.e., able to deliver both nuclear and conventional explosives with resulting variations in range and destructiveness. Manned bombers often span strategic and non-strategic missions if their range permits. The American B-52 force has today a primary strategic nuclear mission, but many of the aircraft were used during the Viet Nam War for conventional area-bombing against targets in South-East Asia. The Soviet Backfire bomber, although probably not intended for use against strategic targets in the United States, has caused problems of definition and accountancy in the SALT negotiations because of its theoretical ability to reach American territory on some missions with in-flight refuelling. Equally, shipbased delivery systems have enjoyed considerable variability -- witness the decision of NATO's Nuclear Planning Group in May 1976 to include Polaris/Poseidon SLMB in the theatre nuclear forces assigned to the Supreme Commander in Europe (SACEUR). So the multi-mission phenomenon is, indeed, not entirely new. But while it had seemed relatively marginal during the development of inter-continental missile systems, it is now becoming much more central, challenging motions that have been essential to arms-control policies of the past twenty years. It is blurring the distinction between strategic and non-strategic weapon systems and making the verifiability of agreements uncertain.

The answer to the problem cannot lie in singling out the latest and most obvious of these new systems, the cruise-missile, and trying to find ways of making it conform to familiar arms-control definitions (for instance, by prohibiting all cruise-missiles, or by so restricting cruise missile sizes that trade-offs between range, guidance, nuclear and non-nuclear use have little or no relevance to the performance). The inapplicability of the approaches of traditional arms control to the cruise missile is a product not so much of any particular characteristic of this specific weapon system as of the technological elements that are responsible for its performance: the miniaturization of guidance and engine, the increased accuracy of delivery, the development of explosives tailored to specific targets and the relatively low cost which allows production in

large numbers. If the cruise missile were banned altogether or in specific configurations, other combinations of these elements would still be conceivable and conceived, and would pose the same problem again, possibly within a short time.

Nor can the answer to the erosion of existing weapons categories -- strategic/theatre, nuclear/non-nuclear -- lie in the setting up of a third or fourth category or of a new arms-control forum designed to cover systems below SALT and above regional negotiations such as MBFR. These systems have often been referred to as 'grey-area weapons', but this is a misleading terms, since it suggests that defining the 'grey area' between strategic and regional arms control would make it possible to subject them to a specific arms-control regime. The particular significance of multi-mission weapons is precisely that they cannot be pinned down in any category; they can span the whole spectrum. Attempts to deal with them with the help of a new category or a new arms-control forum will, therefore, be irrelevant to the problem they pose.

For the same reason, the answer to the challenge of the new technologies is also unlikely to lie in an attempt to squeeze them into the framework of existing arms-control negotiations. Splitting up the 'grey area' between the more SALT-related systems (such as long-range nuclear cruise missiles or versatile medium-range ballistic missiles of the SS-20 type) and systems more related to regional security concerns and regional arms-control forums (such as the short-range cruise missile or the Backfire bomber) can be no more than a temporary and makeshift measure. Not only would verification -- which is which in what context? -- soon provide frustrating but, even if verification were attainable, any arrangement in one forum would deeply affect and disturb the considerations of the other. A severe restriction on cruise missiles in SALT would not only curtail the ability of the superpowers to carry out other military tasks with these systems that they would not want to forgo, but it would also, at least indirectly, circumscribe the use of these weapons by their allies (a problem peculiar to allies of the United States) in purely regional roles and would cause strains in the alliance. conversely, the inclusion of theatre cruise missiles in MBFR, even if compliance were verifiable, is bound to affect the balance of strategic forces discussed in SALT and with its political relations between the super-powers as well as between the United States and her allies. Much of the 'grey-area weapons' technology is not exclusive to the super-powers: refusal by their allies to conform to rules framed by Soviet and American negotiators (leading perhaps to national development of cruise missiles) would limit the scope of super-power agreement while potentially undermining cohesion within the Western alliance.

These, then, are the three problems that technological change poses for the future of East-West arms control: first, the speed of technological change injects a high degree of ambiguity into restrictions directed primarily at quantitative levels of forces, and not only complicate the negotiations but, more important, endangers the political acceptability of their outcome; second, qualitative improvements are often more significant and less

verifiable than quantities of weapons, so that arms-controllers have to choose between agreements that are fully verifiable but increasingly irrelevant for the control of military potential and agreements that may be relevant but cannot be adequately verified; and third, the trend of technological change is towards multi-mission weapons which undermines the definitional categories which have, in the practice of East-West negotiations, been a primary 'organizing principle'. If arms control continues to encompass only the existing categories, it will fail to cover much of the new weaponry, which, as a result, will acquire increasing importance in the arsenals of both sides and will reduce the relevance of existing and future control agreements; if new categories were defined, these would prove equally elusive.

Attempts to cover the whole range from strategic-nuclear to regional-conventional weapons in one framework of negotiation and agreement could scarcely be promising: not only would the process of negotiation be even more cumbersome and agreement delayed beyond relevance but, more important, the wider framework would not do away with the problem of comparing categories and numbers of weapons. The search for strategic stability would be frustrated by the specific concerns of regional security. In this situation the United States may well decide that the former is more important than the latter; that if the security of the regional alliance were to interfere with the Soviet-American strategic relationship, then the alliance would have to take second place. It is a choice which the United States has so far refused to accept.

This analysis of the dilemma is, of course, based on two assumptions: first, that the dilemma matters and that arms control remains an important instrument in the search for East-West security; second, that technological change, which has largely caused the dilemma, cannot be effectively controlled.

II. WHY ARMS CONTROL?

The traditional objectives of East-West arms control have been three: to reduce the likelihood of war by increasing stability; to reduce the damage of war if war does break out; and to reduce the economic cost of preparing for war. If arms control today has lost much of its initial popularity, this is due not only to a greater recognition of the complexities involved, but also to doubts about whether arms control can realistically achieve these objectives.

Current East-West arms-control negotiations -- SALT and MBFR -- are concerned with aspects of the strategic and theatre balance, both of which have, after all enjoyed a relatively high degree of stability in the past. The major change in the strategic relationship between the United States and the Soviet Union has been Soviet accession to parity. But that, it can be argued, is a condition for stability. In spite of the introduction of new weapons on both sides, in spite of a multiplication of deliverable warheads, a dramatic increase in the precision of delivering

destructive power and a combination of symmetries and asymmetries in the force posture of both the Soviet Union and the United States, the post-1970 balance has shown remarkable resilience.

Although a very great deal of thought and diplomatic effort, hard bargaining and political courage has been invested by both sides in the process of strategic arms control, it is difficult to prove that without any of it -- with the possible exception of the Anti-Ballistic Missile (ABM) Treaty -- the stability of the central balance would by now be seriously undermined. The current discussion on limited strategic options, scenarios of limited first strikes against vulnerable ICBMs and the inadequacies of 'mutual assured destruction' concepts for deterrence indicates that the stability of the balance is under strain, and no more. The fact that much of this discussion fails to excite fears and concerns beyond the small society of strategic analysts rather confirms the resilience of the existing strategic relationship between the two superpowers, arms control or no arms control.

The European theatre balance, now the subject of East-West negotiation on force reductions, has shown an equally impressive degree of stability, in spite of the absence of any arms-control agreement. This is not to say that the balance is perfect in all respects, nor that there are not very real and sincere doubts over its future in the light of a continuous Soviet build-up which exceeds NATO efforts. But it does indicate that, in spite of changes in force ratios, political crises and the impact of technological innovation on the military arsenals of both sides, relative stability has in the past been obtained without arms control.

That is, of course, not really surprising. After all, there are other means for obtaining and maintaining stability than arms control, in particular that of offsetting through military efforts any threats to the balance as each side perceives it. The test for arms control is, therefore, not whether stability has been present without it but whether it has contributed to more stable military relationships. Here the record is at least ambiguous. Arms control has made the military relationship between East and West more calculable, and therefore stable, when it has been preclusive in character, i.e. when its aims have been to restrict the emplacement of weapons on the seabed, to prohibit the development and deployment of biological weapons, to reduce anti-ballistic-missile defences to the point of insignificance, as in the 1972 Soviet-American treaty. However, where negotiators have sought not preclusive arrangements but quantitative limitations and reductions of existing arsenals, the contribution to stability has been less evident. Details of military-force relationships have often received emphasis beyond their real strategic significance: reductions seem to have been contemplated primarily in connection with older and more obsolete weapon systems, and new programmes have been entertained both to provide a card in the bargaining with the opponent and to mollify domestic political and military opposition. In this respect, the relevance of arms control to strategic stability has been doubtful. While it is impossible to judge with any certainty what would have been the state of the strategic balance without SALT, it is clear that the

negotiations and the political ambiance they have created have
generated at least some dynamics that have favoured arms
competition rather than control.

In the European context, the effect of quantitative,
systems-oriented arms limitation on stability is equally ambiguous.
While reductions of arms and forces in the potential conflict area
of Central Europe might make war preparations more visible and
therefore perhaps less likely, they could weaken political
stability in a continent where military and political relationships
are so closely intertwined: in Eastern Europe, where Soviet
political control is underpinned by military presence, and Western
Europe, where the strain of negotiations could emphasize
differences between allies at the cost of alliance cohesion, and
where the establishment of certain arms-control zones could lead to
political division. This need not be so -- but the contribution of
arms control to stability is not so clear-cut and obvious as to
warrant, for this reason alone, a major political effort.

Damage Limitation?

Nor is the need for arms control all that obvious when it
comes to the second objective: reducing the damage if war should
break out. Paradoxically, the introduction of new weapons
technology has sometimes been more successful in this respect than
have efforts at controlling arms. The increased accuracy of
delivery systems, both for strategic and theatre use, means that
collateral damage (that is, unintended damage) can be considerably
reduced. New precision-guided weapons with conventional warheads
may, in the European theatre, be able to perform tasks that before
had been allocated to nuclear weapons, thus raising the 'nuclear
threshold'. As strategic systems can be used more selectively,
because of refinements in command and control as well as accuracy,
the threshold of all-out nuclear war is further removed from
regional conflict, and military installations replace urban centres
as the primary targets in the echelon of escalation below that
upper threshold. These technologies may well be 'destabilizing',
in that they remove one barrier against their employment, that of
uncertainty of effect; as the effect of weapons becomes more
calculable, the decision to go to war may also. But if war does
break out, the new technologies allow for a more discriminating and
controlled use -- an important objective of arms control. This
again, is not an argument against arms control; efforts at damage
limitation, like the current Red Cross talks on incendiary and
other weapons, or the negotiations of the United Nations
disarmament Conference in Geneva on chemical weapons, weather
modification and weapons of mass destruction, may also contribute
to making war less indiscriminately destructive. The point is
merely that arms control, contrary to the beliefs and hopes of
some, is not the only, and often not the most effective, way of
achieving this goal.

Reducing Military Costs?

The third objective, that of reducing the economic burden of the military effort, has been the most pragmatic and the least successfully attained to date in East-West arms-control negotiations and agreements. The promise of savings in defence expenditure has been offered by political leaders in East and West every time they have embarked on negotiations over the limitation of arms. Yet the results have rarely matched the promises. In connection with SALT I experience, Allison and Morris have noted:

> After a decade of steady decline in [American] strategic expenditures -- in the absence of a SALT Treaty and attendant principles and agreements -- defence budgets submitted to the Congress [after the 1972 SALT Agreements] . . . called for a levelling off of that decline and indeed, for increasing strategic expenditures.[1]

On the Soviet side, judging by the range of new deployments and newly started strategic programmes, the discrepancy between expressed economic hopes and actual expenditure, although less verifiable, has been no less and probably much greater than in the United States. Even if future SALT negotiations should produce sizeable reductions, as opposed to ceilings without cuts, in the strategic arsenals of both sides, these are not likely to produce major economies but would probably involve the phasing out of old systems in favour of new and more expensive ones. The major exception to the rule has been the ABM Treaty, in which both sides agreed not only to limit, but in reality to forgo the investment for, a functioning ballistic-missile defence, an example to which we shall return later.

No practical experience with mutual arms limitation has so far been gained in the European theatre. The MBER negotiations have been accompanied by publicly expressed hopes that they would result in the maintenance of security at lower costs. This might be the case if negotiations were to lead to a sizeable cut in military manpower; but the Western reductions envisaged by NATO's proposals -- 20,000 United States forces in the first phase and a further 53,000 United States and allied·in the second -- would not go far in producing savings for the six NATO forces involved in the prospective reduction area (even assuming reductions would lead to the units being disbanded rather than redeployed elsewhere). Savings would certainly be much less than the $20,000 million per annum which, it has been argued, could result from NATO weapons standardization. Where not manpower but weapons cuts are considered, as in the December 1975 NATO proposal to withdraw from West European territory 1,000 nuclear warheads with launchers in exchange for a withdrawal of 1,700 Soviet tanks from Eastern Europe, any savings are likely to be largely offset by the cost of modernizing those that remain.

This assessment is, of course, open to the criticism that it

concentrates on savings against actual, but not against potential, expenditure. In the absence of negotiated restrictions, it has been argued, the arms race would have continued unabated and major new weapon investments would have been necessary to keep ahead in the race. This might well be true but it is not self-evident. For one thing, the contention rests on a hypothetical comparison -- between that which is and that which might have been. As the point raised by Allison and Morris makes clear, it is by no means certain that the absence of arms control would have promoted arms competition more than has the negotiation of formal agreements. For another, it assumes that the primary driving force of the arms race is the action-reaction process by which the weapons procurement of each side is a response to that of the other. However, this is an assumption that has been increasingly and persuasively challenged by recent academic studies; at worst it is erroneous, at best too simple.

If the economic rewards of arms control have generally been disappointing, some kinds of arms control seem to have yielded more tangible results. The ABM example is, after all, impressive as a preclusive arms-control agreement which rules out of the legitimate arsenals of both sides the specific military mission of ballistic missile defence and prohibits investment on production and deployment (not research or development) of weapons designed to provide it. Quantitative limitations, however, if they imply reductions at all are likely to produce only marginal savings, because in the bargaining of mutual concessions both sides will tend to seek the smallest common denominator, which often means retention of the largest force. It is also easier to agree on phasing out obsolete weapons which are obsolete precisely because new and more expensive systems have superseded them, thus offering economies in maintenance but not in investment as the most likely saving. Moreover, quantitative restrictions of specific systems encourage the search for alternative, non-restricted systems in a world of technological change. It is therefore not surprising if the economic advantages of quantitative arms control have been less than impressive and represent, by themselves, an insignificant dividend for the effort invested.

Has East-West arms control then outlived its usefulness? The balance in the strategic Soviet-American relationship and in the European theatre is not ideal but it is still relatively stable. Potential damage in war could be reduced with the help of some of the new military technologies that are being introduced over the next few years. The tangible economic dividends of arms control have generally been meagre.

And yet the reasons why, in spite of doubts, disappointments and disillusionment, attempts at arms control between East and West must be continued remain powerful, perhaps more powerful than in the past.

132   Christoph Bertram

Arms Control as Conflict Management

Much of the original American enthusiasm for arms control was shaped in a period of clear American superiority, and more recent disappointments may have much to do with the difficulties of living in a state of nuclear strategic parity. Both the Soviet Union and the United States face a tough learning process. The Soviet Union must learn that catching up with the leader is one thing, gaining superiority over him quite another. The United States must learn that parity is a combination of asymmetries and that marginal advantages on one side or the other do not undermine stability. This learning process will be made even more difficult by the fact that some of the basic elements of nuclear deterrence will be called into question by technological change and will require careful deterrence management. The most important and potentially the most disturbing of these changes is the vulnerability of second-strike forces to strategic counter-force action. With growing missile accuracy, land-based ICBMs (even those in hardened silos) will become, sooner for the United States or later for the Soviet Union, targets that can be destroyed by the other side with a relatively high degree of reliability. As to sea-based nuclear-missile forces, the anti-submarine warfare (ASW) effort continues and may, over time, decrease the margin of invulnerability which they enjoy today. These developments will not only raise the general level of strategic nervousness; they may also reopen the question of ballistic-missile defence which has been presumed closed since the ABM Treaty of 1972. The degree of strategic turbulence will therefore be considerable over the next decade; probably much greater than that provoked by the relatively simple process of adjustment to the Soviet-American parity of secure second-strike force which has marked the previous one. During this period of pronounced sensitivity, with its concomitant risks of miscalculation and misinterpretation, arms control will provide an essential framework of management.

Nuclear Proliferation

The other development which will confront the two strategic superpowers in the decade ahead is nuclear proliferation. As other countries demonstrate their real or potential status as nuclear-weapons powers, the need is becoming manifest for the Soviet Union and the United States to keep their strategic relationship clear of the impact of third-party proliferation. Not that, in the foreseeable future, there will be serious rivals to the status of the superpowers, nor that the next decade is likely to see the emergence of many fully fledged nuclear-weapons states; the situation will be much less clear-cut. Some states will visibly invest in a nuclear-weapons option without proceeding to

breakaways, revolutions, internal feuds, and anarchy. This is aside from the question of external attack, which may threaten any undefended country with resources worth pillaging whether it is underdeveloped or not. While we know that national defense is required for security -- at least in the absence of an international security system -- just how much national defense is required for this purpose cannot be known with any assurance and, moreover, differs from one country to another depending on circumstances.

2) Defense programs also contribute to economic growth by providing close substitutes for civilian goods and services. Some of these are infrastructure (roads, airfields, power lines, hospitals, communication networks, etc.) which may be shared with civilian users. One specially important input is training given to the armed forces which may significantly improve their attitudes, work habits and productivity in civilian employment after demobilization, as well as giving them specific civilian-utilizable skills, such as management, accounting, typing, driving, piloting, and machinery repair. Moreover, a considerable part of defense expenditures go to feed, clothe and house military forces, thereby reducing the number of civilians that have to be fed, clothed, and housed by the civilian economy. Military forces in some developing countries also engage in scientific and technical specialties such as mapping, soil surveys, aerial surveys, dredging, meteorology, etc., which are of use to the civilian economy, and perform certain quasi-civilian activities such as coast guard service, disaster relief, border control, etc., which would otherwise have to be undertaken by civilians. And in some cases they engage in "self-help" production projects (e.g., manufacture of tires or batteries) in which the pooling of defense and civilian demand makes it possible to achieve significant economies of scale.

In the absence of the defense expenditures, the same resources might, no doubt, have provided the same goods and services for the civilian economy, and even more effectively -- though in practice, national motivations being what they are, this would not necessarily occur. This, however, is not the issue; we are considering here the gross economic benefits, rather than the net benefits, of the defense program. Even if we assume that the whole of the defense budget represents an initial loss of potential civilian output, it still remains true that some of the uses of the defense funds contribute something of direct value back to the civilian economy -- beyond military security -- while other military expenditures (e.g., commercial imports of ammunition) do not. This is an important distinction as between the civilian effects of different types of military expenditures; and the distinction is not rendered insignificant by the obvious consideration that spending the same money for optimum uses in the civilian economy would produce still more civilian utility or growth than either type of military use.

3) While shortages of fertile land, skilled labor, capital, administrative capacity, and foreign exchange no doubt provide the primary limitations on achievable growth in most LDCs, there are some indications that inadequate aggregate demand may sometimes also play a limiting role. Thus the raising of aggregate demand

of one soldier would usually suffice to provide general education
and industrial training for a civilian. One can therefore get some
idea of the opportunity cost of defense manpower by considering
that in our sample countries the size of the armed forces is equal
to about an eighth of the population with an elementary education,
almost three-quarters of those with a secondary education, and over
a third of those with jobs in manufacturing. (This is based on
unweighted averages of national ratios.) The implied heavy
opportunity costs are, however, mitigated to the not inconsiderable
extent to which the defense programs themselves serve as a
mechanism for general education, for attitudinal changes favorable
to development, and for training in skills later utilizable in
civilian jobs.

There may be additional adverse growth effects of defense
programs that are not readily quantifiable -- shifting governmental
attention and emphasis from economic to military problems as
defense programs become relatively more important; an increased
danger of a takeover of political power by the military as the
military becomes a relatively larger part of the governmental
apparatus; and diversion of funds from current expenditures on
education, health, etc. -- which are not directly included in our
"investment effect" category.[2] What significance, if any, to
attribute to such factors we do not know. They may at least offset
the exaggeration of the adverse effects of defense expenditures
implicit in our way of calculating the productivity effect, based
on the clearly unrealistic assumption that defense programs
contribute nothing at all to increased civilian productivity.

II. GROWTH BENEFITS OF DEFENSE PROGRAMS

Defense programs also make certain positive contributions to
economic growth. They help to preserve political stability which
is a prerequisite for any economic progress at all. They provide a
number of economic inputs into the civilian economy. In some
cases, they appear to stimulate growth through their
aggregate-demand and price effects. In some cases, they attract
additional foreign aid. They may possibly help to mobilize extra
energies and strengthen national unity and cooperation with
beneficial effects for growth. Unlike some of the adverse effects
and opportunity costs just discussed, these beneficial effects are
not readily quantifiable. Nonetheless, they merit further
examination.

1) The essentiality of the military contribution to the
maintenance of the political stability required for economic
progress is perhaps more readily overlooked in developed countries,
where it may mistakenly appear that a police force would suffice to
maintain national stability and order. Most LDCs, however, are
more obviously exposed to the centrifugal pull of diverse tribal,
caste, religious, and regional loyalties, and might disintegrate
unless possessed of a sufficient force at the center to deter

Series -- for only 1960 to 1965.)

The 44-country sample was not scientifically selected but was based on data availability, which tended to exclude the smaller and new countries. However, the sample included about half of all developing countries and 70-85% of the populations, defense expenditures and GNPs of the less developed countries (LDCs) as a whole -- excluding Communist China. And the mean averages for the sample, with respect to population, GNP and defense expenditure, were not very different than those for all developing countries as a group. The countries included in the sample, and some of the chief indicators of defense and development utilized, are shown in the table on page 9. The statistical analysis was supplemented by a case study of India and brief studies of Argentina, Israel, South Korea, and the UAR.

I. ADVERSE EFFECTS

LDC defense programs have by now come to exceed, as a percent of average GDP, those of developed countries, except the superpowers, and their gross adverse effects on growth have been substantial. Three main types of adverse effects may be distinguished.

There is an "income shift effect" when a rise in defense burdens reduces the part of total GDP that is in the civilian sector and hence the apparent growth of that sector. There is a "productivity effect" as more of the total product is shifted to government services which show negligible rates of measurable productivity increase. And there is an "investment effect" when a rise in defense burdens absorbs resources that otherwise might have gone into civilian investment and contributed to civilian growth.

Econometric analysis of likely values for these three effects suggests that in our sample their combined impact might involve a loss of approximately a quarter of one percent in the civilian growth rate for every one percent of GDP added to the defense program. This is a very strong impact, which would offset about 70% of the additional growth from each one percent of additional GDP going into investment. Such a strong adverse impact would not be inconsistent with the heavy opportunity costs of these programs. Our rough calculations suggest that the industrial-type resources and foreign exchange of particular importance for economic development, was equal to around four percent of the sample countries' gross capital formation, a third of their economic aid receipt, and 20% of their machinery imports.

Moreover, the use of LDC manpower in defense programs also has opportunity costs. Even where unemployment and underemployment, especially in agriculture, are prevalent, it appears that the marginal productivity of vigorous manpower, such as those of the armed forces, remains considerable in seasons of peak agricultural demand, such as in periods of sowing and reaping. Moreover, the amounts invested in the transportation, subsistence, and training

Growth Effects of Defense in Developing Countries

EMILE BENOIT

It has been generally assumed that the use of economic resources for defense programes by developing countries adversely affects their economic growth. A recently completed study showed that the growth effects are more complex than usually supposed.[1] The adverse effects are there, and are of considerable strength. But there are also favorable effects, and the net balance between favorable and unfavorable effects is far from clear. Indeed, I suspect that the net balance may have been favorable for growth in the past, though this need not continue to be the case in the future if defense burdens and procurement costs continue to rise. The composition of defense programs may be as important for economic growth as their size; thus a closer integration of economic and defense planning may be decidedly helpful. This article reports on a few of the study's main conclusions.

The study was mainly based on the statistical and economic analysis of the relations between "B," and the defense burden (average annual defense expenditures as a percent of gross domestic product), and "G," the civilian growth rate (compounded rate of growth in "civilian gross domestic product," i.e., total GDP minus defense expenditures, both at constant prices). The investment rate ("I"), the rate of price increases ("P"), and receipts of bilateral economic aid as a percent of GNP ("R_2") were other economic factors particularly examined in connection with the analysis of the relationship between defense expenditures and growth rates.

The study covered 44 developing countries in the period between 1950 and 1965. (Since data were not available for all countries for the full 16-year period we prepared two sets of estimates, one -- the A Series -- based on an average for each country for all the available years, and another -- the C

From **INTERNATIONAL DEVELOPMENT REVIEW**, 1972/1, (2-10), reprinted by permission of the publisher.

NOTES

1. G. T. Allison and F. A. Morris, in Long and Rathjens (eds.),
   Arms Defence Policy and Arms Control, pp. 99-100, New York,
   Norton, 1976.

its implementation; others will set up a minimum force, primitive by superpower standard but nevertheless frightening to neighbours; other states again will keep the world guessing as to whether or not they have acquired the capability to deliver nuclear weapons against an enemy; and a further group will make their continued non-nuclear status dependent on the co-operative behaviour of others, including the adequate supply of conventional weapons. As a result, nuclear power will be brought into international politics much more actively than before, in spite of the continued military pre-eminence of the United States and the Soviet Union. It is against this background that the superpowers must seek to protect their relationship of mutual deterrence through the continued process of dialogue which is arms control.

Finally, the arms-control process between East and West should be sustained in order to constrain the use of force in the period of international change, potential conflict and gradual adjustment which the world will be facing over the next decade or two. There is a risk that wars in the Third World could embroil the Second and First Worlds as well, that domestic change in East and West European countries could blur the European dividing line and introduce, into a continent which has owed much of its stability of the last thirty years to the predictability of alliances, a degree of unpredictability which could jeopardize security in the short run. And there is a risk that the Soviet Union, faced at home with the dilemma of the continued postponement of needed modernization of her political system for fear of its survival, and abroad with her inability to influence events other than by military force, might seek via the active employment of military resources an expansion of her influence and release from internal deadlock. Arms-control negotiations and agreements will not be capable of repressing the use of force on their own, but they may contribute to restraint, however modestly, in a period when the world will need all the barriers against conflict it can construct.

The requirement for arms control follows, therefore, from the need to manage and control military competition between East and West in the years ahead. Can this not be done adequately by dialogue, by discussion and by the explanation of respective doctrines -- in other words, without specific agreements on subjects which, like force reductions and weapons deployment, are affected by technological change? Dialogue and discussion are, no doubt, an important ingredient of the management of arms competition, but they must be expressed in agreements in order that their success can be assessed and so that they may receive and maintain political support. Results mean visible restrictions, reductions and constraints. As these will be affected by changes in military technology, arms control will either have to develop the means to slow down and control technological change, or it will have to devise other methods of restraint which are less subject to the dynamics of technological innovation and change than the existing method of primarily quantitative limitation.

of one soldier would usually suffice to provide general education and industrial training for a civilian. One can therefore get some idea of the opportunity cost of defense manpower by considering that in our sample countries the size of the armed forces is equal to about an eighth of the population with an elementary education, almost three-quarters of those with a secondary education, and over a third of those with jobs in manufacturing. (This is based on unweighted averages of national ratios.) The implied heavy opportunity costs are, however, mitigated to the not inconsiderable extent to which the defense programs themselves serve as a mechanism for general education, for attitudinal changes favorable to development, and for training in skills later utilizable in civilian jobs.

There may be additional adverse growth effects of defense programs that are not readily quantifiable -- shifting governmental attention and emphasis from economic to military problems as defense programs become relatively more important; an increased danger of a takeover of political power by the military as the military becomes a relatively larger part of the governmental apparatus; and diversion of funds from current expenditures on education, health, etc. -- which are not directly included in our "investment effect" category.[2] What significance, if any, to attribute to such factors we do not know. They may at least offset the exaggeration of the adverse effects of defense expenditures implicit in our way of calculating the productivity effect, based on the clearly unrealistic assumption that defense programs contribute nothing at all to increased civilian productivity.

II. GROWTH BENEFITS OF DEFENSE PROGRAMS

Defense programs also make certain positive contributions to economic growth. They help to preserve political stability which is a prerequisite for any economic progress at all. They provide a number of economic inputs into the civilian economy. In some cases, they appear to stimulate growth through their aggregate-demand and price effects. In some cases, they attract additional foreign aid. They may possibly help to mobilize extra energies and strengthen national unity and cooperation with beneficial effects for growth. Unlike some of the adverse effects and opportunity costs just discussed, these beneficial effects are not readily quantifiable. Nonetheless, they merit further examination.

1) The essentiality of the military contribution to the maintenance of the political stability required for economic progress is perhaps more readily overlooked in developed countries, where it may mistakenly appear that a police force would suffice to maintain national stability and order. Most LDCs, however, are more obviously exposed to the centrifugal pull of diverse tribal, caste, religious, and regional loyalties, and might disintegrate unless possessed of a sufficient force at the center to deter

breakaways, revolutions, internal feuds, and anarchy. This is aside from the question of external attack, which may threaten any undefended country with resources worth pillaging whether it is underdeveloped or not. While we know that national defense is required for security -- at least in the absence of an international security system -- just how much national defense is required for this purpose cannot be known with any assurance and, moreover, differs from one country to another depending on circumstances.

2) Defense programs also contribute to economic growth by providing close substitutes for civilian goods and services. Some of these are infrastructure (roads, airfields, power lines, hospitals, communication networks, etc.) which may be shared with civilian users. One specially important input is training given to the armed forces which may significantly improve their attitudes, work habits and productivity in civilian employment after demobilization, as well as giving them specific civilian-utilizable skills, such as management, accounting, typing, driving, piloting, and machinery repair. Moreover, a considerable part of defense expenditures go to feed, clothe and house military forces, thereby reducing the number of civilians that have to be fed, clothed, and housed by the civilian economy. Military forces in some developing countries also engage in scientific and technical specialties such as mapping, soil surveys, aerial surveys, dredging, meteorology, etc., which are of use to the civilian economy, and perform certain quasi-civilian activities such as coast guard service, disaster relief, border control, etc., which would otherwise have to be undertaken by civilians. And in some cases they engage in "self-help" production projects (e.g., manufacture of tires or batteries) in which the pooling of defense and civilian demand makes it possible to achieve significant economies of scale.

In the absence of the defense expenditures, the same resources might, no doubt, have provided the same goods and services for the civilian economy, and even more effectively -- though in practice, national motivations being what they are, this would not necessarily occur. This, however, is not the issue; we are considering here the gross economic benefits, rather than the net benefits, of the defense program. Even if we assume that the whole of the defense budget represents an initial loss of potential civilian output, it still remains true that some of the uses of the defense funds contribute something of direct value back to the civilian economy -- beyond military security -- while other military expenditures (e.g., commercial imports of ammunition) do not. This is an important distinction as between the civilian effects of different types of military expenditures; and the distinction is not rendered insignificant by the obvious consideration that spending the same money for optimum uses in the civilian economy would produce still more civilian utility or growth than either type of military use.

3) While shortages of fertile land, skilled labor, capital, administrative capacity, and foreign exchange no doubt provide the primary limitations on achievable growth in most LDCs, there are some indications that inadequate aggregate demand may sometimes also play a limiting role. Thus the raising of aggregate demand

and the consequent upward pressure on prices may in some cases provide a positive stimulus to growth.

In the case of India, for example, it appears that the rapid rise in defense expenditures after the Chinese attack led to a temporary liberalization of monetary-fiscal policy with a much more rapid rise in the supply of money and in prices, a fuller utilization of available resources, and a pronounced rise in the growth rate, even of the civilian economy. Moreover, even for the sample as a whole (exclusive of four hyper-inflation countries) we discovered that there was a positive simple correlation between growth rates and the rise in prices or the money supply, and also between the latter and the defense burdens. This suggests that moderate doses of inflation stimulated by heavy defense burdens may have favorable growth effects in a number of countries -- at least up to the point that resources are as fully employed as practicable.

4) An important finding of this study is that there is a strong positive simple correlation between defense burdens and the amounts of bilateral foreign economic aid received, expressed as a percent of GNP (R_2). The main causal relationship explaining this correlation undoubtedly flows from R_2 to B, in that the foreign economic aid received made is possible for the recipients to support larger defense programs than they could otherwise have afforded. However, the causal sequences was not entirely one-way. Certain countries like the Republic of China, South Korea, South Vietnam, and the U.A.R. received so much foreign aid partly because they were maintaining, and were willing to continue to maintain, relatively high defense burdens. This convinced potential donor nations, who believed their own interests would be advanced by those countries maintaining large defense programs, to offer them sufficient aid to facilitate their maintaining large defense programs while making sufficient economic progress to maintain high morale. In short, willingness to cooperate militarily by maintaining a larger than normal defense program may become an important method of attracting aid and thereby of accelerating growth -- at least for a limited number of strategically situated countries.

5) Finally, there is at least the possibility that defense programs in responding to military challenges have a unifying, nation-building effect and may mobilize additional energies and motivation, some of which may spill over into the civilian economy and help to raise the growth rate. This type of dynamic response would be in line with the theories of the psycho-biological school of "ethologists," as well as with the motivational emphasis in the theory of economic development of Albert Hirschman.[3] There is some concrete evidence in the country studies, particularly of India and Israel, that appears to support such a thesis, but it is primarily of an anecdotal and imprecise sort, and the strength of such a tendency, if it really exists, is still unknown.

Regrettably none of the favorable growth effects is directly quantifiable. Some of them (such as the training effects and the contribution made by civic action programs) might be quantifiable in principle, but the data required for making such estimates were not readily available. This lack of information has led some

commentators to assume that such favorable influences are
nonexistent, imaginary, or trivial. Lack of information, however,
should not be confused with lack of influence. Not knowing the
importance of a thing is not identical with knowing it is not
important.

III. THE BALANCE BETWEEN ADVERSE AND FAVORABLE GROWTH EFFECTS

Since it proved impossible to measure the positive influences
directly, we had to resort to statistical analysis in the hope of
shedding light on the question of whether the favorable influences
of defense expenditures on growth surpassed or fell short of the
unfavorable ones. If heavy defense burdens are inversely
correlated with growth rates and if other explanations of the
correlation can be eliminated, then this would imply that heavy
defense programs tend to reduce growth rates, in which case there
might be some presumption that the unfavorable growth effects of
defense would exceed the favorable effects. This is what most
people believe and was the initial hypothesis with which this
investigation began.

If, on the other hand, it should turn out that defense burdens
are positively correlated with growth rates (i.e., if high defense
burdens were reliably accompanied by higher growth rates) and if
other explanations can be eliminated, then this might suggest that,
surprising as it might seem, defense programs tend to reduce growth
rates, in which case there might be some presumption that the
unfavorable growth effects of defense would exceed the favorable
effects. This is what most people believe and was the initial
hypothesis with which this investigation began.

If, on the other hand, it should turn out that defense burdens
are positively correlated with growth rates (i.e., if high burdens
were reliably accompanied by higher growth rates) and if other
explanations can be eliminated, then this might suggest that,
surprising as it might seem, defense programs tended to raise
growth rates, and, in that case, the favorable influences would
presumably be stronger than the unfavorable ones.

Can this latter possibility (i.e., that defense expenditures
might have a net favorable effect on growth) be dismissed a priori
as paradoxical or absurd? An impression to this effect appears to
be based on the consideration that whatever benefits defense
expenditures might have for growth, an equal volume of resources
put into highly productive civilian investments would clearly be
even more beneficial for growth. This consideration, while true,
is not relevant here, since this is not the actual alternative we
confront. Thus this is not a valid criterion for determining the
net balance between favorable and unfavorable effects on growth.

The correct measure of the unfavorable effects is not the
optimum alternative use of the resources for growth but the likely
actual alternative use. In the normal case this will consist of a
mix of consumption and civilian investment, with by far the larger

part going into consumption (including civilian government consumption) with only slight growth effects, and with a substantial part even of the civilian investments going into housing, imports of consumer durables, or other uses with relatively small impacts on growth. Moreover, only about a third of the average LDC defense expenditure is for procurement of equipment, supplies, and construction work. Therefore, a reduction in most LDC defense programs would not readily or quickly translate into an equivalent rise in the investment program, since most of the resources released by the defense program in the event of defense cuts would not be the type of resources required to expand the investment program -- particularly the most efficient and productive sectors of it. In short, it is impossible to say, a priori, whether the net effects of defense expenditures on growth will be negative. It is necessary to analyze the facts.

The B-G' Simple Correlation

A variety of tests of simple correlation showed that the simple correlation between the defense burden and the civilian growth rate was positive and far too strong to be reasonably attributed to chance.[4]

This would point to the likelihood that higher defense burdens stimulated higher growth rates and that there was therefore a net balance of favorable over unfavorable growth effects -- but only if the apparent correlation could not be explained in one of three other ways: 1) The apparent correlation might be false, arising from a systematic bias in the data; 2) the correlation might be valid but explained by the influence of G' on B rather than vice versa; 3) the correlation might be technically "spurious," that is, result from the action of one or more other variables that influenced both G' and B in such a fashion as to explain their correlation. We turn now to a summary consideration of these three possibilities.[5]

Are the Data Biased?

While the quality of the data leaves much to be desired, this is not the same thing as a systematic bias that would explain the correlation. It is not possible with such complex data, of course, to prove that no bias exists, but neither is there any particular reason to suspect that a bias might be present, except in one instance.

One might suspect that countries with military governments spend more on defense than other governments and are also more likely to exaggerate the official estimate of their growth rates.

If so, this might conceivably explain the apparent correlation. Burma, Jordan, and South Vietnam were mentioned by critics as possible examples. Our examination failed to confirm this hypothesis. It was far from clear that countries when taken over by military governments thereafter spent more on defense,[6] and it was also questionable whether such governments actually did exaggerate their growth rates more than other governments -- or that even if they did, this would affect the particular growth estimates we were using. Moreover, when we ran a simple AB-AG' regression analysis with the same sample, but omitting Burma, Jordan, and South Vietnam, we still got a strong positive correlation (r = .52, t = 3.7), nearly as strong as with the whole sample.

Does Growth Stimulate Higher Defense Burdens?

The first way in which a rise in income might tend to increase the share of national product allocated to defense is indicated by the hypothesis that LDCs generally desire larger defense programs, but that only those that grow fastest feel able to afford them -- just as persons who become rich are generally better insured than those who stay poor. If that were the explanation, however, we should expect to find that wealthy countries would generally have proportionately larger defense programs (i.e., higher B's) than poor ones. In fact, no significant correlation between per capita GDP and defense burden was found.

Another hypothesis is that countries with faster growth rates might incur heavier defense burdens because of greater military risks arising from the fear, the envy, or the cupidity of their neighbors, or perhaps from the more adventuresome foreign policies into which they might be tempted. Such a complex hypothesis is not easily tested, but we noted that four of the countries in the top quartile of civilian growth rates were included in the eleven countries with a marked (1% or more) decline in defense burdens from the first to the last year in the series. Another in the top growth quartile showed an 0.8% decline in B, and still another showed a 3% decline from an immediate year. Thus six out of eleven countries in the top growth quartile showed significant declines rather than increases in defense burdens. Incidentally, four of the twelve countries with decided rises in their defense burdens were in the lowest quartile of civilian growth. Moreover, a simple regression analysis relating B (compounded rate of change in B) to G', in the A series, showed no positive correlation, but an inverse correlation (r = -.11445) which, however, was too weak to be significant.

A final hypothesis is that rapid growth might bring about disproportionate increases in government revenues and expenditures, out of which one might expect the military forces, as a potent interest group, at least to get a proportionate share. This too was not sustained by the evidence: no significant correlation was

found between the rise in defense expenditures and in tax revenues as a share of national income; and half the countries with a significant positive year-to-year   D-G correlation and a rising ratio of government expenditures to GDP showed a declining ratio of defense to total government expenditures.

Is the B-G' Correlation Spurious?

In order to analyze the third possibility — that one or more additional variables might explain the simple correlation between B and G' and render it spurious — resort was made to multiple regression analysis. When two additional independent variables were added to the G'-B regression equation — namely, the investment rate (I) and receipt of bilateral economic aid as a percent of GNP (R_2) — they appeared to explain the variation in G' very well, at least in the A series, and reduced the independent explanatory power of B to negligible proportions. At the end of the analysis, AI explained 35% of the variance of AG', AR_2 about 20%, and AB only 3% — less than required for a significant correlation. However, a quite different result was given in the C series, where CB remained a significant explanatory factor despite the presence of CI and CR_2.

In an effort to understand why the results in the A and the C series were so different, the methodology of the multiple regression analysis was examined, especially in the form of stepwise partial regression analysis, which exhibits the results at each stage of the calculations. This examination confirmed the soundness of the views of some statisticians that multiple correlation analysis of a static type can provide only predictive models and offers no valid guidance to the underlying causal structure.

In this particular case, there were specific reasons for doubting that this type of analysis provided valid conclusions on cause-and-effect relations. Thus the final results were found to depend on small initial differences in the relative strength of the simple correlations between the investment rate and growth on the one hand, and the defense burden and growth on the other. As a result of these differences, the defense burden was treated as a proxy of the investment rate in the A series but not in the C series. But it seems quite inappropriate to base a judgment on the existence of a cause-and-effect relationship between the defense burden and growth on the basis of the varying strength of the correlation between investment and growth. It seems particularly unrealistic to treat the defense burden as a proxy of the investment rate since the two are not significantly correlated, and the weak correlation that does exist must be attributed to the influence of the defense burden on the investment rate and not vice versa — defense programs having some construction and other capital items and thus tending to raise the investment rate somewhat when they increase.

IV. A HYPOTHETICAL MODEL OF CAUSATION

All the preceding discussion can show is that B might to some degree be a cause of G', not that it actually is. On the basis of all our research, we suspect that it is, and that the pattern of causal relations among the main variables can be hypothesized as follows:

This model hypothesizes reciprocal influences between G' and I and between R_2 and B. The existence of these influences is well reflected in the positive simple correlations between these variables and is confirmed by a great deal of factual knowledge. The model also hypothesizes a positive but weak influence of B on I that is reflected in a positive but weak correlation between these items and some knowledge of its sources: i.e., that the defense program itself includes an investment component. The model also hypothesizes a significant positive influence of B on G' that is over and above any indirect influence from R_2 that is also transmitted through B and vice versa.

It must be said here that on the last point -- i.e., whether B exerts a positive influence on G' over and above the indirect influences exerted through and by R_2 and I -- the evidence we have developed and analysis we have undertaken do not prove our hypothesis. The statistical evidence, in particular, is highly ambiguous -- it does not lend strong support to our argument nor does it seriously undermine it. Our overall research has strengthened our belief that the hypothesis is a correct one.[7] Hard proof, however, must await further, very complex inquiry.

V. QUALITATIVE ASPECTS

One factor that emerged from the study was the importance of the composition of defense programs in determining their impact for growth. Programs that absorb large amounts of foreign exchange for weapons purchases, or which utilize large amounts of domestic resources for indigenous weapons procurement -- particularly if the weapons are of advanced and sophisticated types -- absorb financial or physical resources particularly strategic for development, and thus heavily burden growth. On the other hand, programs that offer civilian-utilizable training to a large number of men, and release these men early in their working lives back into the civilian labor force, may make a significant contribution to the productivity of the civilian sector.

Table 1

INDICATORS OF DEFENSE AND DEVELOPMENT FOR SAMPLE COUNTRIES

	(1) AB	(2) AG	(3) AΔD	(4) AG'	(5) AI	(6) GMCO	(7) AR_2	(8) AP	(9) Non-AG Output
	(Burden) Def. as % of GDP Av. '50-'65 in current prices	(GDP)	(Def.)	(CivGDP)	Invest. as % of GDP Av. '50-'65	Gross marg. cap. output ratio Av. '60-'65	Bilateral ec. aid receipts as % of GNP	Annual average price change '51-'65	As % of GNP '65
		Cumul. ann. % change constant prices '50-'65							
Argentina	2.49	3.24	-1.10	3.37	19.47	4.7	0.01	25.60	83.4
Brazil	2.63	5.35	5.97	5.16	16.43	5.5	0.53	30.00	71.8
Burma	6.61	5.10	8.39	4.93	18.06	—	1.34	0.06	68.2
Ceylon	0.94	3.32	10.15	3.29	13.29	3.0	0.92	0.80	56.7
Chile	2.69	3.50	-1.21	3.63	10.80	2.6	0.83	33.54	89.6
China (Taiwan)	11.42	8.76	16.50	8.12	17.96	1.8	5.23	9.08	74.0
Colombia	1.59	4.53	7.21	4.50	18.04	4.4	2.04	9.38	67.8
Costa Rica	0.32	4.85	15.34	4.85	18.08	4.1	1.96	-0.04	67.4
Dom. Republic	4.23	4.07	-5.50	4.28	14.49	3.4	2.87	1.66	76.5
Ecuador	2.11	4.63	9.60	4.81	14.10	3.2	0.34	2.44	65.8

Table 1. (continued)

INDICATORS OF DEFENSE AND DEVELOPMENT FOR SAMPLE COUNTRIES

	(1) AB	(2) AG	(3) A⊿D	(4) AG'	(5) AI	(6) GMCO	(7) AR	(8) AP	(9) Non-AG Output
	(Burden) Def. as % of GDP Av. '50-'65 in current prices	(GDP)	(Def.) Cumul. ann. % change constant prices '50-'65	(CivGDP)	Invest. as % of GDP Av. '50-'65	Gross marg. cap. output ratio Av. '60-'65	Bilateral ec. aid receipts as % of GNP	Annual average price change '51-'65	As % of GNP '65
El Salvador	1.41	4.95	6.37	4.95	12.58	3.0	0.71	-0.16	70.5
Ghana	1.18	4.30	9.90	4.23	16.96	4.2	4.20	2.56	47.6
Greece	5.21	6.21	-0.33	6.58	20.68	3.3	3.27	5.84	74.9
Guatemala	0.89	4.73	4.62	4.73	11.01	2.4	0.89	0.72	71.5
Honduras	1.24	3.75	3.21	3.75	14.33	3.4	0.04	1.72	55.8
India	2.46	3.38	10.23	3.20	12.32	3.0	1.22	2.82	55.0
Indonesia	3.10	3.46	-1.95	3.40	15.94	2.7	1.33	55.82	44.0
Iran	4.00	4.73	14.85	4.51	15.25	2.2	1.07	4.90	69.5
Iraq	5.93	6.75	14.91	6.39	16.45	—	1.28	0.34	82.7
Israel	6.08	10.70	11.66	10.47	29.51	3.3	9.97	11.56	91.5
Jordan	16.75	9.01	8.15	10.70	14.97	1.6	24.70	n.a.	75.0
Kenya	0.60	4.93	9.00	4.93	11.50	—	2.02	2.00	61.8
South Korea	5.32	5.66	-2.50	6.23	13.17	2.8	7.88	13.26	59.4
Malaysia	2.68	4.99	7.95	5.00	14.47	3.0	0.46	1.14	66.0
Mexico	0.75	6.13	3.24	6.15	17.25	2.2	0.12	6.30	82.9

Table 1. (continued)

Morocco	3.84	2.43	12.77	2.20	12.88	3.4	2.54	4.54	67.6
Nigeria	0.56	4.21	10.51	3.75	11.98	2.3	1.86	3.68	38.7
Pakistan	3.26	3.56	1.30	3.65	13.37	2.2	3.45	2.80	52.1
Peru	2.70	5.24	3.35	5.25	22.39	2.8	0.21	8.08	78.1
Philippines	1.59	5.10	3.73	5.12	11.11	2.5	1.34	2.00	66.5
South Africa	1.23	4.84	12.11	4.77	20.03	3.6	-0.17	1.09	90.3
Spain	3.26	6.10	2.72	6.20	20.03	—	0.89	5.90	79.2
Sudan	1.59	5.00	13.40	4.92	12.38	2.5	2.10	0.60	42.8
Syria	7.04	5.50	9.86	4.97	16.95	2.0	1.85	-1.38	59.0
Tanzania	2.11	3.08	32.00	2.90	12.20	3.3	-5.53	1.20	45.1
Thailand	3.38	5.86	6.56	5.85	17.37	2.6	0.91	1.54	67.2
Tunisia	1.78	5.52	-2.59	5.68	21.10	3.8	10.22	3.20	77.6
Turkey	4.38	5.74	6.24	5.72	13.22	3.5	2.15	8.10	58.3
Uganda	0.87	3.75	116.50	5.04	9.52	3.2	3.59	3.30	40.8
U.A.R.	6.90	6.46	10.87	6.17	16.60	—	2.97	2.16	69.4
Venezuela	1.88	6.64	9.13	6.65	23.96	3.1	-0.35	1.32	71.5
South Vietnam	10.20	5.34	26.50	3.00	10.33	1.8	32.15	6.18	67.3
Yugoslavia	8.76	8.09	-0.47	8.68	35.85	—	0.60	2.23	71.3
Zambia	1.45	7.05	13.00	8.17	23.66	3.7	-1.29	1.90	90.0
MEAN	3.62	5.24	7.81	5.52	17.15	2.8		6.51	67.3
MEDIAN	2.66	5.00	8.27	4.94	16.07	2.9		2.56	67.8

Sources: Chiefly IBRD, UN, and AID. For details, see *Effect of Defense on Developing Economies, op. cit.*

147

For this reason, military assistance programs that provide military equipment free or at greatly reduced costs may reduce the adverse growth effects of defense on the recipients by making their own defense programs less capital-intensive and more labor-intensive -- a type of specialization conducive to development. While indigenous weapons production may provide some useful industrial learning experience, the benefits are likely to be less than from other types of subsidized industrialization because the secrecy and political intervention usually involved in weapons development and production reduce the diffusion of the industrial know-how that is acquired and shield the continuation of inefficiency and high costs.

Civic action programs which deliberately utilize military forces and equipment for secondary uses on behalf of civilian economic objectives would also appear to have important potential economic benefits, whatever their political merits or demerits. As the defense function becomes increasingly one of deterrence rather than actual fighting, more resources are stockpiled in the military sector than are actually in use for traditional military purposes. Their overhead cost may be reduced by finding secondary and temporary uses for them that contribute to development.

Because of the importance of the composition as well as the size of defense programs, there would appear to be considerable scope for a closer integration of defense planning with economic planning, which in most developing countries have so far very little to do with each other. The introduction of standards of economic efficiency and cost benefit analysis into defense planning might render substantial economic benefits, often with positive improvements in security as well. The introduction of this type of thinking into defense planning would also improve the climate of later arms control agreements among developing countries themselves, which have so far been conspicuously lacking.

NOTES

[1] Emile Benoit with Max F. Millikan and Everett E. Hagen. Effect of Defense on Developing Economies (Cambridge, Mass.: Massachusetts Institute of Technology, Center for International Studies, January 1972, Publication No. C/71-6a). The research for this study was sponsored by the United States Arms Control and Disarmament Agency, which is not responsible for the views and judgments expressed in the study or this article.

[2] Some fiscal effects, however, would be favorable for growth. This would be true, for example, insofar as higher defense expenditure led to more deficit-financed expenditure, raising aggregate demand in cases where it would otherwise be too low to provide an adequate use of available resources. See below, pp. 4-5.

[3] Albert Hirschman. Strategy of Economic Development (New Haven: Yale University Press, 1958).

[4] The basic AB-AG' linear regression equation showed an r of .538 and a t of 4.1, a correlation that could be encountered by accident less than one time in a thousand. The "A" in these symbols, it will be recalled, means the A series (1950-65).

[5] This summary necessarily omits discussion of the methodological complexities involved in this kind of statistical analysis.

[6] Conversely, however, heavy defense spending might make it more likely that a country would get a military government.

[7] Dynamic causal modeling, in which the time sequence of changes in the variables could be identified, might have been more helpful. We were able to go only a short distance in this direction. For useful results it would have been necessary to account in the model for all the variables impinging on G', in order to determine whether B has any independent causal effect on G'. For the less developed countries, a particularly important set of variables are in seasonal and regional variations in rainfall and temperature and other autonomous factors.

The Game of Disarmament

ALVA MYRDAL

Sweden's head delegate to the Geneva Conference of the
Committee on Disarmament sees the disarmament picture as a 'history
of lost opportunities' to bring the nuclear arms race to a dead
stop. She discerns little genuine disarmament progress over the
years, despite certain limited treaties, primarily because the two
superpowers have not really worked for this, but rather to achieve
a balance between themselves. All nuclear-arms-control negotiations have actually been a kind of two-person game -- with the two
superpowers playing strictly between themselves, or teamed against
the rest of the world. So only the non-nuclear-weapons States are
called upon to make the sacrifices in the name of 'arms control'.
     A challenging question has been proposed to me by the editor
of Impact of Science on Society: 'Are the two nuclear superpowers
(United States, U.S.S.R.) really serious about nuclear
disarmament?[1]
     The following article is an attempt to answer this harrowing
question in a personal way, from the vantage point of a participant in ten years of disarmament negotiations, where I have been
representing one of the non-aligned, non-nuclear-weapons states.
The reader should remember that the majority of nations are not
great powers and are either non-aligned or so inclined. Their
views should be taken seriously. The fact that they do not possess
the ultimate weapons of power has put them, since the end of the
Second World War, at the mercy of the nuclear-weapons nations -- if
it should come to the point that issues are decided by military
strength. Thus the whole weight of the interests of these non-
nuclear-weapons States lies in the possibility of regulating world
affairs by other means than violence.
     Let me immediately reveal how the experiences of a decade of
disarmament efforts have gradually led me and many others

From **IMPACT OF SCIENCE ON SOCIETY**, Vol. XXII, No. 3, 1972,
(217-231), reprinted by permission of the publisher.

participating in these efforts to some terrifying conclusions: that
we have accomplished no real disarmament, that we can see hardly
any tangible results of our work, and that the underlying major
cause must be that the superpowers have not seriously tried to
achieve disarmament. The prophesy must then also be made that
there will be no disarmament. (I have elsewhere described the
history of disarmament as a history of lost opportunities [1].) I
am now inclined to describe it as a history of wilfully sqandered
opportunities.)

A statement as sweeping as this should be accompanied by an
explicit qualification: a totally new course of events might, of
course, occur in the wake of some cathartic process of such
intensity that it would amount to a conversion. In the history of
the superpowers, sudden turnabouts, even reversals, have happened,
as when Khrushchev turned the Soviet Union against Stalin or when
Nixon turned the United States towards China. It is conceivable
that the now finally initiated participation of China in the United
Nations and thus in world affairs may call forth the necessary
catharsis. But if a profound about-face is excluded from the
picture of the future, I stand ready to defend as inescapable the
pessimistic prophesy about how little can be expected to be
achieved in the direction of true international disarmament.
('Disarmament' is in this article used in a general way, with the
connotation of capabilities rather than in terms of armed forces
deployed or military budgets.)

This should, however, be taken as my present and possibly
temporary position. I look forward with the keenest interest to
the arguments offered and comments made on this article by the
other authors in this issue[2] as they will surely aid me in
formulating a more final analysis, to which I intend to devote a
forthcoming book.

I. THE CONTINUING INCREASE IN ARMS

As matters stand today, my severe judgement about the lack of
achievement in disarmament negotiations can be fully substantiated
by a simple reference to the steep increase in actual armaments
which has taken place while the talks on disarmament have gone on.
I will insert a quick review of the progress in regard to arming,
before starting my analysis of the failures in regard to
disarmament.

The insane road which the world is taking is most impressively
illustrated by the face that it is now spending some $200,000
million annually on arms, a sum which just about equals the total
national income for the poorer half of mankind.

All nations seem to be bent on continuing down the road to
more abundant and more lethal armaments. But the primary actors
are without doubt the nuclear-weapons superpowers. Their overkill
capacity continues to spiral upwards. The number of nuclear
warheads as well as of their delivery vehicles has increased in an

alarming manner since the start of the disarmament negotiations in Geneva ten years ago. For instance, the number of intercontinental ballistic missiles (ICBMs) has increased by a factor of five. When we started disarmament negotiations in 1962 there were in existence some 500 ICBMs, which it was our task to eliminate; now there are more than 2,600.

The number of nuclear-weapons tests is a similar case in point. They have continued to show an unchecked increase even since an international treaty tried to curtail them by driving them underground. The number and quality of other weapons, misnamed 'conventional', have similarly progressed.

In regard to submarines, it is not so much the number but the effectiveness that has multiplied -- what in cool military parlance is called 'product improvement'. The increase in this factor is something like tenfold during the decade. No small part of this multiplication was achieved by the development of the nuclear-armed, nuclear-propelled Polaris-type submarine, an altogether new phenomenon introduced since 1959. Now these submarines are being fitted in the United States with Poseidon missiles, a weapons system in its turn at least eight times more effective than that previously installed. A similar multiplication of fire-power is occurring in all major powers.

But the acceleration of the armaments race is not confined to the relatively affluent powers. To take just one illustration of this fact: ten years ago only six nations of the Third World had supersonic military aircraft; now at least thirty-two such countries do.

No less significant is the increase in accuracy and destructive power of all weapon types, the automation of systems of targeting and communications, the breakthroughs in military electronic equipment, the vastly improved cameras for spy satellites, etc. This entire unhappy evolution is amply demonstrated in the SIPRI yearbooks [2].

II. THE HISTORY OF THE FAILURE OF DISARMAMENT EFFORTS

Disarmament has not failed for lack of effort. When looking back at the decade of international institutionalized and remarkably sustained disarmament negotiations, one is struck by the high ambitions held at the start in March 1962 of the ENDC (Eighteen Nation Disarmament Committee, as it was then called). Both the United States and the U.S.S.R. each submitted a draft Treaty on General and Complete Disarmament.

The initiative was actively seized in the very first week by the group of newcomers: the non-aligned countries which had just been added to those of the two blocks which had 'off-and-on' been entering into disarmament talks practically since the end of the Second World War. First, they pressed the three nuclear-weapons States present -- U.S.S.R., United Kingdom, United States -- to form a sub-committee in order to produce a convention prohibiting

nuclear-weapons tests. Then, within a month the non-aligned members presented a memorandum (April 1962) offering a new scheme for a comprehensive ban on testing of nuclear weapons. It outlined a radically simplified but effective system for control on a purely scientific and non-political basis, relying mainly on existing or improved means of observations by seismological methods but referring also to the possibility of setting up an international scientific commission for the verification of contested cases of violation.

This attempt at a breakthrough focused the disarmament efforts on a point of major strategic significance, as such a prohibition of weapon testing must have far-reaching disarmament ramifications. A total ban on testing of nuclear weapons would have erected a double barrier of formidable strength: it would have meant the end of the qualitative development of nuclear weapons, thus the end of the competitive race between the nuclear powers, and, in addition an effective block -- for all practical purposes -- against any acquisition of such weapons on the part of non-nuclear-weapons countries which might be tempted to veer away from the narrow path of self-denial staked out for them.

It was for these twin purposes that the global test-ban proposal, which would have profoundly changed our history, had been strategically and ingeniously devised some years earlier. Please note the timing: when it was first proposed by Nehru in 1954, the United States had exploded its first thermo-nuclear device in October 1952 (the U.S.S.R. did the same in August 1954) and in March 1954 the megaton blast on Bikini Atoll had set the world aghast.

Mankind became frightened of the future. The development of terror-engineering was then in such an early phase -- no mass production of nuclear bombs having yet been started -- that a decision to stop testing would have been operationally easy to implement; thus, it would have been much more effective than it could be later when the diabolic knowledge had spread. Burma stated the issue at the time in terms which ring with irony and blame against the insensitive, technocratic fury: 'Cessation of all further experiments designed to produce bigger and better thermo-nuclear and atomic weapons.' In this early stage, we should recall, all the so-called 'threshold nations' -- those which might be on the threshold of developing their own atom bombs -- declared themselves in favour of such a self-sacrificing option.

Soon we could witness the first side-stepping of this crucial issue -- although we have until this day hesitated to acknowledge what happened for what in reality it was. The accent was shifted from stopping tests as a means to stop the further development of nuclear weapons, to stopping them instead in order to avoid the side effects of atomic radiation. A scientific committee was created in the United Nations and studies have since been continuously published on the effects of ionizing radiations upon man and his environment.

Although one cannot ready the history of the ensuing debates [3] without a strong impression of the lack of responsiveness on the part of the superpowers, I do not intend to accuse them of any sinister manoeuvring. The shifting of concern from nuclear-weapons

development to radiation risks was probably rather a result of 'oversell' on the part of those opposed to nuclear testing, which soon got mighty support from public opinion. All those who spoke and marched against the atom bomb were so eager to conjure it out of existence that they exaggerated the radiation scare. Of course, nothing served to arouse the world opinion as much as what befell the crew of the Japanese vessel, Lucky Dragon, whose crew members suffered radiation sickness after being exposed to fall-out from the thermo-nuclear bomb testing on Bikini Atoll in 1954.

That the existence of the nuclear weapons themselves was the larger worry was somehow lost sight of. Anyway, pressure within the United Nations was not enough to get the superpowers to bow down and cease the development, testing and production of nuclear weapons.

To skip the rest of the story about the vagaries of test-ban discussions during their first eight years, suffice it to note that hopes were vigorously renewed in 1962 when ENDC was set up at Geneva. Its non-aligned members made their first important move in transferring the nuclear test-ban issue to ENDC's agenda from that of a preceding body, the Geneva Conference on the Discontinuance of Nuclear Weapons Tests. This latter, consisting of the three nuclear-weapon States plus Canada, had worked inconclusively for four years.

ENDC worked diligently on detailed proposals, encompassing structures and provisions of a comprehensive nuclear test ban, as well as the structure and modalities of a control scheme. Then, in the wake of the Cuba crisis (October 1962) there occurred a spectacular convergence of the American and Soviet positions. For a while only the margin between the two to three or seven annual on-site inspections, obligatory in case of alleged violation, stood in the way of an agreement on a comprehensive test ban. The United States did not, however, accept the offer of two to three on-site inspections which the U.S.S.R. then so unexpectedly held out. A new 'moment of lost opportunities' had to be registered. Evidently we, the smaller nations who after all have most to fear, did not quite understand the seriousness of this refusal on the part of the United States and of the subsequent withdrawal of the Soviet offer to accept any obligatory inspections at all as part of the system.

I must confess that we did not wake up to understand the sombre reality even when the superpowers suddenly, in the summer of 1963, switched the test-ban negotiations from Geneva, where we were in good faith continuing to labour on a total test ban, to bilateral talks in Moscow, where within weeks was produced a partial ban. So doped in hope were we that we euphorically hailed this agreement as one of utmost importance. We took it for granted, as we were told, that it was the first step towards the discontinuance of all tests.

The Preamble of the Moscow Treaty (Partial Test Ban Treaty) explicitly spelt out the commitment of the parties as 'seeking to achieve the discontinuance of all test explosions of nuclear weapons for all time, determined to continue negotiations to this end.' We read the intention to that although the Moscow treaty provisionally excluded underground tests from the partial prohibition, it would nevertheless serve as a disarmament measure

by curtailing further qualitative development of nuclear weapons to a degree which was undetermined but understood to be not insignificant. A representative of the Arab Republic of Egypt has confirmed this interpretation when in Geneva he recently said that the Moscow treaty 'was expected to have a considerable restraining effect on the superpowers.'

It has since become irrefutably clear that the truth is different: the Moscow treaty has not had any restrictive effect whatsoever on nuclear-weapons development or even on the number and yield of tests made by those nations who already possess such weapons. It should be given some credit as a public-health measure, since it has reduced radio-activity in the atmosphere -- even if the degree of such pollution have never been high -- but it can hardly any longer correctly be enumerated among disarmament measures.

Our naievete and credulity were such that we smaller nations did not at the time realize that no disarmament was intended. We evidently did not listen closely enough, for the absence of this intention was clearly stated in President Kennedy's own words when introducing the Moscow treat to the United States Senate. He then explicitly promised the military interests that the country's testing facilities would not be closed: 'The United States has more experience in underground testing than any other nation, and we intend to use this capacity to maintain the adequacy of our arsenal. Our atomic laboratories will maintain an active development program, including underground testing, and we will be ready to resume testing in the atmosphere if necessary [4].'

Outsiders as we were, and just committed to working positively for disarmament, we smaller nations rather paid attention to, and believed, what the President said in his television address to the American people on 26 July 1963, when he did not draw attention to the continuation of testing, except obliquely, saying that the treaty 'permits continued underground testing and prohibits only those tests that we ourselves can police.' Rather Kennedy definitely held out a bright prospect: 'Nevertheless, this limited treaty will radically reduce the nuclear testing which would otherwise be conducted on both sides...it reflects...our common recognition of the dangers in further testing...This treaty can limit the nuclear arms race in ways which, on balance, will strengthen our nation's security far more than the continuation of unrestricted testing...While it may be theoretically possible to demonstrate the risks inherent in any treaty...the far greater risks to our security are the risks of unrestricted testing, the risk of a nuclear arms race, the risk of new nuclear powers, nuclear pollution, and nuclear war [4, p. 251 ff].'[3]

With the hindsight of today the conclusion of the Moscow treaty should perhaps be judged as political mistake. In fact, it introduced the practice of sealing off disarmament schemes with a full stop, as soon as some token measure of success could be registered and sold to the general public -- however partial, one-sided or illusory.

A brief recapitulation of succeeding events will tell us that after 1963 and up to 1965 no result was forthcoming from the Geneva negotiations, that between 1965 and 1968 they were devoted to the

Non-Proliferation Treaty, between 1968 and 1970 to the Treaty on
the Prohibition of Nuclear Weapons on the Seabed, and in 1970-71 to
a Convention on the Prohibition of the Development, Production and
Stockpiling of Bacteriological and Toxin Weapons. Both the last
two deal only with partial disarmament measures.

III. THE REAL SIGNIFICANCE OF THE NON-PROLIFERATION TREATY

To understand both what has happened and what has not happened as
far as disarmament is concerned, an analysis must seek to discern
what interests have been at play. Cui bono is the question that
provides the key to the understanding of the 'game of disarmament'.
    Let us concentrate on the nuclear-weapons field and explore
what has really happened behind what seems to have happened in
relation to the supposedly second most important achievement of
disarmament negotiations. I refer to the Non-Proliferation Treaty
(NPT), which is primarily designed to prevent an increase in the
number of countries possessing nuclear weapons.
    This is a worthwhile purpose per se. But everybody knows that
the greatest dangers spring not from the non-nuclear-weapons
States. Eager as we, the latter, are to promote nuclear
disarmament among the countries which do possess such weapons, we
raised the demand that a ban on 'horizontal proliferation' (spread
of nuclear weapons to more nations) should be combined with one on
'vertical proliferation') further production of such weapons by
States already possessing them). This would mean establishing a
ceiling on the total nuclear-weapon strength in the world at the
level pertaining at the time of concluding the treaty.
    In order to make such a freeze on nuclear-weapons development
complete, Sweden for several years advocated that the package deal
should include as a third element a comprehensive test ban, thus
freezing qualitative as well as quantitative proliferation of
nuclear weapons everywhere.
    On this issue the power position of the superpowers was
asserted even more bluntly than in the case of the Moscow treaty,
which after all carried a semblance of a sacrifice even on their
part, since they restricted themselves to the more cumbersome and
more expensive method of testing their nuclear weapons underground.
In the case of the Non-Proliferation Treaty they accepted not one
iota of sacrifice of present or future nuclear-weapons
capabilities. The only trace of the years of negotiating effort
expended by the smaller countries can be found in an article in the
NPT which enjoins the contracting parties 'to pursue negotiations,
in good faith,' on effective measures relating to cessation of the
nuclear arms race at an early date'. And even that concession had
to be extracted through much patience and perseverance. It was
withheld until the last minute, i.e. the meeting of the General
Assembly itself in the spring of 1968.
    Moreover, because such a pledge was considered insufficient
and also on the ground of other imperfections in the treaty,

several important countries registered abstentions. India went as far as to speak forcefully against the NPT, which was, however, approved by a large majority.

The Non-Proliferation Treaty has not to this date succeeded in becoming the instrument for obtaining the renunciation of nuclear-weapons on the part of the so-called 'threshold countries'. Of the ten to fifteen nations which have the technical and economic capability to produce nuclear weapons only two have ratified the NPT, namely Canada and Sweden. And it should be stressed that their adherence was a foregone conclusion, as they had independently -- treaty or no treaty -- decided and declared their intention of refraining from acquiring nuclear weapons. The ninety-odd other signatures (with only sixty-odd having had the treaty ratified by their parliaments) are those of countries without significant capabilities.

If I state that the adherence to the treaty on the part of threshold countries is still deficient, it is not in order to case suspicion on the reluctant nations of either openly or secretly preparing to manufacture nuclear weapons on their own. Those European countries which belong to EURATOM (European Atomic Energy Community) -- and there are nations as important in this context as Italy, the Netherlands and the Federal Republic of Germany -- have delayed their act of ratification in order to get settled certain technical questions as to how the control over nuclear-fuel elements exerted by EURATOM is to be integrated with the control system operated by the International Atomic Energy Agency (IAEA). The international control system must of course prevail: the burden of control must be made the same for all countries which are hoping to build up an industry and even exports in the nuclear-energy field.

In the case of certain other countries, such as Australia and Japan, the desire to establish such equitable regulations for control, as well as possibly special security considerations in relation to China, may have delayed their ratification. A more worrisome recalcitrance may be that on the part of Israel and South Africa. But for the rest, including such crucial non-aligned countries as Brazil and India, their non-adherence to the NPT seems largely to be motivated by domestic politics, since powerful nationalist groups within these countries voice opposition against being placed under an international and inequitable ban.

In no small measure the reluctance on the part of these countries and the uneasiness felt by most other countries in regard to NPT are connected with a specific difficulty, unresolved if not deliberately implanted in the treaty. I refer to the de facto monopoly it established on nuclear explosions for peaceful purposes. It is true that Article V of the NPT lays down procedures intended to make the potential benefits of peaceful nuclear explosions available to all parties to the treaty. But in reality the nuclear-weapons States are the sole possessors of the know-how and the means necessary to use nuclear devices for such potentially very lucrative activities as digging canals and extracting oil, gas and minerals. Thus, the mighty have a virtual control over the application or non-application of these techniques, a fact that cannot but cast ominous shadows over the

future, if an international licensing system cannot be introduced.

The value of the NPT as an instrument to bring about nuclear disarmament or even just 'non-proliferation' is thus debatable. On the positive side should, however, be recorded a by-product element of the treaty which may become an asset: namely the establishment of an international control machinery within IAEA.

IV. QUESTION: WHY HAVE INTERNATIONAL NUCLEAR-DISARMAMENT TREATIES?

The above reflections on the hopes and disappointments of a non-aligned conscientious collaborator in disarmament striving, when judging the outcomes of two of the major so-called disarmament agreements, can but lead to a bitter verdict. This is that disarmament has for the great powers become an object of super-salesmanship, whose real objective is to get the smaller nations to accept restrictions while -- at least up to now -- not being willing to accept any themselves.

This leads us to ponder over the very 'whys' of international treaties in such a field as nuclear weapons. Why make them international-multinational? What is the point in getting ten countries -- or, yes a hundred -- to sign treaties which cannot possibly apply to their own activities, while at the same time these countries acquiesce in leaving unaffected the activities of those countries which are materially concerned with nuclear weapons?

I can, of course, appreciate that through the multilateral negotiations a certain interest in disarmament as an ideal is kept alive. But simultaneously, the true nature of the power positions which are translated into treaty commitments tend to be concealed.

Furthermore, when their main objective must be to rope in the threshold countries specifically, why are such agreements not tailored and politically anchored so as to secure their adherence? In regard to the NPT this target is obviously missed by a dangerously wide margin as long as such countries as India, Israel, South Africa and Brazil stand obstinately apart -- and the case is even worse if the same remains true of the Federal Republic of Germany and Japan. Did some of these countries ask too high a price, namely that some move should be initiated towards disarming the 'haves', not just the 'have-nots'?

The question as to why disarmament treaties are negotiated multinationally can be put even more pointedly in regard to those agreements which are not only arranged by bilateral superpower accord, such as those just mentioned, but which are in substance relevant only to nuclear-weapons States. Such is the case in regard to another pair of disarmament agreements, the 1970 treaty concerned with keeping the seabed under international waters free of nuclear weapons and the Space treaty of 1967, which similarly safeguards outer space and bodies in space. Both have in common the fact that only the superpowers have practical access to these domains and only the nuclear-weapons countries could, in any case,

have any forbidden objects to place there.

The case of the Space treaty, on the peaceful uses of outer space, is particularly interesting in this respect. The real agreement, which is <u>de facto</u> operational, was a bilateral one announced to the United Nations in October 1963 by Kennedy and Gromyko. Its transformation in 1967 into an international treaty with a number of signatories who cannot, however much they might wish, place nuclear weapons on celestial bodies or in orbit must surely look pointless when this transformation is assessed for its disarmament effect. But it was, <u>mirabile dictu</u>, prescribed that the treaty would only 'enter into force' upon the deposit of ratification instruments by a total of five governments, i.e. any two countries in addition to the depositaries, the U.S.S.R., United Kingdom and United States.

Is it not the truth that to make an international treaty has become an end in itself, the treaty being a magic want to turn away criticism in the United Nations? How long, then, will the majority of the United Nations members keep up the pretence that they believe in this magic when promises about disarmament remain so woefully unfulfilled?

This most intriguing question must really be addressed to the superpowers: Do they wish to keep up multi-national disarmament negotiations in order to offer to the United Nations each year a few homoeopathic drops of something called 'disarmament treaties' at the same time as they are, in deeds, conducting in bilateral secretiveness the only truly important promising negotiations, the Strategic Arms Limitation Talks (SALT)? It want to underline that my criticism is not directed against bilateral negotiations -- their value will be proved by their results -- but against the instituting of multilateral negotiations if they are allowed to be no more than a shadow play, or, as the Ethiopian delegate in Geneva recently said, 'a window-dressing'.

Any attempt at providing my personal and honest response to the question posed as the topic for this article must result in a negative answer, on balance, when weighing the pious talk about disarmament against the harsh reality of the arms race. It becomes unavoidable to conclude that underlying this answer is the lack of any real effort on the part of the superpowers.

Their responsibility for this is also quite formally underlined by the way the Geneva negotiations are structured. When the Eighteen Nation Disarmament Committee was set up, one extraordinary feature was the institution of the co-chairmanship of the United States and the U.S.S.R. It is true that their agreement is in most cases necessary -- but not in all. But has ever any organism where sovereign States are represented been so openly governed by the superpowers? In the Conference of the Committee on Disarmament (which succeeded ENDC in 1969), the co-chairmen have been the ones to decide on the agenda, yes, even the membership of the body itself. The conventions emanating from the Geneva committee have all named the two superpowers, plus the United Kingdom, as 'original parties', or 'depository governments', the signatures of which were required before any agreement could enter into force.

The list of 'achievements' is, therefore, singularly that of

the two superpowers, both symbolically and in substance. That list, short and to a large extent hollow as it is, gives the measure of what the world has obtained during the ten years when the United States and U.S.S.R. were the custodians of disarmament. We can now hope that China will be entering the disarmament negotiations in the United Nations. Then questions ought to be raised as to the proper framework of such negotiations, and the respective roles of great powers and those not so great.

V. WORTHWHILE INTERNATIONAL PACTS RELATED TO DISARMAMENT

My analysis so far has painted a background against which I want to point to the fact that at least two important international agreements, more or less directly related to disarmament, have been arrived at within different contexts.

One is the Anarctic treaty, agreed upon as far back as 1959 -- outside the context of any disarmament negotiations -- between twelve States with interests in that region. It was agreed that Anarctica was to be used for peaceful purposes only, prohibiting any activities of a military nature, opening it for free scientific research, providing for exchange of plans, observations and even personnel, and giving free access at all times to all installations for observers nominated by any of the signatory parties. In many ways, the Anarctic treaty remains a model, never since equalled, of a sound and equitable international pact. Of course, the remoteness of economic and military interest must have made agreement easier.

The other measure taken outside the global disarmament negotiations is the Tlatelolco treaty for the prohibition of nuclear weapons in Latin America, signed in 1967. It was proposed and negotiated on the initiative of the Latin American States themselves. To my mind, its most salient feature is that the parties have succeeded in obtaining engagements from some nuclear-weapons States to the effect that the Latin American States will not be subjected to attacks with nuclear weapons or threats of such attacks. This feature is contained in added Protocol II, which has so far been accepted by the United Kingdom and the United States. The road to similar initiatives for keeping out nuclear weapons, or even weapons of mass destruction in general, lies invitingly open to other regions of the world, where sovereign States can act on their own behalf.

There is a third forward step which may be mentioned in this sequence, although it was initiated in the Geneva conference by its non-aligned members. However, it was not brought to success until we escaped from the tutelage of the co-chairmen, the United States and the U.S.S.R. I am referring to the confirmation by an overwhelming majority vote in 1969 in the United Nations of the Geneva Protocol of 1925 (which is against the use of biological and chemical (B and C) means of warfare) as an instrument which 'embodies the generally recognized rules of international law' and

as encompassing all B and C weapons, including tear gas and herbicides. The resolution which brought on the vote was based on explicit recommendations made by the Secretary-General in the Foreword to the experts' report, 'Chemical and Bacteriological (Biological) Weapons and the Effects of their Possible Use,' which had already defined B and C weapons in an all-inclusive way. This move was engineered wholly by the smaller and particularly the non-aligned nations.

The United Nations resolution has had a direct political impact, for it -- together with the testimony and campaigns of scientists, whose finding were also at the base of our action -- has resulted in the United States Senate's blocking an attempt to append to the proposed American ratification of the Geneva Protocol a clause excluding those chemical agents which have been used in Vietnam on a massive scale. Moreover, the American authorities now seem to be phasing out the use of these weapons for field operations. This affirmation of the Geneva Protocol to prohibit the use of all these horror means of warfare has in addition served to activate the endeavours to prohibit also the production of chemical and biological weapons.

VI. THE SUPERPOWERS' MOTIVATIONS AND THE WIDENING OF THE 'POWER GAP'

In an effort to explain the negotiation behaviour of the superpowers in regard to disarmament, I have already indicated that the reason behind their desire to present some 'positive results' in the shape of international conventions, even when of marginal real value, has been the wish to make some concessions to the clamour of world public opinion. In bleak moments one might think that they just want to keep the would-be disarmers busy: negotiations as a kind of occupational therapy.

The reasons for the 'negative results' -- i.e. the lack of readiness to achieve more -- must be of a very much more complex nature.

I have already repeatedly stated how obviously the disarmament negotiations have been handled by the superpowers as in substance bilateral, even when done within an international framework. This preoccupation of theirs with each other rather than with the world has led them to use two different tactics, depending on whether the game is played between the two of them alone or by both of them against the other nations.

In regard to each other the two superpowers have landed in an arms race which somehow resembles a zero-sum-game: the loss of one is considered the gain of the other. Neither dares to give up a military capability or even an option for a new weapons system lest he may be 'losing ground to the enemy'. During most of the post-war period the field of vision of each has been restricted to the narrow one of its national interests vis-a-vis the other. But in disarmament nothing can be done if one does not consider the

broader, longer-term interests of the world, where one's own security is part of the more general picture.

Evidently the superpowers have had a joint interest in preserving their respective positions and their mutual balance, and in not letting it be disturbed by any disarmament measure for which other nations might be working. The consequence has been that the disarmament negotiations have been used by the superpowers for balancing each other and not for planning disarmament.

While this motive of preserving the mutual balance at the superpower level has been, I believe, the dominating one in the multilateral negotiations, a somewhat different one seems to operate in the bilateral ones. While this is most clearly visible in SALT, it is also evident in the agreements concerning denuclearization of outer space and the seabed. Their common interests here have allowed them to move a bit forward from sheer immobility under a desire to slow down their own pace of nuclear-weapons development and deployment.

But how has this game of satisfying the superpowers' mutual interests been viewed by all those nations which are not great powers? I believe there has occurred a considerable shift in our attitudes over the years.

In the beginning, when the dominant feature of international relations was the Cold War spectre of confrontation between the major nuclear-weapons powers, we did recognize the need for a balance between them. In the disarmament negotiations our energies were therefore directed towards harmonizing their attitudes and presenting possible compromises between their contrary positions, while at the same time endeavouring to keep up the pressure of a more idealistic world opinion that these powers should lower their guards in terms of armaments.

Only gradually has it dawned upon us -- and not least upon me -- that the arms race, however 'balanced', was having as its result an incredible widening of the gap between the superpowers and the rest of the world. Take the situation in regard to nuclear weapons. In the fifties it was still possible for countries to argue for the acquisition of a nuclear-weapon capability on two grounds. One of these was that such weapons had a usefulness for tactical purposes, even in a conflict with a superpower; the other was that they could serve as a deterrent over medium distances, as exemplified by France's force de frappe.

Since 1957, however, the world picture in this respect has irrevocably changed: the launching of the Sputnik demonstrated how far advanced both the two superpowers were as compared to the rest of us. And the subsequent development of ICBMs and the megaton-range nuclear weapons have served further notice on the other nations of the world about the categorical difference between 'them' and 'us', between the 'haves' and the 'have-nots'. Any war can now be won by 'them' alone through the use of nuclear weapons, or maybe simply the threat of such use.

This split into two discontinuous categories of 'superpowers' and 'other nations' has not only become more apparent to us during the disarmament negotiations, it has been made even more bluntly manifest by a conscious design on their part. The best example of this is, of course, the NPT. The major substance of that treaty,

the renunciation of nuclear weapons by the non-nuclear-weapons States, was accepted of their own free will by these States. We signed because we understood the militarily negative value which weak and imperfect nuclear weapons in our hands would have and because we truly wanted to stop nuclear weapons from spreading. But the treaty contained other regulations which we had not desired to accept.

The main effect was, of course, that the NPT in no way infringed upon the nuclear-weapons powers' freedom to develop, test, produce, store, deploy or use these weapons. But we did not even succeed in having accepted a stipulation that they should not be allowed to take deliveries of materials from the non-nuclear-weapons States which would aid in the production of terror weapons over which these latter States were denied all control. Likewise, a Swedish amendment which prescribed safeguard controls on all transfers of the special nuclear materials, including those used for weapons, would have compelled the nuclear-weapons powers to rely on their own resources. But that amendment, too, was defeated through the efforts of the superpowers.

A new incident of overpowering has occurred in relation to the Convention on the Prohibition of the Development, Production and Stockpiling of Bacteriological and Toxin Weapons. It introduced an article on control, which made any investigation, following on complaints about non-compliance, dependent on a decision in the Security Council, where the veto powers of the five permanent members can forestall any such investigation as to their actions and those of their friends. My country, which together with some others had unsuccessfully attempted to make the Secretary-General responsible for the investigations, now finds it difficult to adhere to the treaty on account of its discriminatory character.

VII. THE TECHNOLOGICAL HEGEMENY OF THE SUPERPOWERS
REFERENCES

The mounting discrimination against the smaller nations is, however, not only of concern in regard to the military monopolization of ultimate weapons on the part of the superpowers. It also has considerable spin-off effects in other spheres.

Monopoly over military technology is beginning to play a cardinal role in a similar monopoly over new technologies of immense importance in the economic life of nations and in the relations between powers in general. What we are witnessing today, it seems to me, is the emergence of a duopoly of the two superpowers in regard to modern technology, giving them a more and more dominating hegemony over world affairs. They are the only ones who can wield power over -- and practically the only ones who can have access to -- new provinces of our planet, those which are being opened up thanks to the highly advanced technologies that originate in research and development for military purposes.

Let me briefly enumerate the main fields. One is the

deep-ocean floor.[4] It is now recognized that enormous resources of oil, gas, manganese and other minerals are to be found on and under the seabed in international waters. In the United Nations we have succeeded in getting this rich treasure recognized as the 'common heritage of mankind'. But most of it is accessible only to the two superpowers, thanks to their striking advances in marine technology. Therefore, our plans for economic defence must be outlined together with those of disarmament: the establishment of an international control body which on the one hands sees that armaments are not installed on the deep-ocean floor, and on the other manages the exploration and exploitation of the resources of the deep ocean for the economic benefit of the international community.

A similar situation exists in regard to underground resources which can only become accessible with the aid of nuclear explosives. These devices are the monopoly of the nuclear-weapons States. They are a spin-off from their military research and development. Here we cannot declare all these resources as belonging to 'mankind' -- each nation will want to exploit the subterranean resources of its own territory. But we can and must object to the discretionary power to conduct 'peaceful nuclear explosions', which the superpowers have been trying to reserve for themselves under Article V in the NPT. International agreements in this regard still have to be made.

Again, safety can only be derived from an international control agency with a balanced representation, both geographically and politically, established for both disarmament purposes and to maintain non-discriminatory access to this highly advanced technology. This is what some countries, like Sweden and Mexico, are fighting for in Geneva and in the United Nations, the technical aspects of control of peaceful nuclear explosions already having been appropriately assigned to IAEA.

A third domain presenting the same general features and problems is outer space. Here the demands for international control and management were raised rather late in the day. Satellite developments have gone quite far under what is a near-duopoly of the two superpowers. Some elements of internationalization are, however, discernible, such as the 'World Weather Watch', a programme of the World Meteorological Organization. Actions such as this must be taken as guide-posts along the road to a much more complete internationalization in regard to two other main fields of application, namely earth-resources satellites and communications satellites.

The linkage between military and economic applications is more direct in the case of the earth-resources satellites.[5] Their military counterparts, the reconnaissance satellites, can supervise activities around missile launching pads and underground test sites, as well as the movement of troops. When the satellites are equipped with different forms of apparatus for remote sensings one has an instrument with virtually unlimited capabilities for scanning the earth for hidden deposits of mineral wealth, for deep-water reservoirs, for changes in vegetation and in pollution, etc.

There is an evident risk that such information may be used for

unfair competition, for example by withholding information about certain resources in one country while developing similar ones in another. Such concerns must loom in the minds of all nations that are without a comparable monitoring capability of their own, probably much larger than the slight discomfort of having their military activities put under surveillance by spy satellites. Again, attention is now being increasingly drawn in the United Nations to the need for a true international sharing in these endeavours.

In regard to the telecommunications satellites,[6] the situation has not raised serious misgivings in the present relatively early stages of development, since States have been able to select which activities they wanted to participate in and which programmes of radio and television they wished to transmit to home receivers, since the satellite signals at present are first sent to ground receiver stations for possible re-transmission, and these are under each nation's control.

The United States-dominated Intelsat system has been set up as a service for the world as a whole. There, we other nations have recently begun to increase the non-American influence over certain aspects of its management. (About the U.S.S.R.-based Intersputnik system I am not well informed.)

But when technology leaps forward so as eventually to make possible direct broadcasting from satellites to individual receivers in homes and villages all over the globe, the risk of an information hegemony becomes imminent.

Without ascribing sinister design to any of the two superpowers, the impact of their languages, their viewpoints and their ways of life will make themselves felt by virtue of their near-monopoly over the transmission -- as well as production -- of programmes. Again, the smaller States are working within the United Nations -- although feebly, I regret to say -- to strengthen international collaboration and participation in the management of telecommunications satellite systems.

In this article, I have considered the negative or at least tokenistic, attitude towards true multilateral disarmament on the part of the superpowers as being determined by policy considerations. I stand by the main conclusions of this analysis, even if they sound like a j'accuse. Yet it must be recognized that we have also to reckon with certain other forces which relentlessly generate an escalation. There is the general competitiveness in our world; there are also strong forces that form what may be called the military-industrial-scientific complex. And perhaps one should also take into account as a factor contributing to the present trend, the reluctance on the part of smaller nations to stand up and criticize.

It is not possible to end on a more optimistic note?

I have from the outset pointed to the possibility of sudden mutations in the realm of international politics. SALT might open the way to a change of course; at least, as a starter, these bilateral disarmament talks may establish a foundation for greater confidence between the two parties involved. Political trends towards a detente in Europe may also create a more hopeful climate. Too, while the impact of China's growing participation in world

affairs cannot be estimated, hopefully it might contribute to having disarmament questions treated with greater sincerity or at least realism.

Finally, there always remains the chance that reason may begin to prevail. It may come to dawn on the policy-makers of the world's States that the tremendous waste of resources -- financial, material, technological, or human, in bodies and brains -- on purposes of destruction might be turned into tremendous progress for the benefit of peoples all over the world.

A very special hope which I cannot help nourishing is that scientists, not least those now working for the war machines or on peace research, will begin to oppose more forcibly the present acceptance of the rule of unreason -- so forcibly that they will be heard.

REFERENCES

1. Alva Myrdal. Thank-you speech for the award of the 1970 Peace Prize of the Borsenvereins des Deutschen Buchhandels, Frankfurt am Main, 27 September 1970.
2. SIPRI yearbook of world armaments and disarmaments 1968-1969, and succeeding years. Stockholm, Almqvist & Wiksell, 1969--.
3. The U.N. and disarmament, 1945-1970. New York, N.Y., United Nations, 1970.
4. Documents on disarmaments, 1963, p. 300. Washington, D.C., United States Government Printing Office, 1964. (United States Arms Control and Disarmament Agency, publication 24).

NOTES

[1]This question was originally raised by Milton Leitenberg in his article, "The Classical Scientific Ethic and Strategic-weapons Development," Impact of Science on Society, Vol. XXI, No. 2, 1971. -- Ed.

[2]Unfortunately, as noted in the editorial leading this issue, it has not been possible to circulate the articles in this number to the other authors, as was originally planned. -- Ed.

[3]My italics.

[4]See D.P. O'Connel, "Legal Problems of the Exploitation of the Ocean Floor," Impact of Science on Society, Vol. XXI, No. 3, 1971. -- Ed.

[5]See Thomas O. Paine, "Space Research and a Better Earth," Impact of Science on Society, Vol. XIX, No. 2, 1969. -- Ed.

[6]See Eugene Pepin, "Space Law: Legal Aspects of Direct Broadcasting by Satellite," Impact of Science on Society, Vol. XXI, No. 3, 1971. -- Ed.

The Failure to Disarm: Main Obstacle to Development?

STEPHEN OLUWOLE AWOKOYA

National development, especially among the slowly industri-
alizing nations, depends enormously on the foreign
technical-economic assistance the rich countries of the world can
provide. But much of the reservoir of highly trained scientists,
engineers and technicians has already been tapped by the wealthy
nations for military purposes. It is idle, therefore, to talk
about effective foreign aid so long as the major powers do not
confront squarely the problem of disarmament and arms control. An
orderly procedure is advanced here to enable the opulent peoples on
our globe to transfer science-based knowledge and know-how to those
critically in need of intellectual and material assistance.

National armament and national development, although both
grounded in modern science and technology, are poles apart. The
first conjures up visions of an arsenal of nuclear devices,
chemical and bacteriological weapons capable of wiping out the
human race, research and development producing more and more
weapons, financial and human resources devoted to destruction,
devastated cities and defoliated forests, neglected education,
environmental pollution, heavy taxation, food rationing, war camps
and movement of the population, disruption of trade, national
insecurity and fear and hatred of other nations.

The second brings to mind the concern of the richer and more
industrialized nations for the well-being of the poorer and the
developing, as manifested through programmes of aid provided by
individual countries, regional groupings of nations, and
intergovernmental organizations within the United Nations. This
aid comes in the form of experts, fellowships and equipment in
order to advance education, manpower training and health; road and
other transport development, and telecommunications; industry,
commerce -- and all other forms of economic scientific and

From **IMPACT OF SCIENCE ON SOCIETY**, No. 25, Jan. 1975, (25-35),
reprinted by permission of the publisher.

technical progress.

So development is clearly evidence of international co-operation and philanthropy at their best, and armament is its opposite. Although I have said that they are poles apart, development and armament have a few things in common. The financial resources on which both depend come from the same tax funds; if war expenses increase, development funds decrease. Both require trained men and women, especially scientists, engineers and technicians, managers and planners, and administrators. Since these are in short supply in all countries, military and development services must compete for the available manpower. Natural resources are limited, also, and both military and development projects require them -- but the schemes accorded the highest political priorities usually receive the major share of available resources.

This situation underlines the role of government in determining the priorities to be set for military activities and development programmes, even though the two are separate and distinct exercises. Political considerations play the dominant role in their execution. The factors influencing all decisions are complex, and they vary from nation to nation, with the political party in power, with the personality of the head of State who (often) has the final word as to whether a country goes to war or embarks on the road to social and economic development.

I. WE ARE DEFENSE-READY, YET INSECURE

The strangest aspect of this political dichotomy is that there is no nation in the world that likes war and hates development. Yet all countries spend colossal amounts of money on their so-called defence or security, to the detriment of their own social and economic advancement. By using terms such as 'defence' and 'security', governments rationalize their stand. They delude themselves and become less conscious of the fact that their defence programmes make them potential aggressors, warmongers, enemies of economic and sociocultural development, and dangers to the continued existence of the human race.

Why do governments go to war? Why are nations in the political mess they are today? And why is the world so insecure? An analysis of the situation would be useful. It would probably enable us to know what next to do, how to achieve disarmament and promote development. Two excellent studies have already been published by the United Nations on these problems, The Economic and Social Consequences of the Arms Race and of Military Expenditures and Disarmament and Development [1,2].

It must be admitted that certain individual human beings are warmongers. They are happiest when fighting someone, for something. To them life is a perennial struggle, a survival of the fittest. Unless there is a change in their endocrine or nervous systems, these individuals will continue to be aggressive

all their lives. A nation headed by an individual of this type would be doomed, yet there is no guarantee against such an eventuality. An aggressive representative of a cause can fight his way as its champion from the local to the national level, but it is doubtful that he could achieve international leadership.

Governments, however, go to war for more substantial reasons. They wish to extend their territories or living space, increase population, acquire a broader tax base, control certain mineral resources or assure a water supply, guarantee the procurement of food, augment their sources of cheap labour, attain a 'critical mass' for national development, and generally increase their wealth and their economic prospects. It is all these economic considerations which give meaning and poignancy to many international wars. They are precisely the issues which can be negotiated without wars, and they are never finally settled by military means.

II. THE WORLD'S STOCK OF LETHAL POWER

The perennial excuse in national defence is the so-called security against a possible invasion by another power. The fear and tension created by this feeling of insecurity, real or imaginary, lend impetus to a whole series of socio-economic reactions. Institutions are created that cannot easily be dismantled; industries are established that must continue to produce weapons of war; arsenals are stockpiled with the means to wipe out the totality of humanity; and research and development are undertaken to design still more sophisticated munitions.

The armament race has reached a stage now where -- through technical error, misjudgement or sheer madness -- mankind can cease to exist, as it were, in the twinkling of an eye. The world's stock of lethal power had already reached, by the late 1960s, fifteen tons of trinitrotoluene (TNT) per head of population [3]. Any of the great powers is capable of wiping out the entire race, and a major war involving any one of them could become the end of creation. This is why one must forget everything, even development, in order to talk of disarmament first. Until that is settled, nothing else can be settled; until disarmament is a reality, everything else is insecure and we live in a fool's paradise.

It may sound strange for one coming from a developing country (where everything is underdeveloped) to assign the highest priority to disarmament, but what else is to be done concerning the vast stocks of nuclear weapons? Each of these is more powerful than those which erased Hiroshima and Nagasaki. Each can produce inescapable radioactive fallout that knows no national boundaries. By 1970 there were already 2,160 intercontinental ballistic missiles. How many will there be by the end of this year?[1] Nuclear-powered submarines are capable of delivering 1,800 nuclear warheads at the press of a button. The number of supersonic

fighter aircraft approaches 20,000. There are huge stocks of chemical and bacteriological agents able to eliminate man and beast within minutes; there are defoliants to lay bare our forests, satellites to watch at every moment what supposed enemies are doing in their own countries. The insecurity of man is total. Disarmament is urgent and pressing, the major problem of the hour. We have talked long enough about arms reduction and control; it is now time to act before it is too late.

As disarmament passes to a programme of specific action, it is useful to recall that the United Nations have passed many resolutions to this end. Numerous treaties have been signed to limit strategic arms, to ban nuclear explosions in the atmosphere, outer space and under water (1963), to govern the activities of its members in the exploration and use of outer space, including the moon and other celestial bodies (1967), to prohibit nuclear weapons in Latin America (1967), to forbid the proliferation of nuclear weapons (1968), and to prohibit the emplacement of nuclear arms and other weapons of mass destruction on the sea-bed and in the subsoil thereof (1971) [4]. It is difficult, none the less, to assess the extent to which these agreements have affected the disarmament of individual nations.

III. TO REMOVE THE PERIL OF ANNIHILATION

The two reports of the United Nations already mentioned show that all the nations of the world spend about $208,000 million annually on military expenditures; six countries (the United States of America, the Union of Soviet Socialist Republics, the People's Republic of China, the United Kingdom, the Federal Republic of Germany and France) spend, between them, 89 per cent of this amount. So if mankind is endangered by military investments, 89 per cent of the responsibility can be assigned squarely to these six nations.

I propose that the General Assembly of the United Nations send a delegation to each of the six countries in order to find ways and means to bring to the attention of their heads of State, governments, legislatures and general public that the survival of the human race is in serious jeopardy because of the level of military expenditures made by their government. The world should make it clear to these nations that, unless they wish to destroy mankind, they must not resort to war, nor must they encourage or assist other countries to do so.

Alternatively, the Secretary-General of the United Nations might invite the heads of State of these same countries to meet on a lonely island in order to work out man's fate in terms of world disarmament. In the manner of the cardinals choosing a Pope, the heads of State should remain on the island until they have reached a unanimous decision which they can convey to the rest of the world, thus removing the threat of our total annihilation.

It is idle to pretend that the leaderships of the nations I

have listed are not involved. Although pressure groups favouring a
high level of readiness for war undoubtedly exist, none of the six
countries cited can go to war or spend thousands of millions of
dollars on munitions without the signed approval of their heads of
State. Pressure groups, pro and con, can argue and try to
persuade, but the right of final decision belongs to the chief
executive. Consequently, it is the decision-making apparatus in
six of the globe's nearly 170 countries that means so much to the
lives of hundreds of millions of people -- given the present stage
of development of nuclear and other military armaments.

IV. THE MILITARY-INDUSTRIAL SYNDROME

Most heads of State, individually and personally, are peace
loving; they have the interest of their people at heart. Their
very election presupposes that the public has great confidence in
their ability to direct affairs of State. On the whole, their
concern for human welfare is not in question. But in their anxiety
to prepare for the evil day when a war might be imposed upon them,
these public executives begin to take certain military measures of
security, the cumulative effect of which has been called the
'military-industrial complex' -- a social process perhaps much to
powerful for many heads of State to control. (This is especially
so in the case of the newly appointed chief executive.) Sometimes
elected heads of State and governments, in their political
ambition, seek the assistance of the military-industrial complex
to gain power, thereby becoming the complex's vassal and doing its
bidding.

The $208,000 million spent each year on armaments derive from
the world's gross 'national' product of more than $3 million
million (3×10^{12}) -- about 6.5 per cent of the world's gross
economic product is budgeted to buy arms of destruction. The
actual percentages, for the 'superpowers', are 8.5 per cent for the
United States of America and 6.7 per cent for the Union of Soviet
Socialist Republics. Some of the smaller nations spend relatively
more on weapons: Jordan, 15.8 per cent; Syria, 10.2 per cent;
Israel, 9.8 per cent; Iraq, 9.4 per cent; Bulgaria, 8.7 per cent;
the Arab Republic of Egypt, 8.6 per cent; and Portugal, 6.7 per
cent [1].

The tendency is for these expenses to rise unless a political
decision to disarm is taken -- unless heads of State or government
decide otherwise, unless the military-industrial complex is
dismantled, restructured and re-oriented toward peaceful pursuits.
The challenge of the world today is to take the practical steps
toward the redirection of the munitions -- making complex. If not,
the military-industrial grouping will continue to rule the six
nations that have brought the world to the verge of self-
destruction as well as the other nations following the same
dangerous path. The military-industrial complex, a huge machine
capable of breaking anything in its way, needs to be slowed down

systematically and then dismantled (see box).

Once the military machine has been disassembled and its highly trained body of specialists dismembered and oriented toward new goals, life will be infinitely richer than ever before. Men and women would then be able to channel their energy and creativity in civil industry, in trade and other services and other social institutions. The redeployment of military personnel has been accomplished by many governments, after all, subsequent to past hostilities; we know that it is a highly feasible project. The accomplishment of the transformation proposed here by the end of our century would be a revolution in human development, a rebirth the like of which history has never known. The task is indeed colossal, but one that can only improve life instead of imperiling it.

V. PRIMARY TASK OF THE UNITED NATIONS

The United Nations System has demonstrated, through the year, its capacity to handle the question of peace in the world despite the human (national) obstacles it has encountered. There is no other organization in the world today that can act as the United Nations substitute in the maintenance of peace and security; existing international treaties are ample evidence of this fact. The necessity for universal disarmament offers the occasion to re-examine the United Nations System and the extent to which its present structure and constitution are adapted to attain total disarmament and peace.

The primary function of the United Nations is to keep peace throughout the world; all other activities are subsidiary to this. The functional areas of the United Nations System (labour, health, education, science and technology, culture, agriculture, civil aviation, maritime activities, meteorology, monetary systems, tele-communications, trade and development) are quite properly assigned to appropriate Specialized Agencies within the system, although responsibility for over-all co-ordination remains that of the United Nations. Peace, being a multidisciplinary undertaking, is contributed to by all the Specialized Agencies; but, here again, the United Nations must continue to hold primary responsibility.

International legislation has never been passed by the United Nations, as far as I know, to outlaw war in order to establish peace. The United Nations General Assembly has never been required to transform itself into a legislative body with powers to make world 'laws' for peace, and against war and to punish belligerent nations. With the threat of annihilation now sufficient to rouse the world to the need to make the General Assembly a legislative body for that limited purpose, its Member States should recognize that necessity and invest United Nations with these powers.

The idea is not a new one. Various international bodies have urged this kind of development for the past twenty years. If the United Nations can enact world laws, the universal respect for law

should enable it to carry out its tasks of disarmament and the assurance of peace. It has been suggested that a world legislature of this sort might have two chambers, one of national governments and the other of the people of the world. All governments would have equal numbers in the upper house, and all nations would have representatives in the house of the people proportional to the square-roots of their population.

VI. HOW WOULD THE UNITED NATIONS LEGISLATURE WORK?

Once world laws have been passed by the United Nations, international treaties would be drafted on issues of war and peace within the framework of the laws. These treaties would constitute the statutory instruments of the world laws; their legality could be challenged at the United Nations during their stage of formulation, or at the International Court of Justice when the enforcement of a law is questionable. Similarly, the Specialized Agencies of the United Nations could enact decrees on subjects within their competence, provided there would be no conflict between these decrees and the peace-keeping laws of the United Nations. And the first world laws of the United Nations should be devoted to disarmament and the promotion of peace.

The problem of adjudication would be handled by the court of the United Nations (the International Court of Justice), which the nations of the world, in their wisdom, have already established. The court would try violations of the disarmament treaties and the laws of peace. Heads of State could be tried, leaders of government sued, and national laws which violate world laws could be questioned by the same court. It would have the power to interpret world laws, and punish offending States and their leaders when necessary.

National sovereignty may have been valid four or five centuries ago, but sovereignty which places in jeopardy the whole of the human race is anachronistic. Certainly, sovereignty should not be a licence to foul the earth's atmosphere or the world's ocean, to destroy the animals and the fishes on which we all depend, to defoliate trees and kill vegetables, ultimately to destroy mankind and even remove its traces. In so far as war, disarmament and peace are concerned, the rule of law must be superior to the rights of nation-states and universal in applicability. Until these vital adjustments are made, a report of the Secretary-General of the United Nations cannot be more than a verbal exercise -- merely another resolution emanating from the General Assembly, to be classified by governments, filed in archives, and read by scholars.

If war is to be banned, peace promoted, and disarmament accomplished by the United Nations, a world executive cabinet must be created. The prototype of such an executive already exists in the form of the Security Council which, unfortunately, has no collective responsibility for the peace of the world, as a few

members can veto its resolutions. The executive cabinet I have in mind must include among its members representatives of the 'big six', duly voted into the enlarged council by the General Assembly. Hopefully, all members of the executive cabinet will be committed to the cause of peace and total disarmament.

The administrative Secretariat of the United Nations is a powerful unit, working hard in the service of the United Nations various committees, but the link between this Secretariat and the committees hardly permits the unit to go beyond servicing the committees' activities. Members of an expanded council, on the other hand, could well exercise political responsibility of a ministerial nature in the arena of the United Nations responsibility for peace, disarmament and development. If sufficient funds become available and peace-keeping activities are adequately defined, the staff of the United Nations could well be made responsible for a variety of technical activities to insure world security.

VII. PAYING FOR PEACE

Considering the demands for manpower, the equipment involved, and the operations to be effected, the problems of payment for peace-keeping operations is great. I have already suggested that certain military stockpiles might be transferred to a world authority for security. By the same token, an agreed percentage of military financial appropriations could also be handed over to the United Nations (considering that most nations seem to be committed, in the first place, to world security). Although my suggestions may strike some as being pure fantasy, it will be mankind's happiest day when the 'big six' and the other 138 nations of the United Nations agree to a systematic transfer of national resources to a world pool leading to peace and international co-operation for worldwide development.

Would a United Nations army, navy and air force emerge naturally from all this? Such forces would be procured from all nations, but only the 'big six' could provide the effective power. The United Nations armed force would operate under the supreme command of that body and be responsible solely to it, since existing forces assigned to the United Nations are nothing more than a feeble police organization -- out-gunned, out-equipped, and out-manoeuvred by larger national forces -- and surely incapable of confronting any of the 'big six' should any of these pursue an aggressive policy and choose to hold the rest of the world for ransom. The United Nations without a modern joint military force may well be the laughing-stock of the great powers who now can manage to spend more than $200,000 million yearly on their own conventional and nuclear 'defence and security' establishments.

The problems of peace and disarmament are so acute today that the United Nations needs to invest heavily in the planning, policy formulation, and the forecasting of evolutionary trends in the

field. International meetings organized with a view to identify
the significant areas of research in this sector should be more
numerous. The proposals stemming from such meetings surely would
contribute to lifting the General Assembly from the rut into which
it has fallen -- that of being a resolution-passing machine. The
suggestions I have made would lead to positive action toward peace
and disarmament.

VIII. TURNING ARMS INTO PLOUGHSHARES

It is very tempting for someone from a developing country to
suggest that whatever material (including financial) and human
resources saved by disarmament should be channelled into the
development of the world's less industrialized countries. To hold
such a view would be as selfish and utterably unacceptable as it is
tempting. For even the United States and the U.S.S.R. are
'developing countries' in that they have slums to clear, cities to
build, social services to expand, employment to create, environment
to clean, drug abuse to eliminate, inflation to combat, trade to
expand, the economy to stabilize, and personal consumption to
increase. National requirements alone could well consume all that
can be saved as a result of total disarmament even in the
industrialized countries.

As the world will begin to recover from the spectre of war and
as disarmament becomes reality, one hopes that the necessity to
increase technical assistance to the developing countries will
receive greater attention. The group of experts selected by the
United Nations to study the problem of disarmament and development
suggested that if 20 per cent of the world's annual military
expenditures were converted into an international fund for
development, the developing countries would be able to meet their
urgent needs of building economic and social infrastructure,
reducing the economic and technological gap and, in due course,
closing the gap.

But development is a co-operative task in which both donor and
receiver of aid have certain responsibilities. If these are not
accepted, development assistance may fail. Let me explain briefly.

Many aid-giving agencies know, only too well, that technical
assistance invariably fails when the receiving country is not ready
for it. Administrative readiness is essential if the aid is to be
received at all, but especially there must be political readiness
if the assistance is to be fruitful and appreciated. Otherwise,
appropriate receiving institutions will not be created and whatever
benefits had been anticipated will vanish when the aid ends.
National plans and policy, into which the aid can fit, must already
have been prepared. And all these imply a leadership that is
dissatisfied with the status quo, one dedicated to innovation and
development; the leadership must have, at least implicitly, the
confidence of the country it manages.

Where such leadership does not exist, giving technical

assistance is tantamount to pouring treasure into a bottomless barrel. Leadership is an integration of political, economic, social, cultural, scientific, technical and managerial concerns; it may well be that such integrated, harmonious leadership can be found only in government. Leadership should be committed to the elimination of poverty and ignorance, promotion of scientific and technological training, preservation of health and social welfare, creation of economic and social infrastructures, and the promotion of employment.

IX. LOCAL RECEPTION CENTERS TO REGULATE AID

The least developed countries (of which so much has been said recently) can be helped only if the international organizations coming to their aid work through local leaders. These are accepted and trusted implicitly by their people; they can afford to make honest mistakes, as they will be forgiven. The examples set by these leaders are easily followed: they are at once the catalyst of the society in which they live and the living models copied by youth. Their vision of the future may be limited, but they are accepted for what they are. Outside aid should assist such leadership, enhance its view of the future, and help it formulate the policy and planning of projects in which it believes.

An office for the selection and channelling of various forms of external aid is essential for development. Such a bureau can shape policy, and plan what to ask for and how to receive it. Very often no such unit exists; in the cases where it does, the agency is inadequately staffed and donor groups frequently are obliged to do its work. True international co-operation begins with such an office, and extends to individual projects; bi- and multi-lateral aid can be received, 'digested' and absorbed when an effective clearinghouse exists to channel assistance into the economy's neediest sectors.

Very few developing countries have created an information system whereby the various branches of government can know the different forms of external aid available. Aid-givers are handicapped in getting in touch with needy institutions: first, because they have no means of knowing the indigent national sectors and, second, because they can operate only through the government. For these reasons, the aid bureau must do some promotional work to invite requests for aid from all sectors of the country. Aid received in this fashion is more highly appreciated than otherwise.

All forms of development assistance require from the receiver a substantial contribution of staff, equipment and buildings before help can be effective, and this priority needs to be respected. The situation becomes intolerable when a receiver spends large amounts on 'national security', especially when the possibilities of external invasion and internal commotion are completely imaginary. Developing countries, furthermore, should not upset their foreign exchange position by importing the technology of war

(usually in the form of arms already obsolete), wasting their financial resources and misusing their scanty trained manpower.

Finally, the aid bureau which I have proposed should ensure the diversification of all aid received in conformity with the needs of national development. I mentioned earlier the domains most in need of strengthening, and many developing countries (notably India and Brazil) already have machinery to manage incoming technical assistance. nations which do not could well follow these examples.

X. A FEW FINAL COMMENTS

Most donor countries have given their aid more in the bilateral framework than through the multilateral channel of the United Nations System. There should be, clearly, more of the latter especially when the assistance is intended to support planning and policy formulation in the receiving nations. This form of aid, 'with no strings attached' politically speaking, seems to respect the sovereignty of the receivers. The United Nations Agencies, for their part, should take due cognizance of bilateral aid links already in existence, as too many assistance projects die when these functioning arrangements between two countries are ignored.

It is naive to overlook the fact the 'Western' countries follow their own routes in giving foreign aid, while the 'Eastern' use their own channels. When the two join to co-operate, all is bliss; when they disagree, there is chaos. Most developing countries, their declarations to the contrary notwithstanding, are aligned; perhaps the most difficult aspect of political evaluation of aid is the role played by the former colonial links. In some countries, assistance cannot succeed if room is not provided for the exercise of these old relationships. In others, interference by former colonial powers not only must be avoided, the public needs to know that it is avoided. The same reasoning applies to orders for mechanical equipment, chemicals and the like.

A great problem in making aid available at the right time, in the right place, is the extent to which it affects international trade and the transfer of technology. Very often the choice of experts who will be involved in an assistance programme can affect both the future course of trade of the recipient as well as what kind of (and how much) technology can be transferred. Most aid programmes touch only the fringes of the problems involved, and sometimes the horizontal or geographical transfer of technical know-how (whether in the form of designs, products, processes or services) must be paid for by the receiving country through the buying of patents or their licences. And in many aid-receiving countries there does not yet exist the native infrastructure to permit the vertical transfer of the product of their own R & D laboratories to the production line. Multilateral mechanisms such as the United Nations Industrial Development Organization (UNIDO),

International Labour Organisation (ILO), Conference on Trade and Development (UNCTAD), and Unesco will have to work hard, together, to make reality of the dream of technology transfer.

Disarmament and development in our time are closely interrelated, but real development will depend on a change in the world's political thinking. This is especially so when disarmament policy is involved, especially among the 'big six'. If security and thus peace can be assured through the resolution of conflicts and the settlement of disputes, then the developing countries can progress rapidly to narrow the gap separating them from the industrialized nations.

SCIENTIFIC RESEARCH IN THE MILITARY ARENA

A renewed expansion of world military research has been under way since 1972. The rising costs of producing advanced weapons have led to an increase in co-operative development, especially in Europe where about forty joint projects (usually bilateral or trilateral) have been undertaken.

About 10 per cent of the world's military expenditures are devoted to military research and development. Military R & D lies at the heart of the arms race, leading to the acquisition of more and 'better' weapons. The industrialized countries (especially the United States, the Soviet Union, the United Kingdom and France) support most of this R & D.

The number of arms-producing countries in the developing world is growing, and there is a trend to produce increasingly complex weapons. The 'Third World' nations developing the most advanced industries in conventional arms are Brazil, the People's Republic of China, India, Israel and the Republic of South Africa.

Although the industrially less developed countries have increased their military expenditure by about 17 per cent since 1969, they still account for only 9 per cent of the world's total.

Major imports of weapons to the Third World have increased by about 10 per cent in twenty-five years -- more than twice as fast as the growth of their total gross national product. Almost forty 'developing' countries now possess supersonic or, at least, transonic fighter aircraft.

France, along with the People's Republic of China, is
developing nuclear weapons; their programmes are much
smaller and less advanced than those of the Soviet Union
and the United States. Smaller industrialized countries
(Austria, Czechoslovakia, Italy and Sweden) continue to
contribute to the technical race in conventional arms in
a limited way, by producing qualitative advances in a
restricted range of arms.

> Although the Non-Proliferation Treaty has been in force
> for four years, at least a dozen 'near-nuclear' weapon
> countries (including several in regions of politico-
> military tension) have not formally renounced the option
> to make or bear nuclear armaments.

Stockholm International Peace Research Institute.

BANNING ARMS, IMPROVING LIFE BY SUCCESSIVE HALVES

First, the demand for the weapons of war must be arrested. A
good start will be to transfer existing stockpiles of arms to an
international administration of security under the control of the
United Nations, an organ substantial enough to act as a worldwide
deterrent to the force of arms. The six major powers could be
asked to contribute, as a first move, one-half their stocks in
return for a 'universal assurance of security': that war is
forever barred -- not only among the six -- but throughout the
world. At a later date, one-half of the remaining stocks of
weapons would again be contributed, and so on arithmetically until
complete national disarmament is accomplished.
   Secondly, the war budget should be cut by an equivalent 50 per
cent throughout the world, the savings being used for development
at both the national and international levels. The economic and
social programmes of countries such as the United States, the
U.S.S.R., the United Kingdom, the Federal Republic of Germany,
France and the Republic of China could easily swallow this 50 per
cent and even require more. The savings could help increase food
production, accelerate urban planning and construction of housing,
make educational services and university development available
universally, arrest environmental pollution, and raise the quality
of living and personal consumption. Progressive cuts of 50 per
cent of war budgets will make battle a thing of the past as well as
economic and social development the motivating force of modern
life.
   Third, the specialized manpower trained for military purposes
could then be redeployed to economic and social ends, including
national and international development. Scientists and engineers
engaged in military research and development could be set new tasks
like improved food production, development of housing and the urban
and rural environments, research in medicine and public health,
research in improved education and the social applications of
computers, development of new fuels and energy sources,

amelioration of transport and telecommunications, industrial research in general, and improved means of public information and book production.

INFORMATION, PEACE RESEARCH WITHIN THE UNITED NATIONS

The information system of the United Nations has been given great importance since the outset, yet there remain extensive areas of the world where the so-called educated elite, not to speak of the masses, remain untouched by public information passed through the mass media. It is true that there is an explosion in communication, but the sense of awareness of human catastrophe waiting round the corner is not universal. It would be interesting to add up the sums spent on public information by all the components of the organizations belonging to the United Nations family, then to compare the total with that spent on advertisements by international firms such as General Motors and Unilever. Yet the very survival of the race depends on public information and the public's knowledge of the possibility of our total annihilation.

Research and development within the United Nations directed toward its objective of peace is not as extensive as it should be. Fortunately, national philanthropic bodies have endowed such research privately, notably in the United States of America. Other countries (Canada, France, the Federal Republic of Germany, India, Japan, the Netherlands, Norway, Poland, the United Kingdom and the Union of Soviet Socialist Republics) have contributed to research on peace. Research of this kind should be pursued actively under the United Nations auspices, and the fruits of the research diffused for the information of everyone.

PRIMING THE PUMP OF ASSISTANCE JUST A LITTLE MORE . . .

The vast amount of aid given, bilaterally and multilaterally, by the industrially advanced countries has been tangible evidence of international co-operation. The material benefits are obvious, the social institutions built are visible, the technical know-how is immeasurable -- not to speak of the human and intellectual links thus formed, relations more enduring than those created by official documents. The total impact of the aid is most difficult to assess.

The amount of aid provided is far from being adequate, however, in monetary terms when one compares it with investment in war. Using the ratio $7,000 million to $208,000 million, foreign assistance represents 3.3 per cent of the cost of the world's major war-making potential. Expressed in other terms, aid is only 0.3 per cent of the donor countries' gross national product. If general disarmament comes, the 'security' expenditure will be reduced substantially; and, if international goodwill prevails, more assistance can be made available for the development of less industrialized nations. If only $8,000 million were transferred to

development, the amount available for international aid would be more than doubled -- and there would still be $200,000 million left to assure politico-military security in forms compatible with peace.

The double effect of such a transfer is what has fired the imagination of so many people during this decade of disarmament and development: increasing the chances for peace while helping the developing countries of the world, reducing tension while promoting peaceful co-operation. The thought leads to the expectation that even more resources could be derived from multinational disarmament for development.

Without belabouring the point, it is clear that scientists and engineers (as well as the many technically trained assistants) engaged in military R & D could turn their attention to more ennobling tasks. Chemists, biologists and agronomists, now engaged in chemical and biological warfare programmes, could intensify current research efforts on edible proteins (those which are not toxicogenic), pest control, cancer and communicable diseases. Nuclear scientists could concentrate on peaceful applications, the utilization of solar energy, and explosives for civil engineering projects. The conversion of military engineers needs not be elaborated upon. Military telecommunications could be adapted to airport and other traffic needs in developing countries, in the remote sensing of nature resource reserves, and in natural disaster warning systems. And so on through the marine scientists and system analysts, the aircraft pilots and the technological forecasters. To continue to use all these expensively trained specialists for the purposes of war or national security is inexcusable, criminal folly.

NOTES

[1] By mid-1974, when this article was drafted, the Stockholm International Peace Research Institute reported that the number of nuclear warheads on operational strategic weapons had increased in two years (since the signing of the Salt I talks) from 5,890 to 'nearly 6,000' for the United States of America, from 2,170 to 'about 2,200' for the Union of Soviet Socialist Republics.

REFERENCES

1. UNITED NATIONS. The economic and social consequences of the arms race and of military expenditures. New York, N.Y., United Nations 1972. (Sales no. E72.IX.16).

neighbouring states, but that such techniques could have hostile applications. For example, cloud and rainfall might be deliberately increased in one area in order to create drought and agricultural damage elsewhere. Such operations could be carried out covertly, and would be very hard to detect or counteract. The mere possibility of such actions could poison international relations because of the difficulty in deciding whether a flood, drought or crop failure was due to natural causes of the actions of an enemy.

The hazards of war do not end with the coming of peace. Unexploded mines, bombs and shells can hamper mineral exploitation, make land unsafe to farm, hamper development and endanger people who disturb them. Bomb craters, wrecked vehicles or derelict defences and buildings are a blot on the landscape and reduce its value for recreation. Mines in rivers or at sea can be a serious danger to fishermen, hamper their work, and, if washed ashore, also imperil those living on the coast.

A UNEP survey of the environmental effects of the remnants of war attracted a response from 44 Governments. The volume of munitions left behind in some of their territories by the Second World War is staggering. One Government reported that it had cleared 14,469,600 land mines, and that clearance was continuing at the rate of 300,000 to 400,000 a year. Many thousands of shells, bombs and other munitions also had to be dealt with in various countries. The country most seriously affected reported that the remnants of war had killed 3,834 people, most of them children, and injured 8,384 others of whom 6,783 were children. For the past five years 30 to 40 people had been killed each year and 50 to 80 injured. Some 460 disposal personnel had been killed, and 655 injured. Other replies also indicated serious losses of life, and a cost of clearance running at tens or hundreds of thousands of dollars a year. Costal states reported parallel difficulties with marine mines and with dumped ammunition and wrecked ships (some containing explosives).

Another important aspect of military activity and post-military activity is human migration. The millions of refugees have not only suffered economic and social losses and disruption, but have also exerted pressures on the ecosystems in the areas to which they migrated. In most cases, the living conditions in the new habitat are intolerable in human terms. Since it lacks adequate infrastructures, disease, malnutrition and social disruption have become common problems. In spite of the different international efforts to alleviate the problems of refugees, they will continue to increase in magnitude with increases in tension and military activity.

II. THE PROBLEM

The growing volume and destructive power of the world's weapon stocks poses an obvious risk to man and to his environment. Even

Even worse environmental disruption is likely if new weapons now being developed and tested come into widespread use. Nuclear arsenals are increasing and constitute a major threat to mankind. A full-scale nuclear war would destroy all major cities in the northern hemisphere, and kill the bulk of the urban population in the northern hemisphere by blast and fire and the bulk of the rural population by radiation. It would, in addition, kill many millions in the southern hemisphere by radiation from fallout. The long-term consequences, though unpredictable, could affect the global climate, causing a serious reduction in the ozone layer. In addition, there might well be genetic effects from radiation. Detonation of weapons in the 10-kiloton range causes complete or severe destruction of vegetation over 400–1,300 hectares. Use of these weapons in a full-scale war would destroy vegetation and lead to soil-erosion over large areas, as well as inject huge amounts of radioactive dust into the stratosphere. Ecological recovery in such eroded areas would certainly be extremely slow. Nuclear explosions in the stratosphere would, at least temporarily, deplete ozone concentrations and increase the amount of ultra-violet radiation reaching the earth's surface, increasing the incidence of several effects, harmful to man and ecosystems. The neutron bomb (a low-yield nuclear weapon designed to kill or incapacitate people in armoured vehicles mainly by ionizing radiation rather than blast or heat) would also do appreciable environmental damage. It is estimated that denotation of a one-kiloton bomb 200 metres above the ground will cause death to a wide range of micro-organisms over an area of 40 hectares, to many insects over 100 hectares, to many amphibians and reptiles over 330 hectares, to many species of higher plants over 350 hectares and to many species of exposed mammals and birds over 490 hectares.

The use of chemical and biological weapons could also have serious environmental consequence, since they involve, in effect, deliberate pollution by the release of toxic chemicals or harmful micro-organisms. Chemical deforestation in tropical areas with fragile soils, or semi-arid areas already delicately poised on the brink of desert, could create rapid erosion and irreversible desertification. Wide-scale use of incendiary chemicals, such as napalm, could have similar results. As experience in recent wars in South-east Asia shows, even in areas that are ecologically robust, damage by fire and chemicals to natural vegetation and to crops grown for food and fibre is often long-lasting. If, despite international agreements, chemical, bacteriological or biological weapons are used, the effects of deliberately disseminating quantities of up to a dozen species of highly virulent pathogenic bacteria are less certain (much would depend on whether they attacked livestock or crop species as well as man, on how long they sustained themselves in the wild), but it is easy to see ways in which the agriculture and ecological balance could be disturbed for a long time.

There have been speculations about the possibility of causing economic or other damage to the population of an enemy through environmental modifications. Methods of weather modification are being developed for peaceful purposes, and there is concern not only that those using them could cause accidental damage to

The Environmental Effects of Military Activity

UNITED NATIONS ENVIRONMENT PROGRAM

I. FACTS AND FIGURES

The most obvious and horrifying direct effects of war are on people. But past wars have also had direct and indirect effects through the changes they have brought about in the environment, changing agriculture, shifting the margins of deserts and disturbing the balance of ecosystems.

Most wars have devastated farmlands. The Second World War caused a short-term reduction of 38 percent in the agricultural productivity of 10 nations; recovery progressed at about 8.3 percent per annum. In most recent wars new types of weapons, including high explosive munitions, chemical agents and incendiaries, have been deployed with still greater environmental effects. In South Vietnam chemical herbicides completely destroyed 1,500 square kilometres of mangrove forest and cause some damage to about 15,000 square kilometres more, and natural recovery is proceeding disturbingly slowly. More than 100 kg. of dioxin was inadvertently disseminated as an impurity in one of these defoliants, and this substance has since been linked to human birth defects and miscarriages and to liver cancer. Millions of people in South-east Asia have been displaced from their settlements and cultivated lands, leading to further environmental deterioration including the development of secondary vegetation and collapse of drainage systems. Recovery from these various impacts is likely to take decades. Agricultural pests and vectors of human disease have been spread as another inadvertent consequence of warfare; during the Second World War Italy suffered from the invasion of a moth (Hyphantria cunea) whose larvae defoliate valuable trees.

From **DEVELOPMENT: SEEDS OF CHANGE**, 1982:1, (40-42), reprinted by permission of the publisher.

2. ___, Disarmament and development. New York N.Y., 1972. (Sales no1 E73.IX.1)

3. STOCKHOLM INTERNATIONAL PEACE RESEARCH INSTITUTE. World armaments and disarmament: SIPRI yearbook 1969-70. Stockholm, Almqvist & Wiksell; New York, N.Y., Humanities Press; London, Paul Elek; 1971.

4. UNITED NATIONS. The United Nations and disarmament, 1945-1970. New York, N.Y., 1970. (Sales no. E 70.IX.1.)

TO DELVE MORE DEEPLY

BOUMEDIENE, H. Raw materials and development. Survival, vol. 16, no. 4, July/August 1974.

GREENWOOD, T. Reconnaissance and arms control. Scientific American, vol. 228, no. 2, February 1973.

LEITENBERG, M. The race to oblivion. The bulletin of the atomic scientists, vol. XXX, no. 7 September 1974.

SEGALEN, J. La guerre electronique. La recherche no. 46, June 1974.

STOCKHOLM INTERNATIONAL PEACE RESEARCH INSTITUTE. Resources devoted to military research and development, 1972; The near-nuclear countries and NPT (Non-Proliferation Treaty), 1972; World armaments and disarmament: SIPRI yearbook 1974.

YORK, H. Multiple-warhead missiles. Scientific American vol. 229 no. 5, November 1973.

Even worse environmental disruption is likely if new weapons now being developed and tested come into widespread use. Nuclear arsenals are increasing and constitute a major threat to mankind. A full-scale nuclear war would destroy all major cities in the northern hemisphere, and kill the bulk of the urban population in the northern hemisphere by blast and fire and the bulk of the rural population by radiation. It would, in addition, kill many millions in the southern hemisphere by radiation from fallout. The long-term consequences, though unpredictable, could affect the global climate, causing a serious reduction in the ozone layer. In addition, there might well be genetic effects from radiation. Detonation of weapons in the 10-kiloton range causes complete or severe destruction of vegetation over 400–1,300 hectares. Use of these weapons in a full-scale war would destroy vegetation and lead to soil-erosion over large areas, as well as inject huge amounts of radioactive dust into the stratosphere. Ecological recovery in such eroded areas would certainly be extremely slow. Nuclear explosions in the stratosphere would, at least temporarily, deplete ozone concentrations and increase the amount of ultra-violet radiation reaching the earth's surface, increasing the incidence of several effects, harmful to man and ecosystems. The neutron bomb (a low-yield nuclear weapon designed to kill or incapacitate people in armoured vehicles mainly by ionizing radiation rather than blast or heat) would also do appreciable environmental damage. It is estimated that denotation of a one-kiloton bomb 200 metres above the ground will cause death to a wide range of micro-organisms over an area of 40 hectares, to many insects over 100 hectares, to many amphibians and reptiles over 330 hectares, to many species of higher plants over 350 hectares and to many species of exposed mammals and birds over 490 hectares.

The use of chemical and biological weapons could also have serious environmental consequence, since they involve, in effect, deliberate pollution by the release of toxic chemicals or harmful micro-organisms. Chemical deforestation in tropical areas with fragile soils, or semi-arid areas already delicately poised on the brink of desert, could create rapid erosion and irreversible desertification. Wide-scale use of incendiary chemicals, such as napalm, could have similar results. As experience in recent wars in South-east Asia shows, even in areas that are ecologically robust, damage by fire and chemicals to natural vegetation and to crops grown for food and fibre is often long-lasting. If, despite international agreements, chemical, bacteriological or biological weapons are used, the effects of deliberately disseminating quantities of up to a dozen species of highly virulent pathogenic bacteria are less certain (much would depend on whether they attacked livestock or crop species as well as man, on how long they sustained themselves in the wild), but it is easy to see ways in which the agriculture and ecological balance could be disturbed for a long time.

There have been speculations about the possibility of causing economic or other damage to the population of an enemy through environmental modifications. Methods of weather modification are being developed for peaceful purposes, and there is concern not only that those using them could cause accidental damage to

neighbouring states, but that such techniques could have hostile applications. For example, cloud and rainfall might be deliberately increased in one area in order to create drought and agricultural damage elsewhere. Such operations could be carried out covertly, and would be very hard to detect or counteract. The mere possibility of such actions could poison international relations because of the difficulty in deciding whether a flood, drought or crop failure was due to natural causes of the actions of an enemy.

The hazards of war do not end with the coming of peace. Unexploded mines, bombs and shells can hamper mineral exploitation, make land unsafe to farm, hamper development and endanger people who disturb them. Bomb craters, wrecked vehicles or derelict defences and buildings are a blot on the landscape and reduce its value for recreation. Mines in rivers or at sea can be a serious danger to fishermen, hamper their work, and, if washed ashore, also imperil those living on the coast.

A UNEP survey of the environmental effects of the remnants of war attracted a response from 44 Governments. The volume of munitions left behind in some of their territories by the Second World War is staggering. One Government reported that it had cleared 14,469,600 land mines, and that clearance was continuing at the rate of 300,000 to 400,000 a year. Many thousands of shells, bombs and other munitions also had to be dealt with in various countries. The country most seriously affected reported that the remnants of war had killed 3,834 people, most of them children, and injured 8,384 others of whom 6,783 were children. For the past five years 30 to 40 people had been killed each year and 50 to 80 injured. Some 460 disposal personnel had been killed, and 655 injured. Other replies also indicated serious losses of life, and a cost of clearance running at tens or hundreds of thousands of dollars a year. Costal states reported parallel difficulties with marine mines and with dumped ammunition and wrecked ships (some containing explosives).

Another important aspect of military activity and post-military activity is human migration. The millions of refugees have not only suffered economic and social losses and disruption, but have also exerted pressures on the ecosystems in the areas to which they migrated. In most cases, the living conditions in the new habitat are intolerable in human terms. Since it lacks adequate infrastructures, disease, malnutrition and social disruption have become common problems. In spite of the different international efforts to alleviate the problems of refugees, they will continue to increase in magnitude with increases in tension and military activity.

II. THE PROBLEM

The growing volume and destructive power of the world's weapon stocks poses an obvious risk to man and to his environment. Even

the testing of these weapons can cause serious environmental
damage, as can accidents in their handling, transport or storage.
The use of weapons against the environment -- especially to remove
sheltering forests or to destroy the crops on which an enemy
depends -- brings with it the risk of long-term or even
irreversible damage to soil, agriculture, and the ecological
balance.   If environmental manipulation became an effective agent
of war, a further dimension for damage would be added.

While these direct impacts on man, his settlements, his food
and his habitat have in one form on another been familiar features
of wars down the centuries, wars have become increasingly
disruptive of the environment, and the power of the world's armed
forces to devastate large areas is many times greater now than it
has ever been.   Moreover, the arms race is also having serious
environmental consequences because it is competing for the
resources with other forms of development which are essential if
the quality of life on earth is to be raised to more acceptable
levels.

The current increase in military expenditure is taking place
at a time when 1,500 million people (nearly 40 percent of the
world's population) have no effective medical services, nearly 570
million people are severely undernourished, about 3,000 million
lack access to safe water, and nearly 750,000 die each month from
water-borne diseases.   About 800 million people are illiterate, and
nearly 250 million children under the age of 14 do not attend
school.   Yet it is in the developing countries, where these
problems are most acute, that military expenditure, including
expenditure on arms imports, is growing most rapidly.

The effects of the arms race and military expenditure on
trade, aid, technological and scientific cooperation and other
kinds of exchange between countries are far-reaching.   Political
and strategic considerations distort the flow of trade and aid.
The only politically realistic way for most rich countries to
increase their aid to poor ones is to reduce military spending,
since money cannot be taken from other parts of national budgets.
In the absence of such action, the diversion of resources away from
investment that could increase the wiser use of the environment for
production and growth can only contribute to inflation and economic
crisis and to a widening of the gap between developed and
developing countries.   On any logical analysis the world cannot
afford the arms race -- the developing countries least of all.   Yet
as long as suspicion and uncertainty remain so prevalent in
international affairs, this situation is likely to continue.

III. CONCLUDING REMARKS

It can be stated without hesitation that the questions of
disarmament, development and environmental protection are closely
linked and represent some of the most important issues before the
international community today.   Development can hardly proceed at

the required pace and a healthy environment cannot be guaranteed amidst a widening and constantly escalating arms race. Moreover, development and environmental efforts are threatened by the armaments, especially nuclear weapons, already stockpiled, the use of which either by intent or in error or sheer madness would severely jeopardize mankind's very existence.

One of the most urgent tasks, therefore, is to arrest the technological spiral at the centre of the international arms race and, through substantial and substantive disarmament measures, to pave the way for major reductions, in world military expenditures. A major breakthrough in the disarmament field would release vast financial, technological and human resources for more productive uses in both developing and developed countries in an international political climate of much reduced tension. Even if only 20 percent for example, of annual military expenditures were to be diverted, for instance, to an international fund for sustainable development projects, the developing countries would thus be enabled to attain their socioeconomic objectives more effectively.

In the environmental field, the immediate needs are first to develop means of predicting the kinds of stress various weapons systems will place upon different ecosystems, and second to improve methods for the restoration of lands devastated by war. More needs to be known about the ecological disruption that could be caused through the hostile use of all weapons, especially "mass destruction" weapons, including the deliberate dispersion of pathogenic micro-organisms, and special attention must be given to the possible military use of weather modification techniques. In addition, the restoration of farmlands and international action to ensure the safe disposal of radioactive wastes and obsolete explosives and chemical and biological weapons all merit continuing attention and effective action.

Disarmament and Development: Some Specific Proposals

BARRY M. BLECHMAN
EDWARD R. FRIED

At its twelfth session, held in March/April 1976, the United Nations Committee for Development Planning made a pessimistic assessment of economic prospects over the rest of the current decade for the low-income countries generally and for the poorest among them in particular. "Most disappointing of all", the Committee concluded, "was the performance of the international community in contributing through trade and aid to the development process."[1] The Committee pointed to the high level of world-wide military expenditures as the single most important reason for the failure of the international community to provide adequate development support. For that reason it called for new approaches to a long-sought objective: a reduction in military expenditures and the allocation of a portion of the savings so realized to development assistance.

Much of the attention of the United Nations throughout its history has been devoted to these twin goals: reducing military forces and encouraging development assistance. Each goal is of fundamental importance in its own right and each has been independently pursued. In addition, several proposals have been advanced to link the two, implicitly or explicitly, but without notable success. Although the general proposition of turning swords into ploughshares on a global basis is straightforward enough, the fact that no progress has been made in this direction attests to its complexity.

The most recent discussion of a specific linkage between disarmament and development originated in a proposal made by the Union of Soviet Socialist Republics in 1973 at the twenty-eighth session of the General Assembly. It called on the permanent members of the Security Council to reduce their military expenditures by 10 per cent and to utilize "part of the funds thus

From **JOURNAL OF DEVELOPMENT PLANNING**, No. 12, 1977, (137-153), reprinted by permission of the publisher.

saved to provide assistance to developing countries". Although differences among countries emerged in the debate on this proposal, the Assembly during that session adopted a resolution (a) calling on the permanent members of the Security Council to reduce their military budgets in 1974 by 10 per cent from the 1973 level; (b) appealing to those countries to allot 10 per cent of the savings to development assistance; and (c) expressing the desire that other countries, particularly those with large economies and large military budgets, act similarly.[2] For reasons we note below, the fate of this proposal has been no different from its predecessors; indeed, instead of falling, military expenditures have continued to rise.

It is clear that dramatic changes in attitudes and unconventional measures are necessary if linkages are to be established between disarmament and development. In the present paper we explore some specific proposals towards this end. As a general thesis, we argue that, to be effective, specific actions would have to be taken by many nations, both large and small, and not by just the largest or the most powerful, and that such actions must contribute to easing the underlying political and military tensions that have led to large military budgets. Indeed, worthwhile progress towards lower military expenditures and higher development expenditures will be possible only if responsibility in the attainment of these goals is accepted worldwide and all nations work patiently, over a long period of time, with these common purposes.

I. IS THERE A LINKAGE?

World defence expenditures in 1976 are estimated to have been roughly $388 billion, or perhaps 5.7 per cent of total world output.[3] Over the past decade these expenditures have grown in real terms by an average of about 2.5 per cent a year, one half the rate of growth of the gross world product. It is useful for present purposes to break down these expenditures as follows:

In comparison, expenditures to foster economic growth in the developing countries are small. For the non-OPEC developing countries in particular, excluding China, total net investment probably amounted to no more than $150 billion a year, and the concessional capital received from the industrial and OPEC countries to help sustain this level of investment was only $15 billion a year. Yet these developing countries contain almost half the world's population; hope for a tolerable world order rests in large measure on a marked improvement in their economic prospects.

This striking difference between expenditures on defence and on development is clear evidence from the point of view of the world community as a whole that resources are being misallocated. From the perspective of individual nations, however, these facts in themselves do not demonstrate that priorities are mixed up. Presumably, nations accept the burden of military expenditures

because they believe that otherwise they would be subject to greater risks to their security than would be tolerable. To the extent that the objective of reducing risks is realized, these expenditures fulfil an important national purpose. There may well be less rational reasons for incurring this burden -- aggressive ends, the quest for international prestige, bureaucratic pressures, and misconceptions about the economic consequences of reducing defence expenditures have all been suggested -- but it is the perception about security risks that is usually dominant, and certainly the one that is operationally relevant in negotiations about disarmament. Proposals to reduce military expenditures must convincingly demonstrate to individual nations that at the least such reductions would not make the external environment any more dangerous, and preferably that they would make it less dangerous. Otherwise, these proposals are bound to go nowhere.

Assuming that this fundamental condition could be met, a reduction in military expenditure would release resources for other purposes. What would be the implications for the economic prospects of the poor countries?

Here predominant emphasis is usually placed on actions that should be taken by the industrial countries, notably by the United States of America and the Soviet Union, whose military budgets account for about three fifths of the world total. A negotiated reduction of 10 per cent in United States-Soviet Union military expenditures in 1976 would have meant a "disarmament dividend" for those two countries of approximately $23 billion a year. If this dividend were to be shared in the proportion of 90 per cent for use on social and economic programmes in the United States and the Soviet Union themselves, and 10 per cent for the provision of increased concessional capital to the poorest countries,[4] the consequences for development support would be substantial. Such an action would produce a jump of $2.3 billion, or almost 20 per cent, in official development assistance. Moreover, the restructuring of production in favour of civilian over military goods could mean stronger markets in the world's two largest economies for products exported by the developing countries. And the gains in funds available for domestic purposes in the United States and the Soviet Union resulting from a reduced military burden could make it easier politically for these two countries to support respectable ongoing development assistance efforts. Finally, an agreement of this kind by the two most powerful military protagonists could set the stage for similar actions by their allies in NATO and the Warsaw Pact, with additional benefits for development. In short, the consequences of an agreement between the United States and the Soviet Union to reduce military expenditures, coupled with a development assistance dividend, could add up to a measurable improvement in the international order.

Despite the seeming simplicity of the proposal, the obstacles are formidable. A study of this concept by a United Nations expert panel has brought out the critical problems: (a) the impossibility of verifying expenditure reductions unless much more information were to be provided by the signatories than is now available or is likely to become available; and (b) the danger that expenditure cuts could be allocated in such a way as to be

destabilizing from an arms-control point of view.[5] In other words, when faced with reduced budgets, the United States and the Soviet Union might be tempted to invest relatively more on weapons that provided greater destructive potential -- for example, nuclear systems -- or they might place their forces on a higher alert status, which would increase the incentive to strike first in a crisis. These are disabling deficiencies; an agreement to reduce military expenditures that either party believed would mean heightened military and political dangers would not be negotiable. The United Nations experts also spelt out the difficulties of defining military expenditures and of agreeing on how to value them for comparative purposes. In these latter instances, however, they were able to outline possible ways of resolving the complex issues that are involved, including recommendations for adopting a standardized system for international accounting and reporting of military expenditures.[6] It is important to emphasize that progress along these lines would be useful generally for arms-control negotiations. None the less, the first two problems -- verifying budget cuts and avoiding a less stable allocation of residual defence expenditures -- would continue to be fatal barriers to the conclusion of an agreement.

Expenditure reductions reached by mutual example rather than by formal agreement is another possibility. In 1963-1964 the United States and the Soviet Union apparently undertook parallel actions to reduce their military budgets, but the sharp growth of United States military spending in 1965, resulting from the Vietnamese conflict, eliminated the possibility of judging whether this approach could work, and if so, for how long and to what extent.[7] Here again, the concept is appealing, but applying it would depend in the first instance on whether international tensions had eased to the point where either nation was prepared to reduce its military budget unilaterally, either as a temporary experiment or to move towards a lower spending plateau. In this case, verification of whether the other side had followed suit and, if so, whether it had allocated its budget cut in a stabilizing pattern would depend on unilateral national intelligence systems. Moreover, although agreement on verification procedures would make for a more durable accord, it would not be a necessary condition for initiating unilateral action.

This kind of expenditure reduction initiative could be useful for arms-control purposes, but any formal linkage to development assistance would be damaging. In the event of a linkage, each side would have to establish the size of its budget reduction in order to determine the dividend for development, and this requirement would tend to push them into the very type of negotiation that the unilateral approach is designed to avoid. Furthermore, the requirement to appropriate funds for development as part of an agreement that had not been formalized could arouse; even greater opposition at home than would exist in any case. Thus on two counts, the link to development assistance could be an obstacle to tacitly agreed mutual expenditure reductions and thus could endanger the overriding objective of this approach -- achievement of greater arms control. On the other hand, by reducing military expenditures or obviating the need to increase them, this approach

could improve the political climate and budgetary leeway for development assistance appropriations and in this sense provide an informal link to development support.

What about agreements on specific force reductions, such as the 1972 agreement between the United States and the Soviet Union on strategic arms limitations (SALT I)? If properly constructed, agreements on specific force reductions could serve arms-control purposes by eliminating or reducing components of those military force postures on each side that imply particularly dangerous or immediate threats to the other side's security. In this way they can reduce the risk of war. However, the linkage to development assistance is more obscure, principally because there is no assurance that such arms control agreements will result in lower total military budgets.

Recounting what happened in SALT I illustrates this point. For the United States, the agreement resulted in the termination of anti-ballistic missile (ABM) deployments. It also strengthened arguments for a slow-down in air defence modernization programmes and a reduction in air defence force levels. All told, at 1976 prices, these steps probably saved on the order of $5 billion annually once fully implemented. On the other hand, both kinds of reductions might well have occurred, although at a slower pace, even without the SALT agreements. The margin in the United States Congress favouring ABM deployments was slim and might well have been sustained only by the fact that the negotiations were going on. Similarly, arguments against air defence modernization were compelling even without SALT, and support for the programme within the Executive branch was weak. In any event, expenditures on other components of the United States strategic forces increased after the 1972 agreements, notably on programmes to modernize offensive weapon systems. As a result, in real terms, expenditures on strategic forces as a whole remained nearly constant for several years, and more recently have begun to increase. Still, the 1972 agreements probably brought about net savings as compared to the spending that would have occurred if the negotiations had not taken place at all, or had failed.

Much the same sequence may have occurred in the Soviet Union: specifically, a decline in expenditures on ballistic missile and air defence coupled with a wide-ranging expansion in offensive strategic capabilities. As in the United States, however, the increase in the Soviet strategic budget may have been less than would have occurred without an agreement.

These ambiguous budgetary consequences highlight the dilemma. To have attached the requirement of a development assistance dividend to an agreement that did not produce an absolute and readily apparent budgetary saving would have added considerably to the burden of negotiating SALT I. This would have been unwise, because the agreement was useful for arms-control purposes, whatever its budgetary consequences.

What about military expenditure reductions that could be undertaken by the developing countries? Surprisingly little attention has been paid to this aspect of the linkage between disarmament and development, despite the fact that in these instances the linkage is much more direct. Specifically, a

reduction in military expenditures by developing countries would automatically free an equivalent amount of domestic savings for investment in the civilian economy. Moreover, to the extent that the importation of arms manufactured abroad could also be reduced, there would be an increase in the availability of foreign exchange for development purposes.

Even though the developing countries account for only a small share of world military expenditures, potential savings could make a substantial difference in development prospects. Leaving aside the OPEC countries which, for these purposes, should be placed in a separate category because of the extraordinary investment support they now receive from petroleum revenues, and excluding China, the military budgets of the remaining developing countries represent about 4 per cent of their combined gross national product. Put in different terms, the resources now devoted to military expenditures are equal to one fourth the domestic savings these developing countries are able to mobilize for investment. And the foreign exchange they use for the purchase of arms from abroad is now running at perhaps $3 billion a year, an amount equal to one fourth the capital received from abroad on concessional terms.

These aggregate data mask substantial differences among non-OPEC developing countries in the proportionate emphasis placed on military expenditures and the importation of arms. Nevertheless, the data provide ample evidence of the substantial stimulus that reductions in military expenditures could provide for development, all the more so for certain States in the Middle East, South Asia, and East Asia, which -- for various reasons -- now feel compelled to accept a disproportionately heavy defence burden. In the aggregate, a 10 per cent reduction in the military expenditures of the non-OPEC developing countries, with the savings devoted to investment, could directly benefit their economic prospects about as much as would the proposed development dividend from a 10 per cent reduction in the military expenditures of the industrial countries.

Perceptions that military budget reductions could make the international environment more dangerous are of course the main obstacle to a reordering of spending priorities for the developing countries, just as they are for the industrial countries. In comparison with United States-Soviet Union arms control negotiations, however, some of the technical problems of reaching agreements among pairs or groups of developing countries might prove to be easier to resolve. For one thing, the armed forces involved are comparatively small -- particularly their support establishment, such as research and development laboratories and logistical centres, where the effects of budgetary reductions are particularly hard to assess. This means that negotiated reductions in military budgets could be verified with greater confidence. Secondly, since these nations do not view the size of their military budgets as being in itself a factor in world politics, as the United States and the Soviet Union seem to do, they can confine their assessment of expenditure reduction proposals to the more readily calculated effects on the military balance in specific areas of tension.

Several approaches are possible. The most important,

potentially, would be negotiated reductions of military budgets, or of specific kinds of forces, by pairs or groups of nations that are poised in confrontation. Prominent examples are Greece and Turkey; Egypt, Israel, Jordan and the Syrian Arab Republic; India and Pakistan; Algeria and Morocco; the Democratic People's Republic of Korea and the Republic of Korea; Democratic Kampuchea Thailand and Viet Nam; and possibly Chile, Ecuador and Peru. Or agreements on military budget reductions might be negotiated on a regional basis; an example would be restrictions on weapon modernization programmes or a freeze on force levels in Latin America. Or countries might act unilaterally either because of a change in their assessment of the international environment, or because they believed that their example would be followed by others, or because new economic incentives helped to persuade them to accept the risk at the margin, of reallocating resources from military to civilian purposes.

In short, potential ways for stimulating economic development in the poor countries by reducing world military expenditures are varied and far-reaching, but the linkage is complex and tenuous. Past experience shows that these potentialities will not be realized by exhortation or by concentrating the weight of international opinion solely on the military budgets of the United States and the Soviet Union, dominant as these are in the global total. On the other hand, international pressure might contribute to a break-through in this general area if it were directed towards the creation of a system applicable to all countries, through which the nations of the world acted in common to attain these goals. If developing countries were full participants in a world-wide effort to reduce military expenditures, they could argue more credibly and with greater impact for renewed efforts on the part of the industrial countries to negotiate arms reductions and to link successful negotiations to a development assistance dividend. More importantly, military budget reductions in developing countries that lessened military and political tensions in the developing world would themselves reduce the risk of a military confrontation between the United States and the Soviet Union and, on this account, would strengthen the potential effectiveness of calls for a reduction in the military forces and capabilities of the major military Powers.

II. ELEMENTS OF A GLOBAL SYSTEM

What kind of a framework might lead to collective and cumulative pressure to reduce world military expenditures and increase development capital assistance? We suggest a system in which: (a) all countries accept the obligation to reduce military budgets; and (b) a special fund is established to provide additional capital assistance on a matching basis to those non-OPEC developing countries that can demonstrate they have reduced their military budgets from a specified base level. In such a system

successful arms-control negotiations by one group of countries would both improve the climate and build pressure for other countries to follow suit. For the non-OPEC developing countries, the matching development assistance dividend might serve as an important inducement to enter into arms-control negotiations leading to reduced military budgets or might tip the scales in favour of a unilateral reallocation of domestic resources of such a system, particularly as they relate to the sources and uses of the development assistance dividend?

Funds for the development assistance dividend might come from two sources: (a) from a distribution -- say 10 per cent -- of budgetary savings hypothetically realized as a result of arms-control agreements negotiated by the industrial countries, and (b) from a special tax -- also illustratively 10 per cent -- imposed on all sales of military goods and services by industrial countries to developing countries.

The parties to any arms-control agreement would be under international obligation to state how much the agreement would save in expenditures on the military programmes and forces that it covered, as compared to what would have been spent had the agreement not been negotiated. The parties to the agreement themselves would set this hypothetical value; its determination would have to be negotiated and no doubt would be relatively arbitrary. Savings might be assumed to accrue in equal proportion to the participants when only the United States and the Soviet Union were involved, or on some other rough standard if it covered additional industrial countries. In this way it might be possible to avoid potentially endless disputes over differences in costs among countries and over what costs should be included. Nor would this valuation of savings, however arbitrary, be subject to review by third parties. In effect, the procedure should be loose enough so that the arrangements for assessing the development assistance dividends would not be an obstacle to reaching agreement on the control of arms.

This is not to say that the valuations would necessarily be very small. Indeed, the valuations might be sizable because of the political incentives of the participants to demonstrate the importance of the agreement for both domestic and international consumption, and because in some cases the agreement would indeed bring about actual reductions in military expenditures, which would be evident in subsequent budgets.

The tax on arms sales to developing countries, in addition to being a second source of development funds, could be viewed as a means of discouraging the build-up of expensive weapons systems in the armouries of poor countries. Countries that continued to purchase these arms would be subject to a double penalty; the tax would require them to pay higher prices for the weapons and, because of these higher prices, they would find it that much more difficult to cut their military budgets in order to qualify for matching development assistance. As a new restraining factor in the arms race, the effect of the system might be cumulative. Restraints by countries that had been purchasing more sophisticated weapons would reduce the pressure on their potential adversaries either to modernize their own weapon systems or to take some other

counterbalancing action.

As to the uses of such funds, the logic of the system would confine their distribution to those non-OPEC developing countries that were able to reduce their military budgets. To distribute them generally for development assistance, even to countries, however poor, whose military budgets were increasing, would be contrary to the concept of building a mutually interactive linkage between disarmament and development. Matching funds might be distributed as grants, or possibly as loans on terms comparable to those of the World Bank's soft loan affiliate, the International Development Association.

The United Nations Development Programme might be assigned the task of administering these funds on the understanding that the only conditions for disbursement would be a demonstration by the recipient country that: (a) its military budget had declined from a predetermined base; and (b) the funds would produce a net addition to total investment, or otherwise would be used to improve welfare. Also, it would have to be understood that receipt of these funds would not cause offsetting reductions in the flow of development assistance to these countries from normal bilateral or multilateral channels.

What about possible imbalances between available funds and claims upon them? If funds exceeded claims, not only would the financial inducement for developing countries to reach arms control agreements grow, but this fact would be dramatic evidence that the developing countries were lagging in carrying out their obligation to contribute to a less dangerous international environment. Conversely, if claims exceeded available funds, the claims should be permitted to accumulate, serving as ammunition for the developing countries to charge that industrial countries had failed to live up their obligations under the system.

III. ILLUSTRATIVE CASES

Several illustrations may help to bring out how this global disarmament/development system would work and some of the problems that would have to be faced. We begin with three much-discussed arms-control measures by industrial nations, and then turn to agreements that could be reached among developing States.

Strategic Arms Limitation

The accord initialed by the United States of America and the Soviet Union at Vladivostok in 1974, if implemented, would not be likely to lead to significant reductions in the defence budgets of either signatory. The strategic force levels permitted under the

terms of the accord would require no reductions in planned United
States forces and only minor reductions from present Soviet force
levels. And the few qualitative controls specified in the accord
would have no impact, to speak of, on present weapon modernization
programmes in either nation.

Conceivably, a more far-reaching agreement could be attained
either as a substitute for the Vladivostok accord or as a next step
after the implementation of Vladivostok. Take, for example, an
agreement that required the United States and the Soviet Union to
reduce their strategic forces, over a number of years, to a total
of 1,320 missile launchers and long-range bombers.[8] Such an
agreement would have two significant budgetary effects: it would
bring about savings in operating costs and it would permit a
reduction in the scope and pace of weapon modernization programmes.

In the system we have outlined, the value to be placed on the
agreement would be determined by comparing relevant military
expenditures under its terms to the likely level of expenditures
for those same programmes had the agreement not been reached. In
the case of the United States, for example, a ceiling of 1,320
launchers and bombers could be said to produce annual savings, as
compared to the projected strategic budget in the absence of the
agreement, of between $700 million and $4.9 billion, at 1976
prices. The range is unusually wide because the amount of imputed
savings would depend on which existing forces were cut and which
were retained. For example, bombers, which require substantial
numbers of men to fly and maintain them, are much more expensive to
operate than are missiles.[9] Presumably, savings of a similar
magnitude would become possible for the Soviet Union.

This is not to say that the defence budgets of the signatories
would be reduced by the calculated value of the agreement. Many
other factors would intervene and influence the specific budgetary
decision that would be taken. Indeed, it is possible that all the
money saved on strategic weapons, and even more, would be spent on
other types of military forces. None the less, for purposes of
determining obligations under the system, the signatories would set
a value on the potential savings the agreement could make possible
on the assumption that spending on other forces would not be
increased. The contribution each signatory would make to the
disarmament/development fund would be 10 per cent of that amount.

Mutual Force Reductions

As in the case of strategic arms limitation, the sorts of
agreements now being discussed in the mutual force reductions (MFR)
negotiations would not have significant budgetary implications.
Neither the United States nor the Soviet Union would save money
simply by withdrawing forces from Central Europe, since it does not
cost significantly more for them to station troops there than to
support them at home. For an MFR agreement to have an important
budgetary impact it would have to result not only in the withdrawal

of forces but also in their disestablishment -- that is, in a reduction in the force structure by the amount of the troop withdrawal.

Take, for example, an agreement that called for the withdrawal of 25 per cent of each country's ground forces in Central Europe. On the United States side, that would mean the withdrawal of about 50,000 men; on the Soviet side, perhaps 115,000. To calculate the budgetary value of the agreement it would be assumed that these forces would be phased out of the force structures of the two Powers. For the United States the savings in personnel expenditures alone would then be about $600 million per year (at 1976 prices). The agreement would also result in some savings in other operating costs, such as reduced need for the procurement of such consumable items as fuel. The extent of these savings would depend on the specific units that were assumed to be disestablished. Comparable figures could be calculated for the Soviet Union. This method of valuing the savings achieved by the agreement, and hence of determining the development assistance dividend, would be used whether or not the participants realized the potential savings involved by deactivating the forces that were withdrawn from Central Europe.

At some later stage, MFR might call for reductions in the armed forces of the other members of NATO and the Warsaw Pact. That would lead to similar calculations of the value of such an agreement, of which 10 per cent would go to the disarmament/ development fund.

Naval Limitations in the Indian Ocean

This possible area for the control of arms has also received considerable attention from the United Nations in recent years, although so far there has been little evident progress in moving towards formal negotiations. From an arms control point of view, there would be substantial advantage in an agreement that prohibited extraregional powers from maintaining standing naval forces in the region.[10] The navies of non-littoral states would be permitted to cruise through the region but not to operate there on a permanent basis.

In present circumstances, such an agreement would principally affect the navies of France, the United States of America and the Soviet Union. To calculate the savings potential of such an agreement, it would be assumed that the forces each of these States now maintains in the Indian Ocean and the necessary back-up forces would be phased out of the force structure. Such a reduction would also permit a moderate slow-down in shipbuilding programmes, with additional associated savings. In the case of the Soviet Union, for example, the annual potential value of the agreement -- at 1976 United States prices -- would be roughly $500 million.[11] Similar calculations of potential savings would be made for the United States and France.

Again, none of this is to say that such savings in military
expenditures actually would result following completion of an
Indian Ocean Naval Limitation Agreement -- only that such savings
could result if all other things remained constant. The valuation
of the agreement would be negotiated by the signatories and would
no doubt be set arbitrarily.

The Tax on Arms Sales

Potential revenues from a tax on arms sales to developing
countries -- the second source of financing for the
disarmament/development fund -- could also be sizable. Deliveries
of arms and the provision of military services to the developing
countries, including the OPEC countries, may average $10 billion
annually over the next few years. Perhaps three fourths of this
total will go to countries in the Middle East. Thus a 10 per cent
tax would provide approximately $1 billion a year to the fund. It
would be paid by those countries that insisted on continuing to
escalate the level of weapon sophistication in their regions by
importing foreign military technologies, and thereby put pressure
on other countries to follow suit. It would be distributed to
countries that were exercising restraint in their military
programmes and thereby contributing to a reduction of political and
military tension in the world.

Arms Control in the Developing Countries

Turning to the developing nations, the greatest emphasis on
participation in a disarmament/development system should be on
States now poised in confrontation. Not only do those States
account for the largest share of military expenditures by
developing nations but, more importantly, their confrontations
often carry with them the seeds of regional wars and, ultimately,
of armed and potentially nuclear conflict between the United States
and the Soviet Union. Unfortunately, it is precisely because the
tensions between those developing nations are so acute, and thus
their military expenditures relatively so large, that one cannot be
sanguine about the prospects. What would be necessary first is the
attainment of political understandings between the confrontation
States, which could then lead to the easing of tensions and
reductions in military forces and defence budgets. Disarmament
proposals in themselves are not likely to serve as a catalyst for
the political resolution of long-standing international problems.
Although limited agreements can ease the most dangerous situations
for a while (as did, for example, the 1975 Interim Agreement
between Egypt and Israel), the history of disarmament negotiations

since 1945 shows that successful arms control can only follow
mutual acceptance by the States concerned of the conditions
underlying a political settlement.

   This caution is clearly pertinent to the Middle East. It
would be unrealistic to expect Egypt, Israel, Jordan, and the
Syrian Arab Republic to agree to reduce the size of their armed
forces under the present circumstances. The risks to each would
seem too great. They have fought bitterly, time and again, for
years; the possibility of a renewal of armed conflict among them is
still significant. What is needed in the Middle East is concrete
progress towards a political settlement. Arms reduction can only
parallel or follow -- not precede -- mutual steps towards a peace
agreement.

   Should such a settlement occur, the potential benefits for
development are great. Together, Egypt, Israel, Jordan and the
Syrian Arab Republic spend around $8 billion (at 1976 United States
prices) on defence each year. That is roughly 25 per cent of their
total output -- an extraordinarily heavy burden on their economies.
If, following a political settlement, they could reduce their
defence budgets by 25 per cent as part of a negotiated agreement
among the members of the group, they could support a major increase
in investment. If, in addition, the developing members of the
group (Egypt, Jordan and the Syrian Arab Republic) were to receive
matching contributions from the disarmament/development fund, their
economic prospects would be substantially brightened.

   The situation on the Korean Peninsula provides a close analogy
in this regard to the Middle East. Arms control negotiations
between the Democratic People's Republic of Korea and the Republic
of Korea are not likely to be successful until the two States come
to terms, or at least until they agree to accept the division of
the Peninsula. Following such a political settlement, measures
could be taken to reduce the size of the two military
establishments. Here also, the potential contribution to
development capital would be sizable. Together, the two Koreas
spend perhaps $1.5 billion on defence each year, or roughly 6 per
cent of their combined gross national product. A 25 per cent cut
in these expenditures, matched by capital from the disarmament/
development fund, would enable them to increase investment by 10 to
15 per cent a year and add at least one percentage point to their
rate of growth.

   On the Indian subcontinent, the time for meaningful arms
control may be close at hand. After years of tension and war,
India and Pakistan may now be moving, slowly and largely tacitly,
towards mutual recognition of the need for peace and understanding.
Each nations' decisions will hinge to some extent on attitudes and
actions of third parties, but perhaps these two States could be
among the first "confrontation Powers" in the developing world to
undertake mutual reductions in military expenditures.
Establishment of a global system might enhance this prospect.
Military expenditures are a smaller proportion of gross national
product for these two countries than in the other examples cited
above; none the less, the potential savings would be significant,
particularly in view of their very low per capita incomes and
difficulties such poverty poses for mobilizing resources for

investment. Together, India and Pakistan spend $3.5 billion on defence each year -- or roughly 4 per cent of their combined gross national product. A 25 per cent reduction in this military burden, matched by capital from the disarmament/development fund, would almost be equal to the net flow of concessional and nonconcessional resources these two countries now receive from abroad.

Regional agreements are another possibility. They could take several forms -- for example, a freeze on military force levels, or reductions in military budgets on a negotiated time schedule, or restrictions on the introduction of new generations of weapons or particular types of weapons. The Declaration of Ayacucho, made in December 1974 by the eight Andean countries, is an example of these kinds of arrangements, at least in principle. At that time, Peru proposed that the members of the group negotiate specific limits on the acquisition of offensive armaments, but despite subsequent meetings to establish the groundwork for negotiations, no progress has been made. None the less, the principle is sound and the possibilities are promising. Agreement by regional or subregional groups to achieve negotiated reductions in military forces or expenditures, or to place restraints on weapon modernization, could make it more feasible politically and militarily for each member of the group to act.

The fact that in some countries military expenditures as a percentage of gross national product are comparatively small should not be a reason for slacking off on the effort to reduce the burden. Again, Latin America, where this proportion -- under 2 per cent -- is the lowest among the major regional groupings, is an example. Total military expenditures for the region are over $5 billion a year, of which possibly $500 to $700 million is being spent on arms imports. Reductions in these expenditures would be a new source of development capital, the more so if they were matched by capital assistance from the disarmament/development fund.

Finally, there is the possibility of unilateral budget cuts by countries that are not in areas of political and military tension or otherwise subject to evident threats to their security. In these cases military expenditures are likely to be comparatively low, but a global disarmament campaign, coupled with the possible receipt of a disarmament/development dividend might cause a reappraisal of defence requirements in favour of civilian needs.

Announced military budget reductions would have to be subject to verification, with the dollar amount of the reductions tied to specified cuts in force levels or manpower or weapon programmes. An international body probably would have to verify these reductions by on-site inspections both as a counterpart to the right to draw from the fund and to ensure that budgetary savings from the announced cuts were not used to strengthen other military capabilities. Effective verification procedures, in short, would be necessary both to maintain confidence in disarmament agreements and for the successful operation of the disarmament/development system itself.

IV. CONCLUSIONS

Proposals to link disarmament and development characteristically have an air of unreality, and those we have outlined above may be no different. None the less, in specifying what has to be done, a global disarmament/development system would be much closer to the mark than generalized exhortations to spend less on defence and more on development. It is indeed a melancholy fact that world-wide expenditures on defence are scandalously high when compared to what is spent to improve the material well-being of the poor people of the world. It is also a fact that substantial reductions in military expenditures will depend on hard-headed negotiations to achieve balanced restraining actions by pairs or groups of potential adversaries, as well as on progress in resolving the conditions underlying international tensions. The system we have outlined seeks to take these two propositions into account.

The specifics of such a system are less important than the ground rules that flow from the exercise. We would stress the following:

(a) Build for the long pull. Disarmament takes a long time. It took three years to negotiate the SALT I agreements and it is likely to take about as long to bring the Vladivostok accords to fruition. The MFR negotiations have been going on for four years, with no end in sight. Even so promising and straightforward an initiative as the declaration of Ayacucho among the Andean States has achieved no concrete results in two years;

(b) Arms-control negotiations should not be burdened with a requirement to reduce military budgets. Successful arms-control agreements can diminish the risk of war and lay the groundwork for co-operative political relations between potential adversaries, even though the agreements may be followed by rising rather than falling defence budgets. The benefits are overriding. They can lead to an easing of international tensions, and this in itself is likely to improve prospects for trade, capital flows and development. In time, they will also bring lower military budgets;

(c) A disarmament/development system must involve global participation. Possibilities to reduce international tensions exist virtually everywhere. So do the possibilities for reducing military budgets and thereby increasing the resources available for investment. A system that seeks to establish a linkage between disarmament and development must create both pressures and incentives for all countries to act. A country's participation by example -- that is, by concrete action to reduce its own military expenditures, rather than by calling on others to act -- is the most powerful form of international pressure.

Disarmament and development are critical goals for the international community and each must be pursued as a matter of the highest priority. It should also be possible to link them in a system that improves the prospects of achieving each. Bringing such a system into operation would require new, unorthodox and

concrete approaches to old and familiar problems, and it would take
a long time to accomplish. But a beginning surely is needed
because the problems it seeks to address will not go away -- they
are only likely to become more dangerous.

NOTES

[1]International Finance, Depressed Regions and Needed Progress
(United Nations publication, Sales No. E.76.II.A.8).

[2]General Assembly resolution 3093 A (XXVIII) of 7 December 1973.
For a summary of this episode and a discussion of some of the
issues it raises, see Reduction of the Military Budgets of States
Permanent Members of the Security Council by 10 Per Cent and
Utilization of Part of the Funds thus Saved to Provide Assistance
to Developing Countries (United Nations publication, Sales No. E.
75.I.10).

[3]At the time the present paper was written, official estimates
(made by the United States Arms Control and Disarmament Agency)
were available for no later than 1974. Estimates of world
military expenditures for 1976 are necessarily rough because, in
addition to the usual difficulties caused by differences in the
amount of data countries publish and conceptual problems in
converting those data into a single common monetary denominator,
inherently arbitrary assumptions are required to allow for
inflation and increases in real costs since 1974. None the less,
it seems to us more useful to base the discussion on current
figures, although approximate, than to use the figures for 1974.

[4]As noted previously, this distribution of the disarmament
dividend is suggested in General Assembly resolution 3093 A
(XXVIII) of 7 December 1973.

[5]See especially, Reduction of the Military Budgets of States . . .
annex II.

[6]"Measurement and international reporting of military expenditures: report prepared by the Group of Experts on the Reduction
of Military Budgets" (A/31/222).

[7]An account of this incident is provided by Andrew J. Pierre,
"Limiting Soviet and American conventional forces", Survival,
March 1973, pp. 59-64.

[8]One thousand three hundred twenty is the number of missiles with
multiple warheads permitted under the Vladivostok accord; the

accord would permit a total of 2,400 strategic missile launchers and bombers.

[9]The calculations leading to the low end of the savings range assume that present modernization programmes (B-1 bomber, Trident submarine, and M-X ICBM) would not be affected by the new agreement until the late 1980s. They assume further that only land-based missiles (ICBMs) -- the least expensive system to operate -- would be disestablished in order to reach the lower total launcher limit. Under these assumptions United States strategic force would consist of 656 submarine launched missiles, about 400 bombers and 250 ICBMs. The calculations leading to the high end of the savings range assume that both the M-X and B-1 programmes would be drastically curtailed, and that the United Staets bomber force levels would be reduced to about 100 to meet the terms of the agreement.

[10]See, for example, Barry B. Blechman, The Control of Naval Armaments: Prospects and Possibilities (Washington, D. C., Brookings Institution, 1975).

[11]The Soviet Union typically maintains a total of 16-20 ships in the Indian Ocean, which operate from Soviet Pacific Fleet bases at Vladivostok and Petropavlovsk. A rough rule-of-thumb for the United States Navy is that it requires three ships in the inventory to maintain one ship continuously on station in a distant region. Applying this rule, the total cost (at 1976 United States prices) of the ships necessary to maintain the Soviet Indian Ocean Squadron is between $5 billion and $6 billion. Assuming a 20-year ship lifetime (and not allowing for discounting and similar factors), the Indian Ocean agreement might be said to represent annual shipbuilding savings of perhaps $300 million. Operating costs for this fleet are difficult to estimate, but savings probably would amount to another $200 million, at 1976 United States prices.

Disarmament in the Context of a New International Economic Order

SAM COLE

I. INTRODUCTION: THE WAR SYSTEM AND THE WORLD ECONOMY

The war system is an integral part of the world economic order which facilitates economic and political objectives through both the exercise or threat of war and the production of armaments. thus in any discussion of a just world economic order, the war system -- taken to be the actual set of interactions between military, political, and economic entities which exist within and between states -- cannot be neglected. Escalation in this system must be seen as a facilitating component of escalation in the global economic system as a whole. Nevertheless, in discussion of the NIEO there is a strong tendency not only to leave out questions of the use of war itself as an instrument of policy in conjunction with trade, aid, or technical co-operation, but even to omit discussion or the important role of armaments in the world economic system. Negotiations about armaments tend to be given separate fora, although in practical diplomacy (e.g. the US/Israel/Egypt peace talks) military and economic matters are intertwined.

Such separation of issues in multi-national discussions is not uncommon and usually serves to protect specific interests. While issues of political power at both domestic and international level are implicit in any economic negotiations, to the extent that these do surface they currently reflect concern about the international balance of power. Indeed, the fact that the fora for such discussion (e.g. UN agencies) are obliged to respect national sovereignty protects the interests of the national agents conducting the negotiation. It does this by focussing attention on the global hierarchy of nations and away from internal structures.

From **BULLETIN OF PEACE PROPOSALS**, Vol. 10, No. 3, 1979, (260-265), reprinted by permission of the publisher.

To the extent that these domestic interests are formalised it is in a superficial or peripheral manner, typified by the present campaign on human rights or by previous development policies.

The concept of a just NIEO must carry with it the idea of justice within countries as well as between them. But while there is agreement on the idea that the NIEO, seen as a set of revised global institutions, should reflect this ideal, there are quite contrasting images of what is meant by 'justice' held by different global interest groups, as to what this would mean for an NIEO and even more as to the mechanisms which would be needed to establish a new order. Ultimately these worldviews depend on different notions of human rights in the widest sense -- for example, individualistic versus collective images of human kind. The economic and moral rationale of different actors in the world system is integrally bound up with and dialectically related to their perceptions of the de facto economic and political conditions and desires for change. Thus the adaptation of existing perspectives and the evolution of new perspectives are seen as part of the continuing interactive process. Actors in the world system tend to adopt those rationalisations most directly relevant to their own and allied self-interest.

In many respects the reaction of actors in the world system to the present crisis poses more threats than opportunities for the achievement of a just world order, both within and between countries. The war system is bound up with the competition for worldwide economic growth. In particular, developing countries who can least afford such involvement are being increasingly drawn into this escalation. To ameliorate the effects of the present world crisis on their own economies the industrial countries are, through the export of armaments, shifting much of the burden onto developing countries.

As the industrial countries' markets are increasingly affected by exports from the South and even more so by increasingly differentiated competitiveness between the industrial countries, the importance of exporting arms to the least competitive industrial countries also increases. This has a very differentiated impact within the receiving countries; in addition to the ill affordable expenditure on weaponry, it reinforces repressive and inegalitarian regimes in those countries. Unable to resolve their own internal structural problems, industrial countries are exporting inequality to the South.

Developing countries are being trapped into a process which is economically almost entirely to the advantage of and largely controlled by the industrial countries. Furthermore, it is directly to the advantage of a wider spectrum of the population of the industrial countries. In developing countries it is of advantage economically only indirectly to specific interests. Further, as middle-range developing countries increasingly manufacture and export armaments, so will the burden be pushed systematically down onto the least wealthy in the poorer countries.

As this process continues, technological sophistication in weaponry becomes increasingly important for monopoly of trade in armaments and to the preservation of the military superiority of the North. Through judicious marketing a perceived need is

exaggerated. Product differentiation and innovation become paramount to the manufactures, but because the interests of the state are affected the economic risk for this is carried by national economies. R & D becomes oriented strongly in the direction of 'national security', and technical progress is rapid. Weapons systems become rapidly obsolete. Thus even in the absence of a serious external threat (although the perception of a threat is central to the system) the escalation of weapons systems has a momentum of its own as part of a competition for both relative and absolute economic growth.

Although this takes place against a background of ideological conflict, in an international perspective this conflict provides, in part, only a rationalisation for intervention and manipulation of economic systems to the advantage of the dominant groups, permitting them to regulate and maintain the economic gap between the North and South.

II. SELECTIVE DELINKING FROM THE ARMAMENTS SYSTEM

Industrial countries have become locked into a dynamic of military build up, which now increasingly involves developing countries, and which systematically distorts technological and economic development in all countries. Industrial countries have a strong economic as well as political interest in involving developing countries in the arms race, and as such they may manipulate political and other differences between developing countries to their own advantage. Developing countries are not innocent in this exercise but in seeking economic and political, domestic and international advantage they become locked into an external dynamic. By aggravating a credible threat the industrial countries of East and West attempt to create for themselves a mutually beneficial system of 'divide and rule' based on sophisticated moralistic rationalisations which destroy the possibility of economic linking between neighbouring developing countries and ensure that they remain oriented toward the centre. This build-up of armaments through the present crisis links with the deepening of internal repression in developing and industrial countries, usually serving to rigidify existing inegalitarian and unjust structures.

Injustice in the world is most acute for and in the developing countries (although not uniformly so). To state this is not to overlook the fact that the history of injustice and atrocity by and in the industrial countries even in recent years has exceeded anything of which the developing countries could be accused. Indeed it is exactly the memory and fear of occurrence of such history that motivates to some degree the trade in arms. A just international economic order should be directed to the relief of current injustice as well as to seeking a global peace in the long run. But it is unlikely that present injustice will be relieved by any superficial means. Minor changes to trade agreements or small

amounts of aid are unlikely to have significant impact, and a NIEO
conceived in these terms may only reproduce a variation of the
present world order. For reasons given earlier, small changes are
in many cases as likely to have a deleterious impact not only on
internal income distribution in many developing countries, but on
the overall relative economic well-being of those countries.

If the domestic order in developing countries were to be
changed, the arguments for economic and military links with the
central countries under the present world order would be
diminished. Present arrangements serve to support the existing
power structure and the interests of the industrial countries; they
have a much more marginal benefit to populations at large. Present
development is focused away from the interests of the mass of the
populations and towards the centre. In this respect, the arguments
of the proponents of collective self-reliance become persuasive.

This is not to say that trade, aid, and technological
cooperation in a wide sense with industrial countries is not
advantageous to developing countries. In furtherance of a just
order, external economic relations are best seen as a component of
a development strategy which focuses on internal restructuring of
economies. In the present system, income growth and distribution
within and between countries are intimately linked through markets
and the division of labour. Changes in the system of production in
the North affect distribution and growth in the South, and vice
versa. Because the production of armaments has become an integral
part of this system, it follows that international disarmament too
must be considered in the light of its domestic effects and
unlinked from them for both economic and political reasons. The
possibilities for the selective delinking of the Southern countries
from the North, particularly from the armaments system, or a
genuine restructuring of North-South economic relations, may appear
limited: nevertheless, within the playing out of the present
crisis there may be important opportunities.

III. DISARMAMENT IN A MULTI-POLAR WORLD

Although the outcome of the crisis is unclear, significant
restructuring seems inevitable. A re-establishing of the previous
patterns of dominance is unlikely. Even if the United States
remains as the most powerful world actor, the economic and
political power of its allies is likely to shift dramatically. Of
many possible scenarios, that most widely canvassed for the medium
run is the emergence of a multi-polar system in both the capitalist
and socialist worlds. These would include 'unholy' alliances both
within and between them, based as much on economic and strategic
convenience as on ideological commitment. The stronger developing
countries are as likely to ally with the central countries as with
their weaker neighbours. In its present mood, the United States
seems prepared to play a more humane role, while the Soviet Union's
interests have systematically progressed relative to the US on the

world scene. The European powers who, in the long run, most need to enter into equal collaboration with the developing countries seem unable to throw off their colonialist heritage. In the process of change, however, the ideological basis of these countries will systematically shift. A tendency to world socialism or at least to a significantly different type of capitalism may emerge. In resisting this, capitalist regimes in both industrial and developing countries will deepen the levels of repression employed. Ironically, these techniques are often matched by the regimes which ultimately replace them, and conflicts between adjacent socialist countries are a significant feature of the contemporary world.

From the earlier discussion it is not difficult to devise scenarios of global escalation. It is less easy to discover routes to justice and disarmament, although one may well be found in the course of evolving towards an increasingly multi-polar world.

Although it might reflect a tendency to a less hegemonic and internationally more just world order, a multi-polar world clearly carries with it many dangers. First, the technological competition in weaponry may accelerate. Human ingenuity, given the opportunity, can be expected to upgrade weapons systematically across the whole spectrum. New biological, genetic, and psychological techniques more selective in their application may be added to the chemical and physical. Like the neutron bomb, these may reflect the dominant ideology of their creators. A further danger is that in a multi-polar world, with disputes on many fronts and no well-defined ultimate arbiters, global institutions will be quite unable to cope with the increased level of complexity. Faced with a series of simultaneous confrontations, nations are more likely to become trapped in a series of contradictions irresolvable through negotiation. The already high rate of international warfare may increase and with it the probability of 'all out' global war.

It is admittedly difficult to envisage the complete elimination of weapons. However, it is imperative that the level of armaments be lowered substantially if the threat of global holocaust is to be eliminated and if progressive egalitarian change is to be achieved.

Ironically, in the long run, a multi-polar world offers the most likely structure for a just world order through some global federal structure based on diverse cultural, historical, and economic groupings. In these, national or even geographical boundaries would have no necessary role. Whether under an individualist or collectivist philosophy, such divisions might respect the best aspects of both with a concern for human welfare within and across groupings. This new structure, unlike existing institutions, would not promote the linking of hierarchical power interests across ideologies and countries through the creation of mass insecurity and a sense of aggressive group identity.

To raise such an image in the face of seemingly impossible short-run constraints is to provide at least a direction to negotiation and to some extent to neutralise short term political expedience. To evolve rules for the basis and dynamic operation of such a system requires, if not the unravelling of several thousand

years of history, at least an understanding of it, and probably a
good deal of future painful experiment and experience as well. The
problem ultimately becomes one of an ideology for an NIEO. One
must define a long-term goal for distribution and to set up an
adaptive system which can permit people to achieve, protect, and
develop their own interests.

IV. A 'BASIC NEEDS' DEFENSE SYSTEM

     Development towards a more equal structure could have a
tendency to push weapons production in the direction of either
aggression or defence. The former is more likely if the major
powers take an aggressive stance towards their diminishing status.
It is possible, however, that if military research and development
were oriented strongly towards genuine defence, a de-escalatory
route would be both economically more efficient and more effective
in protecting lives and property.
     As with the present system, a new world order may have a
tendency to develop self-reinforcing cycles of inequality and
oppression. Indeed, there may be a 'natural' tendency for
political and economic systems to become more inegalitarian. It
follows that an egalitarian system, however 'just', may be unstable
and may require policing of the status quo and systematic
correctives. But if a weapons system is required at all, it should
be oriented only to defence and the policing of equality.
     The irony of the situation is that if the purpose of war and
the threat of war is to maintain a world hierarchy, it is the
relative level rather than the absolute level of destructive power
which is important. It is the systematic attempt to change the
international or even the internal order of countries which creates
the ratchet of escalation. Since the order must be changed, the
question of the role of conflict and armaments remains.
     Again, if one considers the (Utopian) end of the story, the
role of weapons systems may be deduced. What is required is the
exploration of the concept of a basic needs defence system
analogous to the concept of 'basic needs' for food, shelter, and
political development. That is, a defence which would allow people
as individuals and groups which would allow them to protect their
own interests yet not destroy the rights of others. A most
important factor is that the more truly egalitarian a global
society, the more likely it is that low-level weaponry would
suffice. Conversely, the greater the inequalities and the
concentrations of wealth, the higher will be the corresponding
levels of armaments.

V. PAPER, STONE AND KNIFE

One answer to the question of how to develop toward and maintain a just world order may lie in the childhood game of paper, stone, or knife -- albeit with a change in rules. As the experience of anticolonialist and other liberation movements has shown, passive resistance (paper) or guerilla-type activities (knife) can often manage to overthrow alien or unwanted regimes, possessing even the most sophisticated 'blunt instrument' weapons (stone). In many respects, the escalated scale of current armaments, exemplified by nuclear weapons but also including many 'conventional' devices, has no function against such opposition. As a consequence, unwanted regimes turn themselves further to propaganda and torture in order to counteract alienation and terrorism. In principle, the desirable situation to be created is one in which it is simply not possible to occupy or repress a country or people against its wishes. As the experiences of anti-colonial liberation movements shown, this appears often to be the case although the suffering in the process has been lengthy and intense.

Given the frequency of international and civil wars in the 'post-war' era, it would be foolish to expect elimination of war or armaments in the foreseeable future. The most conflict-free route is likely to emerge through the reformist prescription of negation and education outlined earlier. That path may certainly not be the most rapid; it may even have an inherent tendency to stagnate without continuous provocation. But if this is to be the route to emerge, then a pattern of thinking which permits change has to be established.

VI. VALUES AND OBJECTIVES

The achievement of this will require a return to base: first, in the sense of a better understanding of different values and perspectives held by world actors and second, in terms of a clearer understanding of long term objectives. To the extent that a separation can be made between means and ends, there is probably more universal agreement on the latter as presently expressed in the various world views. The process of negotiation may be identified in the following stages:

(i) To understand points of view and objectives, including one's own, particularly the relationships between liberty and equality in theories stressing the rights of individuals versus the collective; not to assume that one's own system of values is the best for all people or even for oneself; to understand the implications of one's own actions and theories for others (for example, current trade prescriptions in the interaction between Northern and Southern countries).

(ii) To try to identify what should happen in both the long run and the short run if one were treating all human interests equally in the light of (i) above. In the application of human rights policies, for example, the question may be put more acutely, as to what should happen if there were no self-interest on the part of the actors pursuing the policy. This may require new theories and new models of development. For example, liberals might be persuaded that redistribution before growth would create a market structure more compatible with growth, that developing countries should be encouraged to create monopoly markets for themselves, that the present power structure in capitalist developing or even industrial countries does not present the mass of people with great liberty or the highest social welfare, given even the most flexible assumptions about the impossibility of comparing satisfactions between individuals. Radicals similarly may accept some trade-offs between the pace and the pain of change. For the reformist path (i.e. minimal violence, negotiated) to work, such acceptance is necessary.

(iii) To ask what disinterested intervention at an international level would consist of or whether indeed any external action can further stated goals. Selectivity and disinterestedly used NIEO type proposals on trade, aid, technological assistance and financing could be crucial to the pace of development. But given no internal structural change, such policies may only reinforce present patterns. Thus 'liberals' may question whether they should not be supporting liberation movements or embryonic regimes rather than established power structures. Certainly they and others should question the merits of producing and exporting increasing volumes of armaments and culturally crippling production systems.

(iv) To identify self-interest, particularly the need to protect national security and economy in the short run. Clearly here the build-up of weapons as a threat and the advantages and disadvantages of weapons production have to be identified. It has to be asked whether the development of socialism worldwide is counter to all centre country interests, or only to certain establishment interests.

(v) Finally, there must be an attempt to reconcile interest at both the social and international level.

VII. SUMMARY

The production of armaments is systematically bound up with the competitions for worldwide economic growth. Industrial countries are locked into a dynamic of military build-up which distorts technological and economic development in all countries.

Unable to resolve their own internal structural problems, industrial countries are exporting, through the arms trade, inequality and injustice to the developing world. Developing countries are not innocent in this exercise, but in seeking

economic and political advantage, domestically and internationally they have become locked into an external dynamic. In justifying the build-up of arms and exports to developing countries, the industrial countries employ a series of self-interested arguments to rationalise their continued economic and political influence over developing countries.

It follows from the above that in working through the possibilities for a NIEO, the role of the war system -- the set of interactions between military, political and economic entities which exist within and between states -- must be taken into account far more explicitly than is presently the case in discussions about the NIEO. Neither can the complex of self-interested and moralistic rationalisation and the conflicting underlying perspectives upon development of different world actors be ignored if a workable or 'just' NIEO is to be achieved.

These key features of the relationship between the war system and the political economies of industrial and developing countries structure alternative possibilities for future development. Coupled with the present arms build-up, a tendency toward a 'multi-polar' military and economic world poses several dangers, although it could be the basis of a trend to a less threatening and more equal world order. While it is difficult to envisage the complete elimination of weapons, the level of armaments must be lowered substantially. The more truly egalitarian that global society is, the more likely it is that low-level weaponry would suffice to permit groups and nations to defend their interests yet not destroy those of others. In this paper, some prerequisites for a trend in this direction have been explored.

The Second Disarmament Decade

OLU ADENIJI

I. INTRODUCTION

In writing about the Second Disarmament Decade, it is essential to make a brief historical recollection of the genesis of Disarmament Decades. Obviously when the United Nations took up disarmament where the League of Nations left it, the main preoccupation was the reduction of armaments, not general and complete disarmament. Any idea of phasing the time required into decades was not an immediate factor. The League of Nations' Conference for the Reduction and Limitation of Armaments 1932-35 was primarily concerned with an immediate agreement on a Treaty for the control of armaments. This agreement was to have emerged from the Conference itself and be implemented as soon as the Treaty was signed and ratified by the requisite number of Parties.

The same attitude to the possible control of armaments was carried over to the efforts of the years immediately after the Second World War. This was reflected in the provisions of the Charter of the United Nations. Article 26 of the Charter provides that the Security Council shall be responsible for formulating, with the assistance of the Military Staff Committee plans to be submitted to members of the United Nations for the establishment of a system for the regulation of armaments. Article 47 lists one of the functions of the Military Staff Committee as being to advise and assist the Security Council on the regulation of armaments and possible disarmament.

It was not until 1959 that the United Nations set the basic goal of all its efforts in relation to armaments as general and complete disarmament. After discussion of the item on the Agenda

From **THE ARMS RACE AND DISARMAMENT**, UNESCO Press, 1982, (271-288), reprinted by permission of the publisher.

of the XIVth Session entitled General and Complete Disarmament, the
General Assembly on November 20, 1959 adopted resolution 1378 (XIV)
the essential elements of which are as follows:

The General Assembly

Considering that the question of general and complete
disarmament is the most important one facing the world
today,

Expresses the hope that measures leading towards the goal
of general and complete disarmament under effective
international control will be worked out in detail and
agreed upon in the shortest possible time.

The national and international impact of disarmament became
the focus of attention in the General Assembly following the
adoption of this resolution. Though there was no immediate
agreement on ways and means of carrying it out (as interpretations
differ) it is worthy to note that in the joint Soviet -- United
States statement of Agreed Principles issued in 1961 as a basis for
disarmament negotiations, the first principle stated:

the goal of negotiations is to achieve agreement on a
programme which will ensure that disarmament is general
and complete and war is no longer an instrument for
settling international problems.

The machinery created for negotiation in the following year,
the Eighteen Nation Disarmament Committee, was immediately faced
with two draft Treaties on general and complete disarmament,
proposed by the Soviet Union and the United States respectively.
Both drafts envisaged the accomplishment of general and complete
disarmament in less than ten years, phased into three stages. The
difference in approach evident in the two drafts made immediate
reconciliation impossible and no progress was therefore made in the
negotiation. An alternative approach of negotiation in stages
began to emerge following the impasse on negotiating a treaty on
general and complete disarmament. It was in the context of arms
control negotiations that proposals were first made in the Eighteen
Nation Disarmament Committee for the adoption of "an organic
disarmament programme" and for the "proclamation of a United
Nations Disarmament Decade 1970-1980".

II. UNITED NATIONS DISARMAMENT DECADE: SECRETARY-GENERAL'S COMMENTS AND PROPOSAL

The Secretary-General of the United Nations, U Thant, formally
brought the idea of the Disarmament Decade to the attention of the
General Assembly. In the customary introduction to his annual

report on the work of the United Nations 1968-79, U Thant expressed
grave concern at the ever escalating arms race, the continued
stockpiling of both nuclear and conventional weapons and the
continued growth of military expenditure. The world, he said,
stood at a most critical crossroads. It could either pursue the
arms race at a terrible price to the security and progress of the
peoples of the world, or it could move ahead towards the goal of
general and complete disarmament, a goal that was set in 1959 by a
unanimous decision of the General Assembly on the eve of the decade
of the 1960s. He went on to observe that the diversion of enormous
resources and energy both human and material from peaceful economic
and social pursuits to unproductive and uneconomic military
purposes was an important factor in the failure to make greater
progress in the advancement of the developing countries during the
First United Nations Development Decade. It was his belief that
should the world decide to reverse the trend of the arms race and
move towards the goal of general and complete disarmament, the
security, the economic well-being, and the progress not only of the
developing countries, but also of the developed countries and of
the entire world would be tremendously enhanced.

Secretary-General U Thant then made a proposal:

"I would accordingly propose that the Members of the
United nations decide to dedicate the decade of the 1970s
which has already been designated as the Second United
Nations Development Decade as a Disarmament Decade. I
would hope that the members of the General Assembly could
establish a specific programme and timetable for dealing
with all aspects of the problem of arms control and
disarmament..."

The Secretary-General's proposal received wide support in the
General Assembly. In its resolution 2499 (XXIV) 31 October 1969,
concerning the celebration of the 25th anniversary of the United
Nations, the Assembly endorsed the proclamation of a Disarmament
Decade to coincide with the Second United Nations Development
Decade and entrusted the competent bodies of the Organization with
the task of presenting concrete proposals to the General Assembly
at its 25th Session.

On 16 December 1969, the General Assembly adopted resolution
2602E (XXIV) by which it:

1. Declares the decade of the 1970s a Disarmament
   Decade;

2. Calls upon Governments to intensify without delay
   their concerted and concentrated efforts for
   effective measures relating to the cessation of the
   nuclear arms race at an early date and to nuclear
   disarmament and the elimination of other weapons of
   mass destruction, and for a treaty on general and
   complete disarmament under strict and effective
   international control.

The resolution further requested the Conference of the Committee on Disarmament to work out a Comprehensive Programme of Disarmament, and recommended that consideration be given to channelling a substantial portion of the savings as a result of disarmament measures into economic and social programmes.

III. REVIEW OF THE FIRST DISARMAMENT DECADE

In retrospect, the experiment of the Disarmament Decade for the 1970s failed to achieve its objectives, just as the Second Development Decade was a failure. Though this was the period of detente, which witnessed improved relations between the United States and the Soviet Union, all the hope that this improved climate would manifest itself in the area of arms limitation and disarmament failed to materialize. In 1972, the Soviet Union and the United States of America signed the SALT I agreement, with an undertaking to begin negotiations on SALT II. As it turned out these negotiations were protracted and SALT II was not signed until June 1979. However, it has not been put into force and the chances are very slim that it will be ratified by the American side.

As for multilateral negotiations on disarmament, little progress was made. Through the agreement reached in 1969, the ENDC became the 26-member Conference of the Committee on Disarmament. Throughout the 1970s, the Committee concluded negotiations on only three instruments, namely, the Treaty on the Prohibition of the Emplacement of Nuclear Weapons and other Weapons of Mass Destruction on the Sea-bed and Ocean floor and in the Sub soil thereof (1971); the convention on the Prohibition of the Development, Production and Stockpiling of Bacteriological (Biological) and Toxin weapons and on their destruction (1972); and the Convention on the Prohibition of Military or any other Hostile Use of Environmental Modification Techniques (1977).

Meanwhile the results of military research and development were increasingly evident in the production and deployment of nuclear weapons of greater yield and vastly improved accuracy. Concentration by the multilateral negotiating body on collateral measures in the circumstances was an indication of the powerlessness of that body under the joint United States/Soviet Union control as co-chairmen. Though the one specific element of the Declaration required the Conference of the Committee for Disarmament to work out a Comprehensive Programme of Disarmament, no agreement was reached on the nature of this assignment until 1979 when the Committee set up a Working Group. As there was no substantial measure of disarmament put into effect, there could not have been any diversion of savings to economic and social purposes. Rather, military expenditures grew in constant 1978 prices from 375 billion US dollars to $445 billion during the course of the decade.

IV. FIRST SPECIAL SESSION ON DISARMAMENT

The anxiety of the Non Aligned Countries over the escalating arms race, and their distress at the seeming unwillingness of the superpowers to embark on serious disarmament negotiations, led to the call for the convening of a Special Session of the General Assembly devoted to disarmament. Held from 23 May to 1 July 1978 at the United nations headquarters, the first Special Session devoted to disarmament (Tenth General Assembly Special Session) was quick to deliver a verdict on the Disarmament Decade of the 1970s. In its Final Document the Special Session observed:

"the Disarmament Decade solemnly declared in 1969 by the United Nations is coming to end. Unfortunately, the objectives established on that occasion by the General Assembly appear to be as far away today as they were then, or even further because the arms race is not diminishing but increasing and outstrips by far the efforts to curb it. While it is true that some limited agreements have been reached, 'effective measures relating to the cessation of the arms race at an early date and to nuclear disarmament' continue to elude man's grasp".

The Special Session did not, however, decide upon a follow-up to the Disarmament Decade which was then coming to an end. Any indication of a time frame for the implementation of the Programme of Action agreed upon at the Special Session was couched in vague terms thus: "the present Programme of Action enumerates the specific measures of disarmament which should be implemented over the next few years". A few months after the Special Session, during the 33rd regular session of the General Assembly, an initiative was taken under the regular item "Effective measures to implement the purposes and objectives of the Disarmament Decade". That item had, since 1975, provided the General Assembly with an opportunity to underline the need for the elaboration of the Comprehensive Programme of Disarmament. At the 33rd Session of the General Assembly, however, on the initiative of some Non-Aligned countries, the resolution 33/62, adopted under the item contained an additional element in its para. 3:

"Takes note of the preparations for the third United Nations Development Decade and stresses the need to continue to promote the link between the strategy for disarmament and the strategy for development in view of the close relationship between disarmament and development affirmed by the General Assembly at its Tenth Special Session".

In the final paragraph of the same resolution, the General Assembly decided to include in the provisional agenda of its 34th Session an item entitled "Consideration of the declaration of the

1980s as a disarmament decade".

Opinion in the General Assembly on the Declaration of another Disarmament Decade was by no means unanimously favourable. There were many representatives who expressed doubt as to the usefulness of another "Decade", which would raise expectations that in the end might not be fulfilled. Behind such arguments lay the reluctance to set a deadline for the achievement of specific disarmament measures, evident in the course of the negotiations of the Final Document of the Special Session on Disarmament. They opposed the fixing of the target dates for such highly sensitive and very complicated negotiations in the field of disarmament as being unrealistic and counter-productive. These arguments were to be repeated again during the negotiations of the Elements of the Declaration of the 1980s as the Second United Nations Disarmament Decade by the United Nations Disarmament Commission in 1979.

The overwhelming majority of members, however, were in favour of a second Disarmament Decade. The Non-Aligned countries were particularly anxious to press forward the inter-relationship between disarmament and development, notwithstanding the denial of such link by some militarily significant states. The lack of progress in attaining the objectives of the Disarmament Decade in the 1970s was seen by the Non-Aligned as the result of the lack of political will to reverse the trend of the arms race by the military alliances. The same lack of political will could be discerned as the major obstacle to progress in the implementation of the objectives and the targets of the Second Development Decade. Though the target of the Decade on the transfer of resources in the form of Official Development Assistance was fixed at 0.7 per cent of GNP of each developed country, this figure was not met by the overwhelming majority of those countries. Average annual resources available for multilateral development assistance, as reflected in pledges to the United Nations Development Programme, were $250 million, which represented little more than the average military expenditure every 6 hours during the course of the Decade. As long as military spending escalated, the chances would continue to be severely diminished. Disarmament Decades would therefore continue to be relevant as one of the contributory factors to development on a universal basis.

V. CONSIDERATION AT THE 34TH GENERAL ASSEMBLY

At its 34th Session in 1979, the General Assembly had a fuller exchange of views on the Disarmament Decade under the item: Consideration of the declaration of the 1980s as the Second Disarmament Decade. The reservations of the previous year on the necessity for another decade had by and large given way to widespread support of the proposal as an important element in the strategy for disarmament. By resolution 34/75 adopted on 11 December 1979 the General Assembly:

1. Decides to declare the decade of the 1980s as the
    Second Disarmament Decade.

2. Directs the Disarmament Commission at its substantive
    Session in 1980 to prepare elements of a draft
    resolution entitled Declaration of the 1980s as the
    Second Disarmament Decade and submit them to the
    General Assembly at its 35th Session for
    consideration and adoption.

3. Determines that the Draft resolution should embody
    inter alia an indication of targets during the Second
    Disarmament Decade for accomplishing the major
    objectives and goals of disarmaments as well as ways
    and means of mobilizing world public opinion in this
    regard.

The terms of reference given the United Nations Disarmament
Commission in resolution 34/75 showed several departures from the
procedure for the declaration of the First Disarmament Decade. The
General Assembly was determined that the declaration of the 1980s
should embody an indicative programme of measures to be
accomplished during the decade. Moreover, it was clearly indicated
that in addition to the negotiating process which remains the
primary means of progress in disarmament, due importance is also to
be given to mobilizing world public opinion through education and
information. The Special Session on Disarmament (10th UNGA Special
Session 1978) had given recognition to the role which public
awareness of the true nature of, and the danger implicit in the
arms race could play in making world opinion at large aware of the
necessity for disarmament. Indeed, paragraphs 99-108 of the Final
Document of the Special Session listed a number of measures aimed
at mobilizing world public opinion in favour of disarmament. Among
such measures were:

    call on governmental and non-governmental information
    organs and those of the United Nations and its
    Specialized Agencies to give priority to the preparation
    and distribution of printed and audio-visual material
    relating to the danger represented by the armaments race
    as well as to the disarmament efforts;

    call on the United Nations Centre for Disarmament and
    UNESCO to intensify their activities in the presentation
    of information, in facilitating research and publication
    on disarmament;

    call on Governments, governmental and non-governmental
    organizations, to develop programmes of education for
    disarmament and peace studies at all levels;

    call on UNESCO to step up its programmes aimed at the
    development of disarmament education as a distinct field
    study;

establishment by the United Nations of a programme of
fellowships on disarmament "in order to promote expertise
in disarmament in more member states, particularly in the
developing countries."

VI. THE DECLARATION

The negotiations for the Declaration took place in the United
Nations Disarmament Commission at its May 1980 session. Two
approaches were noticeable in the written views submitted by
members on possible elements for the Declaration. One approach
sought to make governments undertake binding commitment to
undertake negotiations and conclude instruments on specific
disarmament issues to be identified in the Declaration. such
activities would be phased during the decade, earmarking those to
be completed in the first half and those for the second half. The
priority issue of nuclear disarmament was particularly stressed,
and discernible progress was to be made in the first half of the
Decade on specific and identified areas. The second approach
sought to identify only in general terms those measures on which
negotiations should continue or commerce without a prior commitment
as to their conclusion. Naturally, according to this latter view
there could be no prior fixing of the time for the completion of
the negotiation, nor could there be a phasing of the items during
the decade. The proponents of this view believed that the fixing
of a timeframe would be unrealistic in light of the many
imponderables that affect disarmament negotiations, such as the
complexity of any given negotiation, the issue of verification, and
the international situation, especially the political relationship
between the two superpowers. Given such complexities, rigid
targets would only result in unfulfilled expectations. On the
other hand, it was argued that while rigidity certainly ought to be
avoided, it was necessary, for the guidance of negotiators, to
provide a time frame within which they would be expected to
conclude negotiations of specific items. Moreover, it was argued
that the indication of such a timeframe would be a sign of the
commitment of states to make substantive progress in the field of
disarmament. The difference between the Programme of Action of the
Special Session on Disarmament (10th UNGA Special Session 1978) and
the activities of the Decade should lie in part in the timeframe.
While there was no specific timeframe designated for the
implementation of the former, the latter was to be over a ten year
period. Within the overall period, it should be possible to
envisage the phasing of negotiations in such a manner that there
would be a continuous flow of activities throughout the decade. As
will be seen later, a compromise was forged between the two
positions.

A marked novel feature of the Declaration of the Second
Disarmament Decade is that it took the form of a strategy for
disarmament in the period of the 1980s, similar to the strategy for

development. While therefore avoiding a duplication of the Final Document of the Special Session on Disarmament, it nevertheless was elaborated as a self-contained document complete with its own Introduction, Goals and Principles, Activities, and Review and Appraisal Mechanism. Naturally, it is not as extensive as the Programme of Action of the Final Document of the Special Session on Disarmament; it would have been unrealistic if it were to assume that all the elements for the accomplishment of general and complete disarmament could be completed in the 1980s. Nevertheless, it went far beyond the very modest declaration for the 1970s as contained in resolution 2602(e) (XXIV), which left the decision on issues to be negotiated to states themselves, with very little guidance.

The strategy for the Second Disarmament Decade is divided into four parts. The introductory part needs no comments. The second part deals with Principles and Goals. In order to avoid a repetition of the lengthy negotiations during the preparatory stages, as well as at the Special Session on Disarmament, on the Principles that should govern disarmament negotiations, the Declaration of the 1980s confined itself to a reaffirmation of those Principles. Within the overall objective of general and complete disarmament under effective international control, the specific goals set for the Second Disarmament Decade are five-fold:

i.   Halting and reversing the arms race, particularly the nuclear arms race.

ii. The conclusion and implementation of effective agreements which will contribute significantly to the achievement of general and complete disarmament under effective international control.

iii. Development on an equitable basis of the limited results obtained in the field of disarmament in the 1970s in accordance with the provisions of the Final Document of the Special Session devoted to Disarmament.

iv. Strengthening international peace and security in accordance with the Charter of the United Nations.

v.   Making available a substantial part of the resources released by disarmament measures to promote the attainment of the objectives of the Third United Nations Development Decade and in particular the economic and social development of developing countries so as to accelerate the progress towards the New International Economic Order.

VII. ACTIVITIES IN THE SECOND DECADE

The activities earmarked for the Decade include both those to be negotiated in the multilateral disarmament forum -- the Committee on Disarmament -- as well as those negotiations of a bilateral, regional or multilateral nature conducted outside the Committee on disarmament. This was to emphasize the essential unity of disarmament negotiations irrespective of the forum. Thus Part III of the Declaration began as follows:

"The decade of the 1980s should witness renewed intensification by all Governments and the United Nations of their efforts to reach agreement and to implement effective measures that will lead to discernible progress towards the goal of general and complete disarmament under effective international control. In this connection, special attention should be focussed on certain identifiable elements in the Programme of Action as adopted by the General Assembly at its Tenth Special Session which should as a minimum be accomplished during the Second Disarmament Decade both through negotiations in the multilateral negotiating forum, the Committee on Disarmament, and in other appropriate forums...".

Though consensus could not be reached on the proposal to group the measures to be accomplished during the decade into those for the first half up to 1985 and those for the following second half, it was possible nevertheless to indicate some degree of priority as well as a timeframe for accomplishment, albeit in a flexible manner. Thus, the first identifiable period can be said to be 1980-82, the latter year being the year when the Second Special Session devoted to disarmament will be held. The elaboration of the blueprint for disarmament, the Comprehensive Programme for Disarmament, was placed first on the list of measures to be accomplished during the decade. It is a mark of the importance attached to the Comprehensive Programme that it is the only measure for which "a rigid timeframe", was accepted. It is to be completed and adopted in 1982 during the Second Special Session on disarmament. The programme is to encompass all measures thought to be advisable in order to ensure "that the goal of general and complete disarmament under effective international control becomes a reality in a world in which international peace and security prevail and in which the new international economic order is strengthened and consolidated..."

The first group of concrete disarmament measures identified as worthy of priority negotiations by the multilateral negotiating organ ought to have belonged to the same category as the Comprehensive Programme of Disarmament. However, owing to objections on the fixing of a rigid timetable, these measures were recommended as those whose accomplishment would create a very favourable international climate for the second Special Session of the General assembly devoted to disarmament. "All efforts should

be exerted therefore by the Committee on Disarmament urgently to negotiate with a view to reaching agreement, and to submit agreed texts where possible before the second special session devoted to disarmament." Such measures are:

(a) a comprehensive nuclear test ban treaty;

(b) a treaty on the prohibition of the development, production and stockpiling of all chemical weapons and on their destruction;

(c) convention on radiological weapons;

(d) security assurances to non-nuclear weapon states against use or threat of use of nuclear weapons

These are measures of a basic character, that have been under negotiation in the multilateral negotiating body, the Conference of the Committee on Disarmament (CCD) and its successor, the Committee on Disarmament (CD). Considering the many detailed studies that have been carried out, and the equally detailed discussions that have been held on some of these subjects, it was the opinion of many that their early conclusion might well determine the will of states, particularly the militarily significant states to achieve concrete disarmament results in the decade of the 1980s. A particularly sensitive area in the decade will be the issue of nuclear proliferation. It is now obvious that the most important element in the nuclear non-proliferation regime -- the Non-Proliferation Treaty (NPT) -- has been under severe pressure both by Parties and Non-Parties alike. Its essentially discriminatory nature, its "approval" of the possession of nuclear weapons, and the lack of progress in steps for nuclear disarmament, are some of the criticisms made of the NPT. The failure of the Parties to the Treaty to agree on a document at the Second Review Conference in August 1980 was a manifestation of the wide crack that has appeared in the NPT wall.

At the same time reports that various countries are on the threshold of nuclear weapon capability have persisted. In the case of one of such countries -- South Africa -- it was known to have made detailed preparations for exploding a nuclear device in 1977, and believed to have actually detonated one in 1979. In view of these pressures, the need for early progress in developing an international consensus of ways and means to prevent the proliferation of nuclear weapons becomes urgent. It is in this context that the importance and priority nature attached to the Comprehensive Nuclear Test Ban Treaty emerges. It will, on the one hand, make a significant contribution to the aim of ending the further refinement of nuclear weapons and expansion of the stockpile, as well as the development of new types of such weapons. On the other hand, it will prevent the proliferation of nuclear weapons by providing an egalitarian alternative to those countries that have stayed outside the regime of the NPT because of the complaint of its discriminatory character. Even if the Comprehensive Test Ban Treaty cannot by itself alone sustain a Non

Proliferation regime for the 1980s, it will be a more reliable first element for Nuclear Non Proliferation. The political will of the nuclear weapon states is the one crucial missing element in the conclusion of the Treaty. Once that will is demonstrated, this basic but crucial measure can be accomplished early in the decade of the 1980s.

Side by side with the priority instrument under negotiation in the multilateral negotiating forum, the disarmament strategy for the 1980s lists a number of measures on which equally early progress should be made and which are either being negotiated on a bilateral or regional level or, having been already negotiated, are yet to be brought fully into force. These measures are:

Ratification of the Strategic Arms Limitation Treaty (SALT II) signed by the United States and the Soviet Union in 1979.

Negotiations by the United States and the Soviet Union of further limitation of Strategic Arms to result in SALT III.

Strengthening of the Treaty for the Prohibition of Nuclear Weapons in Latin America (Treaty of Tlatelolco) through the ratification of its Additional Protocol I.

Signature and Ratification of the Treaty and Protocols adopted by the United Nations Conference on Prohibitions or Restrictions of use of certain Conventional Weapons which may be deemed to be excessively Injurious or to have Indiscriminate Effects. The Protocols relate to Fragments not detectable by X-rays, Mines and Booby Traps and Incendiary Weapons.

Agreement on Mutual and Balanced Reduction of Arms and Armed Forces in Central Europe.

It is natural that at the top of the list of these measures is the SALT process. Notwithstanding the SALT I agreement concluded in 1972, and the undertaking to negotiate SALT II, both the United States and the Soviet Union took major steps in the development and deployment of strategic nuclear weapons in the 1970s. Given the growing danger represented by these weapons in the light of their greatly improved accuracy as well as explosive yield, the negotiations for their limitation attracted universal interest. The Special Session on Disarmament held by the United Nations General Assembly in 1978 devoted considerable attention to the SALT process. The consensus reached was reflected in paragraph 52 of its Final Document which called upon the USSR and the United States of America to conclude at the earliest possible date their talks on SALT II. The two Powers were invited to follow SALT II promptly by further negotiations on strategic arms limitation "leading to agreed significant reductions of, and qualitative limitations on strategic arms."

The signing of SALT II in 1979 was greeted with some relief

world-wide, notwithstanding the doubts raised in many quarters about its immediate value for limitation of strategic arms. The subsequent refusal by the new American Administration to ratify it, and the gigantic modernization proposals for the 1980s, open the prospect for another round of the strategic weapons race. The important place accorded to negotiations on this category of weapons has become all the most justified. Concerted international pressure is therefore necessary to ensure early resumption of these negotiations with a view to a real limitation of strategic weapons. A related area concerns theatre nuclear weapons in Europe. The deployment of the Soviet SS-20 missiles and the consequent NATO decision to deploy new American cruise and Pershing missiles, open the possibility of a dangerous escalation of the nuclear confrontation in Europe. Commencement of negotiations in the early years of the Second Disarmament Decade may yet obviate the necessity for another round of competition which obviously the Europeans wish to avoid.

The final list of measures "to be pursued as rapidly as possible during the Second Disarmament Decade" included many important items in both nuclear and conventional weapons as well as confidence building. These items are listed in more general terms, partly because of the continuing disagreement on the modalities and prior conditions for their negotiation, and partly because of the necessity for further studies. At the top of this list is the question of nuclear disarmament, in which general areas, identified in the Programme of Action of the First Special Session on Disarmament, were again repeated. Negotiations of agreements at appropriate stages together with adequate measures of verification satisfactory to the States concerned are to be conducted for:

--cessation of qualitative improvement and development of nuclear weapon systems;

--cessation of the production of all types of nuclear weapons and their means of delivery as well as the production of fissionable material for weapons purposes;

--a comprehensive phased programme with agreed timeframes, whenever feasible, for progressive and balanced reduction of stockpiles of nuclear weapons and their means of delivery leading to their ultimate and complete elimination at the earliest possible time.

Alongside of these negotiations, further measures are to be taken for the prevention of the proliferation of nuclear weapons. The development of the Safeguards system of the International Atomic Energy Agency, and the creation of other Nuclear-Weapon-Free Zones are among the steps envisaged. Proposals have already been made and supported by the United Nations General Assembly for nuclear-weapon-free zones in Africa, the Middle East and South Asia. Increasingly, also, suggestions are being made for the establishment of a nuclear-weapon-free zone in central Europe to eliminate once and for all the dangerous situation created by the concentration and mondernization of Soviet and NATO nuclear

weapons in the area. As a further step to save mankind from the
danger of nuclear weapons, it is envisaged during the Decade to
adopt measures for the avoidance of the use of nuclear weapons and
the prevention of nuclear war through the adoption of
confidence-building measures.

In the area of conventional weapons, multilateral, regional
and bilateral measures are to be taken on the limitation and
reduction of conventional weapons and armed forces in accordance
with the relevant provisions of the Final Document of the First
Special Session on Disarmament. The importance of steps in the
area of conventional weapons derives partly from their universal
effect, since all recent conflicts have involved these weapons,
partly from the enormous expenditure they consume (about 80 per
cent of world-wide military expenditure), and partly from their
susceptibility to regional control. Without, therefore, diluting
the priority attached to nuclear disarmament, due to the danger to
mankind's existence which nuclear weapons pose, and mindful of the
need for states to protect their sovereignty and territorial
integrity, appropriate steps towards the reduction of conventional
weapons and armed forces will contribute to the achievement of the
objectives of the Decade. Resolution 35/156A, adopted by the
General Assembly in 1980, in which it requested the
Secretary-General to carry out a study on all aspects of the
conventional arms race and on disarmament relating to conventional
weapons and armed forces, was a useful first step.

Practical steps towards the reduction of military expenditure,
especially by the militarily significant states, will have an
immediate impact in the area of conventional disarmament, will be a
good example to other states, and will contribute to fostering the
inter-relationship between disarmament and development. Peace and
development being indivisible, progress in one will benefit the
other. The existence side by side of mass poverty and desperate
living conditions in the developing countries on the one hand, with
affluence and often lavish life style in the developed countries on
the other, is recognized as a potential threat to international
peace and security. Improvement of the quality of life and the
general economic well-being of the peoples of the developing
countries requires a combination of internal measures as well as a
much-improved international economic co-operation. The economic
difficulties in many of the developed countries in the latter part
of the 1970s have reverberated in their contributions to
international development. These contributions have declined in
real terms; yet expenditures on armaments have consistently
increased, even at the expense of social programmes within
countries.

Bearing in mind the relationship between expenditure on
armaments and economic and social development, the First Special
Session on Disarmament emphasized the need to release real
resources used for military purposes to economic and social
development in the world, particularly for the benefit of the
developing countries. A study which was commissioned on this
subject has focussed on three issues: present-day utilization of
resources for military purposes; economic and social effects of a
continuing arms race and of the implementation of disarmament

measures; and conversion and redeployment of resources released
from military purposes through disarmament measures to economic
purposes. With its forward-looking and policy-oriented approach,
the study can be a stimulus to the necessity for disarmament and
the consequential advantages of conversion and redeployment of
resources from armaments to economic and social programmes. This
process may well facilitate the establishment of the New
International Economic Order.

VIII. DISARMAMENT AND INTERNATIONAL SECURITY

The process of disarmament is both cause and effect of the
general global situation, especially the relationships among the
most advanced military powers. In a period of detente among these
powers, disarmament and arms limitation gain added impetus; the
lack of detente creates a situation where trust is less but the
need for disarmament is even greater, rather than less. In order,
therefore, to create the right atmosphere for sustained disarmament
measures during the Second Disarmament Decade, it is indispensable
that the major Powers refrain from actions that will increase
international tension and threaten the sovereignty and territorial
integrity of states, and the right of peoples under colonial or
foreign domination to self-determination and national independence.
Strict adherence to the provisions of the Charter of the United
Nations on non-intervention in the internal affairs of states will
be necessary to create the right atmosphere. So also will the
development by the United Nations of its capacity for peace-making
and peace-keeping. The institution of confidence-building measures
globally, and as appropriate to particular regional conditions,
should be a continuing process during the Decade.

IX. PUBLIC AWARENESS

An important area which was neglected during the First
Disarmament Decade was the popularization of disarmament
discussions in such a way that those outside the immediate circle
of policy makers and negotiators would take an interest. The First
Special Session on Disarmament was the first major attempt to
democratize disarmament deliberations and negotiations. That
session also aroused a world-wide interest in this otherwise
exclusive subject, which most people had been prepared to leave to
the experts. If was is too important to leave to the policy makers
alone, so is disarmament too important to leave to the policy
makers alone. It is essential that not only governments, but also
the peoples of the world recognize and understand the dangers of
the arms race. The programme of information, education and

research launched by the First Special Session has already yielded some dividends. The United Nations Centre for Disarmament has widely diversified its publications on disarmament issues, as well as the results of studies carried out in this field. It has also undertaken a training programme for young diplomats through the United Nations Fellowship Programme on Disarmament. Disarmament Week is widely observed annually in United Nation member states. Unesco, which in 1980 held a World Congress on Disarmament Education, has proceeded along the way to develop disarmament-related activities during the Decade, including the development of disarmament education. A series of regional training seminars has been planned by Unesco for university teachers. Similarly, the United Nations Centre for Disarmament has been charged by the General Assembly with sponsoring seminars in the different regions of the world at which issues relating to world disarmament in general, and to the particular region concerned will be extensively discussed.

X. THE ROLE OF SCIENTISTS

The role of science and technology is crucial to the maintenance of the arms race. It has been estimated that at least a quarter, and probably much more of the resources, intellectual and financial, available for research in all areas of human activity is devoted to military research and development. This enormous concentration of human and material resources ensures constant sophistication and frequent changes in military technology. By contrast, some of the most devastating scourges of mankind (cancer and malaria, to mention just two), into which research ought to be urgenlty stepped up, often run into problems of attracting the necessary resources. Thus, military research and technology not only contribute to the further insecurity of the world, but also encourage the diversion of intellectual and material resources available from areas more important for the enhancement of the quality of human existence.

No single group is more aware than the scientific community of the destructive capability of the present generation of military hardware, especially nuclear weapons. The ingenuity of man which has created these monster weapons of destruction can be redirected towards their effective control, limitation and ultimate elimination. It is essential that more scientists, individually and collectively, speak out against further development and accumulation of armaments and in favour of disarmament, not as idealists but as realists aware of the danger to present and future generations implicit in the current level of armaments. The annual Pugwash Conferences provide one forum which is increasingly commanding attention. It is encouraging to note that at the 31st Pugwash Conference held in August-September 1981, the participants supported recent proposals for a Committee of distinguished scientists to analyse and make known the dangers of nuclear war.

They also agreed to make the expertise of their members available to the many new groups working to mobilize public opinion for disarmament.

To this end, scientists can make significant contributions to the development of verification measures so essential in disarmament agreements. Moreover, social scientist and Peace Research Institutes can, through research, expose the fallacy underlying many of the concepts and ideas which encourage militarism. The United Nations as well as Unesco should continue to encourage such research.

XI. NON-GOVERNMENTAL ORGANIZATIONS

The role of non-governmental orgnizations in the campaign for disarmament has been widely recognized. A number of these organizations are already active nationally as well as internationally. The strategy for the Second disarmament Decade called upon all segments concerned with information activities -- governmental and non-governmental organs of member states and those of the United Nations and the Specialized Agencies, as well as non-governmental organizations -- to undertake further programmes of information relating to the dangers of the armaments race, as well as to disarmament efforts and negotiations and their results.

XII. WORLD DISARMAMENT CAMPAIGN

These activities may be co-ordinated in the proposed World Disarmament Campaign. Suggested first by the Secretary-General's Advisory Board on Disarmament Studies, the United Nations General Assembly, in its resolution 35/152 I of December 1980, requested the Secretary-General "to carry out a study on the organization and financing of a World Disarmament Campaign under the auspices of the United Nations". If agreement can be reached on the means of financing it, the World Disarmament Campaign may be launched at the forthcoming Special Session of the General Assembly devoted to Disarmament in 1982.

* * *

In conclusion, it should be pointed out that three dates will be important in the context of the implementation of the objectives

of the Second Disarmament Decade. The year of the first major
event of the Decade is 1982, when the Second Special Session of the
General Assembly devoted to Disarmament will be held. That session
is expected to launch the blueprint for disarmament
negotiations -- the Comprehensive Programme of Disarmament. It
should give an added impetus to the process of negotiations in the
multilateral negotiating body, the Committee on Disarmament, as
well as in other forums of negotiation. It should also see the
launching of the World Disarmament Campaign, whereby all segments
of the world population -- men, women, students, professionals,
parliamentarians, religious leaders, labour unions -- would be
included in the disarmament constituency. The second important
date is 1985, the mid-term year when the General Assembly will
undertake a review and appraisal of the implementation of the
measures identified in the Declaration of the 1980s as the Second
Disarmament Decade. The third date, 1990, will not only make the
end of the Second Disarmament Decade but, hopefully, will mark the
half-way stage in the achievement of the general objective of
general and complete disarmament under effective international
control. In the course of negotiating the Comprehensive Programme
for Disarmament, the trend has been strongly in favour of a
twenty-year timeframe. If that trend holds, the world may witness
no more than another and final Disarmament Decade after the current
one. Such an eventuality will lend credibility to the
determination of the member states of the United Nations to live by
the obligation they assumed in declaring Decades for the
achievement of disarmament.

Use of Science and Technology for Arms Control and Peace Keeping

BERNARD FELD

I. INTRODUCTION

"If you want peace, prepare for war". This stupid dictum -- largely responsible for the fall of the Roman Empire -- has, through the ages, led to more misery and bloodshed than all the plagues put together. And still, even now, this calumnious cliche continues to be echoed, blindly, unthinkingly, by political and military leaders throughout the world.

It has been argued in the past that some wars were just wars, and that some even resolved important issues. The Second World War is generally cited as the prime example -- the Allied nations had no choice but to respond by force to Hitler's aggression. But accurate as this statement is, it represent only a part of the story, in so far as it discounts the historical truth that the Second World War would have been entirely unnecessary if the so-called democratic nations had -- instead of permitting the League of Nations to die -- acted in concert early enough, when it would still have been possible to stifle fascist expansion by collective economic actions. Nor has the final verdict of history yet been rendered as to the justification for replacing the Hitlerian policy of genocide by the indiscriminate, so-called strategic bombing of undefended population centres, culminating in the total elimination of two Japanese cities -- Hiroshima and Nagasaki -- by single nuclear weapons in the concluding days of the war.

Indeed, the Second World War -- the bloodiest war in mankind's history, in which more people perished than in all previous wars put together -- was practically predestined by the unsatisfactory

From **THE ARMS RACE AND DISARMAMENT**, UNESCO Press, 1982, (199-215), reprinted by permission of the publisher.

resolution of the European bloodbath of 1914-18. And it is equally
clear that the seeds of the Second World War were planted in the
last war's concluding and immediate postwar years.

Today's situation is, however, radically different from that
which has prevailed until now in the entire checkered and bloody
history of mankind's slow social evolution from the cave to the
skyscraper. In the words of Albert Einstein, one of the spiritual
fathers of Pugwash, "The unleashed power of the atom has changed
everything save our modes of thinking, and thus we drift toward
unparalleled catastrophe."[1] This is in large part the consequence
of indiscriminate technological process.

Indeed, the problem we now face is stark and inescapable.
Again in the words of Einstein (this time, jointly with the British
sage Bertrand Russell): "We have to learn to think in a new
way...Shall we put an end to the human race, or shall mankind
renounce war:"[2].

Another world war could well be mankind's last. The United
States and the Soviet Union have between them (in roughly equal
numbers) some fifty thousand nuclear weapons, most of them vastly
more powerful than the "primitive" bombs that annihilated Hiroshima
and Nagasaki. A nuclear war between these two superpowers, in
which a substantial fraction of this nuclear stockpile were
exploded (and nobody knows whether or how such a nuclear war could
be limited) would, within hours, eliminate the major part of the
populations of the protagonists; the resulting radioactive fall-out
(which could cover with lethal radioactivity an area of
approximately ten million square kilometers) would within days
spread comparable devastation very widely over the rest of the
Northern hemisphere; and the worldwide atmospheric contamination
would raise the level of exposure to radiation from natural sources
by an order of magnitude and could, over a period of months or
years, very seriously raise the burden of damage and defect in the
pool of genetic material, carried by us all, designed by a benign
evolutionary process to ensure the survival and slow improvement of
all species.

But this is only the tale of two giants. Already four other
nations have demonstrated nuclear weapons capabilities; by the end
of this century as many as twenty others will have acquired both
the technical ability and the necessary materials to produce their
own "modest" arsenals of nuclear devastation.

Can any sober individual doubt that war, as a means of
settling anything, is a hopelessly -- no, insanely -- obsolete
concept?

II. SOME HISTORY

It is generally accepted that it is the military application
of science and technology that has placed civilization, not to
speak of the human race itself, in such serious jeopardy. As new
technologies have been exploited in a race to seek military

advantage in an ongoing technological arms competition between the two superpowers, the security of the technological giants, rather than being enhanced, has steadily been diminishing. The dilemma is that each new military advance, heralded by its proponents as the answer to their needs for achieving decisive military superiority, has -- within the relatively short time required for the other side to emulate the originator (the technological "catch-up time" in the past has averaged around 5 years) -- only served as a ratchet for screwing up the spiral of mutual destructability to an even higher and more dangerous level.

Thus, for example, what apparently started out as an attempt by both sides to developed assured retaliatory forces -- to serve as a deterrent against any temptation by the potential antagonist to introduce nuclear forces into one of the periodic confrontations that have been occurring since the end of the Second World War -- has turned into a nightmare of assured escalation of even a conventional confrontation into a large-scale exchange of nuclear annihilation. It has become abundantly clear that the only hope of salvation lies in the superpowers finding some formula for agreement, first to halt this deadly upward spiral of lethal armaments, and then, to reverse it.

The history of the past forty years is characterized by a dreary succession of lost opportunities. In the early 1940s, when the atomic bomb was being conceived, it was widely hoped, by the scientists involved, that the "secret" -- at least, of the existence of a vigorous effort to investigate the feasibility of a fission weapon -- would be exchanged with our Russian allies. But the political leaders in the West, after the untimely death of Roosevelt, were not able to muster the breadth of vision to recognize the vastly greater long-term benefits that would have followed from an open sharing with the Russians of information on the possibility of a nuclear bomb. Instead, they chose the route of secrecy and deception, thus laying the groundwork for the Cold War that poisoned the postwar international atmosphere, and whose echoes still inhibit the achievement of the East-West co-operation necessary for curtailing the ongoing futile and self-destructive race for the accumulation of nuclear overkill.

We now know that all efforts in the West to monopolize the so-called secret of the atomic bomb were completely futile, destined from the start to failure and frustration. First of all, the Soviet scientific community, under the inspired leadership of Igor Kurchatov (see p. 86) and his able team of associates, including Lev Artsimovich and Andrei Sakharov, was thoroughly equal to the task of producing a nuclear weapon from scratch -- especially once they knew that it was possible and they had been released from the immediate exigencies of preventing the German armies from overrunning their homeland. Furthermore, it was not at all necessary for them to go through all the trails and errors of the Manhattan Projects -- even without the inside information provided by an effective espionage network, including Klaus Fuchs and Allan Nunn May -- thanks to the clear and accurate map of the route to the production of an atomic bomb that had been laid out in the official Smyth Report[3].

In retrospect, it is now obvious that once the secret of the

successful achievement of an atomic bomb was out -- and that occurred with its use for the destruction of Hiroshima -- it was merely a matter of a few years before the Soviet scientific community would be able -- even without any additional knowledge from the outside -- to repeat the feat of scientists in the West. Knowledgeable scientists, who had participated in the American, British and Canadian efforts to produce the first atomic bomb, predicted that the time for a technologically competent nation such as the USSR to repeat their feat would not be more than about five years. While this was disputed by the military bureaucracy that had managed the Western effort -- in particular, by General Groves, the head of the wartime Manhattan Project that had organized the American bomb production -- the scientists' estimate turned out to be quite accurate. The Russians achieved their first test explosion of a fission bomb in 1949.[4]

Furthermore, the failure of the United Nations to place nuclear energy under effective international control -- as was envisaged in the Acheson-Lilienthal-Baruch proposals and might well have been possible in the late 1940s -- represents a tragically missed opportunity.

III. THE PROBLEM OF NUCLEAR WEAPONS PROLIFERATION

The historical point is worth emphasizing in view of current discussions on the problems and prospects of nuclear weapons proliferation. There is a great deal of confusion in current discussions between the role of technical secrecy and the role of political constraints in preventing the future spread of nuclear weapons into the Third World. There is no question that, as far as the scientific and technical know-how is concerned, "the cat is out of the bag". There no longer exists any basic "secrets" -- neither scientific nor technical -- concerning the workings of the atomic bomb and the requirements for its production, that are not available in the open literature to any with the minimal technical competence required to understand them. Even a relatively unsophisticated group of technicians in almost any country, given the availability of the requisite quantity of weapons material (some 20 kg of highly enriched uranium-235 or 10 kg of a relatively pure plutonium), would be capable of fabricating a crude atomic bomb by using this material, and the designs are already widely disseminated in the open literature in the West.

There is, however, still a considerable technical effort involved in the application of available knowledge to the actual production of the fissionable materials needed for nuclear bombs.

Unfortunately, for almost any "practical" purpose, it does not much matter whether the weapon produced by some aspiring power elite or terrorist group is highly efficient or relatively inefficient. For almost any purpose important to an aspiring non-superpower nuclear weapons producer, there is no practical difference between a ninety per cent efficient "device"

(approximately 200 thousand tons of TNT equivalent) and a one per
cent efficient (2 thousand tons) "dud". Two thousand tons of high
explosive is more than enough to obliterate the heart of any modern
city.

Under the circumstances, the problem with which the world is
faced is no longer one of maintaining the "secret" in the hands of
a few "reliable" nations, but rather one of preventing the
uninhibited availability of the 10 kg plutonium which would permit
the fabrication of a nuclear "device" by almost any government, or
even any relatively well-organized extra-governmental group with
access to a moderate number of competent technicians and engineers
and the moderate resources needed to support their efforts.

IV. THE SAFEGUARDS PROBLEM

Concern for this problem is part of the rationale for the
establishment of the International Atomic Energy Agency (IAEA) in
Vienna. It was originally intended that all future atomic energy
programmes of all but the nuclear-weapon states would be conducted
under its auspices and control. The hope was that the Agency
should be able to maintain sufficient control over all
weapons-capable fissile materials, to prevent their diversion to
military uses. At the same time, by permitting the Agency access
to the most advanced peaceful technology available, the smaller
nations of the world should find it overridingly in their interests
to accept the IAEA sponsorship, with its concomitant safeguards,
over their atomic energy programmes. Such acceptance would be more
palatable if the same safeguards we also applied to the peaceful
nuclear programmes of the superpowers.

However, it has been recognized from that start that the
Agency concept -- even recognizing the effectiveness of its current
safeguards programmes -- also presents a serious problem. For once
such smaller nations have used the Agency to help build up their
peaceful nuclear power programme, they will also have acquired the
indigenous capability for going it alone, without having to live
with the inhibitions associated with IAEA "safeguards" over their
nuclear programme.

With respect to this problem of the future effectiveness of
IAEA safeguards, the most promising suggestion for the prevention
of nuclear weapons spread appears to lie in the direction of a
"Fort Knox solution" -- that is, a solution which, by putting these
materials under physically effective lock-and-key, prevents any
military significant amounts of plutonium or highly enriched
uranium from falling into the hands of any unauthorized
individuals, groups or governments. Such a solution, it almost
goes without saying, requires the existence of an international
agency that can be universally trusted with the guardianship of
these materials. Presumably, the IAEA -- appropriately
strengthened with the requisite authorities -- would be the
international agency that could eventually assume such a role.

The key to the effectiveness of international safeguards lies in their emphasis on physical protective measures. It would be difficult to make a case for the long-term efficacy of purely accounting measures, or of occasional inspections by International Atomic Energy Agency employees, especially given the political nature of the Agency's charter. None of these approaches is capable of providing the close to 100 per cent assurances against diversion that are required if small nations are to be guaranteed their security against possible surprise nuclear attack by an aggressive neighbour. In the view of most students of the problem there is really no acceptable solution to the nuclear weapons proliferation dilemma short of such complete physical control, but a trusted international agency, over the materials required for nuclear weapons production.

Such controls, and in particular the maintenance of effective and believable inspection procedures, required to guard against unexpected violations of the prohibition against diversion of fissile materials from civil applications to nuclear weapons production, will require a very high order of technological competence on the part of the international inspectorate. The inspectors will need to know at least as much about the workings of uranium separation plants, of nuclear reactors and fuel reprocessing facilities as their designers and operators. They will, of course, also need to have continuous and completely uninhibited access to the relevant plants and their records.

Furthermore, in order to know what kinds of "violations" are most sensitive the inspectorate will also need to have considerable knowledge of the technology of nuclear weapons design and their use. This is a rather "tricky" aspect of the nuclear materials verification problem that may require considerably more study and discussion at the international level.

In any case, whatever the limits on its mission, the IAEA system must be as "fool-proof" as any such system -- even given its built-in restraint on physical access -- can possibly be. This will require the IAEA to call on the most sophisticated technologies available for remote-control monitoring, and for computer-based accounting. For example, the American Arms Control and Disarmament Agency (ACDA) has been developing a regime for the internal monitoring of United States nuclear programmes -- the IAEA problem in microcosm. Many aspects of this programme referred to as RECOVER (Remote Control Verification) are being adapted to IAEA use, with improvements being continuously introduced[5].

The problem of remote-control monitoring or inspection is, of course, not a new one. In the early discussions leading to the nuclear weapons Test Ban Treaty of 1963, the problem of verification of small underground tests was the main obstacle (and remained so) to the conclusion of a comprehensive treaty. The problem of achieving effective "on-site inspection", without providing a licence for uninhibited intelligence activity, was and remains the major stumbling block. At the time, the concept of "black-box inspection" was introduced at one of the Pugwash Conferences at which ideas were exchanged on these issues (see p. 139).

The "black-box" concept is simple: in lieu of the physical

presence of actual inspectors, instruments would be placed at strategic locations in the nation being inspected (i.e. small seismographs for the detection of underground disturbances that could be associated with underground nuclear weapons tests). These instruments would be continuously monitored at stations located outside the borders of the nation under inspection, by an international inspectorate with presumably accepted neutral credentials. Ambiguous signals, if they could not be satisfactorily explained by the nation concerned, would serve as grounds for requests for permission for "on-site inspections" by teams from the international agency. Such requests could not be refused on trivial grounds, but they would also -- by the same token -- require serious reasons before they could be advanced.

Such black-box control came very close to being accepted by both the United States and the USSR in the 1963 negotiations on the test ban, which were initiated in reaction to the Cuban missile crisis. Its acceptance foundered on the inability of the two sides to compromise between the Western insistence on 7 annual mandatory on-site inspections and the Eastern willingness to accept three.

However, the black-box concept should be applicable to many other problems of inspection of arms control agreements without unacceptable intrusion. Technology of detection and communication, in many areas including seismology, has advanced a great deal since 1963. The use of black-box verification may well be a technology whose time has finally come.

In the long run, however, in the absence of significant changes in the international regime of sovereign and independent states, it is difficult to conceive of any international inspection system that would be completely foolproof against determined evasion by a sovereign state. Completely effective inspection requires absolute access to the material and facilities under inspection. Limited measures, requiring national acquiescence -- a situation which has, until now, been the case for practically all the nations involved in international energy programmes -- will work only so long as such national co-operation continues, even assuming complete acceptance of the international control regime. But as the recent Israeli aggression against the Iraqi reactor has demonstrated, not all states are prepared to accept as adequate the present IAEA safeguards.

V. NUCLEAR-WEAPON-FREE ZONES

In spite of verification problems, however, the concept of nuclear-weapon-free zones is becoming increasingly attractive, especially as the superpower rivalry in the accumulation of ever-more sophisticated weapons grows and the concomitant doctrines proliferate for justifying their early introduction into "conventional" conflicts. The classic examples of such areas are Antarctica -- which has been completely demilitarized by formal agreement of all interested parties since 1961 -- and Latin

America, by virtue of the Treat of Tlatelolco of 1967. (Although Brazil has signed the Treaty, it still does not accept it as being in force, since not all Latin American countries (e.g. Cuba) has yet joined.) The Tlatelolco Treaty, although it is a regional agreement, is accompanied by a protocol in which the nuclear weapon states agree to respect the nuclear-weapon-free status of the area.

Serious discussions are taking or have taken place with respect to the possible establishment of such areas in Africa, the Balkans, Europe, the Middle East, the Nordic Area and South-east Asia. However, such discussions have, at least up to now, usually been thwarted by the unwillingness of one or more of the key nations in the region to join in the negotiations. However, as the Latin American case has shown, a treaty can be effective in respect to a given area even if not all the major actors are immediate adherents.

In this regard, it is important to emphasize that the nuclear-weapon-free concept is not wed to the existence of contiguous areas of application. All that is required is the acquiescence to the concept of a sufficient number of nuclearly-capable states in an area. This possibility has sometimes been referred to as the "Swiss cheese" zone concept.

Basically, states will agree to remain non-nuclear -- that is free of nuclear weapons and the facilities for producing them -- so long as it remains in their basic security interests to do so. In this regard, one of the major instruments, available to the nuclear weapons states for promoting this concept of enhanced security deriving from non-nuclear status, is the guarantee of no-first-use of nuclear weapons against such nations.

Until now, the no-first-use pledge of the superpowers have been rather more limited: both have proclaimed the non-use of nuclear weapons against non-nuclear-weapon states which are not aligned or allied with any nuclear weapon states. There would be, however, considerable advantage to the superpowers to extend this concept to all states refusing to acquire or store nuclear weapons, since this would greatly encourage already existing tendencies within both NATO and WTO to reduce, and eventually eliminate, their dependence on so-called tactical or theatre nuclear weapons for their defence.

But beyond such application, it can be persuasively argued that the universal acceptance of the no-first-use concept with respect to nuclear weapons would represent a tremendously important step towards the avoidance of nuclear war. Despite the argument that this would be purely an expository step, without any enforceable or even verifiable aspects -- nor would there be any requirement for associated reduction in nuclear weapon stockpiles and their further development and deployment -- there is an important historical precedent which speaks for the effectiveness of such an agreement.

The Geneva Protocol of 1925 (banning the use of chemical bacteriological and analogous weapons) was very widely interpreted as simply a no-first-use agreement. Nevertheless, it provided very effective inhibitions, especially during the Second World War, against the use, and even development of such weapons. And it laid the groundwork for an eventual Stockpiling of Bacteriological

(Biological) and Toxin Weapons, and providing for the destruction of existing stockpiles (1972). A similar treaty with respect to Chemical Weapons has been under serious negotiation.

With the help of a no-first-use arrangement for nuclear weapons, one might be permitted to hope that international developments (assuming the avoidance of nuclear war) would encourage a universal agreement to ban such weapons and eventually to eliminate them from the arsenals of all nations.

VI. VERIFICATION OF ARMS CONTROL AGREEMENTS

With respect to the proliferation problem, in today's world it is necessary to operate on the assumption that programmes for nuclear power production are destined to be with us for some time, and we must learn to cope with the problems of weapons proliferation associated with such programmes. Just as the most sophisticated technology is today the backbone of the nuclear weapons development and deployment programme of all the major powers, so much a comparable technological sophistication serve as the backbone of any system for the verifiable control, limitation, reduction and eventual elimination of nuclear armaments from the world's military arsenals. For it must stand as given that neither of the superpowers, not so speak of the other nuclear weapon states, will acquiesce to a very substantial reduction, let alone elimination, of its nuclear weapon capability if it not unequivocally sure that no virtual antagonist could possibly maintain a nuclear attack potential at the end of the disarmament process. Verification is the key to any significant nuclear arms limitation, and especially education, now and in the foreseeable future.

Unfortunately, our experience until now with the international verification of arms control arrangements is not too encouraging. Even though problems associated with such verification have received serious consideration, both on the national and international levels, since the late '40s, the history of international acceptance of verification procedures has been uniformly disappointing. It has never been possible for the United States and the USSR to agree on any formal arrangement involving any form of international agency with intrusive inspection capabilities with respect to the two superpowers. Both superpowers have been willing to envisage intrusive IAEA inspection of nations outside their own immediate strategic orbits; but if ever any question of restricting their own national sovereignty has arisen, both of the nuclear giants, as well as the other nations, have come to regard themselves as nuclear powers, have always insisted on "drawing the line". In reality, the world is still a very long way from the acceptance of any of the forms of supranational control over activities of military significance that might signal the initiation of a serious regime of international order.

VII. SATELLITE INSPECTION

Nevertheless, in spite of the determined insistence of all nations on the inviolability of their sovereign territories, a great deal of international inspection has been going on for quite some time. To a large extent, both the Soviet Union and the United States are now capable of continuously monitoring the military potential (and even more) of the other side, by means that lie entirely within their own (national) control. Such monitoring of the capabilities of the other side no longer depends on the effectiveness of clandestine intelligence activities -- efficient as these have become as a result of the use of the most modern surveillance and communications techniques. Beyond the conventional intelligence gathering techniques, the availability to both sides of reconnaissance satellites -- capable of the essentially continuous monitoring of practically the entire area of the other nation by photographic means, coupled with the use of a variety of sensors using other regions of the electromagnetic spectrum -- has resulted in a situation of more-or-less complete openness, as far as the significant physical activities of any nation are concerned. Any major military programme, and especially one that might significantly alter the status quo, would almost certainly be detected through the continuous monitoring of both ground and air-based activities, that is now being carried out by the surveillance satellites of both the Soviet Union and the United States.

The extent of this revolution in observational capabilities that has taken place in the last 20 years or so, since the Soviet launching of the Sputnik in 1957, is still not sufficiently understood in Western defence analysts' circles; the extent to which these revolutionary changes are taken into account in equivalent Eastern "think-tanks" is not known to this author.

The simple fact is that the entire area of both nations is now being continuously scrutinized by the other side, with observational instruments that are capable of reading the numbers on car licence plates, or the headlines of newspapers. Having made this statement of technological capability -- and it is essential that the high level of this capability, now being exercised by both sides, be recognized and accepted -- it is of course necessary, however, to put forth some obvious caveats. Observation by sensors of this degree of resolution cannot be continuous, due to the vicissitudes of weather and the limitation of the number of satellite photographs that can be seriously analysed in a finite time by a finite number of photo-analysts. Nevertheless, it must be accepted as a fact of contemporary international life that any reasonably large-scale enterprise, that would be capable of appreciably altering the military capability of either side, is exceedingly unlikely to escape the almost-continuous scrutiny to which both the United States and the Soviet Union are now subjecting each others' activities.

The capability of reconnaissance systems to detect change is of particular importance. One of the most significant technological

developments of recent years has been in this area. If it were necessary for the military establishments of both sides to analyse all the photographic data on the activities of the other, this would represent an impossible task for any system with finite resources. However, there now exist systems that can provide automatic comparisons between two photographs of the same area, taken at different times, and call attention to any significant differences between these two photographs. Thus, the system need not be capable of analysing the activities in any given area, but only of detecting any "significant" change (which can be appropriately defined in advance) that has taken place in the time interval between the two photographs.

The problems are not simple, of course. Too loose a definition of "change" will result in a swamping of the system by spurious data or could subject the system to easy misdirection by a sophisticated opponent; too tight a definition could permit important evidence to leak through the sieve. However, given the high degree of input into these systems, and the great amount of "redundancy" that has traditionally been built into military systems, it is a good guess that any significant alteration of military capabilities by either side would not excape detection by the sophisticated reconnaissance, surveillance and espionage capabilities of the other for long.

In respect to such reconnaissance satellite systems, it is important that both the United States and the Soviet Union have recognized the value to their own security of maintaining this "open skies" situation. Thus, a number of agreements exist, (e.g. the Outer Space Treaty of 1967, the Direct Communications Link Modernization Agreement of 1971, the Accidents Measures Agreement of 1971, the SALT I and the ABM Agreements of 1972, as well as the International Telecommunications Conventions), some being informal but nonetheless essential, that bind each superpower to respect the satellite verification systems of the other. Other industrialized nations -- in particular France -- also have serious and active satellite reconnaissance programmes under way, so that the superpower monopoly in this field cannot continue indefinitely.

Clearly, in respect to such satellite observation, we are in the midst of a continuing technological race between the "hiders" and the "seekers". Even if techniques can be developed which -- at least for some short time -- may succeed in camouflaging some significant military activity, thus preventing its detection by the other side, any advantages thereby achieved must perforce be short-lived. Meanwhile, however, new techniques are being developed on both sides, mainly of mobile missile deployments (the MX on the part of the United States and the mobile SS-20 and its offshoots, on the part of the USSR), which are deemed by many to threaten the stability of the mutual deterrent posture that, for some time now, has seemed to ensure an accepted balance between the two superpowers.

Of particular concern, with respect to their possible impact on arms control prospects, are three areas of new technical developments: cruise missiles, anti-submarine warfare techniques, and directed energy (particularly laser) sources. The first is, in fact, a rather old idea -- arising from the German V-bombs, of the

Second World War -- which has recently been revived in a much improved manner, mainly through the development of strong, light-weight metallic alloys and highly efficient jet engines. Cruise missiles are pilotless, drone aircraft, travelling at subsonic speeds, capable of delivering conventional and nuclear weapons on specific targets. Owing to modern guidance technology, they can be given pinpoint accuracy, and owing to their ability to fly at rooftop levels, and even to manoeuvre on their course, they are almost invulnerable against conventional anti-aircraft defences. Because of their light weight, they can be launched from aircraft, and dispatched at considerable distance from their intended targets. (They can also be carried by freight trains, ships, submarines, trucks, etc.). They are obviously easy to conceal and almost impossible to verify as to their number. Hence, the deployment of cruise missiles on a large scale will hugely complicate the achievement of a verifiable limitation on numbers of deliverable weapons.

The danger of cruise missile deployments represents a good illustration of a recurring problem of American-Soviet arms control. This is the problem of the "illusive advantage", sometimes referred to as the "fallacy of the last step". The idea -- always an attractive one to military leaders whose horizons rarely extend beyond the last conflict -- is that it is possible to maintain a constant military advantage over the other side by being one step ahead in the race for new weapons technologies. Fortunately, the world has never come to the point of an actual conflict between the United States and the Soviet Union, where some elusive but immediate advantage might count. The actual facts of life have dictated that every new deployment on either side has been followed, within a very short time, by either the deployment of the same system by the other, or the introduction of a new system that has served to counteract the "advantage" of the first. Until now, the Soviet-American military competition has represented a "no-win game".

Another example is the competition, still not definitely resolved, in the realm of anti-submarine warfare (ASW). In the immediate post Second World War period, it was generally believed in the West that the Soviet Union would be content with its pre-eminent status as a major continental power; the control of the seas would remain within the prerogative of the triumphant Western allies of the Second World War.

However, any serious analyst of Soviet military concerns must conclude that the control over the sea lanes in and out of the Soviet Union is a matter of life-or-death concern to Soviet leaders. Hence, the very concept of a submarine threat to surface shipping, and possible means of its denial, would be of immediate concern to the Russians. It is thus rather difficult to understand in retrospect, why almost all studies in the West, to date, on ASW prospects, have completely ignored Soviet concerns. Nevertheless, this has been the case.

Assuming that his deficiency will be remedied in such studies in the future, it is necessary to be concerned with the mutual East-West developments in anti-submarine warfare techniques, not because these represent any possible breakthroughs in new

Towards a Comprehensive Programme of Disarmament

ALFONSO GARCIA-ROBLES

I. INTRODUCTION

The convening of a second special session on disarmament of the United Nations General Assembly (UNSSOD II) was decided by the first special session of the same nature (UNSSOD I) whose Final Document, approved by consensus, stated in its paragraph 119:

"A second special session of the General Assembly devoted to disarmament should be held on a date to be decided by the Assembly at its thirty-third session."

As contemplated in this paragraph, the Assembly subsequently adopted, on 14 December 1978, resolution 33/71 H whereby it decided that UNSSOD II should convene in 1982 at United Nations headquarters in New York, and that a preparatory committee for such a special session should be set up at its thirty-fifth session.

On 3 December 1980, the preparatory committee was established by resolution 35/47 with a composition of seventy-eight Member States appointed by the President of the General Assembly on the usual basis of "equitable geographic distribution".

The Committee held a brief organizational session of three working meetings on 4-5 December 1980 and a second session -- which has been the first devoted to substantive questions -- on 4-15 May 1981. At this session, the Committee began the consideration of the possible content of the provisional agenda of UNSSOD II. This was the task of the next session, 6-16 October 1981, since the Committee had been asked by the above-mentioned resolution to submit to the General Assembly at its thirty-sixth session its

From **THE ARMS RACE AND DISARMAMENT**, UNESCO Press, 1982, (289-299), reprinted by permission of the publisher.

recommendations thereon.

II. AGENDA FOR UNSSOD II

The Preparatory Committee had no difficulty in reaching agreement with regard to the inclusion on the provisional agenda of a series of those items that may be defined as ritual, such as the opening of the session, the holding of a minute of silent prayer or meditation, the election of the President and the adoption of the agenda.

When the discussion went beyond those traditional items, the many different views advanced could be broadly classified in two categories.

The first would comprise all those put forward by delegations which suggested for inclusion on the provisional agenda of the Assembly a large variety of items -- some of them embracing various sub-items -- which comprised mainly the following:

--Review of the implementation of the decisions and recommendations of the first special session devoted to disarmament.
--Consideration of initiatives and proposals of Member States.
--Implementation of the declaration of the 1980s as the second disarmament decade.
--Consideration and adoption of the comprehensive programme of disarmament.
--Strengthening of the role of the United Nations in the field of disarmament.

The main exponent of the second category of views was the Delegation of Mexico which, in addition to the eight ritual procedural items and to a closing one devoted to the "Adoption of the Final Act of the Session", proposed that the agenda should follow the example of UNSSOD I (which, as is well known, had on its agenda only three substantive items dealing with the three main chapters of what was to become its Final Document: a Declaration on disarmament; a Programme of Action for disarmament, and a Machinery for disarmament) and concentrate its efforts on the consideration and adoption of the comprehensive programme of disarmament specifically requested in paragraph 109 of the Final Document and whose draft is being elaborated by the Committee on Disarmament since 1980.

In support of its proposal the Mexican delegation submitted a working paper in which it noted inter-alia the following:

"The experience of the General Assembly at its first special session devoted to disarmament underscored how useful it is, in dealing with a wide-ranging item whose various elements are closely interrelated, to do

everything possible to prevent a dissipation of effort,
and to seek instead a concentration of effort, with a
view to maximum co-ordination.

This experience will be very valuable for the second
special session: the lessons of the experience must be
turned to full account. Such an approach is particularly
advisable considering that the key item on the agenda
will undoubtedly be the comprehensive programme of
disarmament; the programme's structure and content are in
several respects similar to those of the Final Document.
Even more than the latter, they will require a sustained
unity and the necessary correlation between the various
components.

It thus appears most desirable to avoid a
proliferation of items on the agenda of the forthcoming
second session, which would rob it of its distinctiveness
as a 'special' session and make it rather like a regular
session. That would be all the more regrettable
considering the frequency of regular session: the
thirty-sixth session will take place six months before
the second special session, and the thirty-seventh
session barely three months or so after the end of the
special session.

On the other hand, since the comprehensive programme
of disarmament has to be 'self-contained', a thorough
examination and analysis of the content of the programme
by the Assembly at its special session, a <u>sine qua non</u>
for the adoption of the programme by consensus, would,
far from preventing consideration of other less important
related items, make such consideration indispensible."

That this view is well-founded becomes evident if one bears in
mind that the elaboration of the comprehensive programme of
disarmament was expressly provided for in the Final Document of the
first special session of the General Assembly devoted to
disarmament. In paragraph 109 of that Document, the General
Assembly agreed that the programme should encompass:

"All measures thought to be advisable in order to ensure
that the goal of general and complete disarmament under
effective international control becomes a reality in a
world in which international peace and security prevail
and in which the new international economic order is
strengthened and consolidated."

Subsequently, the Committee on Disarmament, in its report to
the General Assembly at its thirty-fifth session (a report welcomed
by the Assembly), affirmed that the comprehensive programme would
have to be "self-contained".

In the light of those statements, borne out by the structure
and content of the programme, which are in general similar to those
of the Final Document of UNSSOD I, it seems obvious, on the one
hand, that the key item on the agenda on the second special session
will be the comprehensive programme of disarmament and, on the

other hand, that the programme itself, by virtue of its
"comprehensiveness", will not only encompass all the elements
included in the Final Document, but will go further than the Final
Document in some respects.

Appropriate consideration of the draft comprehensive programme
prepared by the Committee on Disarmament will therefore require,
inter alia, a review of the implementation of the decisions and
recommendations of the previous special session, and a review of
the status of disarmament negotiations envisaged in the Programme
of Action, particularly those relating to nuclear disarmament. It
will also be necessary to consider the recommendations made by the
Assembly at the previous special session, the follow-up to studies
initiated by it during or after the session, the initiatives and
proposals of Member States, and the manner of implementation of the
declaration of the 1980s as the Second Disarmament Decade.

It will certainly be essential for the General Assembly to
consider another question during its deliberations on the
comprehensive programme: the strengthening of the role of the
United Nations in the field of disarmament, including the
functioning of deliberate organs, ways of enhancing the
effectiveness of the Committee on Disarmament as the sole
multilateral negotiating body in the field of disarmament, and the
consideration of other such institutional arrangements as the
possible convening of a world disarmament conference. Similarly,
the World Disarmament Campaign -- on which a study is at present
being finalized -- will undoubtedly have to be accorded a rightful
place in the work of the General Assembly, like such other
educational and information activities on disarmament as the
holding of seminars and the fellowship programme.

Nevertheless, if all those questions will require attentive
consideration by the General Assembly, they should not be examined
in a haphazard manner as unconnected subjects, but in a coherent
and co-ordinated way as elements of the comprehensive programme of
disarmament and within its framework.

III. ACHIEVEMENT OF UNSSOD I

For a better understanding of what should be the role of
UNSSOD II, it seems appropriate to recall briefly some of the main
achievements of UNSSOD I, which took place in May-June 1978.

First and foremost among those achievements was undoubtedly
the adoption, by consensus, of a Final Document comprising four
sections -- Introduction, Declaration, Programme of Action and
Machinery -- closely intertwined. Its contents, of a much broader
scope than anything previously approved by the United Nations,
provides the elements for what could be called a new disarmament
strategy.

Among these elements, perhaps the most prominent place belongs
to a series of well-founded declarations, and to several
fundamental purposes, principles and priorities which are clearly

defined in the Final Document.

From among them it may be useful to recall as illustrative examples the following.

Concerning international security, which so often has been advanced as a pretext to reject or postpone disarmament, the General Assembly proclaimed that "the increase in weapons, especially nuclear weapons, far from helping to strengthen international security, on the contrary weakens it", and added later on that "enduring international peace and security cannot be built on the accumulation of weaponry by military alliances nor be sustained by a precarious balance of deterrence or doctrines of strategic superiority".

With regard to the dangers involved in the existing situation, the Assembly, after expressing its alarm about "the threat to the very survival of mankind by the existence of nuclear weapons and the continuing arms race", went on to say that "mankind today is confronted with an unprecedented threat of self-extinction arising from the massive and competitive accumulation of the most destructive weapons ever produced" and concluded that: "Removing the threat of a world war -- a nuclear war -- is the most acute and urgent task of the present day. Mankind is confronted with a choice: we must halt the arms race and proceed to disarmament or face annihilation".

As a corollary of the above pronouncements, the Final Document included several provisions intended to underline that "all people of the world have a vital interest in the success of disarmament negotiations", that "all States have the right to participate" in such negotiations; and that "it is essential that not only Governments but also the peoples of the world recognize and understand the dangers in the present situation".

The Assembly also concluded that "it is essential to halt and reverse the nuclear arms race in all its aspects in order to avert the danger of war involving nuclear weapons"; that "the ultimate goal in this context is the complete elimination of nuclear weapons"; that the final goal of "the efforts of States in the disarmament process is general and complete disarmament under effective international control"; and that "progress towards this objective requires the conclusion and implementation of agreements on this cessation of the arms race and on genuine measures of disarmament" which should take place in stages and in such an equitable and balanced manner as to ensure at any stage to each State or group of States "undiminished security at the lowest possible level of armaments and military forces".

In addition to these few illustrative examples, which should rightly be granted priority in any recapitulation of disarmament principles and objectives approved by UNSSOD I, it seems advisable to bear in mind that the Final Document contains many other provisions of the same nature which cover exhaustively all other aspects of this complex matter, such as the following.

Obligation to strictly observe the principles of the UN Charter; negative effect of the arms race on the relaxation of international tension as well as on the exercise of the right of self-determination; necessity to build confidence among States; recognition of the central role of the United Nations in the sphere

of disarmament and the need to strengthen it; affirmation that effective measures of nuclear disarmament and the prevention of nuclear war have the highest priority; elimination of the use or the threat of use of force from international life; effective implementation of the security system provided for in the UN Charter and recourse to procedures of peaceful settlement of disputes; strict observance of an acceptable balance of mutual responsibilities and obligations for nuclear and non-nuclear-weapon States; primary responsibility of nuclear-weapon States, together with other militarily significant States for halting and reversing the arms race; advantages of the creation of nuclear-weapon-free zones and of zones of peaces; adequate measures of verification to be included in disarmament agreements; definition of the following priorities for disarmament negotiations -- nuclear weapons, chemical weapons and other weapons of mass destruction, conventional weapons and reduction of armed forces; close relationship between disarmament and development and incompatibility of the economic and social consequences of the arms race with the implementation of the new international economic order, based on justice, equity and co-operation; urgency to mobilize world public opinion on behalf of disarmament and, to that end, to avoid dissemination of false and tendentious information concerning armaments and to concentrate on a campaign of education and information on the danger of escalation of the arms race and the need for general and complete disarmament under effective international control.

There is no doubt that those and all other similar provisions approved by consensus at UNSSOD I have today the same or even greater validity and will not be in need of any modification by UNSSOD II.

What has just been said regarding principles, objectives and priorities approved by UNSSOD I, is to some extent equally true in connection with the provisions of the Final Document included in its section entitled "Machinery" which are briefly described below.

The General Assembly began by stating the need to "revitalize" the existing disarmament machinery and by rightly pointing out that two kinds of bodies are requested in the field of disarmament, deliberative and negotiating, and that "all Member States" should be represented on the former, "whereas the latter, for the sake of convenience, should have a relatively small membership".

With regard to deliberation, it was declared in the Final Document that the General Assembly had been and should remain "the main deliberative organ of the United Nations", and that its First Committee should deal in the future "only with questions of disarmament and related international security questions", the General Assembly also established, as one of its subsidiary organs, a Disarmament Commission composed of all States Members of the United Nations, which should be a deliberative body and meet every year for a period of four weeks.

Finally, it was also agreed that a second special session of the General Assembly devoted to disarmament should be held at a date to be decided later, and which at present will be June-July 1982.

Concerning negotiations, UNSSOD I declared to be "deeply aware

of the continuing requirement for a single multilateral disarmament negotiating forum of limited size taking decisions on the basis of consensus". As a result of this and other related provisions the Committee on Disarmament and thirty-five other States.

From the procedural stand-point the decisions of UNSSOD I relating to machinery, be it deliberative or negotiating, have proved generally adequate. The fact that both types of organs have been, although with some exceptions, working smoothly, does not mean that there has been progress on disarmament. The absence of political will of the nuclear weapon States -- even if in some cases it has been only of some of them -- gives full validity to the appraisal made in the Final Document. It is a fact that there are now even more reasons than in 1978 to affirm that the disarmament objectives "appear to be as far away today as they were then, or even further because the arms race is not diminishing but increasing and outstrips by far the efforts to curb it".

It should also be recalled that UNSSOD I, bearing in mind that the United Nations "has a central role and primary responsibility in the sphere of disarmament", stressed the necessity of keeping the world organization "duly informed...of all disarmament efforts outside its aegis", whether they are "unilateral, bilateral, regional, or multilateral". The observance of these provisions has so far left much to be desired.

It is in connection with questions such as these, as well as with the mobilization of "world public opinion on behalf of disarmament", also expressly contemplated in the Final Document, that UNSSOD II may perform a most useful task when it reviews the existing disarmament machinery and procedures. Thus, for instance, it could be made mandatory for any President, Chairman or Secretary of a meeting on disarmament held outside the United Nations to send two complete sets of all relevant documents to the UN Secretary-General for transmission to the General Assembly and to the Committee on Disarmament, respectively. The second special session, would likewise provide an excellent opportunity for the solemn launching of the "World Disarmament Campaign" for whose organization and financing the Secretary-General is presently carrying out a thorough study with the assistance of qualified experts, as requested by the thirty-fifth session in 1980. The Assembly could also devise ways and means to prevent paralysis of the negotiating function of the Committee through the abuse of the "consensus" rule on procedural questions.

Nevertheless, whatever may be the significance of any developments and improvements which UNSSOD II may approve on the various types of machinery and procedure briefly outlined above, it seems axiomatic that it is on what was called in the Final Document of 1978 a "Programme of Action" that the forthcoming Assembly should particularly endeavour to secure effective results.

Indeed, none of the priority measures relating to nuclear arms control, not to mention those pertaining to nuclear disarmament, has received even a token implementation.

IV. COMPREHENSIVE PROGRAMME OF DISARMAMENT

In the light of what has happened during the last three years, and of the present alarming conditions of the arms race, pledges like those enshrined in paragraphs 17 ("The pressing need now is to translate into practical terms the provisions of this Final Document and to proceed along the road of binding and effective international agreements in the field of disarmament"), and 42 ("Since prompt measures should be taken in order to halt and reverse the arms race, Member States hereby declare that they will respect the objectives and principles stated above and make every effort faithfully to carry out the Programme of Action") of the Final Document of UNSSOD I, acquire today an ironic flavour. Consequently, it seems imperative that UNSSOD II concentrates its efforts in adopting an all-embracing and specific programme of disarmament, and in securing a binding commitment of all participants States to its faithful implementation.

Fortunately, the Assembly, since the moment when it held its first special session devoted to disarmament, had foreseen this need. Thus, in paragraph 109 of its Final Document it is explicitly provided that "concurrently with negotiations on partial measures of disarmament" it would be necessary to conduct "negotiations on general and complete disarmament", which remains the "ultimate goal of all efforts exerted in the field of disarmament", as emphatically affirmed by the Assembly that adopted at the same time the following far-sighted decision:

"With this purpose in mind, the Committee on Disarmament will undertake the elaboration of a comprehensive programme of disarmament encompassing all measures thought to be advisable in order to ensure that the goal of general and complete disarmament under effective international control becomes a reality in a world in which international peace and security prevail and in which the new international economic order is strengthened and consolidated".

It is in compliance with this decision that the Committee on Disarmament established in March 1980 an ad hoc working group "to initiate negotiations on the Comprehensive Programme of Disarmament...with a view to completing its elaboration before the second special session of the General Assembly devoted to disarmament".

The working group has met regularly since then. It held ten meetings in 1980 and more than twenty in 1981. Since 1980, at an early stage of its deliberations, the working group agreed on a structure for the Comprehensive Programme which is very similar to that of the Final Document, inasmuch as it comprises, in addition to an Introduction or Preamble, sections or chapters devoted to Objectives, Principles and Priorities, Measures with indication of Stages of Implementation, and Machinery and Procedure.

Subsequently, the Committee on Disarmament, in its report to

the thirty-fifth session of the General Assembly (a report welcomed by the Assembly) affirmed that the Comprehensive Programme would have to be "self-contained". Bearing this in mind, as well as the "comprehensiveness" which will have to be one of its essential characteristics, it is clear that the Programme will not only encompass all the elements included in the Final Document but will go further than the latter in some respects. In view of this and of the pressing need to adopt new methods and register appropriate undertakings which permit the implementation of effective disarmament measures, it seems obvious that the key item in the agenda of UNSSOD II will be the Comprehensive Programme of Disarmament.

In the light of the tentative conclusion reached as a result of a "first reading" consideration of all material available to the working group until the middle of July, 1981, it would seem probable that the Comprehensive Programme of Disarmament may comprise four "stages of implementation" of the numerous measures it is going to embrace and the realization of which would have to culminate, as explicitly directed by the Assembly, in general and complete disarmament under effective international control.

As a working hypothesis, the group has provisionally accepted a duration of five years for each of those four stages. This would mean the completion of the Programme by the end of the century, it being understood that, at the end of each stage, a special session of the General Assembly should be convened to review the implementation of the Programme and to make the necessary adjustments for the next stages.

The timeframes thus contemplated, should not however be interpreted as the equivalent of rigid timetables, but rather as the indication of agreed deadlines which represent desirable goals to be aimed at, and for whose attainment all States would thus be accepting a binding undertaking to make every possible effort within their reach.

It is too early to have a clear picture of the results of the ad hoc working group deliberations and negotiations. Nevertheless, it may be safely concluded, in the light of all that has been stated in the present paper, that success or failure of the second special session of the General Assembly devoted to disarmament will rest on whether or not it is able to adopt an adequate Comprehensive Programme of Disarmament which, if it is to be effective, should present the following characteristics.

The Programme must fit the description made of it in paragraph 109 of the Final Document as an instrument which should ensure that the goal of general and complete disarmament under effective international control becomes a reality in a world in which international peace and security prevail, and in which the new international economic order is strengthened and consolidated.

With this purpose in mind, the Programme should encompass all measures thought to be advisable for its achievement and which could be divided into two broad categories. The first would cover what is normally called in the United Nations "Disarmament measures", embracing all types of measures dealing with disarmament, whether they be for the prevention, the limitation, the reduction or the elimination of armaments, or for the

reduction of armed forces. The second category would comprise all other relevant measures -- which could be listed under the general heading "Associated measures" -- such as those aimed at ensuring that disarmament makes an effective contribution to economic and social development and, in particular, to full realization of the new international economic order; those intended to contribute to the strengthening of international procedures and institutions for the peaceful settlement of disputes and for the maintenance of peace and security in accordance with the Charter of the United Nations; those whose main purpose would be to mobilize world public opinion in favour of disarmament through a well organized world disarmament campaign, directed and co-ordinated by the United Nations Secretary-General; and those which are usually referred to as confidence-building measures.

While the Comprehensive Programme would thus contain measures of identical nature to those included in the Final Document, the two documents would, however, present some substantial differences: e.g. due to its comprehensiveness, the measures to be included in the Programme would be more numerous than those contained in the Final Document; the measures would be enunciated in a more concrete manner and described more specifically than they are in the Final Document, and they should be assembled in some -- perhaps four -- stages in order to ensure that the adoption of disarmament measures is carried out in "an equitable and balanced manner" in such a way that the security of all States is guaranteed at progressively lower levels, both qualitative and quantitative, of armaments.

With regard to machinery, some improvements may also be sought, such as longer annual sessions for the Committee on Disarmament and procedural ways and means to avoid the abuse of the consensus rule to paralyse negotiations in the Committee, as well as to secure the practical application of past decisions for keeping the United Nations duly informed of all disarmament efforts outside its aegis.

It would also be most desirable to upgrade the UN Secretariat unit in charge of disarmament matters -- the "UN Centre for Disarmament" -- converting it into a "Department of Disarmament Affairs" which should be placed on the same level as the Department of Political and Security Council Affairs and the Department of International Economic and Social Affairs.

The objectives to be pursued, as well as the principles and priorities for the implementation of the measures which were approved by consensus at UNSSOD I, have today, as already stated, the same or even greater, validity than in 1978. It is therefore safe to assume that those which may be included in the Comprehensive Programme will have to be essentially identical to those contained in the Final Document.

At the outset of the Comprehensive Programme there must certainly be included some introductory material which probably will consist of a descriptive introduction strictu sensu and an analytical preamble. But perhaps one of the most important features, for whose inclusion in the Programme no efforts should be spared, would consist of a firm undertaking of all participant States to abide strictly by the provisions of the programme and of

their recognition of some kind of binding force to such provisions. In this respect it should be recalled that the Final Document of 1978, which, in theory, is an outstanding document, has in practice remained a dead letter because of the absence of political will of the nuclear-weapon States, or at least of some of them. It seems therefore indispensable to avoid, in connection with the Comprehensive Programme of Disarmament, the repetition of such a sad experience. The second special session of the United Nations General Assembly devoted to disarmament is entitled -- as are all the people of the world -- not to be deceived once again.

Strategies for Reconversion of Armaments Industry

MICHEL ROGALSKI
CARLOS YAKUBOVICH

The conversion of armaments producing industries to peaceful uses is a subject of interest to, highly, industrialized countries and underdeveloped countries alike. The consequence of armaments production and conversion differ in each case.

It should be realised that reflections on the nature of armaments industries fit into a <u>wider debate on development planning</u>. If conversion is at the core of the disarmament/development link, it is because it entails reflection on the nature of development. In this regard it is indispensable to establish an exploratory tool to outline simply the choices, constraints and various degrees of freedom involved in implementing a conversion program. This may help those who maintain that militarism is unhealthy for capitalism and who, in a wider sense, hope to improve the latter. It may also aid the more radical viewpoint which cannot envisage conversion without transfer of power from the ruling classes to the workers and society in general, and proposes concrete alternatives by emphasizing the social usefulness of production.

To analyze the problem of converting the armaments industry would suggest two stages in our reasoning.

In the first stage the trade and production of armaments is brought to a standstill. In this way physical infrastructures, equipment and manpower are released for other uses, and cash resources are either withheld (importer) or lost (exporter). The extent of these resources will depend on the size of the armaments industry and its degree of penetration in the production structure and in foreign trade.

In the second stage the armaments industry is converted to non-military activity. This leads to the problem of choosing from among available options to adapt the production apparatus. These

From **DEVELOPMENT: SEEDS OF CHANGE**, 1982:1, (54-57), reprinted by permission of the publisher.

options correspond to differing conceptions of a development strategy.

The dividing line between two categories, development and maldevelopment, like the border between essential and non-essential goods, must be established for each single country and each phase of development, following a detailed study of their consumption structures. Such dividing lines can be established arbitrarily in so far as they are determined by a scale of values outside of strictly economic industry.

The analytical process proposed here consists in creating an exploratory tool to provide the starting point of a program for conversion of the armaments industry.

This tool will help in formulating and identifying conversion problems and will facilitate the identification and treatment of the various typical cases; it will also shed light on the existing strategies and options inherent in such program.

For this purpose we will use a model based on the input-output analysis system. Under this system the economy is divided into three sectors producing goods and services for consumption: Sector C_1: producing consumer goods such as food products, herebelow referred to as essential goods or socially useful goods; Sector C_2: producing luxury and prestige consumer goods, herebelow referred to as non-essential goods; Sector C_3: producing armaments, tools of repression and other means of destruction.

There are two other sectors of the economy, producing Capital goods (sector K) and Intermediate goods (sector I).

Each sector may sell part of its production abroad and, conversely, the supply of each category's goods may be increased through imports. The country may also borrow or lend cash. These foreign trade and monetary transactions with the rest of the world are represented by F, i.e. the country's cash availability at a given moment. Likewise, each sector uses the country's available resources of qualified manpower, science and technology. These resources are represented by S and T. The flow between sectors, including foreign trade and the use of science and technology resources, are set forth in diagram 1, pg. 56.

The graph and its components are so designed that as one moves from right to left, there emerge greater degrees of freedom in the production apparatus. This simplifies selection from among the various options which exist in any process of economic planning.

I. A CONVERSION STRATEGY

Armaments production deprives the economy of resources and diverts these to fabricate tools of destruction; it thus increases competition for resources among the producing sectors, all the while provoking the distortions typical of maldevelopment.

A conversion program must firstly weigh the consequences of the shutdown of armaments production and trade, and then proceed to analyse the possibility of re-using resources released for

non-military use.
Using the diagram, options can be analyzed at two levels:

II. END-USE GOODS SECTORS (C_1, C_2, C_3)

Production equipment and manpower employed in C_3 can be readapted and mobilized to increase production of socially useful goods and services (i.e. towards C_1), within the framework of a strategy of transition towards alternative development.

If on the other hand the production equipment of sector C_3 is mobilized to increase production of luxury and prestige goods (i.e. towards C_2), this brings no change in the development strategy in the sense that resources continue to be detoured and wasted without solving the basic problems and urgent needs of the majority of the population. This option, as with the armaments option, falls within the framework of a maldevelopment strategy.

A third option consists in mobilizing resources of C_3 to expand the production capacity of sector K (equipment) or sector I (intermediate goods) which in turn could increase the production of end-use goods.

III. SECTORS UPSTREAM

A release of resources in sectors upstream of C_1, C_2 and C_3 following the shutdown in armaments production and trade permits mobilization towards the above three options for end-use goods.

A conversion program presents problems at three levels:

-- conversion of companies working in the armaments sector;
-- conversion of military bases;
-- conversion of manpower employed by companies and military bases. As far as conversion of companies and bases is concerned, in the 4-sector diagram only sector C_3 is affected. Thus it becomes a matter of converting the physical infrastructures and equipment operating in sector C_3.

The problem of converting manpower involves two aspects:

-- conversion of unskilled or semi-skilled workers; this regards the problem of work equivalents, i.e. work carried out in sector C_3;
-- conversion of highly-skilled manpower: this regards the availability and relocation of highly qualified manpower resources, i.e. alternative re-use of research personnel (S and T).

IV. CONVERSION OF ARMAMENT COMPANIES

Within the operating logic of companies working for armaments industries in capitalist countries, any conversion program implies a wide range of technical, economic and social problems.

Operating logic refers to the behaviour of the companies as a whole, pressure groups and government which, especially in the United States but also in other industrialized countries, has a rationale totally different from that of companies working in non-military areas.

Domestic or international competition compels non-military companies to abstain from a straightforward policy of price hikes to raise profits because they would risk their competitors' refusal to follow suit and the loss of part of their clientele who could buy substitute products or not buy at all.

To increase profits the non-military companies are obliged to introduce technological innovations leading to higher productivity and lower costs.

V. THE ECONOMIC PROBLEM OF CONVERTING COMPANIES

To convert companies away from armaments production, investment programs must be launched to develop new non-military products for which armaments companies have the necessary equipment and technology. These new products nevertheless should be designed in view of the urgent need for goods and services by the majority of the population. A first problem emerges in the sense that the profit motive and market data in industrialized capitalist or underdeveloped countries are not the best guidelines for devising a conversion program towards non-military production. This brings in the serious risk of converting towards goods of the C_2 type which ultimately multiply inequality without satisfying the need for essential goods of the C_1 type.

A second problem concerns the adaptation of armaments companies accustomed to the rationale of maximizing costs and subsidies, to operating in the private sector where the rationale of profit, marketing and more effective management born of competition calls, for management teams with a different approach.

Even if non-military goods were produced by the armaments companies, production costs in all likelihood would be much higher than those of like products manufactured by private sector companies.

A third problem concerns the barriers encountered when entering new sectors of activity. In view of a conversion program one might compile a list of currently manufactured products for which supply does not satisfy demand. The structure of companies operating in private sectors follows the logic of the oligopoly. Oligopolist companies in the private sector put up barriers to

other firms planning to enter the sector. The barriers are technological, commercial and/or financial, and constitute formidable obstacles for new competitors. Thus if an armaments industry is to be converted to the private sector in one of the country's existing activities and if strict market logic is followed, the above obstacles must be given due consideration.

Nonetheless, armaments industries are equipped to overcome these obstacles provided that when converting to non-military operation they work out in advance objectives and schedule necessary to adapt equipment. This offers two advantages: the introduction of totally new products not previously launched on the market; the possibility of entering a sector in which established companies have totally obsolete plant installations. In this case the converted company can be in a good position to compete in the market-place.

VI. TECHNICAL PROBLEMS IN CONVERTING COMPANIES

A conversion program requires a certain period of time to evaluate possibilities of adapting production equipment, design new products, arrange financing, and adapt manpower to their new job status.

Within the logic of options used the problem of production apparatus inflexibility and time needed for conversion do not emerge very clearly.

On this basis the following problems are seen. Firstly, the technical evaluation of the equipment and infrastructures of armaments factories. This evaluation is an essential step in the conversion process because it reveals the degree of inflexibility of equipment proposed for conversion towards new sectors. Accordingly a distinction must be made between equipment adaptable to any type of industrial activity and more specialized equipment used to produce specific, well-defined goods.

A second problem is the time required for conversion. According to accurate studies conducted in the United States, a two year period is needed to plan all the operations of a company's department once a new product has been selected.

The period therefore is indispensable if a company is to convert with some probability of success. This problem is one of the obstacles to conversion and is frequently cited by armaments manufacturers to justify their opposition to conversion, even when the demand for armaments is on the downturn.

VII. CONVERSION OF MILITARY BASES

The subject of shutting down and converting military bases can

be viewed from differing perspectives:

-- shutdown of military bases and conversion of installations and manpower is implemented solely as a means of improving the effectiveness and quality of a defense system, without reducing the military budget.

Military bases are generally considered important at the regional and local level. They often are situated in isolated areas. Overall, economic policies therefore have little effect on the conversion of such bases. An effective policy to convert military bases must be based above all on an analysis of the impact at the regional and community level.

Conversion of bases requires, as with armaments companies, detailed planning under the guidance of local and governmental authorities, giving due consideration to geographical factors, natural and human resources, and physical installations. Accordingly the closure of military bases can become an important element in latent conflicts between local groups and the central government, and even between national and local military authorities.

However, the policy of closing bases and adapting political, military and industrial leaders to change, has shown a certain flexibility in the politico-military and industrial structures, a flexibility necessary for a more global conversion policy for the armaments industries.

VIII. CONVERSION OF MANPOWER EMPLOYED IN THE SECTOR

A major problem arising from conversion concerns the manpower employed in the armaments industries because of the high portion of qualified manpower working in the sector.

The problem can be viewed at four levels, the first regarding conversion of armaments engineers. Conversion releases a relatively high number of engineers since no private industry employs as many engineers as the military sector. This could force some armaments engineers to leave the region where they live and work.

Secondly, the tasks of armaments engineers are highly specialized and intensive recycling courses would be necessary before they are able to work in non-military industries.

The third problem regards the professional outlook of armaments engineers. They often work to meet a criterium of high performance of systems used by the armed forces or by industrial management with no concern for production costs. The armaments engineer therefore works within a rigid criteria framework and does not have the flexibility needed to introduce project modification liable to affect production costs and improve performance of private sector products.

The fourth problem concerns management personnel. As mentioned above, management criteria in the armaments industries differ completely from management criteria in non-military

industries. Conversion therefore implies recycling part of the personnel but also incorporating new talent suited to management of private sector firms.

Finally the workers, the unskilled labourers and office staff present the least problem for conversion. The majority of this manpower can be redirected to the private sector after attending brief courses.

Conversion of engineers and technicians working in the armaments sector presents the equally serious problem of re-using released resources at the level of research and development of new military products in military or private sector laboratories. In fact, research conversion poses fewer problems than the conversion of industry and depends on governmental decisions for financing and orientation of scientific research.

Conversion of science and technology resources towards the private sector should not pose too many problems given the dual nature of advanced research.

IX. CREATION OF NEW JOBS

Supporters of military expenditure and armaments production oppose the shutdown of production and conversion, arguing that the armaments industry is one of the few sectors unaffected by the present economic crisis and that it generates employment.

It would appear that fewer jobs are created in the armaments industries than in other sectors of the economy (capital investment being equal in both sectors). Studies carried out in the United States are unbending in this regard: military investment generates fewer jobs than does private investment, due above all to hypersophisticated technologies requiring large investment, far higher than those necessary to develop private industries.

Figures emerging from these studies probably differ from country to country. Some examples are given here. In a study of the B1 bomber program Chase Econometric's Associates showed that military production employed, dollar for expenditure dollar fewer workers than private production. In a comparison of the effects in 1980 of the B1 program and of equivalent programs of housing, public expenditures or tax reductions to boost domestic spending, Chase Econometric's projected that the latter three policies would respectively generate 70,000, 60,000 and 30,000 more jobs than would the manufacturers of the giant bombers.

The conclusions drawn from these figures can equally be applied to France and to certain underdeveloped, armaments-producing countries. A group of experts has compiled these figures for all developed countries in a report prepared for the General Secretariat of the United Nations.

Number of direct and indirect jobs created for each expenditure of U.S. $ 1 billion	No. of Jobs
Military production (aircraft, electronic missiles, artillery, naval construction, repairs)	76,000
Machinery production (farm, metalwork, industrial)	86,000
Administration	87,000
Transport	92,000
Construction (individual housing, buildings, public equipment motorways)	100,000
Health sector (hospitals, medical instruments)	139,000
Education	187,000

X. THE OBSTACLES

At the international level we find on the one hand, industrialised countries dominating underdeveloped countries, heavy technological dependence, conditioning of economic aid by politics, and thus the imitation of economic development policies and the armed forces of industrialised countries and on the other hand there is an insane competition in the armaments race among the great powers. Given the present international situation, this creates a difficult obstacle for disarmament and conversion programs.

On the national scale, armaments manufacturers will never initiate conversion programs because of their privileged status and their autarchic operations in highly industrialised countries.

Executives and engineers in the armaments industry tend to preserve their status quo. Their prestige and influence in political and military circles form an important basis for the operation of the military-industrial complex. This is the main obstacle to any conversion initiative.

To accomplish this a certain independence must be gained from the military and industrial groups linked with armaments activity. Technicians, unions, universities, consumer associations and political parties must be given the chance to find a solution to industry conversion to produce goods for which there is a demand. This must be done in the context to of a new concept of lifestyles and allowing at the same time a period of transition towards alternative development.

Beyond the fairly well-known offences of the armaments industries with regard to development -- diversion of resources, inflation, unemployment, parasitism, dependence, etc. and beyond the positive economic and social aspects of disarmaments, questions

remain which we shall not attempt to answer here but which nonetheless are indisputable: What is security? Is there a point past which, security being assured, one can speak of over-armament? What type of defense should be provided?

The above questions are linked to conversion: once technical and economic obstacles are overcome these questions are the last barrier faced by supporters of conversion.

The New International
Economic and Military Orders
as Problems to Peace Research

JAN OBERG

I. INTRODUCTORY REMARKS

This article outlines some of the problems related to studying
Third World armament in a wider framework, one which could
appropriately be called a 'new international military order'
(MIMO). This term is sufficiently close to that of the 'new
international economic order' (NIEO) to stimulate the awareness,
from the very outset, of the structural relationship between
armament and development issues.

At the recent Pugwash Symposium on Problems of
Military-Oriented Technologies in Developing Countries (Feldafing,
22-26 November 1976) some of the participants were surprised that
two days passed before some <u>very basic problems</u> were explicitly
dealt with and treated as basic (which again seemed to surprise
other participants).

Some of these basic problems were the following:

(1) The degree to which global armament is embedded in the
overall dominance-dependence structure -- the present economic
order -- and its conflict formations; and the degree to which it
has a relative autonomy and influences this very structure. (The
'order' problem.)

(2) That disarmament should, ideally, be attained through the
break-up of the present economic order and the establishment of a
true NIEO. (The problem of order transformation.)

(3) That what can be done to curb the rapid quantitative and

From **BULLETIN OF PEACE PROPOSALS**, Vol. 8, No. 2, 1977, (142-149),
reprinted by permission of the publisher.

qualitative development in armament and its trend towards a global reach, especially in the military-industrial field, should primarily begin in and be directed towards the overdeveloped and overarmed center countries, and not find expression in a simple moralistic condemning of peripheral countries' arms efforts. (The problem of policy implications.)

(4) That the relationship between armament/militarism/military technology on the one hand and development -- its various conceptualizations from pure GNP growth to basic needs satisfaction and self-reliance -- on the other is highly complex, and that the role of armament in various types of economies should be the object of more intensive analysis. (The problem of theory in armament research.)

It seems fair to point out that peace researchers and other concerned scientists have been far more aware of the economic and political dimensions of the present world order than of its military dimensions -- especially when it comes to the consequences for the periphery.

It may also be reasonable to maintain that this is reflected in another fact: that the research available today is either primarily quantitative and statistically oriented and lacks explicit theorizing, or is primarily theoretical and lacks empirical analysis. Both orientations have little to say about the question: What should be done?

Thus, at the same time as the relatively new concept of a NIEO comes into focus and develops politically, the armament issues also come into focus empirically as an 'order' problem. The two orders are fundamentally related to each other, although it is difficult to state precisely how and what this interrelationship carries for the future world development.

To treat the two 'orders' and their developments in a larger framework requires some theory and concept development -- in armament theory, imperialism theory, and development theory. These may be the main building-blocks; on the empirical level they correspond, respectively, to the NIMO, the present economic order and a future, truly NIEO.

In the interaction of these theoretical building blocks and their respective 'orders', new problem areas will have to be developed. In the interaction of armament and imperialism it will be increasingly important to employ and clarify the concepts of militarism and militarization -- to understand how militarism is based in the imperialist economic order and how armament militarizes this order.

Likewise, it will be vital to develop appropriate tools to distinguish between the various NIEO concepts and order proposals being produced. We need to differentiate between a 'false' NIEO (one which would develop into a neo-imperialist order establishing a division of labor between centers and periphery at a new level, thereby deepening the underdevelopment trend for the majority) and 'true' NIEO proposals focusing primarily on betterment for the majority and on concepts like basic needs satisfaction and self-reliance.

Thirdly, and perhaps most important for the long-term perspective, some constructive thinking must be stimulated in the relationship between development and armament. What is the conflict and peace potential of various development models and NIEO proposals? Are self-reliance and dissociation from the world market system necessarily peaceful? What new conflict formations are likely to develop? Are certain strategies likely to push armament and militarization upwards? How do we attain a true NIEO with as little violence as possible? On what criteria -- military or non-military, violent or non-violent -- should NIEO proposals and models be judged in the future?

Within the conflict/peace dimension of the relationship between development and armament lies, of course, also the entire problem-area of the role of armament in the economy. This includes the discussion of its so-called beneficial and detrimental effects, its driving forces and possible 'opportunity costs'.

To summarize, the overall theoretical framework for armament studies could ideally look like the representation in Fig. 1 (below).

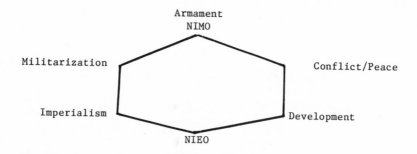

What types of research and what kinds of general approaches are available today? It cannot do justice to the richness of studies when, as in the following, we shall try to group or categorize them under confining headings. What is said for each group does, of course, not necessarily apply to every single contribution mentioned as example of the group. However, by contrasting these approaches, we hope not only to provoke some discussion, but also to point out areas of interest for future research.

II. DEFENSE ECONOMY RESEARCH

Three recent works by Benoit and by Kennedy[1] will serve as examples here. The primary purpose of these studies is to show that neither welfare expenditures nor economic growth are inhibited by defense spending in the 'developing' countries.

The value orientation of such studies is not stated explicitly. However, in both cases, Third World armament is in the end legitimized on the grounds that it does not influence economic growth in an overall negative way. As research ideals the criteria of objectivity and no 'value judgements' are employed. The conservative nature of this approach will be apparent from the quotation at the end of this section.

At the theory level, the problem of the basic conceptualization immediately occurs: What is implied by 'armament' and by 'development'? Armament is seen primarily as something measurable in terms of military expenditures: its wider meaning in relation to societal structures is not analyzed. Concerning the concept of development, we usually meet the traditional quantitative criteria. Kennedy defines it as the growth in GNP or in the per capita product; there are no considerations about basic needs satisfaction, about the distribution of wealth, or the structure of various economic sectors in Third World economies.

Growth in GNP is also the necessary and sufficient indicator of development to Benoit. In addition, he points out that 'the emphasis would be put on bringing about such "modernizing" changes in attitudes and motivation as would lead to a continuous rise in productivity'.[2]

Such modernizing changes are brought about by <u>the military system itself</u>. It contributes to the training of manpower, educating it and giving it skills that can also be employed in civilian fields after demobilization: 'following and transmitting precise instructions, living and working by the clock, noticing and reading signs, spending and saving money, using transportation . . . working with, repairing and maintaining machinery, listening to radio, becoming interested in national and even international news, etc.'[3] .

Most of these changes are not only dubious as positive development values: they are also rather difficult to measure in the manner which Benoit otherwise employs. These changes which more appropriately might be seen as 'positive' effects of militarization of societies and human minds thus represent a special problem to Benoit which we shall return to later.

The same basic value-orientation is found in Kennedy, especially when he is speaking about industrialization:

> The other point of view would regard the establishment of a domestic industry as a part of the programme of industrialization. Without the industrialization programme, the country cannot become independent politically. A defence industry helps to achieve the former -- it develops administrative skills in modern management -- and guarantees the latter.[4]

Why defense industries are better than other industries is not analyzed -- neither whether they really 'guarantee' political independence. It is mentioned that arms industries are protected from competition: this is perhaps true at the national 'market', but far from the case when the country engages in export business.

And most arms-producing countries do -- or are forced to.

Kennedy even maintains that 'mistakes or failures are likely to be set against the hoped-for future political benefits of independence' -- indeed a strange separation of economics and politics, an inversion of the very fact that failures in arms production (and even certain successes) increase dependence on those center countries which help the country develop an arms manufacturing capacity.[5]

There are also some obvious methodological problems in this approach. Countries are treated as homogeneous, independent units of analysis; in consequence they are often grouped in arbitrary ways and on unclear criteria. Kennedy employs comparisons and averages of quantitative indicators like budget expenditures in order to evaluate whether a country is 'high' or 'low' on defense versus welfare spending. He groups a number of countries, finds the average of each group, and comes out with the startling fact that Israel, Lebanon, and Iraq are 'below-average spending' countries in the Middle East;[6] this is maintained despite the fact that they spend, respectively, 26%, 21%, and 30% of their budgets on defense.

Conceptualizations are often superficially journalistic and non-operational, e.g. where Kennedy employs 'the level of insecurity felt by a government' as an important indicator of the relative allocation of resources to civilian and military purposes in countries.

Should one be surprised? Benoit openly states that he was, when arriving at the conclusion of his findings:

> The big surprise of this study was the finding that the evidence does not indicate that defense has had any net adverse effect on growth in developing countries. It even suggests the possibility, though this is not demonstrable, that on balance the defense programs may have stimulated economic growth.[7]

As long as we are speaking of purely economic growth, this finding is hardly surprising. Benoit, of course, is aware that economic growth measured by GNP growth is not necessarily identical with development, but he found no better way of analyzing the subject.[8]

Therefore it may be more telling of the nature of this type of study to look at the value and policy implications which Benoit draws of his study. In addition to speaking about the 'modernizing', positive effects, Benoit maintains that the military establishment in the Third World has a 'revolutionary effect in destroying unquestioned acceptance of local custom and tradition . . .'[9] as it contributes to 'nation building'. Among other benefits from the military establishment, Benoit mentions 'civic action' programs which 'appear to have important potential economic benefits, whatever their possible political difficulties.'[10] Finally Benoit offers some suggestions as to the policy implications of his study, maintaining for instance that the favorable effects of the military influence make 'a stronger case for a much closer coordination between defense planning and

development planning.'[11]

This is, indeed, a strange proposal. First of all, it is a conclusion based on many non-measurable 'favorable effects' of military expenditures in the midst of a quantitative, statistically-oriented study which otherwise does not intend to present 'value judgements'. Secondly, we should notice that here the terminology has changed from 'economic growth' to 'development'. Thirdly, Benoit refrains from discussing the long-term consequences of conscious coordination between armament and development planning. This is the more unfortunate and careless as he has earlier ignored the possible 'political difficulties' of Third World military establishments.

Kennedy concludes his study by stating that violence seems to be embedded in man's nature, and that a world disarmed 'might become the most dangerous place for life that man could create'.[12] With these conclusions in mind, it can hardly surprise the reader that this approach and kind of research does not 'fit' the framework outlined in our triangle: it lacks theoretical foundation in all three building blocks. As to its value orientation and political implications, this approach has already been excellently characterized by Albrecht, Ernt, Lock & Wulf:[13]

> Researches of the Benoit type fulfill functions of a very special kind, not expressed explicitly anywhere, but they can easily be recognized reading between the lines. First of all they are supposed to delineate the potentials and limitations of ways and means of securing the dominance of the existing structure of the capitalist mode of production on a world-wide scale, while analyzing socio-economic reality only partially.

III. POLITICO-MILITARY RESEARCH

This approach is widespread: it is exemplified by the studies by Stockholm International Peace Research Institute (SIPRI), by Stanley and Pearton, by Thayer and several others.[14]

The value orientation is here basically against armament, attempting to show its 'negative' effects. The studies are most often politically neutral. Their purpose is to present 'events' in a reasonably systematic manner, in order to broaden public awareness of global armament issues.

Basically, such politico-military studies are 'documentaristic' and their object is armament itself, as if it were an autonomous phenomenon. The actual driving forces or its economic, social, and political implications are rarely touched upon: this is especially true for consequences of armament, which cannot be quantified.

Concerning theory, the contact with social science is rather limited[15] and the studies seldom discuss theories of armament, imperialism, or development -- not to speak of their relationships.

There is thus little interaction between theory and data.

In order to present data in a reasonably cohesive manner and in a way that can be utilized by others -- scientists, diplomats, politicians, journalists -- this type of study borrows some not-too-clear concepts from political science to categorize and group data.

Methodologically, the following points could be raised: Countries are treated almost exclusively as homogeneous, independent units of analysis, while their position in the global structure is not taken seriously into consideration. Countries 'act' and 'behave', and now and then arms trade is seen as the outcome of acts by nations or individual politicians.

We are left with little real explanation of 'events' because their roots in structures and their dynamics are not analyzed in a deeper sense. What is often given instead is the concept of a 'mix of factors', and frequently the use of explanans and explanandum is mixed up.

Especially SIPRI's research profile is documentaristic, with an underlying 'high science' orientation. In most studies, this institute balances on the tip of our triangle, always careful not to take the plunge into the issues of imperialism or underdevelopment, the relationship between armament and conflict formations, or the constructive thinking about future models of peaceful development and peace-inducing structures. This is the more peculiar as the statues of the Institute state that

> The purpose of the Foundation is to conduct scientific research on questions which are important for international peace and security with the intent to contribute to the understanding of the conditions for peaceful solutions of international conflicts and for a stable peace.[16]

Can this purpose be fulfilled without thorough analysis of the present international structure and its development issues? Can it be fulfilled through primarily stockpiling arms data? And can it be fulfilled as long as the institute adheres to a politically neutral value orientation?

It is somewhat indicative of the research policy of SIPRI that neither its studies nor its yearbooks are objects of stimulating theoretical and political debate, nor is its role in peace research evaluated. This problem cannot be solved merely by popularizing present studies.

It may rather be a matter of shifting priorities from the manifestations and potentials of direct violence to the driving forces, realities, and consequences of structureal violence, and -- more important -- developing an understanding of the deep relationships between the two types of violence.

It should not be concluded that the politico-military type of study is irrelevant for the framework presented in the introduction. Politico-military research can be extremely useful as regards data; also it has an orientation towards peace which is important in de-legitimizing armament and militarization. What is needed is a more integrative, theoretical development, together

with a vitalization of its value-orientation and research methods which could also enhance the potential for constructive development and disarmament thinking.

IV. ARMAMENT-IMPERIALISM RESEARCH

This approach is well exemplified by the contributions of Albrecht, Ernst, Lock and Wulf, Senghaas, Kidron, and others in a more Marxist-oriented tradition.[17] Basically founded in armament and imperialism theories, it seeks to integrate the two. This has been expressed by Senghaas:

> It becomes more and more important to be aware of the symbiotic interlocking between armaments developments on the one hand and societal processes and international structures on the other, but also of the at least practically observable relative autonomy of armament processes within the past few years.[18]

This integrative and very comprehensive approach seems the most fruitful so far. However, it could be highly improved if only the development dimension and the more constructive thinking were allowed to enrich the overall approach. A bit more should be said about this in relation to each of the sides of our triangular model.

First of all, the concepts of militarism and militarization need clarification. They are often employed in concluding and summarizing sections of the contributions, where it is stated that men, nations, and the international structure are being more and more 'militarized' as a consequence of armament trends. The concepts are hardly that simple, but unfortunately we find that the more 'traditional' definitions are not very useful for our study.[19] There is a need for a 'theory of militarization' which can be applied to concepts like economic and military orders at national as well as international levels.

Not only 'theory' is needed. Within the general framework of the World Indicators Program (WIP), for instance, a study of military and militarization indicators is now under way, focusing on such dimensions as the destruction of things and structures (destruction potential), opportunity costs (constructive potential), the basis of legitimization of armament, the relationship between imperialism and militarization, implications for national social structures and developments, and, finally, the military ideology. These are all problems and issues of the problem-area called militarism or militarization, and it will surely take time before these concepts have been properly classified and linked to our basic building blocks. However, the armament-imperialism approach seems the most fit to undertake such efforts.

Secondly, in taking into consideration the development

dimension more substantially, armament research should engage itself in the NIEO discussion and contribute to the integration of armament issues in this discussion.

One concrete way of doing this is to pose analytical questions about the relationship between the specific NIEO issues and the military and armament, e.g.: What is the relationship between world food problems and armament? Between civil and military trade and investment patterns? How much of the Third World debt is caused by the purchase of military equipment and assistance? What is the international flow in military manpower -- 'military brain drain'? How much of so-called development aid is and has been military and paramilitary? What is the relationship between the military and armaments on the one hand and resource flows on the other? What is the military consumption of energy and raw materials? How do civil and military industrialization in the Third World relate to each other? What is the parallel between military and civil transfers of technology? Are transnational corporations the 'carriers' of both the economic and the military world industrial orders in the future?

For example, Kidron has raised the important question of the economic meaning of armament, maintaining that it is 'waste'. This has specific consequences for the periphery in the following way:

> . . . weapons or weapons instruction is not consumed by workers (in the periphery) and can never be. It can never enter the productive process in those countries, however indirectly. It is utterly sterile. What the exchanges have done is shift potentially productive surplus from India to Russia, or from Brazil to the United States, or the Middle East to Britain and waste in the opposite direction. From the point of view of the capitals involved, it is a one-way transfer of investible surplus which takes place even on the assumption of equal exchange.[20]

With an arms trade with the Third World amounting to $15-20 billion a year in pure transfer of hardware, this certainly adds an important dimension to the discussion of unequal exchange between center and periphery which is in focus of the NIEO debate.

Another way is to develop the analytical tools to distinguish between 'true' and 'false' NIEOs and NIEO proposals. If it is true that armament and the emerging NIMO grows out of the present old economic order, it is of paramount importance that armament research should engage in analyzing and proposing ways to transform this order.

If, furthermore, it is true that the best the centers can do to create a true NIEO is to withdraw from this order and make do on their own, it becomes of equal importance that armament research should develop alternative development strategies not only for the Third World but also for the centers: center self-reliance.

This would be the first major advantage of armament studies. It would imply an intensive interest in issues like change of life-styles, definition of maximum living standards, a decrease in the dependence on foreign supplies, reduction in meaningless,

resource-consuming, and luxurious production and reduction in export and import of the same goods, etc. More fundamentally, the self-reliance strategy applied to the overdeveloped center countries would imply work on decentralization, demonopolization, treating human beings as subjects and not as objects, building smaller economic units and circles based on more horizontal exchanges, and developing alternative technology.

What this leads up to in the long-term perspective is an endeavor to reduce the social economic, and political vulnerability of societies.

This is where the second major advantage for armament studies would come in. The discussion of center self-reliance and strategies to reduce the vulnerability of the present society would not only be in accordance with the theoretical assumption that the international economic and military order are fundamentally interlinked: it would also open up new possibilities for developing alternative defense and security concepts and policies based on non-military and non-violent values.

In other words, new thinking about societal and economic and ideological 'defense', assimilated with self-reliant development of the now overarmed and overdeveloped center countries, would make relevant the withdrawal of these countries from the present international economic and military orders.

Thirdly, there is the relationship between development and armament -- of which something has already been said. It will be the task here to outline the implications for armament, militarization, and the military order of various NIEO models and proposals -- true or false. At the moment, the NIEO concept seems to be moving towards 'N' standing for neo-imperialism, i.e. the establishment of an international division of labor on a 'higher' level -- leading to some redistribution of incomes and resources between the centers and the center elites in the periphery, but naturally also furthering the underdevelopment of the masses who hardly participate or are represented in the debate.

The logical scenario may here be that a false NIEO will create more conflicts to be 'solved' in still more violent ways: in other words, that a false NIEO shall contribute to armament and the further development of NIMO. It should be the task of peace researchers, among others, to make such relationships clear and apparent, and increase public awareness about the implications.

On this side of the triangle we also find the need for analyzing the conflict/peace aspects of various development goals and strategies, for instance self-reliance. It is necessarily a more peaceful development, and what strategies could be advocated for it to be so? Again, it is vital to take into consideration both the national and the international level of analysis.

Much more could be said about the possibilities growing out of the armament-imperialism approach. It should be apparent that this approach is the most appropriate. It is stimulating because of its theoretical coverage of two of the three building blocks and because it opens up many new research directions -- also others than those mentioned here.

Obviously there are points of overlapping between the politico-military and the armament-imperialism approaches. They

could fruitfully be integrated.

*

Much of what has been said in this article may seem utopian, or at least aiming at a too-distant goal when seen in relation to the immediate problems facing us. The reasoning has, however, been based on the following chain of argument:

(1) Armament and the emerging New International Military Order (NIMO) is embedded in the present international economic order, but at the same time NIMO has a certain autonomy.

(2) To stop the further development of armament and the NIMO, the present economic order should -- ideally -- be transformed at its very basis and a true NIEO be created, to the benefit of the majority.

(3) A true NIEO can be developed mainly through fundamental changes in the presently overdeveloped and overarmed center countries and through their withdrawal from the imperialist economic order, i.e. through an endeavor to develop more self-reliant strategies and life-styles in center regions as well as nations.

(4) Strategies towards a true NIEO should put a halt to armament. Disarmament is likely to stimulate thinking about completely new non-military, non-violent concepts and policies for 'defense' -- especially economic, political, and societal defense and security. The establishment of much less vulnerable societies as mentioned under point (3) above will be a major step in this direction.

There is a need to broaden the research of global armament and its relationship to the discussion of NIEO. This should also help us in developing criteria for judging about how new is NIEO.

As a first step, armament issues should be integrated in the NIEO discussion -- and the other way around. Secondly, NIEO shall not be called 'true' or 'new' unless it, among other things, puts a halt to world armament and leads to new thinking about defense.

NOTES

[1]Kennedy 1974, The Military in the Third World, Duckworth and Company, London; Benoit, 1973, Defense and Economic Growth in Developing Countries, Lexington Books, Massachusetts; and Benoit, 1976, Growth Effects of Defense in Developing Countries, paper presented at the Pugwash Symposium on Problems of Military-Oriented Technologies in Developing Countries; Feldafing, 22–26 November 1976.

[2]Benoit, 1973, p.x.

[3]Ibid., p. 17.

[4]Kennedy, 1974, p. 283.

[5]See further arguments in Kennedy, op. cit., pp. 292–95.

[6]Ibid., p. 169.

[7]Benoit, 1973, op. cit., p. xix.

[8]At the Pugwash Symposium, Dr. Benoit stated that although GNP is highly criticizable, he found that alternative indicators would have taken too much time to develop.

[9]Benoit, 1976, p. 10.

[10]ibid., p. 15.

[11]Benoit, 1973, op. cit., p. xx.

[12]Kennedy, op. cit., p. 335.

[13]Albrecht et al., 1974 'Armaments and Underdevelopment', BPP, vol. 5, 1974, p. 173.

[14]SIPRI, 1974, The Arms Trade with the Third World, Almquist & Wiksell, Uppsala; SIPRI Yearbooks 1973–76, SIPRI 1975; Arms Trade Registers; Almquist & Wiksell International Stockholm, and Stanley and Pearton, 1972; The International Trade in Arms, Chatto & Windus, London, for the International Institute for Strategic Studies (IISS); and Thayer, The War Business, Paladin, 1969.

[15]This is now being improved at SIPRI by extra-institute contacts and co-operation on projects.

[16]SIPRI, 1976, Prospectus with Report of Activities 1975, quoted from the statues, 2, p. 13.

[17]Albrecht, Ernst, Lock & Wulf, 1976, Rustung and Unterentwicklung, rorooro aktuell, Hamburg, and 'Armaments and Underdevelopment' BPP, 1974; 'Arms Transfer and Arms Production in Peripheral Countries', JPR, 3/1975; Albrecht, 1976, 'Arms Trade with the Third World and Domestic Arms Production'. Instant Research on

Peace and Violence, 1-2/1976; Wulf, Militar and Rusting in Indien, Diplomarbeit 1974. Hamburg; Loch & Wulf, 1976, Consequences of the Transfer of Military Technology on the Development Process, paper presented at the above-mentioned Pugwash Symposium; Senghaas, 1976, Gegenwartige Prozess einer Internationalisierung des Militarismus, paper presented in Ibadan, Nigeria, and 1976, 'Armament Dynamics and Disarmament', Instant Research on Peace and Violence, 1-2; Kidron, 1974, Capitalism and Theory, Pluto Press, London, and 1976, Remarks on the Military and Development in Economically-Weak Countries, paper presented at the above-mentioned Pugwash Symposium.

[18]Senghaas, op. cit.

[19]See for instance Berghahn (ed.), 1975, Militarismus, Kiepenheuer & Witsch, Koln, for such traditional, national approaches to the concept of militarism.

[20]Kidron, 1974, p. 108 -- his arguments and comparative analysis are found in pp. 95-103.

Peace Research

BERT ROLING

I. INTRODUCTION

Peace research is a scholarly pursuit concerned with the
causes of war and the conditions of peace. Peace science, or
polemology, or "Friedenswissenschaft", is a problem-oriented branch
of scholarship. The regular occurrence of war is a social problem.
Peace researchers presume that more knowledge about the causes of
war and about the conditions under which peace can be maintained
will contribute to more rational behaviour in international
relations, and thus contribute to solving this social problem.

Peace research emerged from anxiety rather than curiosity. It
is a branch of the social sciences born in the atomic era. The
introduction of nuclear weapons brought danger to the world
surpassing anything mankind had encountered previously. Awareness
of the extreme danger has generated the peace research movement
throughout the world. When nuclear weapons made war unbearable,
means had to be discovered to eliminate such a confrontation. The
spreading interest in peace research sprang from an urge to
contribute to more rational foreign policies and more peaceful
international relations, through better insight into the causes of
war and the conditions of peace.

The theory of international relations is a well established
branch of scholarship. It originated after the First World War,
which showed the need for a clearer perception of international
relations. This fairly new field of research emphasized state
sovereignty and state power. Government-sponsored "societies for
international relations" appeared in almost all European countries.
Like the League of Nations, their point of departure was the

From **THE ARMS RACE AND DISARMAMENT**, UNESCO Press, 1982, (217-231),
reprinted by permission of the publisher.

maintenance of the status quo, which included the dominance of European states and the United States, over large parts of the non-white world in colonial and imperial relations; the dominance of the victors in the First World War over the vanquished.

It is easy to understand why in the course of time the war-peace problem acquired an evermore prominent place in the theory of international relations. Especially after the Second World War, the awareness grew that maintenance of peace was in the primary national interest. But the approach to the problem of war and peace remained to be based on the traditional standpoint, with emphasis on the significance of the armed power of the national sovereign state. "Peace research" was born out of discontent with the status quo, which was considered to be a dangerous conflict-ridden situation. It was critical in its attitude regarding traditional state policy and questioned the value of the existing concept of national sovereignty. It suspected that the emphasis on national military power would irrevocably lead to arms races, over-kill and weapon-postures, and to increased danger of war. It differed in its paradigmatical approach by taking not the national but the global view-point.

A similar ambiguous relation exists between peace research and "strategic studies", that is research concerning the optimal use of armed power. In principle, both kinds of research should come to the same rational conclusions. The difference in outcome is due to the military origin of "strategic studies" which may explain the trust in power to achieve political ends.

II. THEORIES OF PEACE RESEARCH

Peace research is a recent phenomenon. The science of peace and war is young and as such it has features which are common to most young social sciences. In all social research the tendency exists to give expression to the prevailing value-judgements. A social group which opposes a particular social institution will be tempted to impute a great many social evils to that institution. The kings were seen as the cause of war during the epoch of absolute monarchy. Nowadays, those who have misgivings about the capitalist or the communist system will be inclined to impute the occurrence of war to capitalism or communism. Technology, which at one time was seen as the cure to all social evils, was then regarded as the hoped for road to peace. Today, the inclination exists to ascribe much of the evil to technology, including the arms race and the occurrence of war. For the very reason that social sciences are concerned with evaluations, the prevailing moods may, and will, influence the social scientist.

Another pitfall is the tendency to generalize research findings and to yield to emotion that goes with discovery. Most social scientist start their task by fighting superstitious beliefs and traditional thinking. If they discover a real cause of a social evil they will be inclined to regard it as the cause.

Lombroso's theory of "born criminal" reigned for a long period in criminology. In socialist doctrine each society engenders the crime it deserves. Society is of course to blame, but not for all crimes.

These primitive scientific "truths" were in fact vital errors but they fulfilled the important function of breaking through traditional mistaken opinions. When social science comes to maturity it corrects the generalizations. It becomes more sophisticated, more complicated, more realistic, more aware of the fact that many factors are involved in every social event and that it is often very difficult to determine their relative strength. At this stage the findings of the social sciences are more in conformity with reality but more difficult to adapt by decision makers. The "vital error" is perhaps more effective than the "sterile truth". The history of every social science shows the road it travelled, a road paved with the names of famous scholars who erred in their one-sidedness, but who focussed attention on previously neglected aspects of social phenomena.

It is difficult to establish in which phase peace research finds itself at present. Some radical theories, such as those which label the capitalist system as the cause of war and claim that there can be no peace without the elimination of capitalism, or those which blame structural violence and social injustice as the cause of all evil, would suggest that peace research is still in the early phase. A just world does not necessarily mean a peaceful world! A peaceful world needs a stable structure along with a generally acceptable just order, a structure that is able to withstand a crisis.

In theories which stress specific aspects of a problem, too much may be hidden in the metaphors used in social theory. In his article "Twelve friendly quarrels with Johan Galtung", Kenneth Boulding[1] suggests that many terms used by Galtung, such as negative and positive peace, personal and structural violence, top-dog and under-dog, centre and periphery, are introduced as metaphors and gradually applied as models. A metaphor is the emotionally loaded image of one aspect; a model is the cool simplication of the whole. Boulding states: "perhaps one of the great dilemmas of the human race is that metaphors are persuasive and models are not"[2].

In this connection it is worthwhile to stress the point that the peace researcher tries, as objectively as possible, to describe and analyse the social reality confronting him. Distinction should be made between the "hard facts" and the real world, e.g. the existing weapon potential, and what one might call the "soft facts", the existing perceptions, opinions and evaluations. If one analyses the hard facts it may be possible to discover what would be needed to cope with them. The hard facts determine what society needs if it is to continue and prosper, and the changes necessitated by the "natural law of the atomic age", such as general disarmament and some form of federal world structure. But the soft facts, the attitudes, opinions and short term interests, often prevent the realization of those changes, even if they were considered necessary for survival. These soft facts determine what is possible in human society. William Fulbright[3] stressed the gap

work out their version of a preferred world[15]. A serious effort is
made to exclude all features of cultural imperialism and to
harmonize some basic values within the diversity of cultures,
presupposing different transition periods for different world
regions. Whether cultural imperialism, hidden in the concepts of
socio-political justice and humane governance, can be excluded, is
the main question. This benign form of imperialism may, however,
be inevitable, especially since every region in the world wants the
benefits of technology. The introduction of technology is not
restricted to the transfer of machinery. It inevitably includes
the transfer of many of the accepted values existing in the
developed parts of the world.

V. ARMS CONTROL AND DISARMAMENT

However important futurological peace research may be, we
still live in a world that is rightly called an "endangered
planet"[16]. Its dangers are pressing. Research is badly needed,
particularly to diminish the danger of nuclear war. Mankind cannot
wait until a new world structure has been established, or until a
more just order has been realized. We must ask what can be done,
here and now, within the framework of our conflict-ridden system.
What should be the conduct of states to prevent violent conflicts?
In what manner would it be possible to influence the many causes of
tension: armaments and the arms race, poverty and development,
racial discrimination, violation of human rights, nationalism,
political ideologies, overpopulation? What kind of peace education
and peace action could lead to more rational governmental
decisions?

This is not the place for a survey of the results of peace
research concerning all these different topics. This book deals
with arms control and disarmament, and therefore the discussion
will be restricted to these items of peace research.

Peace research arose out of the anxiety caused by the
emergence of nuclear weapons. A considerable part of peace
research is devoted to the dangers to humanity stemming from the
technological weapon development. For the first time in history
the question of survival has become a serious topic. Much research
and many publications are devoted to the analysis of the dangers
of modern weaponry and the prevailing strategic theories. The
deeper one penetrates into the present weapon situation and the
prevailing military theories, the more worried one becomes. Peace
research has the important task to follow the arms developments
closely and continuously, evaluate these developments and give the
world the much needed information. Governments would presumably
act differently if they were aware of the existing macro-risks.
"Blindness in involvement" plays an important role. The dictum
that between the weapon-reality and its perception lies a gap that
opens the road to Armageddon contains much truth.

Another aspect of research into these matters is concerned

with the factors which play a role in the arming process. What causes governments to spend so much of their resources on arms? National armed power is a logical consequences of an international system consisting of sovereign states which must ensure their own security. But what can be the reason for the excessive armed power existing today? What can explain the existing mindless arms races?

Two extreme theories attempted to supply an explanation. According to one theory the excessive arming stems from an arms race fed by technology and is dominated by an action-reaction process. Fear of new technological developments compel the adversaries to concentrate on technological arms research. Any new development is immediately applied and gives one side a temporary advantage until the other side restores the balance. In a situation like the present Cold War, each side strives for superiority. Hence the current arms race.

The assumption that the strategic arms race follows from the action-reaction syndrome is refuted in the theory of Dieter Senghaas17 which states that to a large extent governments base their armaments and deterrence policies on autonomous, inner-directed motives. Apart from the "military-industrial complex", this theory involves the psychological aspect of social "autism" which leads to a very distorted view of the outside world.

A major proportion of peace research is devoted to the analysis of armaments-dynamics in which internal and external factors intermingle. The lack of sufficient empirical evidence precludes a clear picture of the different forces determining the "deadly logics" of the threat system.

A similar controversy exists in relation to the general theory of the present function of military power.

NATO and WPO account for approximately 70 per cent of the world's arms expenditure, of more than 500 billion US dollars per year. The introduction of weapons of mass destruction, such as nuclear arms and sophisticated rocketry, have made it quite clear that an all-out nuclear war between the two alliances would end in mutual destruction. Such a suicidal war is unacceptable and totally different from von Clausewitz's concept of war, and his description of war as "a continuation of politics". However, such a total war might still occur accidentally or inadvertently, as a war indicating the breakdown of policy. At present the concept of "limited war" keeps creeping up. This is a von Clausewitz type of war which would be fought out in Europe and on the high seas, without the involvement of the devastating central systems strategic nuclear weapons. Opinions are divided about the feasibility of keeping such a war restricted, but experts agree that the risks of escalation are too high.

Modern weapons are so destructive and there is no possibility of real defence, that the reasonable conclusion must be that military power is non-usable. However, it would be wrong to draw the conclusion that national armed power should be abolished. If one of the two major military alliances were to disarm unilaterally, the weapons of the other alliance would then become usable thereby giving the Soviet Union or the United States absolute power. Such a situation is not attractive. History teaches us that a state usually misbehaves according to its might.

Hence the need of countervailing armed power. Modern weapons are unusable but indispensable. This is the problem of present weapons, and it will remain a problem until it is solved by arms control and general disarmament.

What is the function of military power in such a situation[18]? Here, too, there are many different opinions. If any employment of military power carries with it macro-risks, the rational conclusion would be that the function of military power should be restricted to preventing its use in battle, i.e. deterrence. Deterrence aims not only at preventing the factual use of the sword in battle, but as well the rattling of the sword.

Many objections have been raised to such a radical conclusion about the function of armed power. It has been pointed out that military intervention against economic measures exercised by a Third World state, or opposition to ideological developments, may appear attractive. The American "rapid deployment forces" are destined in part to protect economic interests against non-military violations. This is an example of the concept of the political use of military power, the indirect or oblique use of force[19].

Experts may agree that the only function of armed force is to provide for peace and security, but opinions differ about the very concept of security. Security usually means military security with respect to the military power of a possible opponent: this might rather be called "enemy security." But with the present technological weapon developments another danger arises, a danger hidden in the weapon-postures themselves. There are forms of destabilizing weapon-postures, such as the capacity to launch a successful surprise attack. War would be likely if one side acquired a first strike capability; it would be almost inevitable if both acquired it or thought they had acquired it. The premium on haste would have an almost absolute character.

Another aspect of a dangerous premium on haste concerns the situation when war has broken out. If one party has vulnerable weapons of mass destruction, e.g. eurostrategic weapons, the other may be inclined to destroy them immediately. The possessor, on the other hand, may be inclined to put them into action before that destruction. The premium on haste thus leads to a quick escalation, even when both sides have a vital interest in keeping the fighting under strict control, to give diplomatic action a chance.

Another "weapon-danger" is caused by the existing overkill. Use of the nuclear weapons available at present would lead to the total destruction of both sides. Such a threat is not needed for effective deterrence. But if a war started, -- probably an inadvertent war, in a situation in which a local conflict could not be kept under control because of miscalculations or misperceptions -- this overkill might lead to unimaginable disaster.

Thus, military security comprises not only "enemy-security" but also "weapon-security". The distinction is relevant. Steps to enhance enemy-security often diminish weapon-security, not only in bilateral relations. Vertical proliferation of nuclear weapons may easily enhance horizontal proliferation, and the spread of nuclear weapons all over the world would increase the weapon-insecurity.

There is a tendency at present to broaden the concept of security. State interests can be perceived to be violated by means other than military, e.g. by ideological developments or economic measures. Great powers are inclined to protect their interests against such violations by military means, and the military preparations in connection with scarce materials, such as oil, are prominent illustrations. Growing economic interdependence contributes to the fears of the developed nations of the collapse of their economy, through the loss of scarce materials. This has resulted in the ominous revival of the idea of protection of economic interest by military means.

The broadening of the security concept to "economic security" and "ideological security", with its corollary, the extension of the function of military force, may have disastrous effects. Threatened by one of the superpowers, Third World countries may seek protection by turning to the other superpower. This will strengthen the drive for superior military strength and preclude any chance of arms control and disarmament. By the same token, the Third World states may see strong incentives to arm themselves, even to "go nuclear", in an endeavour to prevent great power intervention.

Willingness to use armed force when national interests are threatened or violated by ideological or economic means, indicates a preparedness to disregard the prohibition of the use of force, enshrined in the United Nations Charter, according to which armed force is only to be employed as a reaction against an armed attack. This strict prohibition is reaffirmed in the definition of aggression adopted in 1974 by the General Assembly. The implied elimination of the legal prohibition of the use of force -- the ground-rule of the United Nations structure -- contributes to the misgivings of peace researchers about the broadened concept of security.

If the only legitimate function of national armed power is restricted to providing military security, a progressive development of international law, forbidding military capabilities beyond that function, would be feasible. Offensive, destabilizing and excessive postures would be prohibited. In accordance with the present legal situation of the law of arms control and disarmament that "the right of a state to possess arms is not unlimited", the United Nations General Assembly might be assigned the task of elaborating guiding principles for arms control negotiations, based on the restricted function of armed power. These guiding principles might later harden into binding rules of law: the much needed new chapter of international law restricting the sovereign national freedom of possession of armed force.

A more radical view concerning the present function of military power stresses the need to replace this power by non-violent means of defence, non-violent resistance and non-cooperation. In the domestic field the potential of non-violent resistance is impressive, because the power of a government is based on the obedience of its citizens. If this obedience is collectively renounced, a government becomes powerless. But such a relation of obedience does not apply to international relations, and therefore the prospect of non-violent

resistance has less impact on the behaviour of a would-be aggressor. In a situation of occupation it again becomes a powerful tool to influence the behaviour of the occupying power[20]. How far civilian-based defence -- a term used to indicate a defence policy against foreign invasions and internal take-overs relying on prepared non-cooperation and defiance by the trained civilian population and their institutions to deny the attacker's objections and make lasting control impossible -- can be effective, is questionable. The conclusion of most peace researchers is that more research is needed on this topic[21].

Substantial research is in progress in the area of arms control and disarmament; on the forces which prevent effective arms control and disarmament; on reasonable measures to curb arms proliferation; and on the different methods to achieve results in this field. The usual method is that of negotiation ending in a treaty. The outlook for this method is not promising if one considers the outcome of 35 years of negotiations. Of other methods proposed, the most spectacular alternative is the daring process of "Graduated and Reciprocated Initiatives in Tension Reduction" (GRIT) proposed by Osgood[22]. This method involves a series of relatively small but not negligible unilateral steps taken publicly as a sign of readiness to go further if the opponent follows suit and as an invitation to reciprocate in like form.

The main research pertaining to arms control and disarmament deals with the opposing arguments and with the forces preventing effective agreements and arms control. These are the same forces in society which contribute to arms spending and the arms race, namely the military-industrial complex, the arms technologist, the bureaucracies, the hawks who only believe in power and the martial spirit of the population.

The concept of disarmament is clear. Alva Mydal, in her book The Game of Disarmament[23], uses disarmament as a generic term, with a larger connotation than elimination of armaments. It covers all degrees of reduction of armaments, and it includes the preemption of options for further arms development (non-armament), as well as measures for regulating the production or use of arms quantity or "quality." This extension of the concept of disarmament is perhaps related to her strong rejection of the concept of arms control. Her book gives a fair description of the disarmament failure. She blames the superpowers in particular, who aim to maintain their status of superpower and thus seek to keep the distance between themselves and the rest of the world. She argues conclusively that the small powers have sinned by their silence. Now that the superpowers have failed to achieve substantial disarmament the small powers should take the lead. It is their historic mission to compel the world powers to behave more rationally.

Arms control comprises all measures to assure that armed power can fulfill optimally its reasonable function, which is, to provide for peace and security, by ensuring that the opponent's armed power will not be used for war or for the threat of war. This means the prevention of provocative, offensive features of armed postures, as well as of destabilizing characteristics, arms and arms systems which put a premium on haste to start a war, as in the case of a

disarming first strike capability, or a capability of an effective surprise attack. Thus, as part of the SALT II agreements, the United States and the USSR agreed "to seek measures to strengthen stability by, among other things, limitations on strategic offensive arms most destabilizing to the strategic balance and by measures to reduce and to avert the risk of surprise attack"[24]. Arms control would aim at the right measure of armaments; sufficient to deter, but not leading, in case of failure of deterrence, to mutual annihilation.

To put it another way; arms control implies all measures to ensure that the weapons do not become disfunctional. Technological developments have brought about weapon-postures that can add to the existing tensions and dangers. The first function of arms control is the elimination of the dangers that stem from the weapon-postures themselves, from their offensive character which feeds the arms race, and from their destabilizing character which incites to early action.

The distinction between "arms control" and "disarmament" should be maintained, even though arms control may imply abolishing existing armed power. Arms control has no connection with the existence of detente, or the intensity of existing friendly relations. No "linkage" should be attempted between the willingness to negotiate arms control agreements and the political good behaviour of the other party. Indeed, arms control measures are even more needed in a period of tension or crisis. On the other hand, disarmament, the reduction of armed power to lower levels, aiming at general and complete disarmament, strongly depends on a peaceful climate. Here a "linkage" does exist.

Some balance of power will be needed as long as the anarchical international system is maintained. Disarmament theories are therefore closely related to theories concerning deterrence strategies. The radical analysis leading to the thesis "peace can only be maintained after elimination of deterrence" is less helpful for a rational approach than the search for optimal forms of deterrence. Maximum deterrence is rejected by most researchers, because it leads to endless arms races. A deterrence posture should not scare the opponent into rearmament. Minimal deterrence is preferable. This might take the form of inoffensive deterrence, or defensive deterrence, i.e. enough military power to make war an unacceptable prospect, but not enough military power to be able to start a successful offensive action. If both parties, eager to prevent nuclear war, would accept the strategy of defensive deterrence as a starting point, agreements which would make both parties more secure seem feasible with considerably fewer weapons at considerably less costs. The overkill would be eliminated and with it risk that the disastrous weapons created to deter a von Clauswitz type war, would be used in an unforeseen and unexpected military confrontation, which might occur like a traffic accident in the existing hazardous international traffic.

NOTES

[1] <u>Journal of Peace Research</u>, Oslo, 1977, pp. 75–86. See further elaboration in Boulding's contribution "Metaphors and Models in the International System" in Akkerman, van Krieken and Pannenborg (eds). <u>Declarations on Principles, A Quest for Universal Peace</u>, Leyden 1977, p. 311–321.

[2] <u>Ibid</u>., p. 83.

[3] J. W. Fulbright, <u>Prospects for the West</u>, Cambridge 1963, p. 43.

[4] H. Kissinger at UN General Assembly, 23 September 1974.

[5] J. D. Singer <u>et al: Explaining War</u>. Selected Papers from the Correlates of War Project, Sage Publications, London 1979, also J. D. Singer and M. D. Wallace: <u>To Augur Well, Early Warning Indicators in World Politics</u>. Sage Publications, London, 1979.

[6] J. Dedring, <u>Recent Advances in Peace and Conflict Research, A Critical Survey</u>. Sage Publications, Beverly Hills, London, 1976.

[7] J. van Kan in his L'idee de l'organisation internationale dans ses grandes phases. <u>Recueil des Cours de l'Academie de Droit International</u>, 1938, Vol. IV, p. 259–611.

[8] UN General Assembly Resolution of 4 November 1954.

[9] H. Bull, <u>The Anarchical Society, A Study of Order in World Politics</u>, London 1977.

[10] R. Falk, On Writing a History of the Future, in H-H. Holm and E. Rudeng (eds): <u>Social Science, For What? Festschrift for J. Galtung</u>, Oslo, Bergen, Tromso. 1980, p. 87–91.

[11] S. Hoffman, <u>Primacy or World Order</u>, New York, 1978.

[12] J. Tinbergen, <u>Reshaping the International Order</u>, New York, 1976.

[13] G. Clark & L. B. Sohn, <u>World Peace through World Law</u>, (3rd Ed) 1966.

[14] R. A. Falk, The International Dimension of a New International Order, in A. J. Dolman, <u>Global Planning and Resource Management</u>, Pergamon Press, 1980, p. 87–102.

[15] R. Kothari, <u>Footsteps into the Future</u>, New York, 1974; A. Mazrui, <u>A World Federation of Cultures; an African Perspective</u>, New York, 1976; R. A. Falk, <u>A Study of Future Worlds</u>, New York, 1976; G. Lagos & H. Godov, <u>Revolution of Being: A Latin American View of the Future</u>, New York, 1977; J. Galtung, <u>The True World; A Transnational Perspective</u>, New York, 1980.

[16] R. A. Falk: <u>This Endangered Planet: Prospects and Proposals for Human Survival</u>, New York 1971.

[17]D. Senghaas, Abschreckhung und Frieden. <u>Studien zur Kritik organisierter Friedlosingkeit</u>, Frankfurt, 1972.

[18]IISS Adelphi Paper 102: Force in Modern Societies, Its Place in International Politics, London 1973, and B. V. A. Roling, The Function of Military Power, in <u>Arms Control and Technological Innovation</u>, London, 1977, p. 288-302.

[19]See S. Hoffman, <u>The Acceptability of Military Force</u>, in Adelphi Paper 102, p. 2-13.

[20]G. Sharp, <u>Social Power and Political Freedom</u>, Boston, 1980.

[21]For further elaboration of aspects of "civilian defence" and "social defence", see A. Roberts: <u>The Strategy of Civilian Defence, Non-violent Resistance to Aggression</u>, London 1967; G. Geeraerts (ed), <u>Possibilities of Civilian Defence</u>, Amsterdam and Lisse, 1976.

[22]C. E. Osgood: <u>An Alternative to War or Surrender</u>, University of Illinois Press, 1962.

[23]Alva Myrdal, <u>The Game of Disarmament</u>, New York 1976.

[24]US v USSR Joint statement on SALT II. Vienna, June 18, 1979.

PART II
STATISTICAL
INFORMATION
AND SOURCES

Main purpose of this section is to provide a current bibliography of data sources and statistical data for various indicators of international development, as they relate to disarmament with special reference to the developing countries. An attempt is made to provide the reader with an overview of global trends, based on an analysis of the country data, as it is sometimes difficult to form any such general impression when faced with a general body of highly detailed data.

I. BIBLIOGRAPHY OF INFORMATION SOURCES

AFRICAN STATISTICAL YEARBOOK, UN

Presents data arranged on a country basis for 44 African countries for the years 1965-1978. Available statistics for each country are presented in 48 tables: population; national accounts; agriculture, forestry, and fishing industry; transport and communications; foreign trade; prices; finance; and social statistics: education and medical facilities.

ASIAN INDUSTRIAL DEVELOPMENT NEWS, UN, Sales no. E.74.II.F.16

In four parts: (a) brief reports on the ninth session of the Asian Industrial Development Council and twenty-sixth session of the Committee on Industry and Natural Resources; (b) articles on multinationals and the transfer of know-how, acquisition of technology for manufacturing agro-equipment, fuller utilization of industrial capacity; (c) report of Asian Plan of Action on the Human Environment; and (d) statistical information on plywood, transformers, and transmission cables.

Banks, Arthur S., et al., eds.
ECONOMIC HANDBOOK OF THE WORLD: 1981. New York; London; Sydney
and Tokyo: McGraw-Hill Books for State University of New York
at Binghamton, Center for Social Analysis, 1981.

Descriptions, in alphabetical order, of all the world's independent
states and a small number of non-independent but economically
significant areas (such as Hong Kong). Data are current as of
1 July 1980 whenever possible. Summary statistics for each country
include: area, population, monetary unit, Gross National Product
per capita, international reserves (1979 year end), external
public debt, exports, imports, government revenue, government
expenditure, and consumer prices. Principal economic institutions,
financial institutions, and international memberships are listed
at the end of each description.

BULLETIN OF LABOUR STATISTICS. Quarterly, with supplement 8
times per year. Approx. 150 p.

Quarterly report, with supplements in intervening months, on
employment, unemployment, hours of work, wages, and consumer
prices, for 130-150 countries and territories. Covers total,
nonagricultural, and manufacturing employment; total unemployment
and rate; average nonagricultural and manufacturing hours of
work per week, and earnings per hour, day, week, or month; and
food and aggregate consumer price indexes.

COMPENDIUM OF SOCIAL STATISTICS, 1977. 1980, UN, Sales No. E-F.
80.XVII.6.

Contains a collection of statistical and other data aimed at
describing social conditions and social change in the world.
In four parts. Part 1 includes estimates and projections for
the world, macroregions, and regions. Part 2 comprises data
for countries or areas that represent key series describing social
conditions and social change. Part 3 consists of general
statistical series for countries or areas. Part 4 is devoted
to information for cities or urban agglomerations. Includes
a total of 151 tables, covering population, health, nutrition,
education, conditions of work, housing and environmental
conditions, etc. Provides an overall view of the world social
situation and future trends.

DEMOGRAPHIC YEARBOOK, 1978. (ST-ESA-STAT-SER.R-7) 1979, UN,
Sales No. E-F.79.XIII.I.

--Vol. 1. viii, 463 p. This volume contains the general tables
giving a world summary of basic demographic statistics, followed
by tables presenting statistics on the size distribution and
trends in population, natality, fetal mortality, infant and
maternal mortality, general mortality, nuptiality, and divorce.
Data are also shown by urban/rural residence in many of the tables.
--Vol. 2: Historical supplement.

DEVELOPMENT FORUM BUSINESS EDITION. DESI/DOP, UN, Palais des Nations, CH-1211 Geneva 10, Switzerland. 24 times a yr. 16 p.

A tabloid-size paper, published jointly by the United Nations Department of Information's Divison for Economic and Social Information and the World Bank. Presents articles on all aspects of the development work of the United Nations, with emphasis on specific development problems encountered by the business community. Contains notices referring to goods and works to be procured through international competitive bidding for projects assisted by the World Bank and the International Development Association (IDA). It also includes a Supplement of the World Bank, entitled "Monthly Operational Summary", and a similar supplement of the Inter-American Development Bank (IDB), once a month, which provide information about projects contemplated for financing by the World Bank and IDB, respectively.

DEVELOPMENT FORUM GENERAL EDITION

A tabloid-size paper, published jointly by the United Nations Department of Public Information's Division for Economic and Social Information and the World Bank, having as objective the effective mobilization of public opinion in support of a number of major causes to which the United Nations is committed. Presents articles reporting on the activities of various UN agencies concerned with development and social issues (health, education, nutrition, women in development). Includes a forum for nongovernmental organizations (NGO's) and book reviews.

DEVELOPMENT AND INTERNATIONAL ECONOMIC CO-OPERATION: LONG-TERM TRENDS IN ECONOMIC DEVELOPMENT. Report of the Secretary-General. Monograph. May 26, 1982.

Report analyzing world economic development trends, 1960's-81, with projections to 2000 based on the UN 1980 International Development Strategy, and on alternative low and medium economic growth assumptions. Presents data on GDP, foreign trade, investment, savings, income, population and labor force, housing, education, food and energy supply/demand, and other economic and social indicators.

DIRECTORY OF INTERNATIONAL STATISTICS: VOLUME 1. 1982 Series. Sales No. E.81.XVII.6

Vol. 1 of a 2-volume directory of international statistical time series compiled by 18 UN agencies and selected other IGO's. Lists statistical publications, and machine-readable data bases of economic and social statistics, by organization and detailed subject category. Also includes bibliography and descriptions of recurring publications, and technical descriptions of economic/social data bases.

VOLUME 2: INTERNATIONAL TABLES. Sales No. E.82.XVII.6, Vol. II

Statistical Information and Sources

Presents analytical summary of major income and product accounts for approximately 160 countries, by country and world region.

ECONOMIC AND SOCIAL PROGRESS IN LATIN AMERICA: 1980-81 REPORT. 1981, IDB.

Provides a comprehensive survey of the Latin America economy since 1970, with particular emphasis on 1980 and 1981. Part One is a regional analysis of general economic trends, the external sector, the financing of development from internal and external sources, regional economic integration, and social development trends (women in the economic development of Latin America). Part Two contains country summaries of socioeconomic trends for 24 States members of IDB. Statistical appendix includes data on population, national accounts, public finance, balance of payments, primary commodity exports, external public debt, and hydrocarbons.

ECONOMIC AND SOCIAL SURVEY OF ASIA AND THE PACIFIC, 1977. The International Economic Crises and Developing Asia and the Pacific. 1978, UN, Sales No. E.78.II.F.1.

In two parts: (a) review of recent economic developments and emerging policy issues in the ESCAP region, 1976-1977; and (b) the impacts of the international economic crises of the first half of the 1970's upon selected developing economies in the ESCAP region and the market and policy response thereto. Topics discussed include: the food crisis; the breakdown of the international monetary system; fluctuations in the international market economy comprising the primary commodities export boom, the associated inflation and the subsequent recession, and, finally the sharp rise in the price of petroleum.

ECONOMIC AND SOCIAL SURVEY OF ASIA AND THE PACIFIC, 1979. Regional Development Strategy for the 1980's. 1981, UN, Sales No. E.80.II.F.1.

Analyzes recent economic and social development in the UN ESCAP region, as well as related international developments. Focuses on economic and social policy issues and broad development strategies. In two parts: (a) recent economic developments, 1978-1979, covering the second oil price shock economic performance of the developing countries of the ESCAP region, inflation, and external trade and payments; and (b) findings of a two-year study dealing with regional developmental strategies, covering economic growth, policies for full employment and equity, energy, technology, implementation systems, international trade, shipping, international resource transfers, and intraregional cooperation.

ECONOMIC SURVEY OF ASIA AND THE FAR EAST, 1973. 234 p. (also issued as Economic Bulletin for Asia and the Far East, vol. 24, no. 4), 1974, UN, Sales No. E.74.II.F.1.

Contains a general summary followed by Part One, which covers: education and employment--the nature of the problem; population, labor force and structure of employment and underemployment in the ECAFE [ESCAP] region; the role of location--assumptions underlying the education policies of developing countries in the ECAFE region; momentum and direction of expansion of education; structuring the flow of workers into the modern science of education for self employment--the traditional and informal sectors; and the search for new policies--a review of current thinking. Part Two covers: current economic developments--recent economic developments and emerging policy issues in the ECAFE region, 1972/73; and current economic developments and policies in 28 countries of the ECAFE region.

ECONOMIC SURVEY OF LATIN AMERICA. Series.

Series of preliminary annual reports analyzing recent economic trends in individual Latin American countries. Each report presents detailed economic indicators, including GDP by sector, agricultural and industrial production by commodity, foreign trade, public and private sector finances, and prices. Also includes selected data on employment and earnings.

THE ECONOMIST. THE WORLD IN FIGURES. Third edition. New York: Facts on File, Inc., 1980.

Compendium of figures on economic, demographic, and sociopolitical aspects of over 200 countries of the world. The first part is a world section with information on population, national income, production, energy, transportation, trade, tourism, and finance. The second part is organized by country (grouped by main region), containing statistics on location, land, climate, time, measurement systems, currency, people, resources, production, finance and external trade, and politics and the economy. The data, from many sources, cover through 1976. Country name and "special focus" indices.

FACTS OF THE WORLD BANK. Monthly (current issues).

A compilation of figures on World Bank lending, giving cumulative amounts and amounts for the current fiscal year of commitments by number of projects and by sector, as well as for each country by region. Also gives figures on sales of parts of Bank loans and IDA credits and on World Bank borrowings by currency of issue, original and outstanding amounts, and number of issues.

IMF SURVEY. Biweekly.

Biweekly report on international financial and economic conditions; IMF activities; selected topics relating to exchange rates, international reserves, and foreign trade; and economic performance of individual countries and world areas.

MAIN ECONOMIC INDICATORS: HISTORICAL STATISTICS, 1960-1979. 1980, OECD, Sales No. 2750 UU-31 80 20 3.

Bilingual: E-F. Replaces previous editions. Base year for all indicators is 1970. Arranged in chapters by country, the tables cover the period 1960 to 1979, and are followed by short notes describing some major characteristics of the series, and, where applicable, indicating breaks in continuity. Note: Supplements the monthly bulletin Main Economic Indicators.

MONTHLY BULLETIN OF STATISTICS. Monthly.

Monthly report presenting detailed economic data including production, prices, and trade; and summary population data; by country, with selected aggregates for world areas and economic groupings, or total world. Covers population size and vital statistics; employment; industrial production, including energy and major commodities; construction activity; internal and external trade; passenger and freight traffic; manufacturing wages; commodity and consumer prices; and money and banking. Each issue includes special tables, usually on topics covered on a regular basis but presenting data at different levels of aggregation and for different time periods. Special tables are described and indexed in IIS as they appear.

POPULATION AND VITAL STATISTICS REPORT. Quarterly.

Quarterly report on world population, births, total and infant deaths, and birth and death rates, by country and territorial possession, as of cover date. Also shows UN population estimates for total world and each world region.

QUARTERLY BULLETIN OF STATISTICS FOR ASIA AND THE PACIFIC. Quarterly.

Quarterly report presenting detailed monthly and quarterly data on social and economic indicators for 38 ESCAP member countries. Includes data on population; births and deaths; employment; agricultural and industrial production; construction; transportation; foreign trade quantity, value, and direction; prices; wages; and domestic and international financial activity.

1978 REPORT ON THE WORLD SOCIAL SITUATION. 1979, UN, Sales No. E.79.IV.1.

Deals with the global issues of population trends and employment; growth and distribution of income and private consumption; the production and distribution of social services; and changing social concerns. A supplement reviews the patterns of recent governmental expenditures for social services in developing countries, developed market economies, and centrally planned economies.

STATISTICAL INDICATORS FOR ASIA AND THE PACIFIC.   Quarterly.

Quarterly report presenting selected economic and demographic indicators for 26 Asian and Pacific countries. Covers, for most countries, population size, birth and death rates, family planning methods, industrial and agricultural production, construction, transport, retail trade, foreign trade, prices, money supply, currency exchange rate, and GDP.

STATISTICAL YEARBOOK, 1979/80.   1981, UN, Sales No. E/F.81.XVII.1.

A comprehensive compendium of the most important internationally comparable data needed for the analysis of socioeconomic development at the world, regional and national levels. Includes tables (200) grouped in two sections: (a) world summary by regions (17 tables); and (b) remaining tables of country-by-country data, arranged in chapters: population; manpower; agriculture; forestry; fishing; industrial production; mining and quarrying; manufacturing; construction; development assistance; wholesale and retail trade; external trade; international tourism; transport; communications; national accounts; wages and prices; consumption; finance; energy; health; housing; science and technology; and culture. For this first time, this issue contains three new tables on industrial property: patents, industrial designs, and trademarks and service marks. Note: This issue is a special biennial edition, covering data through mid-1980, and in some cases for 1980 complete.

STATISTICAL YEARBOOK FOR ASIA AND THE PACIFIC, 1978.   1979, UN, Sales No. E-F.79.II.F.4.

Eleventh issue. Contains statistical indicators for the ESCAP region and statistics for period up to 1978 available at the end of 1978 for 34 countries and territories members of ESCAP, arranged by country, covering, where available: population; manpower; national accounts; agriculture, forestry, and fishing; industry; consumption; transport and communication; internal and external trade; wages, prices, and household expenditures; finance; and social statistics.

STATISTICAL YEARBOOK FOR LATIN AMERICA, 1979.   1981, UN, Sales No. E/S.80.II.G.4.

In two parts. Part 1 presents indicators of economic and social development in Latin America for 1960, 1965, 1970 and 1975-1978, including: population; demographic characteristics; employment and occupational structure; income distribution; living levels; consumption and nutrition; health; education; housing; global economic growth; agricultural activities; mining and energy resources; manufacturing; productivity; investment; saving; public financial resources; public expenditure; structure of exports and imports; intra-regional trade; transport services; tourist services; and external financing. Part 2 contains historical series in absolute figures for the years 1960, 1965 and 1970-1978

on population; national accounts; domestic prices; balance of
payments; external indebtedness; external trade; natural resources
and production of goods; infrastructure services; employment;
and social conditions.

SURVEY OF ECONOMIC AND SOCIAL CONDITIONS IN AFRICA, 1980-81 AND
OUTLOOK FOR 1981-82: SUMMARY

Examines growth in GDP, agricultural and industrial production,
trade and balance of payments, resource flows, energy
production/consumption, and selected other economic indicators,
1979-80, with outlook for 1981-82 and trends from 1960's.

TECHNICAL DATA SHEETS

Provides up-to-date information about projects as they are approved
for World Bank and IDA financing. In addition to a description
of the project, its total cost, and the amount of Bank financing,
each technical data sheet describes the goods and services that
must be provided for the project's implementation and gives the
address of the project's implementing organization. On the
average, 250 such sheets will be issued annually. Requests for
sample copies are to be addressed to: Publications Distribution
Unit, World Bank, 1818 H St., N.W., Washington, D.C. 20433,
U.S.A.

UNESCO STATISTICAL YEARBOOK, 1978-79, 1266 p. 1980, UNESCO.

Composite: E/F/S (introductory texts). Presents statistical
and other information for 206 countries on education; science
and technology; libraries; museums and related institutions;
theater and other dramatic arts; book production; newspapers
and other periodicals; film and cinema; radio broadcasting; and
television. In this edition, the summary tables relating to
culture and communications, previously given in the introduction
to each of the corresponding chapters, have been grouped together
in a separate chapter.

World Bank. ANNUAL REPORT, 1982. 1982, WBG.

Presents summary and background of the activities of the World
Bank Group during the fiscal year ended 30 June 1982, covering:
the International Bank for Reconstruction and Development (IBRD);
the International Development Association (IDA); and the
International Finance Corporation (IFC). Chapters cover: brief
review of Bank operations in fiscal 1982; a global perspective
of the economic situation; Bank policies, activities and finances
for fiscal 1982; 1982 regional perspectives; and Executive
Directors. Lists projects approved for IBRD and IDA assistance
in fiscal 1982 by sector, region and purpose. Also reviews trends
in lending by sector for 1980-82 and includes statistical annex.

WORLD BANK COUNTRY STUDIES. Series.

Series of studies, prepared by World Bank staff, on development issues and policies, and economic conditions in individual developing countries. Studies may focus on specific economic sectors or issues, or on general economic performance of the country as a whole.

The World Bank.
WORLD DEVELOPMENT REPORT, 1978. August 1978.

First volume in a series of annual reports designed to provide a comprehensive, continuing assessment of global development issues. After an overview of development in the past 25 years, the report discusses current policy issues and projected developments in areas of the international economy that influence the prospects of developing countries. Analyzes the problems confronting policy makers in developing countries, which differ in degree and in kind, affecting the choice of appropriate policy instruments, and recognizes that development strategies need to give equal prominence to two goals: accelerating economic growth and reducing poverty. Reviews development priorities for low-income Asia, sub-Saharan Africa, and middle-income developing countries.

The World Bank.
WORLD DEVELOPMENT REPORT, 1979. Washington, D.C.

Second in a series of annual reports designed to assess global development issues. Focuses on development in the middle income countries, with particular emphasis on policy choices for industrialization and urbanization. Part one assesses recent trends and prospects to 1990 and discusses capital flows, and energy. Part two focuses upon structural change and development policy relevant to employment, the balance between agriculture and industry, and urban growth. Part three reviews development experiences and issues in three groups of middle income countries: semi-industrialized nations; mineral primary-producing countries; and predominantly agricultural primary-producing countries. Maintains that progress toward expanding employment and reducing poverty in developing countries lies not only in internal policy choices but also in a liberal environment for international trade and capital flows.

The World Bank.
WORLD DEVELOPMENT REPORT, 1980. New York: Oxford University Press for the World Bank, 1980.

Third in a series of annual reports. Parts one examines economic policy choices facing both developing and developed countries and their implications for national and regional growth. Projects, to the year 2000 but particularly to the mid to late 1980's, growth estimates for oil-importing and oil-exporting developing countries; and analyzes the fundamental issues of energy, trade, and capital flows. Part two focuses on the links between poverty, growth, and human development. It examines the impact of

education, health, nutrition, and fertility on poverty; reviews
some practical lessons in implementing human development programs;
and discusses the trade-offs between growth and poverty and the
allocation of resources between human development and other
activities. Stresses the views that growth does not obviate
the need for human development and that direct measures to reduce
poverty do not obviate the need for economic expansion. Concludes
that world growth prospects have deteriorated in the past year,
but higher oil prices have impoved the outlook [for the first
half of the 1980's] for the fifth of the developing world's
population that lives in oil-exporting countries; however, the
four-fifths that live in oil-importing countries will experience
slower growth for the first half of the decade. Includes a
statistical appendix to part one; a bibliographical note; and
a very lengthy annex of World Development Indicators.

The World Bank.
WORLD DEVELOPMENT REPORT, 1981. New York: Oxford University
Press for the World Bank, 1981.

With the major focus on the international context of development,
examines past trends and future prospects for international trade,
energy, and capital flows and the effects of these on developing
countries. Presents two scenarios for the 1980's, one predicting
higher growth rates than in the 1970's and one lower. Analyzes
national adjustments to the international economy, presenting
in-depth case studies. Concludes that countries pursuing
outward-oriented policies adjusted more easily to external shocks.
Contends that whichever scenario prevails, income differentials
will increase between the industrial and developing countries.
Low income countries have fewer options and less flexibility
of adjustment, therefore requiring continued aid from the more
affluent countries. Advocates policies to channel increased
resources to alleviate poverty.

The World Bank.
WORLD DEVELOPMENT REPORT, 1982.

The Report this year focuses on agriculture and food security.
As in previous years there is also a section on global prospects
and international issues, as well as the statistical annex of
World Development indicators.

The World Bank.
WORLD TABLES 1980: FROM THE DATA FILES OF THE WORLD BANK. Second
edition. Baltimore and London: Johns Hopkins University Press
for the World Bank, 1980.

A broad range of internationally comparable statistical information
drawn from the World Bank data files. Includes historical time
series for individual countries in absolute numbers for most
of the basic economic indicators for selected years (1950-77
when available); also presents derived economic indicators for
selected periods of years and demographic and social data for

selected years.   Although the number of social indicators is
fewer than those in the 1976 edition the quality of the data
has been improved through the use of more uniform definitions
and concepts, greater attention to population statistics, and
better statistics on balance of payments and central government
finance.   Includes an index of country coverage.

WORLD ECONOMIC OUTLOOK: A SURVEY BY THE STAFF OF THE INTERNATIONAL
MONETARY FUND.   1980, IMF.

An in-depth forecast of the world economy in 1980 and a preliminary
summary for 1981.   Chapters discuss: a profile of current
situation and short-term prospects; global perspectives for
adjustment and financing; industrial countries; developing
countries--oil-exporting and non-oil groups; and key policy issues.
Appendixes include country and regional surveys; technical notes
on the world oil situation, estimated impact of fiscal balances
in selected industrial countries, and monetary policy and
inflation; and statistical tables.

WORLD ECONOMIC OUTLOOK: A SURVEY BY THE STAFF OF THE INTERNATIONAL
MONETARY FUND.   [1982 ed.]   1982, IMF.

A comprehensive analysis of economic developments, policies,
and prospects through June 1981 for industrial, oil exporting
and non-oil developing countries.   It highlights persistent
imbalances in the world economy, high inflation, rising
unemployment, excessive rates of real interest, and unstable
exchange rates.   Appendix A includes supplementary notes providing
information on selected topics in greater depth or detail than
in the main body of the report: country and regional surveys;
medium-term scenarios; fiscal development; monetary and exchange
rate development; world oil situation; growth and inflation in
non-oil developing countries; developments in trade policy; and
commodity price developments and prospects.   Appendix B presents
statistical tables on: domestic economic activity and prices;
international trade; balance of payments; external debt;
medium-term projections; and country tables.

The World Bank.
WORLD BANK ATLAS.   Fourteenth edition.   1979.   Annual.

Presents estimates of gross national product (GNP) per capita
(1977), GNP per capita growth rates (1970-77), and population
(mid-1977), with population growth rates (1970-77) for countries
with populations of one million or more in three global maps;
a computer-generated map shows GNP per capita (1977) by major
regions.   Six regional maps give the same data for 184 countries
and territories, as well as preliminary data for 1978.   The base
years 1976-78 have been used for the conversion of GNP for both
1977 and 1978.   A Technical Note explains in detail the methodology
used.

The World Bank.
WORLD DEVELOPMENT INDICATORS. June 1979. 71 pages.

A volume of statistics prepared in conjunction with and
constituting the Annex to the World Development Report, 1979
to provide information of general relevance about the main features
of economic and social development, reporting data for a total
of 125 countries whose population exceeds one million. Countries
are grouped in five categories and ranked by their 1977 per capita
gross national product (GNP) levels. The volume contains 24
tables covering some 110 economic and social indicators. The
choice of indicators has been based on data being available for
a large number of countries, the availability of historical series
to allow the measurement of growth and change, and on the relevance
of data to the principal processes of development.

The World Bank.
WORLD ECONOMIC AND SOCIAL INDICATORS. Quarterly (current issues).

Presents most recent available data on trade, commodity prices,
consumer prices, debt and capital flows, industrial production,
as well as social indicators and select annual data (by countries
where applicable). Each issue contains an article on topics
of current importance. Strategies for improving the access to
education of the disadvantaged rural poor by serving areas out
of range of existing schools are discussed and programs in four
projects financed by the World Bank are described.

WORLD ECONOMIC OUTLOOK: A SURVEY BY THE STAFF OF THE INTERNATIONAL
MONETARY FUND. Annual. April 1982. (Occasional Paper No. 9)

Annual report on economic performance of major industrial and
oil exporting and non-oil developing countries, 1970's-81 and
forecast 1982-83, with some projections to 1986. Includes analysis
of economic indicators for selected industrial countries, world
economic groupings, and world areas, primarily for IMF member
countries. Covers domestic economic activity, including prices,
GNP, and employment; international trade; balance of payments;
and foreign debt. Also includes financial indicators for selected
industrial countries, including government budget surpluses and
deficits, savings, money supply, and interest rates.

WORLD ECONOMIC SURVEY. 1978, UN, Sales No. E.78.II.C.1.

Provides an overview of salient developments in the world economy
in 1977 and the outlook for 1978. Focuses on policy needs for
improving the tempo of world production and trade. Examines
in detail the course of production and trade and related variables
in the developing economies, the developed market economies,
and the centrally planned economies.

WORLD ECONOMIC SURVEY 1979-80. 1980, UN, Sales No. E.80.II.C.2.

A survey of current world economic conditions and trends, with

chapters on salient features and policy implications; the growth of world output, 1979-80; the accelerating pace of inflation; world trade and international payments; world economic outlook, 1980-1985; and adjustment policies in developing countries. Annexes cover external factors and growth in developing countries--the experience of the 1970's; supply and price of petroleum in 1979 and 1980; and prospective supply and demand for oil.

YEARBOOK OF NATIONAL ACCOUNTS STATISTICS, 1980. Annual. 1982.

Annual report presenting national income and product account balances for approximately 170 countries, and for world areas and economic groupings, selected years 1970-79, often with comparisons to 1960 and 1965. Data are compiled in accordance with the UN System of National Accounts (SNA) for market economies, and the System of Material Product Balances (MPS) for centrally planned economies. SNA data include GDP final consumption expenditures by type; production, income/outlay, and capital formation accounts, by institutional sector; and production by type of activity. MPS data include material and financial balances, manpower and resources, and national wealth and capital assets.

STATISTICAL NEWSLETTER. Quarterly.

Quarterly newsletter on ESCAP statistical programs and activities, and major statistical developments in ESCAP countries. Includes brief descriptions of meetings, working groups, upcoming international statistical training programs, and regional advisory services; and an annotated bibliography of recent ESCAP and UN statistical publications.

THE UNITED NATIONS DISARMAMENT YEARBOOK. Vol. 5: 1980. UN, 1981, Sales No. E.81.IX.3.

Comprises a review of deliberations, negotiations and other developments which took place during 1980 in UN bodies or under the auspices of the UN, and in the Committee on Disarmament. In five parts: (a) comprehensive approaches to disarmament; (b) nuclear disarmament; (c) prohibition or restriction of use of their weapons; (d) other approaches to disarmament and arms limitation; and (e) studies and information.

UNESCO YEARBOOK ON PEACE AND CONFLICT STUDIES, 1980. Greenwood Press/UNESCO, 1981.

Reflecting UNESCO's long-term commitment to supporting, disseminating and exchanging the findings of peace researchers, this first volume of a projected series investigates a wide range of topics relevant to the study of conflict and conflict prevention by groups, societies, and the world at large. New approaches to the study of war--from societal, political, and economic and statistical points of view--are examined in detail, utilizing new research in psychology, philosophy, military affairs,

international relations, and other fields. Also reviews new methods of processing and documenting data on peace and war and recent institutional developments in the field of peace studies.

DIRECTORY OF UNITED NATIONS INFORMATION SYSTEMS. IOB for UN, 1980.

Vol. 1: Information Systems and Data Bases. This volume gives particulars of United Nations family organizations and their information systems, together with the practical details, such as the address to contact for information, the conditions of access, the type of services that can be obtained. Details are provided on where to obtain bibliographies, indexes and other publications which are frequently available in several languages. The information systems covered include libraries, referral centres, clearing-houses, data banks, statistical information systems and other data collections, computerized or manual.
Vol. 2: Information Sources in Countries. Gives information by country, to facilitate contact between users and organizations' systems and services. More than 2,500 addresses in 167 countries are given. The addresses include organizations' offices, centres contributing information or serving as contact points to the various systems, and depository libraries where the publications or organizations can be found. Information is given on the publications and papers of the different organizations held in depository libraries and in United Nations Information Centres, and on the related services provided.

II. STATISTICAL TABLES AND FIGURES

This section focuses attention on some of the major economic and social indicators from a global and developing country perspective. It's aim is to highlight some generalizations made in the first part of this book as pointers to needed policies. The limited extent to which statistical information is cited in this book is solely for illustrative purposes. Most of the statistical information in the following pages have been reproduced from the following sources:

WORLD TABLES 1980: FROM THE DATA FILES OF THE WORLD BANK, Baltimore: Johns Hopkins University Press for the World Bank, 1980, (Reprinted by permission of the World Bank and Johns Hopkins University Press).

WORLD ECONOMIC AND SOCIAL INDICATORS, October 1978. Report No. 700/78/04. Washington, D.C.: WORLD BANK.

GLOBAL INDICATORS

TABLE 1. SOCIAL INDICATORS BY INCOME GROUP OF COUNTRIES

(ADJUSTED COUNTRY GROUP AVERAGES)

DEVELOPING COUNTRIES EXCLUDING CAPITAL SURPLUS OIL EXPORTERS

INDICATOR	LOW INCOME			LOWER MIDDLE INCOME			INTERMEDIATE MIDDLE INCOME		
	1960	1970	MOST RECENT ESTIMATE	1960	1970	MOST RECENT ESTIMATE	1960	1970	MOST RECENT ESTIMATE
GNP PER CAPITA (IN CURRENT US $)	67.4	107.4	162.0	136.1	239.6	398.6	225.6	410.9	817.9
POPULATION									
GROWTH RATE (%) - TOTAL	2.2	2.4	2.4	2.7	2.7	2.6	2.7	2.7	2.5
- URBAN	5.3	4.7	4.7	4.4	4.4	9.8	5.4	4.9	5.1
URBAN POPULATION (% OF TOTAL)	10.4	14.0	14.8	17.7	21.6	26.1	33.7	41.4	46.1
VITAL STATISTICS									
CRUDE BIRTH RATE (PER 1000)	47.5	46.9	45.2	47.1	45.5	42.6	44.6	41.2	38.2
CRUDE DEATH RATE (PER 1000)	26.1	21.7	18.2	21.4	16.1	12.7	18.6	13.5	11.1
GROSS REPRODUCTION RATE	2.9	3.1	3.1	3.4	3.2	3.3	3.0	2.8	2.6
EMPLOYMENT AND INCOME									
DEPENDENCY RATIO - AGE	0.8	0.9	0.9	0.9	0.9	0.9	0.9	0.9	0.9
- ECONOMIC	1.0	1.1	1.1	1.3	1.4	1.4	1.6	1.6	1.5
LABOR FORCE IN AGRICULTURE (% OF TOTAL)	65.4	62.0	59.3	70.4	65.9	62.5	62.8	54.5	47.0
UNEMPLOYED (% OF LABOR FORCE)	4.7	4.0	3.1	6.3	8.4	5.5	6.1	6.0	5.8
INCOME RECEIVED BY - HIGHEST 5%	24.5	23.3	20.3	25.1	23.1	25.5	31.5	27.0	19.3
- LOWEST 20%	4.6	5.1	6.5	4.8	4.9	4.8	4.4	3.9	5.7
HEALTH AND NUTRITION									
DEATH RATE (PER 1000) AGES 1-4 YEARS	43.6	33.0	33.0	9.3	6.8	7.5	8.5	3.6	2.7
INFANT MORTALITY RATE (PER 1000)	129.0	121.3	102.8	84.6	79.9	58.4	88.6	65.8	55.0
LIFE EXPECTANCY AT BIRTH (YRS)	39.2	43.8	46.0	45.0	50.8	53.2	51.1	57.0	59.1
POPULATION PER - PHYSICIAN	21790.7	15219.9	13235.9	16767.4	11977.3	10586.0	3299.7	2549.2	2412.7
- NURSING PERSON	8472.3	5215.0	4830.9	4078.2	1921.9	1683.8	3394.0	2205.1	1502.1
- HOSPITAL BED	1386.7	1267.8	1236.2	1037.6	815.3	793.1	721.8	629.2	507.1
PER CAPITA PER DAY SUPPLY OF:									
CALORIES (% OF REQUIREMENTS)	89.8	91.5	94.5	85.1	93.3	102.3	94.4	101.8	103.9
PROTEIN (GRMS) - TOTAL	50.5	51.6	53.9	47.4	53.0	56.9	54.4	58.7	60.6
- FROM ANIMALS & PULSES	14.9	14.4	16.4	17.7	18.1	18.8	21.8	22.1	23.0
EDUCATION									
ADJ. ENROLLMENT RATIOS - PRIMARY	37.4	48.4	59.0	60.7	74.0	92.7	77.8	95.3	99.9
- SECONDARY	4.8	10.3	13.9	4.8	12.7	22.6	14.5	26.7	29.4
FEMALE ENROLLMENT RATIO (PRIMARY)	34.6	39.0	43.3	45.6	75.0	77.5	65.8	87.8	87.6
ADULT LITERACY RATE (%)	24.4	32.0	33.8	41.0	60.0	63.0	49.8	57.8	62.3

TABLE 1. Social Indicators by Income Group of Countries (Continued).

(ADJUSTED COUNTRY GROUP AVERAGES)

DEVELOPING COUNTRIES EXCLUDING CAPITAL SURPLUS OIL EXPORTERS

INDICATOR	LOW INCOME 1960	1970	MOST RECENT ESTIMATE	LOWER MIDDLE INCOME 1960	1970	MOST RECENT ESTIMATE	INTERMEDIATE MIDDLE INCOME 1960	1970	MOST RECENT ESTIMATE
HOUSING									
PERSONS PER ROOM - URBAN	2.5	2.0	2.8	2.6	2.5	2.2	2.3	2.2	1.6
OCCUPIED DWELLINGS WITHOUT WATER	62.2	69.8	..	68.7	64.6	67.8	74.6	64.2	58.9
ACCESS TO ELECTRICITY (%) - ALL	..	..	..	17.3	23.3	40.4	28.4	49.6	71.9
- RURAL	..	..	..	..	..	..	5.6	26.7	34.1
CONSUMPTION									
RADIO RECEIVERS (PER 1000 POP.)	4.5	14.4	23.1	11.9	62.3	70.4	48.8	96.2	102.6
PASSENGER CARS (PER 1000 POP.)	1.3	2.5	3.0	3.0	6.5	8.6	4.2	7.5	11.1
ENERGY (KG COAL/YR PER CAPITA)	62.0	83.4	104.8	99.6	220.1	265.2	258.7	489.2	586.2
NEWSPRINT (KG/YR PER CAPITA)	0.2	0.4	0.3	0.6	0.8	0.8	1.1	1.8	2.4

INDICATOR	DEV'G CTRIES. EXCL. CAP. SURP. OIL EXP. — UPPER MIDDLE INCOME 1960	1970	MOST RECENT EST.	HIGH INCOME 1960	1970	MOST RECENT EST.	CAP. SURP. OIL EXP. 1960	1970	MOST RECENT EST.	INDUSTRIALIZED COUNTRIES 1960	1970	MOST RECENT EST.
GNP PER CAPITA (IN CURRENT US $)	401.2	817.1	1648.7	689.4	1564.2	2911.1	1054.3	2858.9	5710.5	1417.4	3096.8	5297.7
POPULATION												
GROWTH RATE (%) - TOTAL	1.6	1.3	1.5	2.1	3.1	2.9	4.5	2.4	2.7	0.9	0.9	0.9
- URBAN	3.3	3.4	2.8	4.5	3.9	3.5	..	5.8	6.8	1.6	1.3	1.3
URBAN POPULATION (% OF TOTAL)	43.4	51.1	53.1	63.0	82.1	88.6	24.6	20.0	39.0	66.1	70.5	73.8
VITAL STATISTICS												
CRUDE BIRTH RATE (PER 1000)	26.4	28.5	20.8	41.7	37.4	33.6	48.3	49.4	45.0	21.3	20.0	18.7
CRUDE DEATH RATE (PER 1000)	10.4	9.1	8.9	9.6	8.3	8.0	21.2	22.8	14.7	9.7	9.0	8.8
GROSS REPRODUCTION RATE	1.7	1.8	1.8	2.3	2.5	1.8	..	3.5	3.3	1.3	1.3	1.2

TABLE 1. Social Indicators by Income Group of Countries (Continued)

(ADJUSTED COUNTRY GROUP AVERAGES)

INDICATOR	DEV'G CTRIES. EXCL. CAP. SURP. OIL EXP. UPPER MIDDLE INCOME			DEV'G CTRIES. EXCL. CAP. SURP. OIL EXP. HIGH INCOME			CAP. SURP. OIL EXP.			INDUSTRIALIZED COUNTRIES		
	1960	1970	MOST RECENT EST.	1960	1970	MOST RECENT EST.	1960	1970	MOST RECENT EST.	1960	1970	MOST RECENT EST.
EMPLOYMENT AND INCOME:												
DEPENDENCY RATIO - AGE	0.7	0.7	0.6	0.8	0.6	0.6	0.9	0.9	0.9	0.5	0.6	0.4
- ECONOMIC	1.3	1.7	1.6	1.2	1.2	1.2	1.8	1.7	1.7	0.9	0.9	0.8
LABOR FORCE IN AGRICULTURE (% OF TOTAL)	48.5	42.5	36.3	26.1	17.8	21.0	54.7	44.5	29.0	19.8	13.2	10.0
UNEMPLOYED (% OF LABOR FORCE)	7.4	3.3	4.0	9.0	5.4	5.1	7.4	2.0	3.0	2.1	1.5	1.9
INCOME RECEIVED BY - HIGHEST 5%	32.5	28.2	21.3	18.9	16.1	..	13.3	..	..	19.3	14.0	15.5
- LOWEST 20%	4.2	3.8	4.7	5.8	6.6	..	10.1	..	..	4.2	7.0	5.7
HEALTH AND NUTRITION												
DEATH RATE (PER 1000) AGES 1-4 YEARS	4.8	2.9	1.9	..	1.3	..	..	3.6	3.6	1.2	0.9	0.8
INFANT MORTALITY RATE (PER 1000)	74.4	51.3	37.9	44.9	27.8	23.2	45.4	134.3	80.3	27.9	17.0	15.0
LIFE EXPECTANCY AT BIRTH (YRS)	64.6	67.3	68.4	66.2	64.0	68.2	..	44.9	52.9	69.5	71.4	72.5
POPULATION PER - PHYSICIAN	1625.8	967.5	718.2	1117.5	888.9	756.0	9833.7	6323.4	1260.0	895.2	825.6	656.0
- NURSING PERSON	1690.7	1279.6	1028.5	1165.0	605.9	683.5	5140.0	2856.8	460.0	279.6	194.6	167.1
- HOSPITAL BED	209.9	180.4	185.8	170.0	162.5	170.0	1093.2	727.5	230.0	96.1	86.0	81.9
PER CAPITA PER DAY SUPPLY OF:												
CALORIES (% OF REQUIREMENTS)	104.5	114.4	111.5	106.3	107.2	113.6	83.9	90.3	104.9	118.7	118.7	119.5
PROTEIN (GRMS) - TOTAL	75.5	84.0	77.8	78.5	79.2	89.9	53.6	57.0	65.1	90.3	94.1	94.8
- FROM ANIMALS & PULSES	27.0	29.0	27.5	33.0	40.1	48.0	11.0	14.8	18.2	49.7	55.0	54.9
EDUCATION												
ADJ. ENROLLMENT RATIOS - PRIMARY	94.6	97.9	95.7	104.4	120.1	107.6	18.2	47.1	145.0	106.7	104.3	103.3
- SECONDARY	22.7	36.6	46.7	18.1	40.1	46.2	3.1	12.4	47.0	59.5	79.1	79.8
FEMALE ENROLLMENT RATIO (PRIMARY)	89.7	87.9	86.1	100.2	100.0	102.0	3.5	31.6	40.4	111.4	104.6	104.0
ADULT LITERACY RATE (%)	51.4	67.8	66.1	81.8	86.2	87.2	25.2	17.1	..	98.0	99.0	99.0
HOUSING												
PERSONS PER ROOM - URBAN	1.4	1.2	..	1.1	..	..	..	1.9	..	0.8	0.7	0.9
OCCUPIED DWELLINGS WITHOUT WATER	59.1	75.3	67.1	57.1	20.0	..	..	69.0	..	7.2	3.1	4.3
ACCESS TO ELECTRICITY (%) - ALL	50.6	47.4	59.8	79.3	91.0	..	..	24.0	..	97.3	98.9	99.1
- RURAL	26.9	..	..	57.0	58.0	..	..	..	..	91.4	95.2	94.8
CONSUMPTION												
RADIO RECEIVERS (PER 1000 POP.)	76.3	137.2	200.4	170.7	174.3	185.6	13.8	17.5	18.4	277.1	359.7	379.3
PASSENGER CARS (PER 1000 POP.)	11.2	29.2	42.3	14.1	41.3	54.4	7.6	16.6	113.7	90.7	233.3	266.5
ENERGY (KG. COAL/YR PER CAPITA)	676.2	1426.1	1618.7	798.4	1755.1	2467.6	302.5	1003.1	1419.4	2624.7	4575.2	4997.3
NEWSPRINT (KG/YR PER CAPITA)	1.4	1.9	2.3	3.5	8.7	6.6	0.2	0.2	0.1	16.4	22.3	22.2

TABLE 2. SOCIAL INDICATORS BY GEOGRAPHIC AREAS (DEVELOPING COUNTRIES)

INDICATOR	EUROPE			LATIN AMERICA & CARIBBEAN			(ADJUSTED COUNTRY GROUP AVERAGES) N. AFRICA & MIDDLE EAST		
	1960	1970	MOST RECENT ESTIMATE	1960	1970	MOST RECENT ESTIMATE	1960	1970	MOST RECENT ESTIMATE
GNP PER CAPITA (IN CURRENT US $)	496.6	1018.0	2070.3	362.0	626.8	1015.6	307.7	579.0	1290.3
POPULATION									
GROWTH RATE (%) - TOTAL	1.0	0.8	0.9	2.5	2.7	2.6	2.7	2.9	3.0
- URBAN	3.8	2.8	2.1	4.2	4.1	4.2	6.4	4.5	5.1
URBAN POPULATION (% OF TOTAL)	32.1	40.7	38.7	48.3	54.3	58.5	33.8	39.6	44.3
VITAL STATISTICS									
CRUDE BIRTH RATE (PER 1000)	23.3	20.5	19.2	40.9	39.0	36.8	48.3	47.2	45.7
CRUDE DEATH RATE (PER 1000)	10.5	9.0	9.0	14.1	10.9	9.2	22.6	18.0	15.3
GROSS REPRODUCTION RATE	1.4	1.3	1.3	2.7	2.6	2.6	2.3	3.4	3.4
EMPLOYMENT AND INCOME									
DEPENDENCY RATIO - AGE	0.6	0.6	0.4	0.9	1.0	0.9	0.9	1.0	1.0
- ECONOMIC	1.0	1.1	1.0	1.6	1.5	1.7	1.6	2.0	1.9
LABOR FORCE IN AGRICULTURE (% OF TOTAL)	47.9	31.8	27.4	48.3	41.0	36.9	52.6	43.4	42.9
UNEMPLOYED (% OF LABOR FORCE)	3.0	4.0	6.0	7.6	6.2	8.8	6.3	3.4	4.1
INCOME RECEIVED BY - HIGHEST 5%	21.8	24.5	25.0	37.1	30.4	31.7	24.0	25.0	21.0
- LOWEST 20%	5.4	3.9	3.9	3.9	3.5	2.0	4.4	4.2	5.2
HEALTH AND NUTRITION									
DEATH RATE (PER 1000) AGES 1-4 YEARS	4.7	2.8	1.7	10.6	7.7	6.6	..	6.0	..
INFANT MORTALITY RATE (PER 1000)	60.4	39.7	34.5	77.4	67.3	56.2	127.8	111.6	97.8
LIFE EXPECTANCY AT BIRTH (YRS)	65.8	68.6	69.1	55.8	60.6	62.5	45.5	50.3	52.8
POPULATION PER - PHYSICIAN	1004.0	821.3	694.4	2058.1	1866.8	1796.9	5690.8	5760.2	4774.7
- NURSING PERSON	1343.2	653.9	339.2	4542.1	3389.5	2804.5	3286.6	2564.7	2383.1
- HOSPITAL BED	190.5	168.0	170.5	444.1	392.3	405.6	670.8	661.6	700.0
PER CAPITA PER DAY SUPPLY OF:									
CALORIES (% OF REQUIREMENTS)	109.3	118.0	118.0	97.6	103.2	105.5	80.9	91.0	96.0
PROTEIN (GRMS) - TOTAL	85.9	90.7	90.0	63.7	59.8	60.7	54.5	58.3	63.1
- FROM ANIMALS & PULSES	27.0	29.0	33.0	29.0	28.0	28.2	17.5	15.0	15.6
EDUCATION									
ADJ. ENROLLMENT RATIOS - PRIMARY	105.0	102.1	104.3	85.0	101.7	105.1	51.5	75.6	80.5
- SECONDARY	25.5	50.5	49.2	15.0	27.6	36.0	10.3	20.4	22.2
FEMALE ENROLLMENT RATIO (PRIMARY)	98.9	99.4	100.4	85.6	98.3	98.1	30.8	50.2	52.3
ADULT LITERACY RATE (%)	64.9	75.0	88.2	61.4	74.6	75.7	17.7	26.9	40.6
HOUSING									
PERSONS PER ROOM - URBAN	1.4	1.5	1.4	1.9	1.3	2.1	1.8	2.3	3.0
OCCUPIED DWELLINGS WITHOUT WATER	67.0	63.3	59.5	65.5	67.0	66.4	62.2	77.1	90.5
ACCESS TO ELECTRICITY (%) - ALL	51.4	46.3	57.9	44.4	54.2	53.1	40.1	31.0	39.1
- RURAL	18.1	20.9	33.8	9.3	12.5	12.6			

TABLE 2. Social Indicators by Geographic Areas (Developing Countries), Continued

(ADJUSTED COUNTRY GROUP AVERAGES)

INDICATOR	AFRICA SOUTH OF SAHARA			SOUTH ASIA			EAST ASIA AND PACIFIC		
	1960	1970	MOST RECENT ESTIMATE	1960	1970	MOST RECENT ESTIMATE	1960	1970	MOST RECENT ESTIMATE
GNP PER CAPITA (IN CURRENT US $)	94.9	137.0	207.4	54.1	88.2	131.4	141.8	290.0	568.3
POPULATION									
GROWTH RATE (%) – TOTAL	2.2	2.4	2.6	2.2	2.6	2.1	3.0	2.8	2.3
– URBAN	5.6	6.0	6.0	5.2	4.1	4.3	5.4	5.0	5.2
URBAN POPULATION (% OF TOTAL)	9.1	12.5	13.5	7.8	9.8	12.4	28.1	27.1	38.1
VITAL STATISTICS									
CRUDE BIRTH RATE (PER 1000)	48.8	48.1	47.1	47.4	45.8	45.1	42.3	40.7	32.0
CRUDE DEATH RATE (PER 1000)	26.7	23.7	21.2	26.4	21.4	17.3	19.2	12.4	8.7
GROSS REPRODUCTION RATE	2.9	3.1	3.0	3.2	3.0	2.9	3.0	2.5	2.3
EMPLOYMENT AND INCOME									
DEPENDENCY RATIO – AGE	0.9	0.9	0.9	0.8	0.8	0.8	0.9	0.9	0.7
– ECONOMIC	1.1	1.1	1.1	1.5	1.4	1.2	1.4	1.4	1.3
LABOR FORCE IN AGRICULTURE (% OF TOTAL)	79.8	75.0	73.1	61.8	60.8	63.0	67.9	59.5	48.4
UNEMPLOYED (% OF LABOR FORCE)	5.1	4.6	5.1			11.0	5.1	5.1	4.1
INCOME RECEIVED BY – HIGHEST 5%	28.2	26.4	25.7	24.6	23.2	18.6	22.7	20.5	19.8
– LOWEST 20%	5.2	3.9	5.7	4.6	5.2	7.8	5.5	5.8	6.6
HEALTH AND NUTRITION									
DEATH RATE (PER 1000) AGES 1–4 YEARS								3.4	2.0
INFANT MORTALITY RATE (PER 1000)	153.9	129.6	127.5	136.2	124.3	104.0	61.2	31.1	27.4
LIFE EXPECTANCY AT BIRTH (YRS)	36.9	41.5	43.4	40.6	45.2	48.1	52.5	59.1	61.6
POPULATION PER – PHYSICIAN	31886.1	24906.5	21616.5	9920.9	8519.2	7412.6	3429.3	2268.9	2208.9
– NURSING PERSON	4558.4	3088.7	2496.5	14566.1	9168.6	8339.3	3096.6	1935.5	1465.5
– HOSPITAL BED	1234.7	819.9	799.9	2885.8	1998.5	1908.0	1270.8	921.7	662.1
PER CAPITA PER DAY SUPPLY OF:									
CALORIES (% OF REQUIREMENTS)	89.6	90.7	91.9	89.1	97.6	96.0	90.0	99.4	106.5
PROTEIN (GRMS) – TOTAL	56.6	59.0	60.6	47.8	53.2	50.8	48.1	53.4	55.6
– FROM ANIMALS & PULSES	19.2	19.8	23.1	15.0	16.0	15.5	19.0	22.1	22.1
EDUCATION									
ADJ. ENROLLMENT RATIOS – PRIMARY	27.7	42.4	50.0	36.9	47.9	55.2	95.0	105.7	110.0
– SECONDARY	1.9	5.6	6.9	9.1	15.5	20.0	17.3	26.9	51.1
FEMALE ENROLLMENT RATIO (PRIMARY)	21.7	37.4	43.2	22.2	53.8	44.5	88.5	102.0	104.7
ADULT LITERACY RATE (%)	9.8	17.4	18.4	16.0	20.0	21.0	47.7	66.4	72.6
HOUSING									
PERSONS PER ROOM – URBAN	2.7	2.4	1.7				2.5	2.3	
OCCUPIED DWELLINGS WITHOUT WATER							83.7	69.5	60.3
ACCESS TO ELECTRICITY (%) – ALL							22.6	40.7	50.5
– RURAL							12.0	20.1	23.4

GLOBAL INDICATORS

TABLE 3. COMPARATIVE SOCIAL INDICATORS FOR DEVELOPING COUNTRIES (BY GEOGRAPHIC AREA AND COUNTRY)

AREA AND COUNTRY	POP. GROWTH RATE % (65-75)	URBAN POP. % OF TOTAL	CRUDE BIRTH RATE (/000)	CRUDE DEATH RATE (/000)	LABOR IN AGR. % OF TOTAL	INCOME RECD BY HIGHEST 5% HH	INCOME RECD BY LOWEST 20% HH	LIFE EXPECT. YRS AT BIRTH	CALORIE SUPPLY %/CAP REQD.	PROTEIN SUPPLY GR/DAY /CAP	PRIMARY SCHOOL ENROLL RATIO %	FEMALE ENROLL. RATIO PRIMARY	ADULT LITERACY RATE % OF TOTAL
EUROPE													
CYPRUS	0.6	42.2	22.2	6.8	34.0	12.1	7.9	71.4	113.0	86.0	71.0	72.0	85.0
GREECE	0.6	64.8	15.4	9.4	34.0	18.7	6.3	71.8	132.0	102.0	106.0	104.0	82.0
MALTA	0.2	94.3	17.5	9.0	6.0	..	..	69.6	114.0	89.0	109.0	109.0	87.0
PORTUGAL	0.3	28.8	19.2	10.5	32.5	56.3	7.3	68.7	118.0	85.0	116.0	94.0	70.0
ROMANIA	1.2	43.0	19.7	9.3	36.0	..	..	69.1	118.0	90.0	109.0	109.0	98.0
SPAIN	1.0	59.1	19.5	8.3	23.0	18.5	6.0	72.1	135.0	94.1	115.0	115.0	94.0
TURKEY	2.6	42.6	39.4	12.5	52.5	28.0	3.5	56.9	113.0	75.7	104.0	94.0	55.0
YUGOSLAVIA	0.9	38.7	18.2	9.2	39.0	25.1	6.6	68.0	137.0	97.5	97.0	93.0	85.0
ALL COUNTRIES - MEDIAN	0.8	42.8	19.4	9.3	34.0	18.6	6.5	69.4	118.0	89.5	107.5	99.0	85.0
LATIN AMERICA & CARIBBEAN													
ARGENTINA	1.4	80.0	21.8	8.8	15.0	21.4	5.6	68.3	129.0	107.1	108.0	109.0	93.0
BAHAMAS	3.6	57.9	22.4	5.7	7.0	20.7	3.4	66.7	100.0	87.0	135.0	..	93.0
BARBADOS	0.4	3.7	21.6	8.9	18.0	19.8	6.8	69.1	133.0	82.5	117.0	116.0	97.0
BOLIVIA	2.7	34.0	44.0	19.1	65.0	36.0	4.0	46.8	77.0	48.5	74.0	65.0	40.0
BRAZIL	2.9	59.1	37.1	8.8	37.8	35.0	3.0	61.4	105.0	62.1	90.0	90.0	64.0
CHILE	1.9	83.0	27.9	9.2	19.0	31.0	4.8	62.6	116.0	78.3	119.0	118.0	90.0
COLOMBIA	2.8	70.0	40.6	8.8	39.0	27.2	5.2	60.9	94.0	47.0	105.0	108.0	81.0
COSTA RICA	2.8	40.6	31.0	5.8	36.4	22.8	5.4	69.1	113.0	60.8	109.0	109.0	89.0
DOMINICAN REPUBLIC	2.9	45.9	45.8	11.0	53.8	26.3	4.3	57.8	98.0	45.4	104.0	105.0	51.0
ECUADOR	3.4	41.6	41.8	9.5	43.5	..	..	59.6	93.0	47.4	102.0	100.0	69.0
EL SALVADOR	3.4	39.4	42.2	11.1	55.0	38.0	2.0	65.0	84.0	50.3	75.2	69.0	63.0
GRENADA	1.0	..	27.4	6.8	30.8	..	..	..	89.0	57.0	99.0	..	85.0
GUATEMALA	3.2	37.3	42.8	13.7	56.0	35.0	5.0	54.1	91.0	52.8	62.0	56.0	47.0
GUYANA	2.1	40.0	32.4	5.9	30.9	18.8	4.3	67.9	104.0	58.0	114.0	114.0	85.0
HAITI	1.6	23.1	35.8	16.3	77.0	..	..	50.0	90.0	39.0	70.0	37.0	20.0
HONDURAS	2.7	31.4	49.3	14.6	60.3	28.0	2.5	53.5	90.0	56.0	90.0	88.0	53.0
JAMAICA	1.7	37.1	32.2	7.1	26.9	30.2	2.2	69.5	118.0	68.9	111.0	112.0	86.0
MEXICO	3.5	63.3	42.0	8.6	41.0	27.9	3.4	64.7	117.0	66.9	112.0	109.0	76.0
NICARAGUA	3.6	48.0	48.3	13.9	48.0	42.4	3.1	52.9	105.0	68.4	85.0	87.0	57.0
PANAMA	3.2	49.6	36.2	7.1	30.0	22.2	4.6	66.5	105.0	61.0	124.0	120.0	82.2

TABLE 3. COMPARATIVE SOCIAL INDICATORS FOR DEVELOPING COUNTRIES (BY GEOGRAPHIC AREA AND COUNTRY) Continued

AREA AND COUNTRY	POP. GROWTH RATE % (65-75)	URBAN POP. % OF TOTAL	CRUDE BIRTH RATE (/000)	CRUDE DEATH RATE (/000)	LABOR IN AGR. % OF TOTAL	INCOME RECD BY HIGHEST 5% HH	INCOME RECD BY LOWEST 20% HH	LIFE EXPECT. YRS AT BIRTH	CALORIE SUPPLY %/CAP REQD.	PROTEIN SUPPLY GR/DAY /CAP	PRIMARY SCHOOL ENROLL RATIO %	FEMALE ENROLL. RATIO PRIMARY	ADULT LITERACY RATE % OF TOTAL
PARAGUAY	2.6	37.4	39.8	8.9	49.0	30.0	4.0	61.9	118.0	74.5	106.0	102.0	81.0
PERU	2.9	55.3	41.0	11.9	40.0	28.8	3.1	55.7	100.0	61.7	111.0	106.0	72.0
TRINIDAD & TOBAGO	1.0	25.1	27.3	5.9	13.5	..	..	69.5	114.0	66.0	111.0	111.0	90.0
URUGUAY	0.4	80.6	20.4	9.3	13.2	19.0	4.4	69.8	116.0	98.1	95.0	94.0	94.0
VENEZUELA	3.3	75.7	36.1	7.0	21.0	21.8	3.6	66.4	98.0	63.1	96.0	96.0	82.0
ALL COUNTRIES - MEDIAN	2.7	43.7	36.2	8.9	37.8	27.9	4.0	63.0	104.0	61.7	105.0	105.0	81.0
NORTH AFRICA & MIDDLE EAST													
ALGERIA	3.3	39.9	48.7	15.4	42.8	..	..	53.3	88.0	57.2	77.0	72.0	35.0
BAHRAIN	3.3	78.1	49.6	18.7	..	..	..	44.5	..	..	..	..	..
EGYPT	2.4	44.6	37.8	14.0	43.9	21.0	5.2	52.4	113.0	70.7	72.0	55.0	40.0
IRAN	2.9	43.0	45.3	15.6	41.0	29.7	4.0	51.0	98.0	56.0	90.0	67.0	50.0
IRAQ	3.3	62.0	48.1	14.6	51.0	35.1	2.1	52.7	101.0	60.4	93.0	63.0	26.0
JORDAN	3.4	42.0	47.6	14.7	19.0	..	..	53.2	90.0	65.0	83.0	77.0	62.0
KUWAIT	7.7	88.0	45.4	..	2.0	..	..	64.0	..	..	90.0	86.0	55.0
LEBANON	2.8	60.1	39.8	9.9	17.8	26.0	4.0	63.3	101.0	67.9	132.0	125.0	68.0
LIBYA	4.2	30.5	45.0	14.7	19.5	13.3	10.1	52.9	117.0	62.0	145.0	135.0	27.0
MOROCCO	2.4	40.1	46.2	15.7	50.0	20.0	4.0	53.0	108.0	70.5	61.0	44.0	28.0
OMAN	3.1	5.0	49.6	18.7	48.0	..	..	47.0	..	..	44.0	..	20.0
QATAR	10.5	85.0	..	..	..	..	..	..	..	..	112.0	..	21.0
SAUDI ARABIA	1.9	17.9	50.2	24.4	61.0	..	..	42.0	86.0	56.0	34.0	27.0	15.0
SYRIAN ARAB REP.	3.1	46.2	45.4	15.4	49.9	17.0	5.0	56.0	104.0	66.7	102.0	81.0	40.0
TUNISIA	2.3	47.0	40.0	13.8	37.4	..	..	54.1	102.0	67.4	95.0	75.0	55.0
UNITED ARAB EMIRATES	13.1	80.0	..	..	73.0	..	..	37.0	83.0	58.3	75.0	..	21.0
YEMEN ARAB REP.	1.7	7.0	49.6	20.6	42.9	..	..	44.8	84.0	57.0	25.0	6.0	10.0
YEMEN PEOP. DEM. REP.	3.1	35.3	49.6	20.6	..	..	..	..	..	..	78.0	48.0	27.1
ALL COUNTRIES-MEDIAN	3.1	43.8	46.9	15.6	42.9	21.0	4.0	52.8	101.0	62.0	83.0	70.5	28.0
AFRICA SOUTH OF SAHARA													
BENIN PEOP. REP.	2.7	13.5	49.9	23.0	47.5	31.4	5.5	41.8	87.0	56.0	44.0	28.0	20.0
BOTSWANA	2.1	10.7	45.6	23.0	83.0	28.1	1.6	43.5	85.0	65.0	85.0	93.0	25.0
BURUNDI	2.0	3.7	48.0	24.7	86.0	..	..	39.0	99.0	62.0	23.0	17.0	10.0
CAMEROON	1.9	28.5	40.4	22.0	82.0	..	..	41.0	102.0	59.0	111.0	97.0	6.0
CENTRAL AFRICAN EMPIRE	2.2	35.9	43.4	22.5	91.0	..	..	41.0	102.0	49.0	79.0	53.0	15.0

TABLE 3. COMPARATIVE SOCIAL INDICATORS FOR DEVELOPING COUNTRIES (BY GEOGRAPHIC AREA AND COUNTRY)   Continued

AREA AND COUNTRY	POPULATION & VITAL STATISTICS				EMPLOYMENT AND INCOME			HEALTH & NUTRITION			EDUCATION (MOST RECENT ESTIMATE)		
	POP. GROWTH RATE % (65-75)	URBAN POP. % OF TOTAL	CRUDE BIRTH RATE (/000)	CRUDE DEATH RATE (/000)	LABOR IN AGR % OF TOTAL	INCOME RECD BY HIGHEST 5% HH	INCOME RECD BY LOWEST 20% HH	LIFE EXPECT. YRS AT BIRTH	CALORIE SUPPLY %/CAP REQD.	PROTEIN SUPPLY GR/DAY /CAP	PRIMARY SCHOOL ENROLL RATIO %	FEMALE ENROLL. RATIO PRIMARY	ADULT LITERACY RATE % OF TOTAL
CHAD	2.0	13.9	44.0	24.0	90.0	21.5	7.7	38.5	75.0	60.2	37.0	20.0	15.0
CONGO PEOP. REP.	2.3	38.0	45.1	20.8	56.0	..	..	43.5	98.0	44.0	153.0	140.0	50.0
EQUATORIAL GUINEA	1.3												
ETHIOPIA	2.5	11.2	49.4	25.8	85.0	..	..	41.0	82.0	58.9	23.0	14.0	7.0
GABON	1.5	32.0	32.2	22.2	58.0	45.3	3.2	41.0	98.0	49.3	199.0	197.0	12.0
GAMBIA	2.3	14.0	43.3	24.1	79.6	..	..	40.0	98.0	64.0	32.0	21.0	10.0
GHANA	2.6	32.4	48.8	21.9	52.0	..	..	43.5	101.0	53.4	60.0	53.0	25.0
GUINEA	2.8	19.5	44.6	22.9	84.1	..	..	41.0	84.0	42.7	28.0		7.0
IVORY COAST	4.1	34.3	45.6	20.6	80.0	30.9	9.0	43.5	113.0	64.5	86.0	64.0	20.0
KENYA	3.4	13.0	48.7	16.0	84.0	20.2	3.9	50.0	91.0	59.6	109.0	101.0	40.0
LESOTHO	2.2	3.1	39.0	19.7	90.0	61.7	5.3	46.0	109.0	67.6	121.0	144.0	40.0
LIBERIA	3.3	27.6	43.6	20.7	72.0	41.0	5.2	43.5	87.0	39.0	62.0	44.0	15.0
MADAGASCAR	2.9	14.5	50.2	21.1	83.0	29.5	5.7	43.5	105.0	57.0	85.0	80.0	40.0
MALAWI	2.5	6.4	45.7	23.7	86.0	..	..	41.0	103.0	68.4	61.0	48.0	25.0
MALI	2.2	13.4	50.1	25.9	88.7	..	..	38.1	75.0	64.0	22.0	16.0	10.0
MAURITANIA	2.6	23.1	44.8	24.9	85.0	31.0	4.5	38.5	81.0	63.2	17.0	9.0	10.0
MAURITIUS	1.4	48.3	25.1	7.8	30.3	..	..	65.5	108.0	55.8	80.0	78.0	80.0
MOZAMBIQUE	2.2	55.0	43.3	21.4	73.0	23.0	6.0	41.0	94.0	41.0	46.0		
NIGER	2.7	9.4	52.2	25.5	91.0	..	..	38.5	78.0	62.1	17.0	12.0	5.0
NIGERIA	2.5	26.0	49.3	22.7	62.0	..	..	41.0	88.0	46.3	49.0	39.0	25.0
RWANDA	2.8	3.8	50.0	23.6	93.0	36.8	3.2	41.0	90.0	51.3	58.0	54.0	23.0
SENEGAL	2.7	38.8	47.6	23.9	73.0	36.2	1.1	40.0	97.0	67.1	43.0	33.0	10.0
SIERRA LEONE	2.3	15.0	44.7	20.7	73.0	..	..	43.5	97.0	50.9	35.0	28.0	15.0
SOMALIA	2.4	28.3	47.2	21.7	77.0	..	..	41.0	79.0	55.1	58.0	41.0	50.0
SUDAN	2.2	13.2	47.8	17.5	66.5	20.9	5.1	48.6	88.0	60.4	40.0	27.0	15.0
SWAZILAND	3.2	14.3	49.0	21.8	83.0	..	..	43.5	89.0		103.0	102.0	50.0
TANZANIA	2.8	7.3	47.0	20.1	83.1	33.5	2.3	44.5	86.0	47.1	57.0	46.0	49.0
TOGO	2.7	15.0	50.6	23.3	75.0	..	..	41.0	96.0	52.1	98.0	68.0	12.0
UGANDA	3.1	8.4	45.2	15.9	86.0	20.0	6.2	50.0	90.0	54.0	44.0	43.0	25.0
UPPER VOLTA	2.2	12.1	48.5	25.8	89.0	..	..	38.0	78.0	59.2	14.0	11.0	7.0
ZAIRE	2.7	26.4	45.2	20.5	77.0	23.0	..	43.5	85.0	32.0	88.0	87.0	15.0
ZAMBIA	2.9	36.3	51.5	20.3	52.0	..	3.8	44.5	89.0	58.8	88.0	86.0	43.0
ALL COUNTRIES-MEDIAN	2.5	14.8	47.4	22.1	82.5	30.9	4.5	41.0	90.0	57.0	58.0	47.0	15.0

TABLE 3. COMPARATIVE SOCIAL INDICATORS FOR DEVELOPING COUNTRIES (BY GEOGRAPHIC AREA AND COUNTRY)   Continued

AREA AND COUNTRY	POPULATION & VITAL STATISTICS				EMPLOYMENT AND INCOME			HEALTH & NUTRITION			EDUCATION (MOST RECENT ESTIMATE)		
	POP. GROWTH RATE % (65-75)	URBAN POP. % OF TOTAL	CRUDE BIRTH RATE (/000)	CRUDE DEATH RATE (/000)	LABOR IN AGR. % OF TOTAL	INCOME RECD BY HIGHEST 5% HH	INCOME RECD BY LOWEST 20% HH	LIFE EXPECT. YRS AT BIRTH	CALORIE SUPPLY %/CAP REQD.	PROTEIN SUPPLY GR/DAY /CAP	PRIMARY SCHOOL ENROLL RATIO %	FEMALE ENROLL. RATIO PRIMARY	ADULT LITERACY RATE % OF TOTAL
SOUTH ASIA													
AFGHANISTAN	2.2	14.3	51.4	30.7	52.9	16.7	..	40.3	83.0	61.5	23.0	7.0	14.0
BANGLADESH	2.3	8.8	49.5	28.1	78.0	..	7.9	45.0	93.0	58.5	73.0	51.0	23.0
BURMA	2.2	22.3	39.5	15.8	67.8	14.6	8.0	50.1	103.0	58.0	85.0	81.0	67.0
INDIA	2.2	20.6	37.0	17.0	69.0	25.0	4.7	49.5	89.0	48.0	65.0	52.0	36.0
NEPAL	2.1	4.8	42.9	20.3	94.4	..	..	43.6	95.0	50.0	59.0	10.0	19.2
PAKISTAN	2.9	26.0	47.4	16.5	54.8	17.3	8.4	49.8	93.0	54.0	51.0	31.0	21.0
SRI LANKA	2.0	24.3	28.2	7.9	55.0	18.6	7.3	67.8	97.0	48.0	77.0	77.0	78.1
ALL COUNTRIES-MEDIAN	2.2	20.6	42.9	17.0	67.8	17.3	7.9	49.5	93.0	54.0	65.0	51.0	23.0
EAST ASIA & PACIFIC													
CHINA REP.	2.6	51.1	23.0	4.7	35.0	13.3	8.8	68.6	111.0	68.0	104.0	110.0	82.0
FIJI	2.2	38.5	25.0	4.3	43.3	19.0	5.1	70.0	..	43.8	111.0	75.0	75.0
INDONESIA	2.3	18.2	42.9	16.9	69.0	33.7	6.8	48.1	98.0	43.8	81.0	109.0	62.0
KOREA	2.1	48.5	28.8	8.9	44.6	18.1	7.2	68.0	115.0	75.7	109.0	109.0	92.0
LAO P.D.R.	2.7	15.0	44.6	22.8	85.0	..	..	40.4	94.0	58.0	57.0	47.0	20.0
MALAYSIA	2.7	30.2	31.7	6.7	45.2	28.3	3.5	59.4	115.0	56.5	93.0	91.0	60.0
PAPUA NEW GUINEA	2.5	12.9	40.6	17.1	83.0	..	..	47.7	98.0	48.2	59.0	44.0	31.0
PHILIPPINES	2.9	29.8	43.8	10.5	52.6	28.8	5.5	58.5	87.0	50.0	105.0	103.0	87.0
SINGAPORE	1.7	90.2	21.2	5.2	2.8	..	..	89.5	122.0	74.7	111.0	108.0	75.0
THAILAND	3.1	16.5	37.6	9.1	76.0	22.0	5.6	58.0	107.0	50.0	78.0	75.0	82.0
VIET NAM	2.6	21.5	36.9	6.7	67.0	..	..	58.0	100.0	52.7	91.0	..	97.8
WESTERN SAMOA	1.9												
ALL COUNTRIES-MEDIAN	2.6	29.8	36.9	8.9	52.6	22.0	5.6	58.5	103.5	53.6	93.0	91.0	75.0

COMPARATIVE ECONOMIC DATA

TABLE 4. Selected Economic Development Indicators: Population and Production
(Average annual real growth rates)

Income group/ region/country	Population 1950-60	1960-65	1965-70	1970-77	Gross domestic product 1950-60	1960-65	1965-70	1970-77	GDP per capita 1950-60	1960-65	1965-70	1970-77
Developing countries	2.2	2.4	2.5	2.4	4.9	5.6	6.4	5.7	2.7	3.1	3.8	3.2
Capital-surplus oil-exporting countries	2.3	3.2	3.7	4.1	..	..	11.0	6.7	..	..	7.2	3.0
Industrialized countries	1.2	1.2	0.9	0.8	3.8++	5.3	4.9	3.2	2.5++	4.0	4.0	2.4
Centrally planned economies	1.7	1.8	1.6	1.4	..	6.2+	7.7+	6.4+	..	4.8+	6.7+	5.6+
A. Developing countries by income group												
Low income	2.0	2.4	2.4	2.2	3.8	3.8	5.3	4.0	1.8	1.4	2.8	1.7
Middle income	2.4	2.5	2.5	2.5	5.3	6.1	6.6	6.0	2.8	3.5	4.0	3.4
B. Developing countries by region												
Africa south of Sahara	2.3	2.5	2.5	2.7	3.6	5.0	4.9	3.7	1.3	2.4	2.3	0.9
Middle East and North Africa	2.4	2.6	2.7	2.7	5.1	6.4	9.4	7.1	2.6	3.7	6.5	4.3
East Asia and Pacific	2.4	2.6	2.5	2.2	5.2	5.5	8.0	8.0	2.8	2.8	5.4	5.7
South Asia	1.9	2.4	2.4	2.2	3.8	4.3	4.9	3.2	1.8	1.9	2.4	1.0
Latin America and the Caribbean	2.8	2.8	2.7	2.7	5.3	5.2	6.1	6.2	2.4	2.3	3.3	3.4
Southern Europe	1.5	1.4	1.4	1.5	6.1	7.5	6.5	5.3	4.5	6.0	5.0	3.8
C. Developing countries by region and country												
Africa south of Sahara												
Angola	1.6	1.5	1.6	2.3	..	5.9	3.2	-9.4	..	4.3	1.6	-11.5
Benin	2.2	2.5	2.7	2.9	..	3.1	2.7	2.7	..	0.6	0.0	-0.1
Botswana	1.7	1.9	1.9	1.9	2.9	4.2	9.8	15.7	1.2	2.2	7.8	13.5
Burundi	2.0	2.3	2.4	2.2	-1.3	2.8	5.8	2.3	-3.2	0.5	3.3	0.4
Cameroon	1.4	1.7	1.9	2.1	1.7	2.9	7.3	3.4	0.3	1.2	3.3	1.2
Cape Verde	3.1	3.1	2.7	2.2	..	..	..	..	..	..	5.3	..
Central African Republic	1.4	2.2	2.2	2.2	2.6	0.4	3.5	3.1	1.1	-1.7	1.3	0.9
Chad	1.4	1.8	1.9	2.2	..	0.5	1.6	1.2	..	-1.3	-0.3	-0.9
Comoros	3.0	3.2	3.3	3.8	..	9.5	3.2	-1.5	..	6.1	-0.1	-5.2
Congo, People's Republic of the	1.6	2.1	2.2	2.5	1.1	2.7	3.4	3.9	-0.5	0.6	1.2	1.4
Equatorial Guinea	1.5	1.7	1.9	2.2	..	13.8	2.0	-3.0	..	11.8	0.1	-5.0
Ethiopia	2.1	2.3	2.4	2.5	3.9	5.1	3.7	2.6	1.7	2.7	1.2	0.1
Gabon	0.2	0.5	0.7	0.9	11.5	3.9	5.3	9.1	11.3	3.3	4.6	8.1

TABLE 4. COMPARATIVE ECONOMIC DATA (Continued)

Income group/ region/country	Population				Gross domestic product				GDP per capita			
	1950-60	1960-65	1965-70	1970-77	1950-60	1960-65	1965-70	1970-77	1950-60	1960-65	1965-70	1970-77
Gambia, The	2.0	3.3	3.2	3.1	1.3	5.2	4.3	8.2	-0.7	1.9	1.1	4.9
Ghana	4.5	2.7	2.1	3.0	4.1	3.3	2.5	0.4	-0.4	0.6	0.4	-2.5
Guinea	2.2	2.7	3.0	3.0	...	3.9	3.0	5.4	...	1.2	0.0	2.4
Guinea-Bissau	0.2	-1.1	-0.2	1.6	...	...	...	...	...	...	...	...
Ivory Coast	2.1	3.7	3.8	6.0	3.6	10.1	7.4	6.5	1.5	0.1	3.5	0.5
Kenya	3.3	3.4	3.5	3.8	4.0	3.6	8.0	4.8	0.7	0.2	4.9	1.0
Lesotho	1.5	1.8	2.2	2.4	4.4	8.7	2.1	8.0	2.8	6.7	-0.1	5.5
Liberia	2.8	3.1	3.2	3.4	10.5	3.1	0.4	2.7	7.4	0.0	3.1	-0.6
Madagascar	1.8	2.1	2.3	2.5	2.3	1.4	4.9	-0.7	0.5	-0.7	2.5	-3.2
Malawi	2.4	2.7	2.9	3.1	...	3.3	4.5	6.3	...	0.6	1.5	3.1
Mali	2.1	2.5	2.4	2.5	3.2	3.2	2.9	4.7	1.0	0.7	0.5	2.1
Mauritania	2.2	2.5	2.6	2.7	...	9.9	4.6	2.2	...	7.2	2.0	-0.5
Mauritius	3.3	2.7	1.9	1.3	0.1	5.4	-0.3	8.2	-3.0	2.7	-2.2	6.8
Mozambique	1.4	2.1	2.3	2.5	3.1	2.3	8.3	-3.7	1.7	0.2	5.9	-6.1
Namibia	...	2.4	2.6	2.8	...	...	...	...	...	...	...	...
Niger	2.3	4.0	2.7	2.8	...	6.6	-0.3	1.2	...	2.5	-2.9	-1.5
Nigeria	2.4	2.5	2.5	2.6	4.1	5.3	4.5	6.0	1.6	2.7	1.9	3.3
Réunion	...	3.3	2.5	1.8	...	...	...	...	...	...	...	...
Rhodesia	4.1	4.2	3.7	3.3	...	3.2	6.1	3.2	...	-0.9	2.4	-0.1
Rwanda	2.3	2.5	2.7	2.9	1.0	-2.9	8.5	5.2	-1.2	-5.3	5.6	2.2
Senegal	2.2	2.4	2.5	2.6	...	3.6	1.3	2.8	...	1.1	-1.2	0.2
Sierra Leone	1.8	2.1	2.3	2.5	3.6	4.3	3.9	1.5	1.8	2.1	1.6	-1.0
Somalia	2.0	2.4	2.5	2.3	12.8	-0.5	3.4	1.2	10.6	-2.8	0.9	-1.1
South Africa	3.0	2.5	2.7	2.7	2.9	6.6	5.9	4.0	-0.1	4.0	3.1	1.2
Sudan	1.9	2.2	2.4	2.7	5.5	1.5	1.3	5.4	3.5	-0.7	-1.0	2.7
Swaziland	2.0	2.3	2.1	2.5	8.4	13.6	6.3	6.2	6.3	11.0	4.1	3.7
Tanzania, United Republic of	2.2	2.6	2.8	3.0	6.0	5.2	5.9	5.2	3.7	2.6	3.1	2.1
Togo	2.2	2.7	2.7	2.6	1.3	8.4	6.7	4.0	-0.9	5.6	3.9	1.4
Uganda	2.8	3.8	3.7	3.0	3.3	5.7	5.9	0.5	0.5	1.8	2.2	-2.4
Upper Volta	1.9	1.6	1.6	1.6	1.6	2.7	3.3	0.5	-0.3	1.0	1.6	-1.0
Zaïre	2.3	1.9	2.1	2.7	3.4	3.7	4.3	1.0	1.1	1.7	2.2	-1.7
Zambia	2.4	2.8	2.9	3.0	5.6	5.4	2.8	2.8	3.1	2.6	-0.1	-0.2

TABLE 4. COMPARATIVE ECONOMIC DATA (Continued)

Income group/ region/country	Population				Gross domestic product				GDP per capita			
	1950-60	1960-65	1965-70	1970-77	1950-60	1960-65	1965-70	1970-77	1950-60	1960-65	1965-70	1970-77
C. Developing countries by region and country (cont.)												
Middle East and North Africa												
Algeria	2.1	2.0	3.7	3.2	6.5	0.8	8.1	5.4	4.4	-1.2	4.2	2.2
Bahrain	3.5	4.2	2.9	7.1	··	··	··	10.7[d]	··	··	··	3.2[d]
Egypt, Arab Republic of	2.4	2.5	2.1	2.1	3.3	7.6	3.2	6.4	0.9	4.9	1.1	4.2
Iran	2.5	2.7	2.8	3.0	5.9	9.2	12.6	7.4	3.3	6.3	9.5	4.3
Iraq	2.8	3.1	3.2	3.4	9.9	7.7	4.1	8.1[e]	6.9	4.5	0.9	4.7[e]
Jordan	3.2	3.0	3.2	3.3	··	··	··	7.0[f]	··	··	··	3.6[f]
Lebanon	2.6	3.0	2.8	2.5	··	··	··	··	··	··	··	··
Morocco	2.7	2.5	2.9	2.7	2.0	4.2	5.7	0.4	-0.7	1.7	2.8	3.6
Syrian Arab Republic	2.7	3.1	3.3	3.3	··	8.8	5.0	9.6	··	5.4	2.3	6.2
Tunisia	1.8	1.9	2.1	2.0	··	5.2[c]	4.9	8.5	··	3.3[c]	2.8	6.4
Yemen, Arab Republic of	2.0	2.1	1.5	1.9	··	··	··	8.4	··	··	··	6.4
Yemen, People's Democratic Republic of	1.9	1.9	1.9	1.9	··	··	··	6.8[d]	··	··	··	4.8[d]
East Asia and Pacific												
Fiji	3.1	3.3	2.3	1.8	2.8	3.7	7.4	5.0	-0.3	0.3	5.0	3.1
Hong Kong	4.5	3.7	1.3	2.0	9.2	11.7	8.0	8.0	4.5	7.7	6.6	5.9
Indonesia	2.1	2.2	2.2	1.8	4.0	1.6	7.5	8.0	1.9	-0.6	5.2	6.1
Korea, Republic of	2.0	2.6	2.2	2.0	5.1	6.7	10.3	9.9	3.1	4.0	7.9	7.8
Malaysia	2.5	2.9	2.9	2.7	3.6	6.8	5.9	7.8	1.0	3.7	2.9	4.9
Papua New Guinea	1.8	2.3	2.4	2.4	4.8	6.4	5.7	5.0	2.9	4.0	3.3	2.5
Philippines	2.7	3.0	3.1	2.7	6.5	5.2	5.2	6.3	3.6	2.2	2.1	3.5
Singapore	4.8	2.8	2.0	1.6	··	5.5	13.0	8.6	··	2.6	10.7	6.9
Solomon Islands	2.6	2.6	2.6	3.5	10.7	3.7	2.5	5.4	7.9	1.1	-0.1	1.8
Taiwan	3.5	3.0	2.4	2.0	7.6	8.9	9.2	7.7	4.0	5.8	6.7	5.6
Thailand	2.8	3.0	3.1	2.9	5.7	7.4	8.4	7.1	2.8	4.2	5.1	4.0
South Asia												
Afghanistan	1.5	2.2	2.2	2.2	··	1.7	2.3	4.5	··	-0.4	0.2	2.2
Bangladesh	2.4	2.8	3.0	2.5	··	4.6	3.4	2.3	··	1.8	0.4	-0.1

TABLE 4. COMPARATIVE ECONOMIC DATA (Continued)

Income group/region/country	Population				Gross domestic product				GDP per capita			
	1950-60	1960-65	1965-70	1970-77	1950-60	1960-65	1965-70	1970-77	1950-60	1960-65	1965-70	1970-77
Bhutan	..	1.9	2.1	2.3	..	..	..	3.6	..	..	..	1.4
Burma	1.9	2.1	2.2	2.2	6.3	4.4	2.3	3.1	4.3	2.2	0.1	1.0
India	1.9	2.3	2.4	2.1	3.8	4.0	5.0	2.6	1.9	1.7	2.6	0.4
Nepal	1.2	1.9	2.2	2.2	2.4	2.7	2.2	2.6	1.2	0.8	0.0	0.7
Pakistan	2.3	2.7	2.9	3.1	2.4	7.2	6.9	3.8	0.1	4.4	3.8	1.1
Sri Lanka	2.6	2.5	2.3	1.7	3.9	4.0	5.8	2.9	1.3	1.5	3.4	1.5
Latin America and the Carribean												
Argentina	1.9	1.5	1.4	1.3	2.8	3.0	4.5	2.8	0.9	1.4	3.1	1.5
Bahamas	3.6	4.8	4.4	2.7	..	..	..	..	..	..	..	..
Barbados	0.9	0.3	0.3	0.5	5.9	4.5	7.9	2.0	4.9	4.1	7.6	1.4
Belize	3.1	2.8	2.8	0.9	..	..	..	6.0	..	..	..	5.0
Bolivia	2.1	2.5	2.6	2.7	6.9	5.0	4.8	5.9	3.7	2.5	2.1	3.1
Brazil	3.1	2.9	2.9	2.9	4.0	4.0	8.0	9.9	2.6	1.1	5.0	6.8
Chile	2.2	2.3	1.9	1.7	4.6	4.9	3.6	0.1	1.4	2.6	1.7	-1.6
Colombia	3.1	3.3	2.8	2.1	..	4.7	5.9	5.7	..	1.4	2.9	3.6
Costa Rica	3.7	3.7	3.2	2.5	5.8	5.3	6.9	6.0	1.5	1.6	3.6	3.3
Dominican Republic	2.9	2.9	2.9	3.0	..	4.6	6.6	8.0	..	1.6	3.6	4.9
Ecuador	2.9	3.0	3.0	3.0	4.4	..	5.8	9.2	1.5	..	2.7	6.0
El Salvador	2.8	3.4	3.5	3.1	3.1	6.7	4.3	5.3	0.3	3.2	0.7	2.1
Honduras	3.3	3.5	2.8	3.3	8.1	4.9	4.2	3.2	1.4	1.4	1.4	-0.1
Jamaica	1.5	1.6	1.2	1.7	5.6	3.7	5.1	0.0	2.1	2.1	3.9	-1.7
Mexico	3.2	3.3	3.3	3.3	..	7.4	6.8	4.9	..	3.9	3.5	1.5
Netherlands Antilles	1.7	1.7	1.4	1.2	5.2	..	4.1	5.8	2.2	..	2.7	..
Nicaragua	2.9	3.0	3.0	3.3	4.9	10.4	7.8	5.8	1.9	7.2	4.6	2.4
Panama	2.9	3.1	3.1	3.1	2.7	7.9	4.3	3.5	0.1	4.7	1.6	0.4
Paraguay	2.6	2.6	2.7	2.9	4.9	4.5	4.3	7.0	2.2	1.9	1.4	4.0
Peru	2.6	2.9	2.9	2.8	5.3	7.1	7.0	4.5	4.1	4.1	5.6	1.7
Puerto Rico	0.6	1.6	1.3	2.8	..	8.1	3.3	3.6	..	6.5	5.6	0.7
Trinidad and Tobago	2.8	3.0	1.1	1.2	1.7	4.7	1.9	2.2	0.3	1.6	2.2	1.0
Uruguay	1.4	1.2	1.0	0.2	8.0	0.6	1.9	1.6	-0.6	-0.6	1.0	1.3
Venezuela	4.0	3.6	3.3	3.4	8.0	7.4	4.9	5.6	3.8	3.7	1.6	2.2

TABLE 4. COMPARATIVE ECONOMIC DATA (Continued)

Income group/ region/country	Population				Gross domestic product				GDP per capita			
	1950-60	1960-65	1965-70	1970-77	1950-60	1960-65	1965-70	1970-77	1950-60	1960-65	1965-70	1970-77
C. Developing countries by region and country (cont.)												
Southern Europe												
Cyprus	1.5	0.6	0.8	0.7	4.0	3.7	8.1	1.0	2.5	3.0	7.2	0.3
Greece	1.0	0.5	0.6	0.7	6.0	7.7	7.2	4.6	5.0	7.2	6.6	3.9
Israel	5.3	3.9	3.0	2.8	11.3	9.8	8.7	5.0	5.6	5.6	5.5	2.2
Malta	0.5	-0.6	0.5	0.3	3.3	0.3	9.0	11.4	2.7	0.9	8.5	11.1
Portugal	0.7	0.2	-0.2	0.8	4.1	6.4	6.4	4.6	3.4	6.1	6.6	3.7
Spain	0.8	1.0	1.1	1.0	6.2	8.0	6.3	4.7	5.3	7.5	5.1	3.6
Turkey	2.8	2.5	2.5	2.5	6.3	5.3	6.3	7.3	3.4	2.8	3.7	4.6
Yugoslavia	1.2	1.1	0.9	0.9	5.6	6.6	6.2	6.2	4.4	5.4	5.2	5.2
D. Capital-surplus oil-exporting countries												
Kuwait	6.2	11.1	9.6	6.2	..	4.7[h]	5.7	-0.1	..	-5.8	-3.5	-6.0
Libyan Arab Republic	2.7	3.8	4.2	4.1	..	..	..	6.8	..	..	..	3.5
Oman	2.0	2.5	2.7	3.2	..	5.7	39.7	..	..	3.2	36.0	..
Qatar	2.4	7.1	6.9	10.3	..	..	..	..	..	..	..	..
Saudi Arabia	2.0	2.5	2.8	3.0	..	..	9.1	12.7	..	..	6.1	9.4
United Arab Emirates	2.4	9.3	13.7	16.7	..	..	..	12.5[i]	..	..	..	-2.1[i]
E. Industrialized countries												
Australia	2.3	2.0	1.9	1.7	4.7[i]	5.3	6.2	3.3	2.3[i]	3.2	4.2	1.6
Austria	0.2	0.6	0.5	0.2	5.6	4.3	5.1	4.0	5.4	3.7	4.6	3.8
Belgium	0.6	0.7	0.4	0.3	3.1[i]	5.2	4.8	3.7	2.5[i]	4.5	4.4	3.4
Canada	2.7	1.9	1.7	1.2	4.0[i]	5.8	4.8	4.7	1.3[i]	3.8	3.0	3.4
Denmark	0.7	0.8	0.7	0.4	3.6[i]	5.1	4.5	2.8	2.9[i]	4.3	3.7	2.4
Finland	1.0	0.6	0.2	0.4	4.9	5.0	5.1	3.4	3.9	4.4	4.9	3.0
France	0.9	1.3	0.8	0.7	4.8	5.9	5.3	3.8	3.8	4.5	4.5	3.1
Germany, Federal Republic of	1.0	1.3	0.6	0.2	7.3[i]	4.8	4.5	2.4	6.3[i]	3.5	3.9	2.2
Iceland	2.1	1.8	1.2	1.3	..	7.1	1.1	4.6	..	5.2	-0.2	3.2
Ireland	-0.5	0.3	0.5	1.2	..	4.0	5.3	3.4	..	3.7	4.7	2.3
Italy	0.7	0.7	0.7	0.7	5.5[g]	5.0	6.1	2.9	4.8[g]	4.3	5.4	2.2

TABLE 4. COMPARATIVE ECONOMIC DATA (Continued)

Income group/ region/country	Population				Gross domestic product				GDP per capita			
	1950-60	1960-65	1965-70	1970-77	1950-60	1960-65	1965-70	1970-77	1950-60	1960-65	1965-70	1970-77
Japan	1.3	1.0	1.1	1.2	8.0[l]	10.1	12.4	5.0	6.6[l]	9.0	11.2	3.7
Luxembourg	0.6	1.1	0.4	0.8	..	3.3	3.6	2.3	..	2.2	3.2	1.5
Netherlands, The	1.3	1.4	1.2	0.9	4.7	4.9	5.7	3.2	3.3	3.5	4.4	2.3
New Zealand	2.2	2.1	1.4	1.7	..	5.0	2.6	2.9	..	2.9	1.2	1.2
Norway	0.9	0.8	0.8	0.6	3.4[l]	5.1	4.8	4.8	2.5[l]	4.3	3.9	4.1
Sweden	0.6	0.7	0.8	0.4	3.4	5.3	3.9	1.7	2.7	4.6	3.1	1.3
Switzerland	1.3	2.1	1.1	0.2	4.6	5.2	4.2	0.2	3.2	3.0	3.1	0.0
United Kingdom	0.4	0.7	0.3	0.1	2.8	3.2	2.5	1.9	2.3	2.4	2.2	1.7
United States	1.7	1.5	1.1	0.8	3.3	4.7	3.2	2.8	1.5	3.2	2.1	1.9
F. Centrally planned economies[k]												
Albania	2.8	3.0	2.8	2.5	..	..	..	..	..	..	..	..
Bulgaria	0.8	0.8	0.7	0.6	..	7.0	8.6	7.5	..	6.2	7.8	6.9
China	1.9	2.0	1.8	1.6	..	..	..	..	..	..	..	..
Cuba	2.6	2.1	1.9	1.6	..	..	..	..	..	..	..	..
Czechoslovakia	1.0	0.7	0.3	0.7	..	..	6.6[a]	5.2	..	..	6.3[a]	4.5
German Democratic Republic	-0.6	-0.3	0.0	-0.2	..	2.7[l]	5.5[l]	5.1[l]	..	5.9	5.5	5.3
Hungary	0.7	0.3	0.4	0.4	..	4.5	6.8	6.2	..	4.2	6.4	5.8
Korea, Democratic People's Republic of	0.8	2.8	2.8	2.6	..	..	..	..	..	..	..	..
Mongolia	2.2	2.8	3.1	3.0	..	6.0	6.0	8.7	..	4.6	5.4	7.6
Poland	1.8	1.3	0.6	1.0	..	8.8	7.7	10.7	..	8.0	6.2	10.1[m]
Romania	1.2	0.7	1.4	0.9	..	6.6	8.2	6.1	..	5.0	7.1	5.5[m]
Union of Soviet Socialist Republics	1.8	1.5	1.0	0.9	..	..	..	..	..	..	..	..

+ Weighted average of the country growth rates; GDP in US dollars were used as weights; these are not strictly comparable to other group averages.   ++ 1955-60.   a. 1966-70.   b. 1967-70.   differences in national accounting system   l. Based on NMP index (1960=100) constructed from 1975 constant price series.   m. 1970-78.

TABLE 4. COMPARATIVE ECONOMIC DATA (Continued)

	Gross production							
	Agriculture				Manufacturing			
	1950-60	1960-65	1965-70	1970-77	1950-60	1960-65	1965-70	1970-77
Developing countries	3.9	2.6	3.4	2.7	4.9	7.6	7.5	7.4
Capital-surplus oil-exporting countries	..	..	2.2	4.4	..	..	..	..
Industrialized countries	2.3+	2.0	2.2	2.1	..	5.9	5.8	2.8
Centrally planned economies	..	..	3.2+	2.4+	6.1+	8.0+	8.3+	7.4+
A. Developing countries by income group								
Low income	..	1.6	4.1	2.2	..	8.4	3.3	5.2
Middle income	4.5	3.1	3.0	3.0	4.7	7.5	7.9	7.2
B. Developing countries by region								
Africa south of Sahara	4.8	2.6	2.4	1.3	..	8.3	8.0	5.6
Middle East and North Africa	..	1.3	3.6	2.8	..	10.0	0.9	12.1
East Asia and Pacific	4.8	4.6	3.4	4.1	..	4.8	11.9	11.6
South Asia	3.2	1.1	4.7	2.1	6.4	8.8	3.5	4.3
Latin America and the Caribbean	..	3.5	2.8	3.3	4.0	5.6	6.7	5.8
Southern Europe	4.4	3.2	3.2	3.1	8.4	11.4	9.3	6.1
C. Developing countries by region and country								
Africa south of Sahara								
Angola	..	3.2	2.0	-3.4	..	..	..	..
Benin	3.3	1.9	5.2	1.5	..	..	..	..
Botswana	..	2.4	0.4	4.5	..	..	..	..
Burundi	-1.5	1.7	1.7	2.0	..	..	..	..
Cameroon	3.7	7.2	4.4	1.8	..	..	10.7*	6.2
Cape Verde	..	..	..	..	..	..	..	..
Central African Republic	..	-1.2	3.3	2.1	..	4.1	8.1	6.0
Chad	..	0.9	-0.3	0.2	..	..	2.0^b	5.7
Comoros	..	..	..	..	..	..	..	..
Congo, People's Republic of the	..	0.0	2.9	2.8	..	3.4	7.7	2.3
Equatorial Guinea	..	4.8^c	-3.1	-4.9	..	..	..	..
Ethiopia	4.1	1.8	1.9	-0.1	..	..	..	..
Gabon	..	3.2^c	1.9	1.3	..	..	..	..

TABLE 4. COMPARATIVE ECONOMIC DATA (Continued)

	Gross production							
	Agriculture				Manufacturing			
	1950-60	1960-65	1965-70	1970-77	1950-60	1960-65	1965-70	1970-77
Gambia, The	0.4	7.1	-0.3	1.7	..	3.1	8.9	4.3
Ghana	7.0	3.5	3.8	-0.4	4.6	10.8	12.5	-1.9
Guinea	2.7	1.9	3.5	0.0	..	..	..	..
Guinea-Bissau	..	..	..	..	..	..	..	..
Ivory Coast	9.3	11.3	3.7	4.5	..	14.2	8.0	7.5
Kenya	4.7	2.9	1.1	3.0	..	..	..	..
Lesotho	..	0.1	1.5	2.0	..	..	..	..
Liberia	2.6	3.0	3.0	2.3	..	..	14.1	5.5
Madagascar	3.9	4.1	1.8	2.7	..	..	..	1.2
Malawi	..	3.8	3.4	3.8	..	..	..	10.6
Mali	1.8	2.3	3.2	2.7	..	..	4.0	9.2
Mauritania	..	3.4	2.2	-3.3	..	..	35.1	2.9
Mauritius	..	3.1	-1.4	2.6	..	..	..	..
Mozambique	..	0.8	4.4	-1.6	..	..	..	..
Namibia	..	..	..	..	..	..	..	..
Niger	5.5	5.2	0.6	0.4	..	14.6	8.8	8.6
Nigeria	5.1	2.1	1.7	1.7	..	11.1	10.4	8.1
Réunion	..	..	..	..	..	..	..	..
Rhodesia	..	2.9	0.0	3.9	5.0	6.2	7.5	3.8
Rwanda	..	-1.6	8.4	3.6	..	..	..	..
Senegal	4.8	4.1	-4.5	5.0	..	0.4	1.2	8.2
Sierra Leone	0.3	4.7	2.2	2.0	..	..	2.7	3.6
Somalia	..	2.7	1.9	0.0	..	..	..	..
South Africa	4.1	1.5	3.9	2.2	5.0	8.4	6.7	3.2
Sudan	-0.4	5.4	6.0	2.3	..	17.1[c]	21.9	7.3
Swaziland	..	4.6	7.0	3.6	..	..	..	..
Tanzania, United Republic of	6.9	2.9	3.0	1.2	..	..	..	..
Togo	9.3	31.3	1.4	-5.5	..	..	6.7	11.3
Uganda	6.9	1.4	4.2	0.8	..	..	..	..
Upper Volta	-0.2	7.2	2.2	1.6	..	..	3.8[b]	7.1
Zaire	1.0	-2.2	2.3	1.9	..	..	0.3	1.1
Zambia	..	1.2	1.9	4.7	..	12.1	8.6	1.7

TABLE 4. COMPARATIVE ECONOMIC DATA (Continued)

| | Gross production | | | | | | | |
| | Agriculture | | | | Manufacturing | | | |
	1950-60	1960-65	1965-70	1970-77	1950-60	1960-65	1965-70	1970-77
C. Developing countries by region and country (cont.)								
Middle East and North Africa								
Algeria	-0.5	-2.2	4.1	0.4	..	..	..	..
Bahrain	..	..	1.6	4.0	..	..	..	..
Egypt, Arab Republic of	3.4	3.6	3.5	0.7	8.8	20.0	3.8	6.3
Iran	2.1	2.7	4.1	4.2	..	9.5	13.4	16.0
Iraq	1.5	4.0	4.0	-2.3	..	..	..	..
Jordan	..	20.7	-15.3	-1.6	..	..	..	..
Lebanon	5.0	9.1	0.7	-0.5	..	..	..	..
Morocco	3.0	5.1	4.1	-2.0	5.2	3.3	5.8	6.5
Syrian Arab Republic	2.1	10.8	-1.7	9.8	6.3	9.2	4.8	8.3
Tunisia	4.5	3.6	-0.5	5.6	..	2.9	4.8	5.6
Yemen, Arab Republic of	..	1.2	-4.3	3.1	..	..	..	..
Yemen, People's Democratic Republic of	..	2.6	1.2	3.8	..	..	..	..
East Asia and Pacific								
Fiji	..	11.2^c	3.3	-0.4	..	..	5.4	3.0
Hong Kong	..	0.9	-0.3	-10.3	..	12.4	18.6	4.0
Indonesia	2.6	3.9	3.3	3.1	..	1.0	7.9	12.5
Korea, Republic of	5.5	6.3	3.1	4.9	10.4	13.9	25.6	23.5
Malaysia	0.9	5.2	6.4	4.3	..	..	11.5	12.6
Papua New Guinea	..	4.2	2.8	3.1	9.7^g	..	..	..
Philippines	3.3	2.8	3.2	5.8	..	6.2	4.4	5.2
Singapore	..	1.4	15.8	1.0	..	7.7	15.8	11.2
Solomon Islands	..	1.4	0.9	1.9	..	..	..	..
Taiwan	4.8	4.8	2.9	3.1	15.4	13.6	21.0	13.3
Thailand	3.8	6.0	3.1	4.7	6.4	10.8	10.2	11.8
South Asia								
Afghanistan	..	1.6	1.0	4.0	..	..	8.0	9.3
Bangladesh	..	3.1	3.1	1.8	..	5.8	7.4	5.7

TABLE 4. COMPARATIVE ECONOMIC DATA (Continued)

	Gross production							
	Agriculture				Manufacturing			
	1950-60	1900-65	1965-70	1970-77	1950-60	1960-65	1965-70	1970-77
Bhutan	2.5	3.1	3.1	1.6	..	..	..	..
Burma	3.2	0.5	4.9	2.1	6.6	5.6	1.7	4.4
India	..	0.9	1.7	1.2	..	9.0	2.8	4.6
Nepal	..	4.6	5.9	2.6	..	12.1	9.4	2.6
Pakistan	..	3.6	2.1	2.4	..	6.1	5.6	2.7
Sri Lanka	2.3	..	..	..	-0.9	..	..	..
Latin America and the Carribean								
Argentina	..	3.0	3.0	3.3	0.4	3.9	6.1	3.0
Bahamas	..	..	-2.5	-2.7	..	..	..	..
Barbados	..	3.6	5.4	2.6	..	..	1.6*	6.5
Belize	..	13.7	4.2	4.4	..	..	..	..
Bolivia	4.5	4.1	2.7	4.4	1.3	7.0	3.4	7.1
Brazil	2.9	3.2	2.5	1.7	9.1	3.7	10.4	9.6
Chile	..	2.2	3.6	3.9	5.7	6.7	1.5	-4.4
Colombia	..	2.8	5.6	3.5	0.5	5.7	6.2	6.5
Costa Rica	..	3.4	5.9	2.0	..	9.2	8.0	8.1
Dominican Republic	..	-2.7	3.0	3.5	5.0	1.5	11.4	8.8
Ecuador	..	5.8	0.4	3.3	..	..	7.2	10.6
El Salvador	..	2.9	5.3	1.3	5.7	17.0	5.0	8.3
Honduras	..	4.5	-1.3	1.1	7.0	3.0	4.9	5.6
Jamaica	2.9	3.2	2.0	2.1	..	7.6	3.0	0.6
Mexico	5.4	5.9	3.1	9.7	7.0	9.6	8.4	5.9
Netherlands Antilles	..	1.2	1.2	5.0	..	..	..	..
Nicaragua	1.1	13.0	6.5	3.5	10.7	..	..	..
Panama	..	4.3	2.4	4.6	..	12.6	9.0	1.2
Paraguay	..	4.9	2.3	0.7	..	3.5	5.9	3.1
Peru	3.6	2.4	..	..	7.3	9.7	6.7	5.8
Puerto Rico	..	..	..	-0.5	..	..	..	..
Trinidad and Tobago	..	2.8	1.4	..	..	..	6.1	-1.1
Uruguay	0.3	2.3	3.1	0.4	3.2	1.0	2.4	2.7
Venezuela	..	5.6	5.7	2.2	13.0	9.5	3.6	5.6

TABLE 4. COMPARATIVE ECONOMIC DATA (Continued)

| | Gross production | | | | | | | |
| | Agriculture | | | | Manufacturing | | | |
	1950-60	1960-65	1965-70	1970-77	1950-60	1960-65	1965-70	1970-77
C. Developing countries by region and country (cont.)								
Southern Europe								
Cyprus	3.8	7.7	5.4	0.8	..	2.5	10.1	1.4
Greece	4.7	6.5	2.4	3.8	7.9	7.9	8.7	7.7
Israel	12.0	8.1	5.8	4.9	11.6	13.6	11.6	6.1
Malta	..	2.7	6.7	0.4	..	..	..	..
Portugal	2.1	3.7	1.1	-1.1	6.7	8.7	8.9	1.2
Spain	2.9	2.6	3.3	3.4	8.8	12.6	10.1	7.9
Turkey	4.7	2.9	4.0	3.7	8.6	12.7	11.6	10.1
Yugoslavia	6.2	2.5	3.1	4.6	10.4	11.7	6.1	8.2
D. Capital-surplus oil-exporting countries								
Kuwait	..	..	3.0	1.5	..	..	..	..
Libyan Arab Republic	3.9	7.2	-2.0	11.4	..	..	..	..
Oman	..	..	2.8	2.1	..	..	..	..
Qatar	..	..	..	..	..	..	..	..
Saudi Arabia	..	2.8	2.9	2.8	..	..	11.9	4.0
United Arab Emirates	..	..	..	..	..	..	..	..
E. Industrialized countries								
Australia	3.8	0.5	3.6	1.9	6.3	6.1	4.9	1.3
Austria	4.7	0.7	3.0	1.9	7.5	4.5	6.4	3.3
Belgium	1.3	0.7	4.3	0.9	4.1	6.3	6.0	2.6
Canada	2.5	5.0	-1.2	2.8	3.5	6.3	4.9	3.7
Denmark	1.5	0.8	-1.1	1.2	3.5	6.9	4.6	1.8
Finland	3.4	2.4	1.4	1.4	6.4	6.2	7.5	3.3
France	3.2	2.7	1.6	1.3	6.8	5.5	9.6	2.8
Germany, Federal Republic of	3.3	0.8	3.7	0.4	9.8	5.7	6.5	1.6
Iceland	..	..	..	3.2	..	..	..	..
Ireland	2.2	0.3	3.2	3.9	3.0	6.6	7.1	4.1
Italy	2.2	3.0	2.4	1.0	9.3	6.3	7.3	3.0

TABLE 4. COMPARATIVE ECONOMIC DATA (Continued)

| | Gross production | | | | | | | |
| | Agriculture | | | | Manufacturing | | | |
	1950-60	1960-65	1965-70	1970-77	1950-60	1960-65	1965-70	1970-77
Japan	2.4	3.2	3.3	2.1	18.3	11.5	10.3	2.9
Luxembourg	1.3	0.7	4.5	0.9	4.4	1.8	4.5	0.0
Netherlands, The	2.9	0.1	6.6	3.0	5.9	6.2	7.4	2.1
New Zealand	3.0	3.0	2.2	1.0	..	..	..	..
Norway	0.6	-0.8	0.8	1.6	4.8	5.8	4.2	2.2
Sweden	-0.2	0.3	0.7	2.5	3.0	7.4	4.9	2.0
Switzerland	1.1	-0.9	2.5	1.9	6.0	5.1	5.8	-1.0
United Kingdom	2.7	3.1	1.1	0.8	3.5	3.4	3.0	0.5
United States	1.8	1.7	1.5	3.1	3.4	6.3	3.8	3.3
F. Centrally planned economies								
Albania	..	..	4.2	3.4	..	..	..	..
Bulgaria	..	..	1.5	1.6	..	11.0	11.0	8.4
China	..	..	2.5	3.0	..	..	..	..
Cuba	..	..	4.0	0.0	..	..	..	..
Czechoslovakia	..	..	3.8	2.9	..	4.5	6.8	6.7
German Democratic Republic	..	..	1.2	3.6	..	5.7	6.4	6.3
Hungary	..	..	2.7	3.7	..	7.7	5.9	6.2
Korea, Democratic People's Republic of	..	..	2.1	6.7	..	..	..	..
Mongolia	..	..	-2.0	2.3	..	..	..	..
Poland	..	..	1.6	1.3	..	8.7	8.9	10.7
Romania	..	..	-0.4	6.9	..	..	..	..
Union of Soviet Socialist Republics	..	..	4.1	1.8	..	8.4	8.6	7.2

c. 1961-65. d. 1973-77. e. 1970-75. f. 1972-77. g. 1951-60. h. 1962-05. i. 1952-00. j. 1953-00. k. GDP data are not strictly comparable to those of other countries because of

TABLE 5. Tables of World Military Expenditure, Arms Importers and Exporters

Rank order of all major-weapon exporters to the Third World, 1970–79[1]

Exporting country	Total value	Percentage of Third World total
United States of America	27 727	45
USSR	16 914	27.5
France	5 894	10
United Kingdom	3 044	5
Italy	1 868	3
Third World exporters	1 805	3
Federal Republic of Germany	1 444	2.3
China	787	1.3
Netherlands	515	0.8
Australia	421	0.7
Canada	323	0.5
Sweden	196	0.3
Czechoslovakia	154	0.2
Spain	110	0.2
Ireland	87	0.1
Poland	80	0.1
Switzerland	55	—
Yugoslavia	47	—
New Zealand	13	—
Belgium	5	—
Japan	3	—
TOTAL	≃ 61 000	100.0

1. Figures are SIPRI trend-indicator values, as expressed in constant $ millions, at constant 1975 prices.
Source : SIPRI Yearbook, 1980.

TABLE 5. Tables of World Military Expenditure, Arms Importers and Exporters (continued)

World military expenditure. Middle East in constant price figures (figures are in $ millions, at 1978 prices and exchange-rates)

	1950	1955	1960	1965	1970	1975	1976	1977	1978	1979
Bahrain				16.8	13.9	21.4	29.9	41.1	[44.7]	[47.8]
Cyprus						23.2	22.7	30.1	[23.2]	[17.4]
Egypt	206	489	513	974	2 271	5 756	5 004	5 239	[3 325]	[2 840]
Iran	212	291	577	862	1 906	10 168	11 031	8 902	9 506	(4 943)
Iraq	58	140	313	563	841	2 049	2 010	2 100	1 988	
Israel	57	49	189	385	2 016	3 160	3 158	2 726	2 377	(3 063)
Jordan	56	109	181	191	279	246	232	275	307	387
Kuwait			53	97	393	860	1 073	1 189	1 091	
Lebanon	13	27	38	68	94	165	137	85		
Oman					36	698	785	686	767	[695]
Saudi Arabia				1 035	2 094	(9 430)	[11 375]	[11 900]	(12 700)	(14 640)
Syria	58	68	170	242	429	1 088	1 086	1 097	1 151	(1 937)
United Arab Emirates						74	(153)	(904)	(1 066)	(1 195)
Yemen Arab Republic				12	58	(102)	(122)	(134)	(132)	
Yemen, Democratic					45.8	38.2	52.1	57.9	74.6	
TOTAL MIDDLE EAST	[800]	[1 400]	[2 400]	[4 500]	(10 506)	33 879	36 271	35 366	(34 636)	[33 103]

Source: SIPRI Yearbook, 1980.

TABLE 5. Tables of World Military Expenditure, Arms Importers and Exporters (continued)

Rank order of Third World major arms importers, 1975–79

Importing region	Percentage of Third World total	Largest recipient countries	Percentage of region's total	Largest supplier to each country	Largest suppliers per region
Middle East	48	Iran	31	United States	United States
		Saudi Arabia	14	United States	USSR
		Jordan	13	United States	France
		Iraq	12	USSR	United Kingdom
		Israel	10	United States	
		Syria	6	USSR	
Far East	16	Republic of Korea	38	United States	United States
		Viet Nam	16	USSR	USSR
		Taiwan	13	United States	France
		Malaysia	5	United States	China
		Philippines	5	United States	
		Indonesia	5	United States	
North Africa	11	Libya	65	USSR	USSR
		Morocco	20	France	France
		Algeria	14	USSR	United States
		Tunisia	1	Italy	United Kingdom
Sub-Saharan Africa	10	South Africa	24	France	USSR
		Ethiopia	13	USSR	France
		Angola	9	USSR	United States
		Mozambique	9	USSR	United Kingdom
		Sudan	6	France	
		Nigeria	5	United Kingdom	
South America	9	Brazil	24	United States	United States
		Peru	20	USSR	United Kingdom
		Argentina	17	United Kingdom	France
		Chile	14	France	Italy
		Venezuela	13	Italy	
		Ecuador	8	France	
Indian subcontinent	5	India	52	USSR	USSR
		Pakistan	28	France	France
		Afghanistan	13	USSR	United Kingdom
		Bangladesh	3	China	China
		Nepal	0.3	France	
		Sri Lanka	0.2	France	
Central America	1.5	Cuba	45	USSR	USSR
		Mexico	28	United Kingdom	United Kingdom
		Bahamas	6	United States	United States
		Honduras	5	United States	France
		El Salvador	5	Israel	
		Guatemala	4	Israel	
Oceania	0.02	Papua New Guinea	63	Australia	Australia
					United States
		Fiji	37	United States	

TABLE 5. Tables of World Military Expenditure, Arms Importers and Exporters (continued)

World military expenditure summary, in constant price figures (figures are in $ millions at 1978 prices and exchange-rates)

	1950	1955	1960	1965	1970	1975	1976	1977	1978	1979
United States	39 475	98 252	100 001	107 192	130 872	110 229	104 261	108 540	108 357	110 145
Other NATO	27 885	44 328	50 386	60 891	63 094	74 699	76 669	78 183	80 438	81 728
Total NATO	67 360	142 580	150 387	168 083	193 966	184 928	180 930	186 723	188 795	191 873
USSR	[37 700]	[51 200]	[48 000]	[65 900]	[92 500]	[99 800]	[102 700]	[104 200]	[105 700]	
Other WTO	...	...	3 388	5 423	8 263	10 530	11 138	11 756	12 006	12 256
Total WTO	[40 700]	[54 200]	[51 388]	[71 323]	[100 763]	[110 330]	[112 438]	[114 456]	[116 206]	[117 956]
Other Europe	(2 800)	(5 140)	(5 867)	7 552	8 595	10 579	11 111	11 052	11 139	11 544
Middle East	[800]	[1 400]	[2 400]	[4 500]	(10 500)	33 879	36 271	35 366	(34 636)	[33 103]
South Asia	[1 240]	[1 415]	[1 555]	3 376	3 424	4 037	4 558	4 541	(4 648)	[4 747]
Far East (excl. China)	[4 400]	[5 200]	[6 100]	8 000	11 990	15 771	[16 880]	[18 780]	[20 275]	[21 580]
China	[12 900]	[11 800]	[13 100]	[25 300]	[37 900]	[40 300]	[40 400]	[41 700]	[42 900]	[44 200]
Oceania	987	1 583	1 485	2 279	3 068	3 232	3 194	3 206	3 204	3 175
Africa (excl. Egypt)	[125]	[400]	[900]	2 898	5 330	9 134	(9 720)	(9 950)	[10 130]	[10 250]
Central America	[400]	[420]	[575]	742	987	1 266	[1 500]	[1 825]	[2 070]	[2 275]
South America	[2 000]	[2 250]	(2 485)	(3 312)	3 981	5 489	5 858	[6 120]	[5 950]	[5 455]
WORLD TOTAL	133 710	226 390	236 245	297 265	380 510	418 945	422 860	433 719	439 953	446 158

Source : SIPRI Yearbook 1980

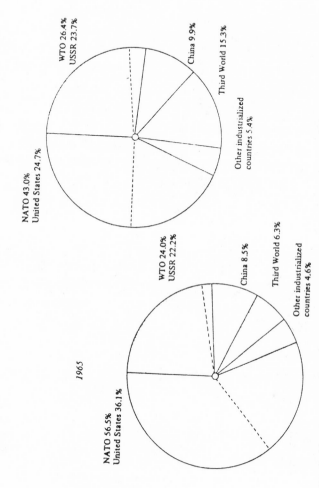

FIGURE 1. Distribution of World Military Expenditure, 1965 and 1979

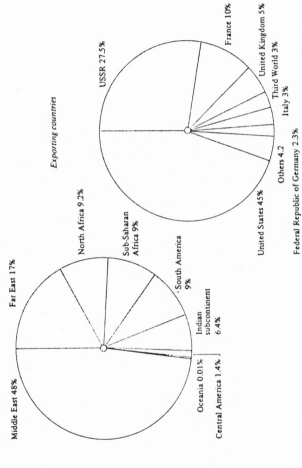

Third World importing regions

Exporting countries

Far East 17%

North Africa 9.2%

Sub-Saharan Africa 9%

Middle East 48%

South America 9%

Indian subcontinent 6.4%

Oceania 0.01%

Central America 1.4%

USSR 27.5%

France 10%

United Kingdom 5%

Third World 3%

Italy 3%

Others 4.2

United States 45%

Federal Republic of Germany 2.3%

FIGURE 2. The Importers' and Exporters' Shares of Major Weapon Suppliers to the Third World, 1970–79

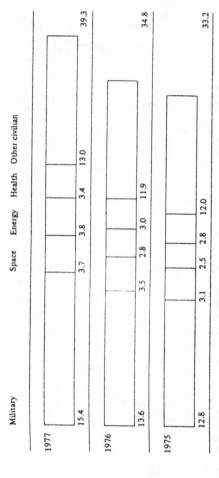

FIGURE 3. Government Financing of Research in the United States and the European Community (in \$1,000 million)

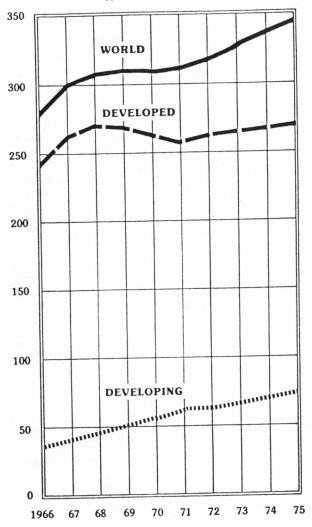

FIGURE 4. World Military Expenditures
($ Billions (constant 1974)

Source: U.S. Arms Control and Disarmament Agency, *World Military Expenditures and Arms Transfers, 1966-1975* (Washington, D.C.: Government Printing Office, 1976),

PART III
RESOURCE
BIBLIOGRAPHY

This bibliography is entirely restricted to publications in English language and covers the literature since 1970. In a bibliography of this nature, it is essential that the material be as contemporary as possible, while at the same time it was thought desirable to provide a balanced weight of materials discussed over the last decade.

With respect to classification of the material, a bibliographic subject index by item number has been provided at the end of this section.

First part of this bibliography entitled, DEVELOPMENT (GENERAL) has been classified for the general reader, according to the following categories. This classification is arbitrary, however, much cross indexing has been done in the bibliographic subject index following this section of the book.

A. Problems, Issues and Trends;
B. Analytical Methods;
C. Strategies and Policies; and
D. Country Studies.

Many of the annotations in this section have been compiled from the Journal of Economic Literature, World Bank Publications, IMF-IBRD Joint Library Periodicals, Finance and Development, U.N. Documents and Publisher's Book Promotion Pamphlets.

I. BOOKS

DEVELOPMENT (GENERAL)

01   Abraham, M. Francis
A B   PERSPECTIVES ON MODERNIZATION: TOWARD A GENERAL THEORY
      OF THIRD WORLD DEVELOPMENT
      Washington, D.C.:   University Press of America, 1980.

02   Adelman, Irma and Morris, Cynthia Taft
B   ECONOMIC GROWTH AND SOCIAL EQUITY IN DEVELOPING COUNTRIES
      Stanford, Calif.:   Stanford University Press, 1973.

      A quantitative investigation of the interactions among
      economic growth, political participation, and the
      distribution of income in noncommunist developing nations.
      The study is based on data (presented in the earlier
      study, Society, politics, and economic development) from
      74 countries which is given in the form of 48 qualitative
      measures of the [countries] social, economic, and political
      characteristics, and it includes the use of discriminant
      analysis in an examination of the forces tending to
      increase political participation and the use of a stepwise
      analysis of variance technique in analyzing the
      distribution of income.

03   Albin, Peter S.
A B   PROGRESS WITHOUT POVERTY; SOCIALLY RESPONSIBLE ECONOMIC
      GROWTH
      New York: Basic Books, 1978.

      Examines the relationship among important social
      tendencies, growth processes, and growth policies and
      argues for the return of the growth economy, with the
      caveat that social objectives and policy directions be

reformulated to avert ecological disaster and to improve economic welfare. Using a dualistic imbalance framework, explores the style and impact of unbalanced growth in modern industrial capitalism, focusing on educational policy, income distribution, and the control of technology, poverty, and urban decay. Concludes with policy recommendations for a program of social and technical advance that is geared to the intelligent management of a growth economy and the renovation of its distributive mechanisms. An appendix presents a dualistic-imbalance model of modern industrial growth.

04   Alexander, Robert J.
A B C   A NEW DEVELOPMENT STRATEGY
          Maryknoll, N.Y.: Orbis Books, 1976.

Focusing on the demand side of the development equation, this monograph concerns itself with an economic development strategy of import substitution where industries are established to manufacture products for which a home market has already been created by imports. Analyzing the effect on development of this assured demand, and exploring the limit to which this strategy can be used, the author, looks in detail at the prerequisites for the use of this method (substantial imports and protection for newly created industries) and discusses the priorities for private and public investment in this phase. Contends that this process provides a basis for developing countries to decide which projects should be undertaken first and which can be postponed until later.

05   Alvarez, Francisco Casanova
A C   NEW HORIZONS FOR THE THIRD WORLD
          Washington, D.C.: Public Affairs Press, 1976.

Presents the factors leading to approval of the Charter of Economic Rights and Duties of States by the United Nations General Assembly on 12 December 1974. Shows that the charter, with the main objective of overcoming the injustice prevailing in economic relations between nations and [elimination of] the dependence of Third World countries on industrial nations, owes its origin and adoption to President Luis Echeverria of Mexico. Argues that the developing nations remain essentially colonized and dependent entities of the industrialized world. Concludes that the future world will be less unjust and less ridden with anxiety, more secure and better able to care for its own if we respect the principles of the charter.

06   Anell, Lars and Nygren, Birgitta
A B C   THE DEVELOPING COUNTRIES AND THE WORLD ECONOMIC ORDER
          New York: St. Marin's Press, 1980.

Explores the possible form, functioning, and enforcement
of a New International Economic Order (NIEO). Provides
an account of the demands of developing countries for
a better allocation of the world's resources and considers
the early cooperation between developing and developed
countries, particularly resolutions passed at various
U.N. General Assembly sessions. Also analyzes and comments
on the central NIEO demands. Among the possible actions
the authors suggest developing countries could take are:
(1) force industrialized countries to increase the flow
and quality of aid by threatening trade discrimination;
(2) establish a list of honest consultancy firms and
a file of information on technology procurement; and
(3) feel free to steal patents from big corporations
and make use of copyrights without compensation.

07   Angelopoulos, Angelos T.
A C   FOR A NEW POLICY OF INTERNATIONAL DEVELOPMENT
        New York: Praeger, 1977.

08   Angelopoulos, Angelos T.
A C   THE THIRD WORLD AND THE RICH COUNTRIES;
        PROSPECTS FOR THE YEAR 2000
        Translated by N. Constantinidis and C. R. Corner
New York: Praeger, 1972.

An examination and projection of the gap in incomes between
the developed and underdeveloped countries of the world.
The author brings data on and discusses the indicators
of poverty, the population explosion in the developing
world, the main causes of economic backwardness, the
"myth" of development aid, the need for a new international
development strategy, various strategies of development
financing, precipitating factors in the emergence of
the Third World, economic growth and forecasts of world
income in the year 2000, and the possibilities of China
becoming the spokesman for the Third World.

09   Arkhurst, Frederick S., ed.
B C D   AFRICA IN THE SEVENTIES AND EIGHTIES;
        ISSUES IN DEVELOPMENT
        New York and London: Praeger in cooperation with the
        Adlai Stevenson Institute of International Affairs, 1970.

Eleven experts in various fields express their views
in a symposium "Africa in the 1980's" which met in Chicago
in early 1969 under the auspices of the Adlai Stevenson
Institute of International Affairs. The purpose...was
to attempt to draw a portrait of Africa in the 1980's
on the basis of the experience of the past decade and,
also, on the basis of current trends in the area of
politics, economic development, population, agriculture,
trade, education and law - all viewed as composite and
interactive factors in the development process.

10   Arndt, H. W., et al.
A B C   THE WORLD ECONOMIC CRISIS: A COMMONWEALTH PERSPECTIVE
          London: Commonwealth Secretariat, 1980.

          Report of a group of experts from Commonwealth countries
          on obstacles to structural change and sustained economic
          growth, with recommendations for specific measures by
          which developed and developing countries might act to
          reduce or eliminate such constraints. Focuses on the
          implications of the world economic crises - inflation,
          slowdown of economic growth, and staggering disequilibria
          in balance of payments - for the developing countries
          of the Third World. Stresses the need for collective
          action in view of the interdependence of the world economy.

11   Bairoch, Paul
A C D   THE ECONOMIC DEVELOPMENT OF THE THIRD WORLD SINCE 1900
          Translated from the fourth French edition by Cynthia
          Postan
          Berkeley: University of California Press, 1975.

          The author covers a wide range of factors important to
          development, namely population, agriculture, extractive
          industry, manufacturing industry, foreign trade, education,
          urbanization, the labor force and employment, and
          macroeconomic data. Particular attention is devoted
          to the development of agriculture. Comparison is drawn
          between the economic progress of Third World countries
          and developed countries at a similar stage of
          industrialization. Twenty-four countries were selected
          for the analysis, representing 80 percent of the population
          of the Third World. These include seven countries from
          each of Africa, Latin-America, and Asia respectively,
          and three countries from the Middle East.

12   Bairoch, Paul and Levy-Leboyer, Maurice, eds.
A B   DISPARITIES IN ECONOMIC DEVELOPMENT SINCE THE INDUSTRIAL
          REVOLUTION
          New York: St. Martin's Press, 1981.

          Collection of thirty-five previously unpublished essays
          presented at the 7th International Economic History
          Congress in Edinburgh in August 1978. Main theme deals
          with disparities in economic development. Concerns
          differences in income at micro-regional and international
          levels. In four parts: (1) discussing economic
          disparities among nations (two papers on international
          disparities: ten on the Third World and five on the
          developed world); (2) covering regional economic
          disparities (eight essays on northern, western, and central
          Europe; three on France; two on Southern Europe and one
          on the Third World); (3) detailing relations between
          regional and national disparities (two papers); and (4)
          discussing the methodological aspects of measurement
          of economic disparities (two papers).

13   Baldwin, Robert E.
B C   ECONOMIC DEVELOPMENT AND GROWTH
        New York, London, Sydney and Toronto: John Wiley and
        Sons, Inc., 1972.

        This short text seeks to provide "an analysis of economic
        development that in terms of breadth and sophistication
        lies between the usual elementary and advanced approaches
        to the development topic." It is organized around three
        themes, i.e., what the nature of growth problem is, what
        the main theories of growth and development are, and
        what the main policy issues facing less developed countries
        are. Therefore, the chapters deal with the characteristics
        of poverty, various classical development theories
        relatively more recent contributions to development theory,
        national and sectoral policies for growth, and issues
        in the financing of development.

14   Bauer, P.T.
B C   DISSENT ON DEVELOPMENT. STUDIES AND DEBATES IN DEVELOPMENT
        ECONOMICS
        Cambridge, Mass.: Harvard University Press, 1972.

        A collection of previously published articles, essays,
        and book reviews, some of which have been rewritten and
        expanded, dealing with various theoretical and empirical
        issues in economic development. Part One ("Ideology
        and Experience") examines general problems of concept
        method, analysis, historical experience and policy in
        economic development, such as the vicious circle of
        poverty, the widening gap, central planning, foreign
        aid, Marxism, etc. Part Two ("Case Studies") features
        five of the author's studies on developing countries,
        particularly Nigeria and India. Part Three ("Review
        Articles") brings book reviews on such well known books
        as W. Arthur Lewis' The Theory of Economic Growth, Benjamin
        Higgins' Economic Development, Walt W. Rostow's The Stages
        of Economic Growth, Thomas Balogh's The Economics of
        Poverty, and other volumes by Gunnar Myrdal, John Pincus,
        Harry G. Johnson, E.A.G. Robinson, B.K. Madan and Jagdish
        Bhagwati.

15   Bauer, P.T.
A B   EQUALITY, THE THIRD WORLD AND ECONOMIC DELUSION
        Cambridge, Mass.: Harvard University Press, 1981.

        Critique of methods and finding of contemporary economics,
        particularly development economics, arguing that there
        is a hiatus between accepted opinion and evident reality.
        All but four chapters are extended and/or revised versions
        of previously published articles. In the three parts:
        equality, the West and the Third World, and the state
        of economics. Criticizes economics and especially
        development economics for disregard of personal qualities

and social and political arrangements as determinants
of economic achievement and for ignoring the role of
external contracts in extending markets. Notes that
the benefits of mathematical economics have been bought
at the cost of an uncritical attitude, which has led
to inappropriate use and in some cases to an emphasis
on form rather than substance.

16   Berry, Leonard and Kates, Robert W., eds.
A C   MAKING THE MOST OF THE LEAST
          New York: Holmes and Meier Publishers, 1979.

The poverty faced by Third World countries today seriously
challenges the stability of the world order. The
contributors look torward the restructuring of the present
economic order by establishing "harmonious linkages"
between the industrialized and nonindustrialized worlds.
A welcome addition to the literature on economic
development.

17   Bhatt, V. V.
A B C   DEVELOPMENT PERSPECTIVES: PROBLEM, STRATEGY AND POLICIES
          Oxford; New York: Sydney and Toronto: Pergamon Press,
          1980.

Discusses the dynamics of the socioeconomic system in
terms of the cumulative and cyclical changes in economic
institutions, ideologies, and technology. Stresses the
importance of: upgrading traditional technology and
adapting modern technology to given situations; the
financial system, since it affects savings and shapes
the pattern of resource allocation; and upgrading of
agricultural organization and technology. Sets forth
as necessary for the development process: the stability
of the international currencey and the international
monetary system, which the author proposes be linked
to prices of primary products; the shaping of the
international monetary-financial-trade system to be
consistent with LDC's development strategy; and viewing
the process of socioeconomic development as an integral
part of nation-building and of building the international
community.

18   Brown, Lester R.
A C   THE GLOBAL ECONOMIC PROSPECT: NEW SOURCES OF ECONOMIC
          STRESS
          Worldwatch Paper no. 20
          Washington, D.C.: Worldwatch Institute; New York, 1978.

Considers the relationship between the expanding global
economy and the earth's natural systems. Discusses the
increase in fuel costs, suggesting that the world is
running out of cheap energy; diminishing returns in grain
production and to fertilizer use; overfishing; global

inflation; capital shortages; unemployment; and the
changing growth prospect. Concludes that future economic
policies must shift from growth to sustainability; not
advocating abandonment of growth as a goal, but with
concern for carrying capacities of biological system.
Fisheries, forests, grasslands, and croplands, require
development of alternative energy sources and population
policies consistent with resource availability.

19
A B C   Chenery, Hollis and Syrquin, Moises
PATTERNS OF DEVELOPMENT, 1950-1970
Assisted by Hazel Elkington
New York and London: Oxford University Press, 1975.

Examines principal changes in economic structure that
normally accompany economic growth, focusing on resource
mobilization and allocation, particularly those aspects
needed to sustain further growth. These aspects are
treated in a uniform econometric framework to provide
a consistent description of a number of interrelated
types of structural change and also to identify systematic
differences in development patterns among countries that
are following different development strategies. The
major aim of the research is to separate the effects
of universal factors affecting all countries from
particular characteristics. The authors use data for
101 countries in the period 1950 to 1970. Countries
are grouped into three categories: large country, balanced
allocation; small country, industry specialization.
Chapter 5 compares the results obtained from time-series
data with those observed from cross-sectional data.
Results are obtained from regression techniques, where
income level and population are treated as exogenous
variables. The demographic variables show how the movement
of population from rural to urban areas and lowering
of the birth rate and death rate have influenced demand
and supply of labor. A technical appendix discusses
the methods used, the problems encountered, and all the
regression equations specified in this study.

20
A B C   Chenery, Hollis B., et al., eds.
STUDIES IN DEVELOPMENT PLANNING
Cambridge, Mass.: Harvard University Press, 1971.

Attempts to bring together the contributors' varied
backgrounds in both field work and the use of quantitative
techniques and show how modern methods can be used in
operational development planning.

21
A B   Chodak, Szymon
SOCIETAL DEVELOPMENT: FIVE APPROACHES WITH CONCLUSIONS
FROM COMPARATIVE ANALYSIS
New York: Oxford University Press, 1973.

A sociologist analyzes the development and change of societies using five different conceptual approaches, attempting to view the processes of development in society from a multidimensional synthesizing perspective. These five approaches are called: "Evolutionary Theories," "Development - The Growing Societal Systemness," "Development and Innovation in the Search for Security," "Economic and Political Development," and "Modernization." The author gives references to the societal development which has taken place in various parts of the world and under different political systems.

22   Colman, David and Nixson, Frederick
A B C ECONOMICS OF CHANGE IN LESS DEVELOPED COUNTRIES
       New York: Wiley, Halsted Press, 1978.

Analyzes the changes that are occurring in the less-developed countries (LDC's); considers the problems generated by change; and examines the agents of change. Emphasizes the internal (rather than the international) aspects of development and focuses on economic inequality within LDC's and the impact on the development process in agriculture and industry of different income distributions. Although recognizing the impact of transnational corporations on the nature and characteristics of development within the LDC's, the authors argue that it is the LDC government that is responsible for the economic policies pursued. Also outlines the concepts and measurement of development, and reviews the literature on economic theorizing about development. A final chapter discusses inflation and migration in LDC's. Authors note that too often policy recommendations ignore political acceptability and recommend that the economist should cooperate with the political scientist in the study of inflation and with the sociologist in the study of rural urban migration.

23   Corbet, Hugh and Jackson, Robert, eds.
A B C IN SEARCH OF A NEW WORLD ECONOMIC ORDER
       New York and Toronto: Wiley, Halsted Press, 1974.

Focuses on the reform of the international commercial systems for further liberalizations of world trade. Papers are grouped into four categories: (1) introduction, (2) general factors affecting negotiations, (3) outside issues of significance, (4) issues on the agenda.

24   Fields, Gary S.
A B C D POVERTY, INEQUALITY, AND DEVELOPMENT
       New York and London: Cambridge University Press, 1980.

Focuses on the distributional aspects of economic development and explores the impact of the rate and type of growth on poverty and inequality in poor countries. Findings show that in general growth reduces poverty, but a high aggregate growth rate is neither necessary nor sufficient for reducing absolute poverty or relative inequality. Uses case studies of distribution and development in Costa Rica, Sri Lanka, India, Brazil, the Phillippines, and Taiwan to examine which combinations of circumstances and policies led to differential performance. Concludes that a commitment to developing to help the poor does not guarantee progress, but it helps a great deal. In its absence, the flow of resources to the haves, with only some trickle down to the have-nots, will be perpetuated.

25   Finger, J. M.
A B D INDUSTRIAL COUNTRY POLICY AND ADJUSTMENT TO IMPORTS FROM DEVELOPING COUNTRIES
World Bank Staff Working Paper no. 470, July 1981.

A background study for World Development Report 1981. Reviews and interprets recent analyses of the policies established by industrial countries in response to increasing imports from developing countries.

26   Finger, Nachum
A C D THE IMPACT OF GOVERNMENT SUBSIDIES ON INDUSTRIAL MANAGEMENT: THE ISRAELI EXPERIENCE
New York: Praeger, 1971.

27   Fitzgerald, E. V.
A B   PUBLIC SECTOR INVESTMENT PLANNING FOR DEVELOPING COUNTRIES
New York: Holmes and Meier, 1978.

28   Florence, P. Sargant
A B C ECONOMICS AND SOCIOLOGY OF INDUSTRY: A REALISTIC ANALYSIS OF DEVELOPMENT
Baltimore, Md.: Johns Hopkins University Press, 1969.

29   Frank, Andre Gunder
A B C CRISIS IN THE THIRD WORLD
New York: Holmes and Meier, 1981.

30   Frank, Andre Gunder
A B   DEPENDENT ACCUMULATION AND UNDERDEVELOPMENT
New York and London: Monthly Review Press, 1979.

Explains underdevelopment by an analysis of the production and exchange relations of dependence. Distinguishes the three main stages or periods in this world embracing process of capital accumulation and capitalist development: mercantilist (1500-1770), industrial capitalist (1770-1870), and imperialist (1870-1930). Analyzes each period

in terms of history, trade relations between the metropolis and the periphery, and transformation of the modes or relations of production, and the development of underdevelopment in the principal regions of Asia, Africa, and the Americas.

31   Frank, Charles R., Jr., and Webb, Richard C., eds.
A B D   INCOME DISTRIBUTION AND GROWTH IN THE LESS-DEVELOPED COUNTRIES
Washington, D.C.: Brookings Institution, 1977.

Fourteen previously unpublished essays representing part of the results of a project undertaken jointly by the Brookings Institution and the Woodrow Wilson School of Public and International Affairs at Princeton University, dealing with the relation between income distribution and economic growth in the developing countries. The first two articles present an overview of income distribution policy and discuss the causes of growth and income distribution in LDC's, respectively. The next nine examine the relation between income distribution and different economic policies and factors, including: industrialization, education, population, wage, fiscal, agricultural, public works, health and urban land policies.

32   Gant, George F.
A B   DEVELOPMENT ADMINISTRATION - CONCEPTS, GOALS, METHODS
Madison, Wisconsin: The University of Wisconsin Press, 1979.

Growth and modernization in the less developed countries (LDC's) during the past three decades has frequently depended upon the state's ability to plan and manage a range of developmental activities. Gant's study of development administration looks at some of the issues that could be of concern to managers in LDC's: in particular, coordination, budgeting, the selection of personnel, training, etc. He also delves into the administrative side of certain specific governmental concerns, such as family planning and education, drawing on examples from a number of Asian countries. This is not a book which goes into much technical detail. Nor does it tell one how to design an efficient administrative setup. Primarily for the general reader interested in an overview of these topics.

33   Garbacz, Christopher
A B D   INDUSTRIAL POLARIZATION UNDER ECONOMIC INTEGRATION IN LATIN AMERICA
Austin, Texas: Bureau of Business Research, Graduate School of Business, The University of Texas, 1971.

The author discusses the problem of increased disparities in the levels of regional economic development that tend

to come about as a result of economic integration. The
political and economic implications of industrial
polarization are studies within the context and experience
of the Central American Common Market and the Latin
American Free Trade Association. Finally, the author
considers the problem in the light of the planned Latin
American Common Market, discussing the various measures
that could be taken as well as the implications for the
future.

34   Garzouzi, Eva
A B C   ECONOMIC GROWTH AND DEVELOPMENT: THE LESS DEVELOPED
        COUNTRIES
        New York: Vantage Press, 1972.

        Essays to consolidate into one readable text the whole
        of the economics of growth and development. Part I
        discusses the meaning and theories of economic development,
        outlines historical patterns of development, and summarizes
        the impact of capital, agriculture, industry, monetary
        and fiscal policies, international trade, and foreign
        aid on economic growth. Part II presents comparative
        analyses of developing regions, including Latin America,
        the Middle East and North Africa, Africa south of the
        Sahara, and Southeast Asia.

35   Geithman, David T., ed.
A B C D FISCAL POLICY FOR INDUSTRIALIZATION AND DEVELOPMENT IN
        LATIN AMERICA
        Gainesville: University Presses of Florida.

        Collection of 10 previously unpublished papers (and related
        comments) presented at the Twenty-First Annual Latin
        American Conference held in February 1971. Central theme
        of the conference was the analysis and evaluation of
        the interaction among fiscal problems, fiscal tools,
        and fiscal systems in the industrializing economies of
        Latin America.

36   Ghai, D. P.
A B C   THE BASIC-NEEDS APPROACH TO DEVELOPMENT: SOME ISSUES
        REGARDING CONCEPTS AND METHODOLOGY
        ILO, Geneva, 1977.

        Contains five papers which discuss issues which arise
        in the formulation of criteria and approaches for the
        promotion of employment and the satisfaction of the basic
        needs of a country's population. Presents the first
        results of the research and conceptual work initiated
        by the ILO to help countries implement the basic
        needs-oriented strategy recommended by the World Employment
        Conference in 1976.

37   Gianaris, Nicholas V.
A B C   ECONOMIC DEVELOPMENT: THOUGHT AND PROBLEMS
          North Quincy, Mass.: Christopher Publishing House, 1978.

          Part one examines the process of development, the
          historical perspective, mathematical models, and modern
          theories of development; part two considers domestic
          problems of development, specifically land and other
          natural resources, human resources (particularly the
          role of education), capital formation and technological
          change, the allocation of resources, and the role of
          government and planning; part three discusses the
          international aspects of development (foreign trade,
          aid, investment, and multinationals) and current issues
          such as environmental problems, the status of women,
          income inequalities, and discrimination.

38   Giersch, Herbert, ed.
A B C D   INTERNATIONAL ECONOMIC DEVELOPMENT AND RESOURCE TRANSFER:
          WORKSHOP 1978
          Tubingen, Germany: J. C. B. Mohr, 1979.

          Twenty-four previously unpublished papers from a workshop
          held in June 1978 at the Institut fur Weltwirtschaft,
          Kiel University. Contributions organized under ten
          headings: Rural Industrialization, Employment and Economic
          Development; Choice of Techniques and Industries for
          Growth and Employment; Agricultural Patterns and Policies
          in Developing Countries; Hypotheses for the Commodity
          Composition of East-West Trade; The Relationship Between
          the Domestic and International Sectors in Economic
          Development; Patterns of Trade in Services and Knowledge;
          Changes in Industrial Interdependencies and Final Demand
          in Economic Development; Public Aid for Investment in
          Manufacturing Industries; Institutional and Economic
          Criteria for the Choice of Technology in Developing
          Countries; and Problems of Measuring the Production and
          Absorption of Technologies in Developing Countries.

39   Gierst, Friedrich and Matthews, Stuart R.
A B C   GUIDELINES FOR CONTRACTING FOR INDUSTRIAL PROJECTS IN
          DEVELOPING COUNTRIES
          New York: United Nations Publications, 1975.

          Designed to serve public and private organizations in
          developing countries as a guide in preparing contracts
          concerned with industrial investment projects. Examines
          various stages involved in the preparation of an industrial
          project and discusses the basic types of contacts involved
          (i.e. those with financial institutions, with consultants
          and with contractors).

40   Gill, Richard T.
A B C   ECONOMIC DEVELOPMENT: PAST AND PRESENT

Third Edition. Foundations of Modern Economics.
Englewood Cliffs, N.J.: Prentice-Hall, 1973.

Third edition of an introductory textbook with revisions
of the discussions. The Green Revolution, two-gap analysis
of foreign aid, Denison-Jorgenson-Griliches studies of
factors affecting United States economic growth and
Leibenstein's "X-efficiency" concept have been added.
Statistical tables have been updated to include figures
on Chinese economic growth. Six chapters cover: 1)
General factors in economic development, 2) Theories
of development, 3) Beginnings of development in advanced
countries, 4) Growth of the American economy, 5) Problems
of underdeveloped countries, and 6) Development in China
and India.

41   Goulet, Denis
A B C   THE CRUEL CHOICE: A NEW CONCEPT IN THE THEORY OF
        DEVELOPMENT
        Cambridge, Mass.: Center for the Study of Development
        and Social Change, Atheneum, 1971.

This work is intended to probe moral dilemmas faced by
economic and social development. Its central concern
is that philosophical conceptions about the "good life"
and the "good society" should be of more profound
importance in assessing alternative paths to development
than economic, political, or technological questions.
The theoretical analysis is based on two concepts:
"vulnerability" and "existence rationality." Vulnerability
is defined as exposure to forces that can not be
controlled, and is expressed in the failure of many
low-income countries to attain their development goals,
as well as in manifestations of mass alienation in certain
societies where prosperity has already been achieved.
Existence rationality denotes those strategies used by
all societies to possess information and to make practical
choices designed to assure survival and satisfy their
needs for esteem and freedom. These strategies vary
with a country's needs and are conditioned by numerous
constraints.

42   Griffin, Keith
A B C   INTERNATIONAL INEQUALITY AND NATIONAL POVERTY
        New York: Holms & Meier, 1978.

Nine essays, seven previously published between 1970
and 1978. Challenges the classical assumption that
unrestricted international intercourse will reduce
inequality and poverty. Argues that forces creating
inequality are automatic, and not due to malevolence
of developed nations or corporations, but that the motor
of change in the contemporary world economy is technical
innovation. Since the advances tend to be concentrated

in the developed countries where they are applicable
to their technology, rich countries are able to extract
supra-normal profits and rents from the poor countries
through trade. The high level of factor earnings in
rich countries attract the most valuable financial and
human resources of the poor countries through induced
international migration. Divided into two parts, part
one deals with international inequality and discusses:
the international transmission of inequality; multinational
corporations; foreign capital, domestic savings, and
economic development; emigration, and the New International
Economic Order. The essays in part two focus on national
poverty, discussing the facts of poverty in the Third
World, analyzing models of development, and assessing
the Chinese system of incentives.

43   Griffin, Keith B. and Enos, John L.
A B C   PLANNING DEVELOPMENT
          Reading, Mass.; Don Mills, Ontario; Sydney; London; and
          Manila: Addison-Wesley. 1971.

          Part of a series intended to serve as guidebooks on
          development economics, this book deals with practical
          problems of planning and economic policy in underdeveloped
          countries. Consists of four parts: 1) the role of
          planning, 2) quantitative planning techniques, 3) sector
          policies, and 4) planning in practice with reference
          to Chile, Columbia, Ghana, India, Pakistan and Turkey.

44   Hagen, Everett E.
A B C   THE ECONOMICS OF DEVELOPMENT
          Revised Edition. The Irwin Series in Economics.
          Homewood, Ill.: Irwin, 1975.

          Revised edition with two new chapters added, one dealing
          with the earth's stock of minerals and economic growth,
          and the other on the relationships between economic growth
          and the distribution of income. Chapters on population
          and economic planning have been extensively revised,
          with the former focusing on the relationship of food
          supply to continued world growth. Additional changes
          include: reorganization of the discussion of growth
          theories; a considerably augmented discussion of
          entrepreneurhsip; and a reorganization of the chapters
          on import substitution versus export expansion and external
          finance.

45   Helleiner, G. K., ed.
B C   A WORLD DIVIDED: THE LESS DEVELOPED COUNTRIES IN THE
          INTERNATIONAL ECONOMY
          Perspectives on Development, no. 5
          New York; London and Melbourne: Cambridge University
          Press, 1976.

Twelve papers discussing the new policies and instruments
needed if the interests of poor nations are to be met.
Within the realm of trade, consideration is given to
the possibility of increased cooperation through: supply
management schemes; bargaining capacity and power; closer
ties with other less developed countries; and the
development of alternative marketing channels and joint
sales efforts. Relations between the less developed
countries and transnational firms is then considered
with special attention given to the factors affecting
the bargaining position of the countries. Issues in
international finance and monetary policy are: the
borrowing of Eurodollars by less developed countries,
internationally agreed upon principles for an honorable
debt default, and interests of less developed countries
in a new international monetary order. Another paper
considers means by which a self-reliant but poor country
can seek to conduct its economic affairs in the face
of a most inhospitable and uncertain international
environment. The concluding paper considers the
implication of the new mood in the less developed countries
for future international organisation.

46   Hermassi, Elbaki
A C D   THE THIRD WORLD REASSESSED
         Berkeley: University of California Press, 1980.

47   Horowitz, Irving Louis, ed.
A B C   EQUITY, INCOME, AND POLICY: COMPARATIVE STUDIES IN THREE
         WORLDS OF DEVELOPMENT
         New York and London: Praeger, 1977.

Ten previously unpublished papers by sociologists and
economists on the multiple ideologies of development
and the drive toward equity congruent with different
social systems. Six essays address the problems of the
"First World," i.e. those types of societies dominated
by a free market and an open society, where the main
problem would seem to be how to maintain growth and
development while providing distributive justice. Two
papers look at the "Second World" of socialism; these
assume the central role of state power as imposing its
will to produce equity. The remaining papers consider
the Third World, examining in particular income
distribution in Tanzania and economic equality and social
class in general.

48   Jalan, Bimal
A B C   ESSAYS IN DEVELOPMENT POLICY
         Delhi: S. G. Wasani for Macmillan of India, 1975.

A common theme of the 11 essays (some previously published)
is the explicit reference to political philosophies
involved in the choices of means and objectives of

development and social change. Essays include: discussion of self-reliance objectives; trade and industrialization policies; distribution of income; the project evaluation manual of Professors Little and Mirrlees; UNIDO guidelines for project evaluation; criteria for determination of appropriate terms of aid assistance; the definition and assessment of performance in developing countries; the history of the United Nations Capital Development Fund, the World Bank, and the International Development Association; and an analysis of the principal recommendations of the Pearson Commission Report (1969).

49   Jumper, Sidney R.; Bell, Thomas L. and Ralston, Bruce A.
B C   ECONOMIC GROWTH AND DISPARITIES: A WORLD VIEW
Englewood Cliffs, N.J.: Prentice-Hall, 1980.

The authors emphasize understanding of real world differences in levels of human development, rather than sophisticated analytical procedures. In seven parts: geographical concepts; the factors influencing variations in levels of development; world food supplies; minerals; factors affecting intensity of manufacturing development; the service industries; and a summary of the role of geographers in facing these development problems.

50   Kahn, Herman
A B C   WORLD ECONOMIC DEVELOPMENT: 1979 AND BEYOND
With the Hudson Institute.
Boulder: Westview Press, 1979.

Examines economic prospects focusing on the period 1978-2000, and particularly the earlier part of the period. In two parts, part one presents the general historical framework, concepts, and perspectives on economic growth and cultural change. Part two examines the major trends and problems of the real world, focusing on the elements of change and continuity in both the advanced and developing economies. Rejects attempts by some to stop the world and argues for and suggests strategies for rapid worldwide economic growth, for Third World industrialization, and for the use of advanced (or at least appropriate) technology.

51   Kasdan, Alan R.
A B C   THE THIRD WORLD: A NEW FOCUS FOR DEVELOPMENT
Cambridge, Mass.: Schenkman Publishing, 1973.

52   Kindleberger, Charles P. and Herrick, Bruce
B   ECONOMIC DEVELOPMENT
Third Edition. Economics Handbook Series.
New York; London; Paris and Tokyo: McGraw-Hill, 1977.

Textbook that survey[s] the present panorama of international poverty, the applications to it of economic analysis, and the policies for improvement that the analysis implies. This edition which has been completely rewritten and updated, includes new chapters on: population, urbanization, collective international action, employment, income distribution, and the theories of economic development.

53   Leipziger, Danny M., ed.
A B C   BASIC NEEDS AND DEVELOPMENT
        Foreword by Paul P. Streeten
        Cambridge, Mass.:   Oelgeschlager, Gunn & Hain, 1981.

Five previously unpublished essays discuss the potential contribution of the basic needs approach to developmental theory and practice. Michael J. Crosswell gives his views in two essays on a development planning approach and on growth, poverty alleviation, and foreign assistance. Maureen A. Lewis discusses sectional aspects of the linkages among population, nutrition, and health. Danny M. Leipziger writes about policy issues and the basic human needs approach. Martha de Melo presents a case study of Sri Lanka focusing on the effects of alternative approaches to basic human needs. The authors are all economists.

54   Leontief, Wassily, et al.
A B C   THE FUTURE OF THE WORLD ECONOMY: A UNITED NATIONS STUDY
        New York: Oxford University Press, 1977.

Investigates the interrelationships between future world economic growth and availability of natural resources, pollution, and the impact of environmental policies. Includes a set of alternative projections of the demographic, economic, and environmental states of the world in the years 1980, 1990, and 2000 with a comparison with the world economy of 1970. Constructs a multiregional input-output economic model of the world economy. Investigates some of the main problems of economic growth and development in the world as a whole, with special accent on problems encountered by the developing countries. The findings include: (1) target rates of growth of gross product in the developing regions...are not sufficient to start closing the income gap between the developing and the developed countries; (2) the principal limits to sustained economic growth and accelerated development are political, social and institutional in character rather than physical; (3) the necessary increased food production is technically feasible, but dependent on drastically favorable public policy measure; (4) pollution is not an unmanageable problem.

55   Lin, Ching-Yuan
A C D   DEVELOPING   COUNTRIES   IN   A   TURBULENT   WORLD: PATTERNS
        OF ADJUSTMENT SINCE THE OIL CRISIS
        New York: Praeger, 1981.

        Examines national authorities' policy reactions to changes
        in the world economy since 1973, to determine whether
        differences in national economic performances can be
        explained in terms of differences in their policy
        reactions.   Investigates global patterns of absorption,
        production, and adjustment since the oil crisis; global
        expenditure flows before and after the crisis; and
        international bank transactions and world trade.   Reviews
        the experiences of developing countries during the period,
        focusing on non-oil countries.   Finds that collectively
        the non-oil developing countries experienced a much milder
        contraction of domestic demand and real ouput than the
        more developed countries after the disturbances in 1973-75,
        although individual experiences varied; however, inflation
        remains persistent.   Argues that most developing countries
        did not pursue demand management policies early enough
        to counteract sharp changes in external demand.

56   Madhava, K. B., ed.
A B C D INTERNATIONAL DEVELOPMENT, 1969:   CHALLENGES TO PREVALENT
        IDEAS ON DEVELOPMENT
        Dobbs Ferry: Oceana for Society for International
        Development, 1970.

        Contains the proceedings of the 11th World Conference
        of the Society for International Development held in
        1969 in New Delhi.   The theme "Challenges to Prevalent
        Ideas on Development" was carried out through roundtable
        discussions centering on: the redefinition of goals;
        foreign aid; manpower, education, and development;
        population communication; social communication; political
        and social-cultural requisites; and challenges to theorists
        and strategists.

57   May, Brian
A C D   THE THIRD WORLD CALAMITY
        London and Boston: Routledge & Kegan Paul, 1981.

        Assessment of social conditions, politics, economics,
        and cultural barriers in the Third World, with particular
        reference to India, Iran, and Nigeria.   Contends that
        the "chronic socio-economic stagnation" that characterizes
        these countries is not attributable to Western imperialism,
        maintaining that fundamental change in Third World
        countries was and is blocked by psychological and cultural
        facts.   Compares relevant factors in Europe and in the
        three countries to show the constraints that block
        significant socioeconomic change.

58   McGreevey, William Paul, ed.
A B C   THIRD-WORLD POVERTY: NEW STRATEGIES FOR MEASURING
        DEVELOPMENT PROGRESS
        Lexington, Mass.:   Heath, Lexington Books, 1980.

Five previously unpublished papers on the problems of measuring progress in alleviating poverty in the Third World, originally part of a series of seminars (1976-79) sponsored by the Agency for International Development. Editor McGreevey reviews the development progress from both a human capital and poverty alleviation standpoint; Gary S. Fields looks at absolute-poverty measures (i.e., those not depending on income distribution considerations); Harry J. Bruton considers the use of available employment and unemployment data in assessing government poverty policy, and G. Edward Schuh and Robert L. Thompson discuss measures of agricultural progress and government commitment to agricultural development. The fifth paper by Nancy Birdsall is a summary of discussion in two seminars on time-use surveys and networks of social support in LDC's. The authors find in part that: (1) existing data are inadequate to judge progress; (2) the best data gathering method is multipurpose household surveys; and (3) networks of social support are important (and unmeasured) means of income transfer between households.

59   McHale, John and McHale, Magda C.
A B C   BASIC HUMAN NEEDS: A FRAMEWORK FOR ACTION
        New Brunswick, N.J.:   Rutgers University, Transaction
        Books, 1978.

60   Meadows, Dennis L., ed.
A B C   ALTERNATIVES TO GROWTH--I: A SEARCH FOR SUBSTAINABLE
        FUTURES: PAPERS ADAPTED FROM ENTRIES TO THE 1975 GEORGE
        AND CYNTHIA MITCHELL PRIZE AND FROM PRESENTATIONS BEFORE
        THE 1975 ALTERNATIVES TO GROWTH CONFERENCE, HELD AT
        THE WOODLANDS, TEXAS
        Cambridge, Mass.:   Lippincott, Ballinger, 1977.

Seventeen previously unpublished interdisciplinary papers on the transition from growth to a steady-state society i.e., a society with a constant stock of physical wealth and a constant stock of people. In four parts: the relation between population and food or energy; economic alternatives; the rationales, mechanisms, and implications of various long-term planning proposals; and analysis of the determinants, nature, and implications of current paradigms, norms, laws, and religion.

61   Melady, Thomas Patrick and Suhartono, R. B.
A B   DEVELOPMENT -- LESSONS FOR THE FUTURE
        Maryknoll, New York: Orbis Books, 1973.

Investigation of what determines, economically, which
countries are developing, based on examination of
characteristics of nations agreed to be undergoing this
experience. The study examines such facets of development
as the nonhomogeneity of the developing countries; factors
affecting economic growth, the sectoral aspect of growth
(industry and agriculture), measurements of the phenomenon,
and the applicability of economic theory in this work;
and the effects of economic development on man and his
role in society.

62   Morawetz, David
A B D   TWENTY-FIVE YEARS OF ECONOMIC DEVELOPMENT, 1950 TO 1975
        Johns Hopkins University Press for IBRD, 1977.

Assesses development programs of developing countries
and global development targets adopted by international
organizations over the past 25 years. Chapters cover:
a) changing objectives of development; b) growth in GNP
per capita, population and the gap between rich and poor
countries; c) reduction of poverty, including employment,
income distribution, basic needs, nutrition, health,
housing and education; d) self-reliance and economic
independence; and e) conclusions, hypotheses, and
questions.

63   Morgan, Theodore
B C   ECONOMIC DEVELOPMENT: CONCEPT AND STRATEGY
        New York and London: Harper & Row, 1975.

Textbook in economic development with emphasis on policy,
its appropriate definition, its targets, and its
improvement of application. Diverts focus from GNP and
average income growth rates and into issues such as income
distribution, nutrition, disease, climate, and population
increases and their effects on development. Surveys
existing theoretical literature. Discusses development
planning and the importance of the statistical foundation
of decision-making, and planning techniques such as
cost-benefit analysis. Provides sporadic data for
less-developed countries, mostly for the post-World War
II period, on various national variables.

64   Ramati, Yohanan, ed.
A B C   ECONOMIC GROWTH IN DEVELOPING COUNTRIES--MATERIAL AND
        HUMAN RESOURCES: PROCEEDINGS OF THE SEVENTH REHOVOT
        CONFERENCE
        Praeger Special Studies in International Economics and
        Development
        New York and London: Praeger in cooperation with the
        Continuation Committee of the Rehovot Conference, 1975.

Collection of 49 papers presented in September 1973.
The papers are grouped into five sections following the

structure of the conference. Part I includes papers setting the framework to analyze natural and human resources as factors in development and problems of planning and the quality of life. Part II includes papers on resources, technology, and income distribution. Part III deals with external constraints on development. Part IV examines planning and implementation. Part V contains the very brief closing addresses by Simon Kuznets and Abba Eban. Participants included 99 experts and policy makers for developing countries in Africa, Latin America, and Southeast Asia.

65   Rubinson, Richard, ed.
A B   DYNAMICS OF WORLD DEVELOPMENT
        Political Economy of the World-System Annuals, vol. 4
        Beverly Hills and London: Sage, 1981.

Twelve previously unpublished papers, almost all by sociologists, presented at the Fourth Annual Political Economy of the World-System conference at Johns Hopkins University, June 1980. Papers are based on the assumption that the world's history is the history of capitalist accumulation; and that capitalist development is the development of a single...modern world-system. Papers cover: development in peripheral areas; development in semiperipheral states; development and state organization; cycles and trends of world system development; theooretical issues; and dynamics of development of the world economy.

66   Sachs, Ignacy
A C   THE DISCOVERY OF THE THIRD WORLD
        Cambridge, Mass., and London: M. I. T. Press, 1976.

Focusing on a redefinition of development theory, discusses the role of ethnocentrism and domination by European and Western ideas in such areas as science, technology, and economics. Argues that discussions regarding economic development strategies attempt to apply Western theories and ignore the fact that Third World growth, unlike capital-intensive European growth, must be based on the use of labor. Proposes a general development theory to bridge the gap between European theory and Third World practice and discusses problems such as economic surplus and economic aid. Recommends that the U.N. assess Western nations and funnel the money to Third World nations on a "no-strings" basis.

67   Shafei, Mohamed Z.
A B   THREE LECTURES ON ECONOMIC DEVELOPMENT
        Beirut, Lebanon: Beirut Arab University, 1970.

The first lecture focuses on the characteristics of developing countries. The second traces the process

of economic development in the U.A.R. (Egypt) since 1952.
The third is on the foreign assistance needs of developing
countries.

68   Singer, H. W.
A C   THE STRATEGY OF INTERNATIONAL DEVELOPMENT: ESSAYS IN
THE ECONOMICS OF BACKWARDNESS
Edited by Sir Alec Cairncross and Mohinder Puri
White Plains, N.Y.: International Arts and Sciences
Press, 1975.

A collection of 13 papers by the author, all published
in past years, dealing with some of the central problems
of economic development and development policy. Papers
cover such issues as gains distribution among borrowing
and investing countries, dualism, international aid,
trade and development, employment problems, income
distribution, science and technology transfers, etc.
Introduction to the author's work and career by editor
Sir Alec Cairncross.

69   Singer, Hans W. and Ansari, Javed A.
A   RICH AND POOR COUNTRIES
Baltimore and London: Johns Hopkins University Press,
1977.

Examines the changes that are required if the relationship
between rich and poor countries is to make a more effective
contribution to the development of the poor countries.
Part one describes the structure of international economy
and the nature of development process. Part two discusses
the importance of the international trade sector to
development in the poorer countries and reviews the trade
policies of the rich and poor countries. Part three
deals with the role of aid in the development process;
and part four is concerned with international factor
movement. Stresses the need for the formulation of an
international development strategy...by the rich countries
(both old and new), providing assistance in an increasing
flow of resources through trade, aid capital and the
transfer of skills and technology to the poor countries.
Argues that such a strategy first must provide for some
discrimination in international trade in favor of poor
countries to provide more resources and secondly to enable
the importation of more appropriate technologies.

70   Spiegelglas, Stephen and Welsh, Charles J., eds.
A B   ECONOMIC DEVELOPMENT; CHALLENGE AND PROMISE
Englewood Cliffs, N.J.: Prentice-Hall, 1970.

A collection of 33 reprinted readings, each representing
an outstanding contribution, controversial issue, or
synthesis of ideas in economic development. Major sections

include: an   introduction;   nature   and   techniques   of
planning;   strategy   and   policy;   and   trade   or   aid.   The
selection   of   topics   in   these   sections   reflects   recent
increased   emphasis   on   practical   development   problems,
particularly   on   human   resources   development   and   the   need
to   create   exportable   manufactured   goods.   A   matrix   showing
how   each   selection   fits   into   the   scheme   and   sequence
of   the   seven   widely   used   development   textbooks   is   included.

71   T. N. Srinivasan
A B C D   DEVELOPMENT, POVERTY, AND BASIC HUMAN NEEDS: SOME ISSUES
          World Bank Reprint Series, 76
          IBRD, 1977.

Reprinted   from   Food   Research   Institute   Studies,   vol.
XVI,   no.   2   (1977),   pp.   11-28.   Deals   with   the   raising
of   standard   of   living   of   the   poorest   sections   of   the
population   in   developing   countries.   Discusses   aid
problems,   distributional   aspects   of   economic   growth,
employment   goals,   and   the   new   perceptions   of   development.

72   Stein, Leslie
A C D   ECONOMIC REALITIES IN POOR COUNTRIES
          Sydney, London and Singapore: Angus and Robertson, 1972.

This   book   surveys   the   problems   of   growth   faced   by   the
developing   countries   of   the   world.   The   first   part   of
the   book   describes   the   economic   and   social   characteristics
of   Third   World   countries   and   presents   some   theories   of
development,   including   Baran's   Marxian   view,   W. W.   Rostow's
non-Marxist   alternative,   balanced   growth   theory,   and
Myrdal's   view   which   considers   non-economic   as   well   as
economic   factors   of   growth.   Succeeding   chapters   discuss
population   growth,   problems   of   education,   the   role   of
agriculture   and   industrial   development,   obstacles   to
trade,   and   government   plans   which   have   been   used   in
developing   countries.   Designed   for   use   as   a   text   or
for the layman.

73   Streeten, Paul
A B D   DEVELOPMENT PERSPECTIVES
          New York: St. Martin's Press, 1981.

A   combination   of   17   previously   published   articles   and
7   new   chapters,   in   five   parts: concepts,   values,   and
methods   in   development   analysis;   development   strategies;
transnational   corporations;   the   change   in   emphasis   from
the   growth   approach   to   the   basic   needs   approach;   and
two   miscellaneous   chapters   on   taxation   and   on   Gunnar
Myrdal.   Newly   written   chapters   cover: the   results   of
development   strategies   for   the   poor,   alternatives   in
development,   the   New   International   Economic   Order,   the
basic   needs   approach,   human   rights   and   basic   needs,   the

search for a basic-needs yardstick (with Norman Hicks), and transnational corporations and basic needs.

74   Thomson, W. Scott, ed.
A C   THE THIRD WORLD: PREMISES OF U.S. POLICY
San Francisco: Institute for Contemporary Studies, 1978.

75   Tinbergen, Jan
A B   THE DESIGN OF DEVELOPMENT
The Johns Hopkins University Press, 1958.

Formulates a coherent government policy to further development objectives and outlines methods to stimulate private investments.

76   Todaro, Michael P.
A B C   ECONOMIC DEVELOPMENT IN THE THIRD WORLD: AN INTRODUCTION TO PROBLEMS AND POLICIES IN A GLOBAL PERSPECTIVE
London and New York: Longman, 1977.

In four parts: Part one discusses the nature of underdevelopment and its various manifestations in the Third World, and parts two and three focus on major development problems and policies, both domestic (growth, income distribution, population, unemployment, education, and migration) and international (trade, balance of payments, and foreign investment). The last part reviews the possibilities and prospects for Third World development.

77   Todaro, Michael P.
A B   DEVELOPMENT PLANNING: MODELS AND METHODS
Series of undergraduate teaching works in economics, Volume V.
London, Nairobi, and New York: Oxford University Press, 1971.

This is the last in a series of undergraduate teaching works in economics developed at Makere University, Uganda. This book is an introduction to development planning, with emphasis on plan formulation rather than implementation.

78   United Nations Department of Economic and Social Affairs
THE INTERNATIONAL DEVELOPMENT STRATEGY: FIRST OVER-ALL REVIEW AND APPRAISAL OF ISSUES AND POLICIES. REPORT OF THE SECRETARY-GENERAL
New York: United Nations, 1973.

Deals with the issues and policies in the field of economic and social development...of prime concern in the first two years of the Second United Nations Development Decade. Emphasis is upon changes in the following areas: priorities of objectives, techniques of production, trade

and aid relationships, and the external environment in which economic and social development takes place.

79
A C
United Nations Department of Economic and Social Affairs
SHAPING ACCELERATED DEVELOPMENT AND INTERNATIONAL CHANGES
New York: United Nations Publications, 1980.

Contains views and recommendations of the UN Committee for Development Planning relating to the international development strategy for a third UN development decade. Chapters cover general premises and basic objectives; priority areas for action; means and implementation; and key goals and needed changes.

80
A C
United Nations Department of Economic and Social Affairs
DEVELOPMENT IN THE 1980'S: APPROACH TO A NEW STRATEGY; VIEWS AND RECOMMENDATIONS OF THE COMMITTEE FOR DEVELOPMENT PLANNING
New York: United Nations Publications, 1978.

Reviews development issues for the 1980's with a discussion of the current situation and preliminary comments relating to a development strategy for the 1980's. Discusses economic cooperation among developing countries, covering trade, economic integration and other arrangements for economic cooperation.

81
A B C
United Nations Industrial Development Organization
INDUSTRIALIZATION FOR NEW DEVELOPMENT NEEDS
New York: United Nations Publication, 1974.

Emphasizes the reshaping of industrial development in the light of new development needs that the pervasive problems of unemployment, maldistribution of income, and poverty in general have brought to the fore in the developing countries.

82
A B C
UNRSID
THE QUEST FOR A UNIFIED APPROACH TO DEVELOPMENT
UNRSID: 1980.

Provides background information on UNRSID's efforts to formulate a unified approach to development analysis and planning, an approach which would bring together all the different aspects of development into a set of feasible objectives and policy approaches. Chapters cover: styles of development--definitions and criteria; strategies; the findings of the Expert Group; an assessment by Marshall Wolfe, former Chief of the Social Development Division of UN ECLA; and an annex containing the final report on the project by the UN Commission for Social Development, covering questions of diagnosis, monitoring, indicators, and planning and capicitation.

83   Uri, Pierre
A B C   DEVELOPMENT WITHOUT DEPENDENCE
        New York: Praeger for the Atlantic Institute for
        International Affairs, 1976.

        Monograph on foreign aid. Contends that the aid programs
        of the 1950's and 1960's were lopsided and failed to
        address the needs of the truly poor. According to Bundy,
        the author argues that although effective transfer of
        resources and skill remains a vital part of the need...such
        nation-to-nation aid...can only help to foster the very
        feelings of dependence...that are the deepest grievance
        of the developing world. Discusses control of population
        growth, the role and necessary scale of official foreign
        aid, stabilization of the raw materials market so as
        to assist consumers and producers alike, and the types
        of industries the developing countries should strive
        to build as a part of a rational world division of labor.
        Examines the control and regulation of multinational
        corporations and, focusing on Latin America, the extent
        to which regional cooperation can be developed. Recommends
        that development planning be based on future population
        growth and distribution.

84   Varma, Baidya Nath
A B C   THE SOCIOLOGY AND POLITICS OF DEVELOPMENT: A THEORETICAL
        STUDY
        International Library of Sociology Series
        London and Boston: Routledge & Kegan Paul, 1980.

        The author critically examines theories of development
        and presents his own theory. Considers general criteria
        used for evaluating the modernization process; describes
        a model for a general paradigm of modernization; surveys
        other models encompassing ideological, social scientific,
        anthropological and activistic theories; and discusses
        theoretical problems of planning and national
        reconstruction. Summarizes views of theorists in various
        social science disciplines and features of modernization
        in terms of guidance provided for economic, political,
        educational, and bureaucratic decision-making in a
        developing country. Concludes that both the socialist
        and capitalist systems of modernization are viable models
        for Third World countries.

85   Vogeler, Ingolf and De Souza, Anthony R., eds.
A C   DIALECTICS OF THIRD WORLD DEVELOPMENT
        Montclair: Allanheld, Osmun, 1980.

        Collection of previously published (some revised) papers
        designed for use by students of economics, political
        science, and development. Representing a variety of
        ideas and arguments relevant to Third World
        underdevelopment, the readings discuss climate and

resources, cultural traditions, European colonialism
(i.e., plantation agriculture), population, tourism,
and imperialism. An appendix provides "awareness"
exercises.

86   Wallman, Sandra, ed.
A B   PERCEPTIONS OF DEVELOPMENT
        New York: Cambridge University Press, 1977.

87   Ward, Richard J.
A C   DEVELOPMENT ISSUES FOR THE 1970'S
        New York and London: Dunellen, 1973.

An assessment of key issues and problems which emerged
from the Decade of Development and which will continue
to absorb the attention of students of development in
the present decade. The author, former Chief of Planning
of the U.S. Agency for International Development, presents
much data which has not been previously released and
which is unavailable elsewhere. The book is divided
into three parts: "Food and Human Welfare," "Development
Problems for This Decade," and "Planning Programs and
Strategies." The chapters specifically discuss such
issues as labor absorption in agriculture, means of
population control, the burden of debt service, the role
of foreign aid, big-push development, etc.

88   Waterston, Albert
A B   DEVELOPMENT PLANNING; LESSONS OF EXPERIENCE
        The Johns Hopkins University Press, 1979.

Analyzes the success of the development planning experience
in over 100 countries in Asia, Africa, Europe, and the
Americas. In two parts. Part 1 describes and analyzes
the problems associated with the implementation of planning
programs, the provision of basic data, the role of national
budget, and administrative obstacles. Part 2 contains
an extensive and comparative discussion of the experience
of the countries under review in setting up organizations
and administrative procedures for preparing and
implementing development projects; the distribution of
planning functions, types of central planning agencies,
and subnational regional and local planning bodies.

89   Watts, Nita, ed.
A B   ECONOMIES OF THE WORLD
        New York: Oxford University Press.

The purpose of this new series is to provide a brief
review of economic development during the post-war period
in each of a number of countries which are of obvious
importance in the world economy, or interesting because
of peculiarities of their economic structure or experience,
or illustrative of widespread economic development

problems. The series will be of interest to economists
in universities, and in business and government.

90   Wilber, Charles K., ed.
A B   THE POLITICAL ECONOMY OF DEVELOPMENT AND UNDERDEVELOPMENT
        New York: Random House, 1973.

Emphasis in approach and content is on political economy
in the sense of attempting to incorporate such noneconomic
influences as social structures, political systems, and
cultural values as well as such factors as technological
change and the distribution of income and wealth. Readings
are radical in that they are willing to question and
evaluate the most basic institutions and values of society.
Divided into eight groups concerned with methodological
problems, historical perspective, trade and imperialism,
agricultural and industrial institutions and strategies,
comparative models of development, the human cost of
development, and indications for the future.

91   Worsley, Peter
A C   THE THIRD WORLD
        Chicago: University of Chicago Press, 1972.

92   Wriggins, W. Howards and Adler-Karlsson, Gunnar
AC   REDUCING GLOBAL INEQUALITIES
        New York: McGraw-Hill, 1978.

Two papers, plus an introduction on the role that
developing countries themselves take to reduce the gap
between rich nations and poor and to eliminate mass poverty
within their own societies. W. Howard Wriggins, U.S.
ambassador to Sri Lanka and formerly professor of political
science at Columbia University, analyzes the various
bargaining strategies open to developing countries such
as developing commodity or regional coalitions, or a
variety of threats to developed countries. The future
is likely to see continued efforts at coalition building,
but also periodic outbreaks of irregular violence against
local opponents, neighbors, or Northern centers of power.

93   Zuvekas, Clarence, Jr.
A B C   ECONOMIC DEVELOPMENT: AN INTRODUCTION
        New York: St. Martin's Press, 1979.

Text written from an interdisciplinary perspective
stressing policy and empirical findings rather than an
overall development theory. Aims at balance between
theory and policy, including historical development and
empirical evidence. After discussing the terminology
of and the obstacles to development, the author examines
population growth, trade and development, and the role
of government. Also covers: the problems of agriculture

industry, income distribution, employment, mobilization of domestic and foreign savings, manipulation of trade to the advantage of the developing country, and with the limits to growth controversy. Presumes acquaintance with basic macro and micro theory.

DISARMAMENT AND DEVELOPMENT

94   Adelman, Irma and Morris, Cynthia
ECONOMIC GROWTH AND SOCIAL EQUITY IN DEVELOPING COUNTRIES
Stanford, CA: Stanford University Press, 1973.

95   Albrecht, Ulrich, et al.
NEW TRENDS IN THE ARMS TRANSFER PROCESS TO PERIPHERAL COUNTRIES; SOME HYPOTHESES AND RESEARCH PROPOSALS
Hamburg, 1975.

96   Albrecht, U.; Eide, A.; Kaldor, M; Leitenberg, M. and Robinson, J. P.
A SHORT RESEARCH GUIDE ON ARMS AND ARMED FORCES
London: Croom Helm, 1978.

97   Albrecht, Ulrich, et al.
ARMAMENTS AND UNDERDEVELOPMENT
Rowalt, 1976.

98   Alcock, N.
THE WAR DISEASE
Ontario: CPRI Press, 1972.

99   Alexander, A. S. et al.
THE CONTROL OF CHEMICAL AND BIOLOGICAL WEAPONS
New York: Carnegie Endowment for International Peace, 1971.

100   Allison, G. T.
QUESTIONS ABOUT THE ARMS RACE: WHO'S RACING WHOM? A BUREAUCRATIC PERSPECTIVES
Cambridge, MA: Harvard University, Public Policy Program, 1974.

101   Alford, J.
THE FUTURE OF ARMS CONTROL: CONFIDENCE-BUILDING MEASURES
London: IISS, 1979.

102   Andren, N. and Birnbaum, K., eds.
BEYOND DETENTE: PROSPECTS FOR EAST-WEST COOPERATION IN EUROPE
Leiden: A. W. Sitjhoff, 1976.

103   Ansari, Javed and Kaldor, Mary
MILITARY TECHNOLOGY AND CONFLICT DYNAMICS: THE BANGLADESH CRISIS OF 1971

104   Arkhurst, Frederick S., ed.
ARMS AND AFRICAN DEVELOPMENT: PROCEEDINGS   OF   THE   FIRST
PAN-AFRICAN CITIZENS' CONFERENCE
New York and London: Praeger for the Adlai Stevenson
Institute of International Affairs, 1972.

105   ARMS CONTROL IN EUROPE: PROBLEMS AND PROSPECTS
Laxenburg: Austrian Institute for International Affairs,
1980.

106   Askari, Hossein and Glover, Michael C.
MILITARY EXPENDITURES AND THE LEVEL OF ECONOMIC DEVELOPMENT
Austin: University of Texas, Bureau of Business Research,
1977.

107   Ayoob, Mohammed
CONFLICT AND INTERVENTION IN THE THIRD WORLD
New York: St. Martin's Press, 1980.

108   Bailey, S. D.
PROHIBITIONS AND RESTRAINTS IN WAR
London: Oxford University Press, 1972.

109   Baker, Philip Noel
DISARMAMENT
Kennikat, 1970.

110   Barbera, H.
RICH NATIONS AND POOR NATIONS IN PEACE AND WAR
Lexington, MA: Lexington Books, 1973.

111   Barnaby, F. and Schaerf, C.
DISARMAMENT AND ARMS CONTROL: PROCEEDINGS OF THE THIRD
COURSE GIVEN BY THE INTERNATIONAL SUMMER SCHOOL ON DISARMAMENT
AND ARMS CONTROL OF THE ITALIAN PUGWASH MOVEMENT
New York: Gordon and Breach Science Publishers, 1972.

112   Barnaby, F. and Huisken, R.
ARMS UNCONTROLLED
Harvard University Press, 1975.

113   Barnet, R.
ROOTS OF WAR
New York: Atheneum, 1972.

114   Barnet, R.
THE ECONOMY OF DEATH
New York: Atheneum, 1970.

115   Barnet, R. J.
THE GIANTS: RUSSIA AND AMERICA
New York: Simon & Schuster, 1977.

116   Barnett, A. Doak

CHINA AND THE MAJOR POWERS IN EAST ASIA
Washington, D.C.: Brookings Institution, 1977.

117 Barringer, R.
WAR: PATTERNS OF CONFLICT
Cambridge, MA: MIT Press, 1972.

118 Barton, J. H. and Weiler, L. D., eds.
INTERNATIONAL ARMS CONTROL: ISSUES AND AGREEMENTS
Stanford, CA: Stanford University Press, 1976.

119 Becker, Abraham S.
MILITARY EXPENDITURE LIMITATION FOR ARMS CONTROL: PROBLEMS
AND PROSPECTS: WITH A DOCUMENTARY HISTORY OF RECENT PROPOSALS
Cambridge, MA: Lippincott, Ballinger, 1977.

120 Beer, Francis A.
PEACE AGAINST WAR: THE ECOLOGY OF INTERNATIONAL VIOLENCE
San Francisco: Freeman, 1981.

121 Beer, F.
HOW MUCH WAR IN HISTORY: DEFINITIONS, ESTIMATES,
EXTRAPOLATIONS AND TRENDS
Beverly Hills, CA: Sage, 1974.

122 Benoit, Emile
DEFENSE AND ECONOMIC GROWTH IN DEVELOPING COUNTRIES
Lexington, MA: Lexington Books, 1973.

123 Bertram, C., ed.
THE DIFFUSION OF POWER; I: PROLIFERATION OF FORCE
London: IISS, 1977.

124 Bienen, Henry, ed.
THE MILITARY AND MODERNIZATION
Chicago: Aldine Publishing, 1971.

125 Birnbaum, K. E., ed.
THE POLITICS OF EAST-WEST COMMUNICATION IN EUROPE
Westmead: Saxon House, 1979.

126 Black, C. and Falk, R. A.
CONFLICT MANAGEMENT: THE FUTURE OF INTERNATIONAL LEGAL
ORDER; VOL. II
Princeton, NJ: Princeton University Press, 1971.

127 Blainey, G.
THE CAUSES OF WAR
London: Macmillan, 1973.

128 Blechman, B. M. and Kaplan, S. S., eds.
FORCE WITHOUT WAR: UNITED STATES ARMED FORCES AS A POLITICAL
INSTRUMENT
Washington, D.C.: The Brookings Institution, 1978.

129   Bloomfield, L. P.
      THE POWER TO KEEP PEACE: TODAY AND IN A WORLD WITHOUT WAR
      Berkeley: World Without War Council, 1971.

130   Bondurant, J. V.
      CONFLLICT: VIOLENCE AND NON-VIOLENCE
      Chicago: Aldine-Atherton, 1971.

131   Boserup, A. and Passmore, J. R.
      WAR WITHOUT WEAPONS: NON-VIOLENCE IN NATIONAL DEFENSE
      New York: Schocken, 1975.

132   Boulding, E.; Passmore, J. R. and Gassler, S. R.
      BIBLIOGRAPHY ON WORLD CONFLICT AND PEACE
      Boulder, CO: Westview Press, 1979.

133   Boulding, K.
      PEACE AND THE WAR INDUSTRY
      Chicago: Aldine-Atherton, 1970.

134   Boulding, Kenneth E.
      COLLECTED PAPERS; VOLUME V: INTERNATIONAL SYSTEMS: PEACE,
      CONFLICT RESOLUTION, AND POLITICS
      Boulder: Colorado Associated University Press, 1975.

135   Bredow, W. Von, ed.
      ECONOMIC AND SOCIAL ASPECTS OF DISARMAMENT
      Oslo: BPP Publication, 1975.

136   Brown, S.
      NEW FORCES IN WORLD POLITICS
      Washington, D.C.: Brookings Institute, 1974.

137   Buchan, A.
      POWER AND EQUILIBRIUM IN THE 1970'S
      New York: Praeger, 1973.

138   Burton, J.
      WORLD SOCIETY
      London: Cambridge University Press, 1972.

139   Butterworth, R. and Nye, J. S.
      CONFLICT MANAGEMENT BY INTERNATIONAL ORGANIZATIONS
      Harristown, NJ: General Learning Press, 1972.

140   Carlton, D. and Scharf, C.
      THE DYNAMICS OF THE ARMS RACE
      London: Croom Helm, 1975.

141   Carlton, D. and Scharf, C.
      ARMS CONTROL AND TECHNOLOGICAL INNOVATION
      London: Croom Helm, 1978.

142   Choucri, N. and Robinson, T.
      FORECASTING AND INTERNATIONAL RELATIONS
      San Francisco: W. H. Freeman, 1976.

143   Choucri, N.
      NATIONS IN CONFLICT: POPULATION, EXPANSION AND WAR
      San Francisco: W. H. Freeman, 1974.

144   Choucri, N.
      POPULATION DYNAMICS AND INTERNATIONAL VIOLENCE: PROPOSITIONS,
      INSIGHTS AND EVIDENCE
      Lexington, MA: Lexington Books, 1974.

145   Choucri, N. and North, R.
      NATION IN CONFLICT: NATIONAL GROWTH AND INTERNATIONAL
      VIOLENCE
      San Francisco: Freeman, 1975.

146   Choucri, N.; Laird, M. and Meadows, D.
      RESOURCE SCARCITY AND FOREIGN POLICY: A SIMULATION MODEL
      OF INTERNATIONAL CONFLICT
      Cambridge, MA: MIT Press, 1972.

147   Clarke, R.
      THE SCIENCE OF WAR AND PEACE
      London: Jonathan Cape, 1971.

148   Coffey, J. I.
      ARMS CONTROL AND EUROPEAN SECURITY: A GUIDE TO EAST-WEST
      NEGOTIATIONS
      London: Macmillan, 1979.

149   Cox, A. M.
      THE DYNAMICS OF DETENTE: HOW TO END THE ARMS RACE
      New York: W. W. Norton, 1976.

150   Cranston, Maurice W.
      PEACE AND CONVICTIONS: A COMMENTARY ON A UNESCO FORUM
      Paris: UNESCO, 1977.

151   Cuenod, M. A. and Kahne, S.
      SYSTEMS APPROACHES TO DEVELOPING COUNTRIES
      Pittsburgh: Instrument Society of America, 1973.

152   Curle, A.
      MAKING PEACE
      London: Tavistock, 1971.

153   Curtis, Michael, ed.
      PEOPLE AND POLITICS IN THE MIDDLE EAST
      New Brunswick, NJ: Transaction Books, 1971.

154   Deutsch, M.
      THE RESOLUTION OF CONFLICT: CONSTRUCTIVE AND DESTRUCTIVE
      PROCESSES

New Haven: Yale University Press, 1973.

155 Dietz, Henry A.
     POVERTY AND PROBLEM-SOLVING UNDER MILITARY RULE: THE URBAN
     POOR IN LIMA, PERU
     Austin and London: University of Texas Press, 1980.

156 Dougherty, J. E.
     HOW TO THINK ABOUT ARMS CONTROL AND DISARMAMENT
     New York: Crane, Russak, 1973.

157 Eide, A. and Thee, M., eds.
     PROBLEMS OF CONTEMPORARY MILITARISM
     London: Croom Helm, 1980.

158 Einaudi, Luigi; Heymann, Hans, Jr.; Ronfeldt, David and
     Sereseres, Cesar
     ARMS TRANSFERS TO LATIN AMERICA: TOWARD A POLICY OF MUTUAL
     RESPECT
     Santa Monica, CA: Rand Corporation, 1973.

159 Enthoven, A. and Smith, W.
     HOW MUCH IS ENOUGH? SHAPING THE DEFENSE PROGRAM
     New York: Harper and Row, 1971.

160 Epstein, W.
     THE LAST CHANCE: NUCLEAR PROLIFERATION AND ARMS CONTROL
     New York: The Free Press, 1976.

161 Epstein, William
     DISARMAMENT: TWENTY-FIVE YEARS OF EFFORT
     Canadian Institute of International Affairs, 1971.

162 Etchison, Don L.
     THE UNITED STATES AND MILITARISM IN CENTRAL AMERICA
     New York: Praeger, 1975.

163 Falk, R. and Mendlovitz, S. H.
     REGIONAL POLITICS AND WORLD ORDER
     San Francisco: W. H. Freeman, 1973.

164 Falk, R. A. and Kim, S. S., eds.
     THE WAR SYSTEM: AN INTERDISCIPLINARY APPROACH
     Boulder, CO: Westview Press, 1980.

165 Farrar, L. L., ed.
     WAR: A HISTORICAL, POLITICAL AND SOCIAL STUDY
     New York: Oxford University Press, 1978.

166 Feierabend, I.; Feierabend, R. and Gurr, T. R.
     ANGER, VIOLENCE AND POLITICS: THEORIES AND RESEARCH
     Englewood Cliffs, NJ: Prentice Hall, 1972.

167   Feld, L. T., et al. (ed.)
      IMPACT OF NEW TECHNOLOGIES ON THE ARMS RACE
      Cambridge, MA: MIT Press, 1971.

168   Fidel, Kenneth, ed.
      MILITARISM IN DEVELOPING COUNTRIES
      New Brunswick, NJ: Rutgers University, Transaction Books,
      1975.

169   Fromm, E.
      THE ANATOMY OF HUMAN DESTRUCTIVENESS
      New York: Holt, Rinehart and Winston, 1973.

170   Galtung, J.
      ESSAYS IN PEACE RESEARCH I: PEACE RESEARCH, EDUCATION,
      ACTION; II: PEACE, WAR AND DEFENCE
      Copenhagen: Christian Ejlers, 1975/76.

171   Gardiner, R. W.
      THE COOL ARM OF DESTRUCTION: MODERN WEAPONS AND MORAL
      INSENSITIVITY
      Philadelphia: Westminster Press, 1974.

172   Glagloev, I.
      WHY WE NEED DISARMAMENT
      Moscow: Novosti Press, 1973.

173   Goody, Jack
      TECHNOLOGY, TRADITION AND THE STATE IN AFRICA
      Oxford: Oxford University Press, 1971.

174   Grieves, F.
      CONFLICT AND ORDER: AN INTRODUCTION TO INTERNATIONAL
      RELATIONS
      Boston: Houghton, Mifflin, 1977.

175   Griffith, F. and Polanyi, J. C., eds.
      THE DANGERS OF NUCLEAR WAR
      Toronto: University of Toronto Press, 1979.

176   Gurr, T. R.
      WHY MEN REBEL
      Princeton University Press, 1970.

177   Haas, M.
      INTERNATIONAL CONFLICT
      New York: Bobbs-Merrill, 1974.

178   Haberman, F. W., ed.
      NOBEL LECTURES: PEACE; VOL. I: 1901-25, VOL. II: 1926-50,
      VOL. III: 1951-70
      Amsterdam: Elsvier, 1972.

179 Hamilton, M. P.
     TO AVOID CATASTROPHE: A STUDY IN FUTURE NUCLEAR WEAPON
     POLICY
     Grand Rapids, MI: William B. Erdmans, 1977.

180 Harkavy, R. E.
     THE ARMS TRADE AND INTERNATIONAL SYSTEMS
     Cambridge, MA: Ballinger, 1975.

181 Harrison, R.
     WARFARE
     Minneapolis: Burgess, 1973.

182 Hawker, Guy J. and Associates
     IN SEARCH OF SELF RELIANCE: U.S. SECURITY ASSISTANCE TO
     THE THIRD WORLD UNDER THE NIXON DOCTRINE
     Santa Monica, CA: Rand Corporation, 1973.

183 Hazelwood, A. D.
     ECONOMIC INTEGRATION: THE EAST AFRICAN EXPERIENCE
     London: Heineman.

184 Holst, J. J. and Nerlich, U., eds.
     BEYOND NUCLEAR DETERRENCE: NEW AIMS, NEW ARMS
     New York: Crane Russel, 1977.

185 I.L.O.
     MEETING BASIC HUMAN NEEDS
     Geneva: ILO, 1977.

186 International Institute of Strategic Studies
     THE MILITARY BALANCE
     London: Annual.

187 INTERNATIONAL WORKSHOP ON DISARMAMENT
     New Delhi: Center for the Study of Developing Societies,
     1978.

188 Jack, H. A.
     THE UNITED NATIONS SPECIAL SESSION AND BEYOND
     New York: World Conference on Religion and Peace, 1978.

189 Johansen, R. C.
     THE NATIONAL INTEREST AND HUMAN INTEREST: AN ANALYSIS OF
     UNITED STATES FOREIGN POLICY
     Princeton: Princeton University Press, 1980.

190 Johnson, Stuart E.
     THE MILITARY EQUATION IN NORTHEASTERN ASIA
     Washington, D.C.: Brookings Institution, 1979.

191 Jolly, Richard
     DISARMAMENT AND WORLD DEVELOPMENT
     New York: Pergamon, 1978.

192 Kaldor, Mary
     TOWARDS A THEORY OF THE ARMS TRADE: PAPER PRESENTED TO
     THE CONFERENCE ON ALTERNATIVE TRADE THEORIES AT THE INSTITUTE
     OF DEVELOPMENT STUDIES
     University of Sussex, 1975.

193 Kaldor, Mary
     EUROPEAN DEFENCE INDUSTRIES: NATIONAL AND INTERNATIONAL
     IMPLICATIONS
     Institute for the Study of International Organizations,
     Sussex, 1972.

194 Kalyadin, A.
     NUCLEAR ENERGY AND INTERNATIONAL SECURITY
     Moscow: Novosti Press, 1970.

195 Kay, David A., ed.
     THE CHANGING UNITED NATIONS: OPTIONS FOR THE UNITED STATES;
     PROCEEDINGS OF THE ACADEMY OF POLITICAL SCIENCE
     New York: The Academy of Political Science, 1977.

196 Kende, I.
     TWENTY-FIVE YEARS OF LOCAL WARS IN ASIA, AFRICA AND LATIN
     AMERICA: 1945-1969
     Budapest: Hungarian Academy of Sciences, 1972.

197 Kennedy, Gavin
     THE MILITARY IN THE THIRD WORLD
     London: Duckworth, 1974.

198 Khrushchev, Nikita S.
     DISARMAMENT AND COLONIAL FREEDOM
     Greenwood, 1975.

199 Kinkade, W. H. and Porro, J. D., eds.
     NEGOTIATING SECURITY, AN ARMS CONTROL READER
     Washington, D.C.: The Carnegie Endowment for International
     Peace, 1979.

200 Kothari, R.
     FOOTSTEPS INTO THE FUTURE
     New York: The Free Press, 1975.

201 Kuhlman, Charles
     THE MILITARY IN THE DEVELOPING COUNTRIES: A GENERAL
     BIBLIOGRAPHY
     Bloomington: Indiana University, 1971.

202 Laszlo, Ervin and Keys, Donald
     DISARMAMENT: THE HUMAN FACTOR
     New York: Pergamon, 1981.

203 Lefever, Ernest W.
     NUCLEAR ARMS IN THE THIRD WORLD: U.S. POLICY DILEMMA
     Washington, D.C.: Brookings Institution, 1979.

204   Leiss, A. O. and Associates
      ARMS TRANSFERS TO LESS DEVELOPED COUNTRIES
      Cambridge, MA: Center for International Studies, MIT, 1970.

205   Leitenberg, M.
      NATO AND WTO LONG RANGE THEATER NUCLEAR FORCES in K. E.
      Birnbaum,   ed.,   Arms   Control   in   Europe: Problems   and
      Perspectives
      Laxenburg: Austrian   Institute   for   International   Affairs,
      1980.

206   Lider, J.
      ON THE NATURE OF WAR
      Farnborough: Saxon House, 1977.

207   Lin, P.
      ON THE CREATION OF A JUST WORLD ORDER
      New York: The Free Press, 1975.

208   Lock, Peter and Wulf, Herbert
      A REGISTER ON ARMS PRODUCTION IN DEVELOPING COUNTRIES
      Hamburg: Study   Group   on   Armaments   and   Underdevelopment,
      1977.

209   Long, F. and Rathjens, G. W., eds.
      ARMS, DEFENSE POLICY, AND ARMS CONTROL
      New York: Norton, 1976.

210   Lokshin, G., ed.
      SOCIO-ECONOMIC PROBLEMS OF DISARMAMENT
      Vienna: International Institute for Peace, 1978.

211   Lowenthal, Abraham F., ed.
      THE PERUVIAN EXPERIMENT: CONTINUITY AND CHANGE UNDER MILITARY
      RULE
      Princeton, NJ: Princeton University Press, 1975.

212   Luttwak, E. N.
      STRATEGIC POWER: MILITARY CAPABILITIES AND POLITICAL UNITY
      London: Sage Publications, 1976.

213   Manontov, V.
      DISARMAMENT: THE COMMAND OF THE TIMES
      Progress Publishers, 1979.

214   Marks, A. W., ed.
      NPT: PARADOXES AND PROBLEMS
      Washington,   D.C.:   Carnegie   Endowment   for   International
      Peace, 1975.

215   Mastny, Vojtech
      DISARMAMENT AND NUCLEAR TESTS, 1964-69
      New York: Fact on File, 1970.

216 M'Bow, Amadou-Mahtar
     CONSENSUS AND PEACE
     Paris: UNESCO, 1980.

217 McNamara, Robert S.
     ADDRESS ON "DEVELOPMENT AND THE ARMS RACE"
     Chicago: University of Chicago, May 22, 1979.

218 Midlarsky, M.
     ON WAR: POLITICAL VIOLENCE IN THE INTERNATIONAL SYSTEM
     New York: The Free Press, 1975.

219 Myradal, Alva
     THE GAME OF DISARMAMENT: HOW THE UNITED STATES AND RUSSIA
     RUN THE ARMS RACE
     New York: Pantheon Books, 1976.

220 NEW CONVENTIONAL WEAPONS AND EAST-WEST SECURITY
     London: Macmillan, 1979.

221 Northedge, F. S. and Donelan, M. D.
     INTERNATIONAL DISPUTES: THE POLITICAL ASPECTS
     New York: St. Martin's Press, 1971.

222 NUCLEAR PROLIFERATION FACTBOOK
     Washington, D.C.: United States Govt. Printing Office,
     1977.

223 Parry, V. J. and Yapp, M. E., eds.
     WAR, TECHNOLOGY AND SOCIETY IN THE MIDDLE EAST
     New York: Oxford, 1975.

224 Pikisuk, M.
     INTERNATIONAL CONFLICT AND SOCIAL POLICY
     Englewood Cliffs, NJ: Prentice-Hall, 1972.

225 Polner, Murray
     DISARMAMENT CATALOGUE
     Pilgrim, 1982.

226 Pranger, R. J., ed.
     DETENTE AND DEFENCE: A READER
     Washington, D.C.: American Enterprise Institute for Public
     Policy Research, 1976.

227 Primakov, E., et al.
     INTERNATIONAL DETENTE AND DISARMAMENT: CONTRIBUTIONS BY
     FINNISH AND SOVIET SCHOLARS
     Tampere, Finland: Tampere Peace Research Institute, 1977.

228 RACE TO OBLIVION: A PARTICIPANT'S VIEW OF THE ARMS RACE
     New York: Simon and Schuster, 1970.

229   Rana, Swadesh
      OBSTACLES TO DISARMAMENT AND WAYS OF OVERCOMING THEM
      Paris: UNESCO, 1981.

230   Ranger, R.
      ARMS AND POLITICS 1958-78:   ARMS CONTROL IN A CHANGING
      POLITICAL CONTEXT
      Toronto: Macmillan of Canada, 1978.

231   Raskin, M. G.
      THE POLITICS OF NATIONAL SECURITY
      New Brunswick: Transaction Books, 1979.

232   Rosen, S., ed.
      TESTING THE THEORY OF MILITARY-INDUSTRIAL COMPLEX
      Lexington, MA: Lexington Books, 1970.

233   Rosencrance, R.
      STRATEGIC DETERRENCE RECONSIDERED
      London: IISS, 1975.

234   Rummel, R.
      UNDERSTANDING CONFLICT AND WAR; VOL. I-III
      London: Sage, 1975, 1976, 1977.

235   Russet, B. M., ed.
      PEACE, WAR AND NUMBERS
      London: Sage Publications, 1972.

236   Sampson, A.
      THE ARMS BAZAAR
      London: Hodder and Stoughton, 1977.

237   Sarkesian, S., ed.
      THE MILITARY-INDUSTRIAL COMPLEX: A REASSESSMENT
      London: Beverly Hills, 1972.

238   Schaerf, Barnaby
      DISARMAMENT AND ARMS CONTROL
      Gordon, 1972.

239   Sharp, G.
      EXPLORING NON-VIOLENT ALTERNATIVES
      Boston: Porter Sargent, 1970.

240   Sharp, J., ed.
      OPPORTUNITIES FOR DISARMAMENT
      Washington, D.C.:   Carnegie Endowment for International
      Peace, 1978.

241   Simon, Sheldon W.
      MILITARY AND SECURITY IN THE THIRD WORLD: DOMESTIC AND
      INTERNATIONAL IMPACTS
      Boulder, CO: Westview Press, 1978.

242 Sims, N. A.
     APPROACHES TO DISARMAMENT
     London: Quaker Peace and Service, 1979.

243 Sirard, Ruth
     WORLD MILITARY AND SOCIAL EXPENDITURES 1974
     New York: Institute for World Order, WMSE Publications,
     1974, 1976, 1978, 1979.

244 Smith, D.
     THE DEFENCE OF THE REALM IN THE 1980'S
     London: Croom Helm, 1980.

245 Stanton, J. and Pearton, M.
     THE INTERNATIONAL TRADE IN ARMS
     London: Chatto & Windus, 1972.

246 Stockholm International Peace Research Institute
     ARMAMENTS AND DISARMAMENTS IN THE NUCLEAR AGE: A HANDBOOK
     Humanities Press, 1976.

247 Stockholm International Peace Research Institute
     THE ARMS TRADE WITH THE THIRD WORLD
     Stockholm: Almquist and Wicksell, 1971.

248 Stockholm International Peace Research Institute
     YEARBOOK ON ARMAMENT AND DISARMAMENT
     Stockholm: Almquist and Wicksell, Annual.

249 Stockholm International Peace Research Institute
     ARMS TRADE REGISTERS
     Stockholm: Almquist and Wicksell, MIT Press, 1974.

250 Thee, M., ed.
     EUROPEAN SECURITY AND THE ARMS RACE (Special Issue of the
     Bulletin of Peace Proposals, Vol. 10, No. 1), 1979.

251 Thee, Marek
     ARMSAMENTS: ARMS CONTROL AND DISARMAMENT
     Paris: UNESCO, 1981.

252 Udis, B., ed.
     THE ECONOMIC CONSEQUENCES OF REDUCED MILITARY SPENDINGS
     Lexington, MA: D. C. Heath & Co., 1974.

253 UNA - USA National Policy Panel On Conventional Arms Control
     CONTROLLING THE CONVENTIONAL ARMS RACE
     New York: Nov. 1976.

254 United Nations
     BASIC PROBLEMS OF DISARMAMENT; REPORTS OF THE SECRETARY-
     GENERAL
     New York: UN, 1970.

255 United Nations
     DISARMAMENT AND DEVELOPMENT REPORT OF THE GROUP OF EXPERTS
     New York: UN, 1981.

256 United Nations
     DISARMAMENT AND DEVELOPMENT REPORT OF THE GROUP OF EXPERTS
     ON THE ECONOMIC AND SOCIAL CONSEQUENCES
     New York: UN, 1972.

257 United Nations
     ECONOMIC AND SOCIAL CONSEQUENCES OF THE ARMS RACE AND OF
     MILITARY EXPENDITURES
     New York: UN, 1972.

258 United Nations
     THE UNITED NATIONS AND DISARMAMENT 1945-1970
     New York: UN, 1970.

259 United Nations Center for Disarmament
     THE UNITED NATIONS DISARMAMENT YEARBOOK; 1976-1981
     New York: UN, Annual.

260 United Nations
     REDUCTION OF THE MILITARY BUDGETS OF THE PERMAMENT MEMBERS
     OF THE SECURITY COUNCIL BY 10 PERCENT AND UTILIZATION OF
     PART OF THE FUNDS TO PROVIDE ASSISTANCE TO DEVELOPING
     COUNTRIES
     New York: UN, 1974.

261 United Nations
     DISARMAMENT; Vol. 4, No. 2
     Unipub, 1981.

262 United Nations
     DISARMAMENT: A PERIODIC REVIEW BY THE U.N.; Vol. 4, No. 1
     Unipub, 1981.

263 United Nations
     DISARMAMENT: A SELECT BIBLIOGRAPHY, 1967-1972
     Unipub, 1973.

264 United Nations
     DISARMAMENT: A SELECT BIBLIOGRAPHY, 1973-77
     Unipub, 1978.

265 United Nations
     STATUS OF MULTILATERAL ARMS REGULATIONS AND DISARMAMENT
     AGREEMENTS: SPECIAL SUPPLEMENT TO THE UNITED NATIONS
     DISARMAMENT YEARBOOK, VOL. 2: 1977
     New York: UN, 1978.

266 United Nations
     DISARMAMENT: PROGRESS TOWARDS PEACE
     Unipub, 1974.

267 United Nations
     COMPREHENSIVE STUDY OF THE QUESTION OF NUCLEAR-WEAPON-FREE
     ZONES IN ALL ITS ASPECTS
     New York: UN, 1976.

268 United Nations
     ECONOMIC AND SOCIAL CONSEQUENCES OF THE ARMS RACE AND OF
     MILITARY EXPENDITURES: UPDATED REPORT OF THE SECRETARY-
     GENERAL
     New York: UN, 1978.

269 United Nations
     DISARMAMENT: THE IMPERATIVE PEACE
     Unipub, 1970.

270 UNESCO
     PEACE RESEARCH: TREND REPORT AND WORLD DIRECTORY
     Paris: UNESCO, 1979.

271 UNESCO
     THREAT OF MODERN WARFARE TO MAN AND HIS ENVIRONMENT
     Paris: UNESCO, 1979.

272 United States Library of Congress; Congressional Research
     Service
     UNITED STATES POLICY ON THE USE OF NUCLEAR WEAPONS, 1945-75
     Washington, D.C., 1975.

273 United States Arms Control and Disarmament Agency
     ECONOMIC IMPACT OF MILITARY BASE CLOSINGS
     Washington, D.C.: ACDA, 1970.

274 United States Congress
     ECONOMIC ISSUES IN MILITARY ASSISTANCE
     Washington, D.C.: Jan. and Feb., 1971.

275 Viera Gallo, J. A., ed.
     THE SECURITY TRAP: ARMS RACE, MILITARISM AND DISARMAMENT:
     A CONCEPT FOR CHRISTIANS
     Rome: IDOC International, 1979.

276 Wallensteen, P., ed.
     EXPERIENCES IN DISARMAMENT: ON CONVERSION OF MILITARY
     INDUSTRY AND CLOSING OF MILITARY BASES
     Uppsala, Sweden: Uppsala University, 1978.

277 Wangborg, Manne
     DISARMAMENT AND DEVELOPMENT: A GUIDE TO LITERATURE RELEVANT
     TO THE UNITED NATIONS STUDY
     Stockholm: Foravarets Forskningsanstalt (FOA), 1980.

278 Weidenbaum, M. L.
     THE ECONOMICS OF PEACETIME DEFENCE
     New York: Praeger, 1974.

279 Wolpin, Miles D.
     MILITARY AID AND COUNTER REVOLUTION IN THE THIRD WORLD
     Lexington, MA: Lexington Books, 1973.

280 Wolpin, Miles D.
     MILITARISM AND SOCIAL REVOLUTION IN THE THIRD WORLD
     Allanheld, 1982.

281 WORLD MILITARY EXPENDITURES
     Washington, D.C.: Annual up to 1973.

282 WORLD MILITARY EXPENDITURES AND ARMS TRADE, 1963-73
     Washington, D.C., 1974.

283 Wright, Q.
     A STUDY OF WAR
     Chicago: University of Chicago Press, 1971.

284 Wulf, C., ed.
     HANDBOOK ON PEACE EDUCATION
     Frankfurt: International Peace Research Association, 1974.

285 Yarmolinsky, A.
     THE MILITARY ESTABLISHMENT
     New York: Harper and Row, 1971.

286 York, H. F., ed.
     ARMS CONTROL
     San Francisco: Freeman, 1973.

287 York, H.
     RACE TO OBLIVION
     New York: Simon & Schuster, 1970.

288 Young, E.
     A FAREWELL TO ARMS CONTROL?
     Hammondsworth: Penguin, 1973.

289 Zinnes, D.
     CONTEMPORARY RESEARCH IN INTERNATIONAL RELATIONS
     New York: Macmillan, 1976.

II. SELECTED PERIODICAL ARTICLES

290 Abrahamsson, Bengt
     A model for the analysis of inter-group conflict, in Conflict
     Control and Conflict Resolution, ed. Hoglund and Ulrich,
     pp. 72-85.

291 Afheldt, Horst
     Political conclusions of the study "The consequences of

war and the prevention of war," JOURNAL OF PEACE RESEARCH No. 3:259-64.

292   Afheldt, Horst and Sonntag, Philipp
Stability and deterrence through strategic nuclear arms.
JOURNAL OF PEACE RESEARCH No. 3:245-50, 1973.

293   Albrecht, Ulrich
The costs of armamentism. JOURNAL OF PEACE RESEARCH No. 3:265-84, 1973.

294   Albrecht, Ulrich; Galtung, Johan; Joenniemi, Pertti; Senghaas, Dieter and Verona, Sergiu
Is Europe to demilitarize? INSTANT RESEARCH ON PEACE AND VIOLENCE No. 4:181-246, 1972.

295   Albrecht, Ulrich and Associates
Armaments and underdevelopment. BULLETIN OF PEACE PROPOSALS Vol. 5, 1974.

296   Alcock, Norman Z. and Lowe, Keith
The Vietnam war as a Richardson process. JOURNAL OF PEACE RESEARCH No. 2:105-12, 1969.

297   Alker, Hayward R., Jr. and Brunner, Ronald D.
Simulating international conflict: a comparison of three approaches. INTERNATIONAL STUDIES QUARTERLY 13, No. 1:70-110, March 1969.

298   ALTERNATIVES: A JOURNAL OF WORLD POLICY 1, No. 1, March 1975.

299   Ashworth A.
The sociology of trench warfare, 1914-18. BRITISH JOURNAL OF SOCIOLOGY 19, No. 4:407-23, 1968.

300   Balke, W.; Hammond, K. and Meyer, G. D.
An alternate approach to labor-management relations. ADMINISTRATIVE SCIENCE QUARTERLY 18, No. 3, Sept. 1973.

301   Bank, A.
Patterns of domestic conflict: 1919-39 and 1946-66. JOURNAL OF CONFLICT RESOLUTION 16:41-50, 1972.

302   Banks, A. and Gregg, P.
Dimensions of political systems: factor analysis of a cross-polity survey. AMERICAN POLITICAL SCIENCE REVIEW 59:602-14, 1965.

303   Barnaby, F.
Arms and the Third World: the background. DEVELOPMENT DIALOGUE, 1977.

304   Barrea, Jean
The counter-core role of middle powers in processes of

external political integration. WORLD POLITICS 25, No. 2:274-87, Jan. 1973.

305 Barsegov, Yuri and Khairov, Rustem
A study of the problems of peace. JOURNAL OF PEACE RESEARCH Nos. 1/2:71-80, 1973.

306 Beitz, Charles R.
Justice and international relations. PHILOSOPHY AND PUBLIC AFFAIRS 4, No. 4, Summer 1975.

307 Bixenstine, Edwin V. and Gaebelein, Jacquelyn W.
Strategies of "real" opponents in elicitiing cooperative choice in a Prisoner's Dilemma game. JOURNAL OF CONFLICT RESOLUTION 15, No. 2:157-66, June 1971.

308 Boasson, Charles; Galtung, Johan and Amad, Adnan
Discussion on Galtung's "The Middle East and the theory of conflict." JOURNAL OF PEACE RESEARCH Nos. 1/2:133-54, 1973.

309 Bonacich, Phillip
Putting the dilemma into Prisoner's Dilemma. JOURNAL OF CONFLICT RESOLUTION 14, No. 3:379-87, Sept. 1970.

310 Bonham, G. Matthew
Simulating international disarmament negotiations. JOURNAL OF CONFLICT RESOLUTION 15, No. 3:299-315, Sept. 1971.

311 Boulding, Elise
New careers and new societies: challenges for college peace studies programs. JOURNAL OF WORLD EDUCATION, 1975.

312 Boulding, Elise
The study of conflict and community in the international system: summary and challenges to research. JOURNAL OF SOCIAL ISSUES 23, No. 1, Jan. 1967.

313 Boudling, Elise
Peace research: Dialetics and development. JOURNAL OF CONFLICT RESOLUTION 16, No. 4:469-73, Dec. 1972.

314 Bozeman, A.
War and the clash of ideas. ORBIS 20, No. 1:61-102, 1976.

315 Brecher, Michael; Steinberg, Blema and Stein, Janice
A framework for research on foreign policy behavior. JOURNAL OF CONFLICT RESOLUTION 13, No. 1:75-101, March 1969.

316 Bwy, D.
Dimensions of social conflict in Latin America. AMERICAN BEHAVIORAL SCIENTIST 11:39-50, 1968.

317 Campbell, Thomas W.
     Nationalism in America's UN policy, 1944-45.   INTERNATIONAL
     ORGANIZATION 7, No. 1:25-44, Winter 1973.

318 Cantori, Louis J. and Spiegel, Steven L.
     The analysis of regional international politics: the
     integration   versus   the   empirical   systems   approach.
     INTERNATIONAL ORGANIZATION 27, No. 4:465-94, Autumn 1973.

319 Carroll, Berenice
     Peace research: the cult of power.   JOURNAL OF CONFLICT
     RESOLUTION, Dec. 1972.

320 Cattell, R. and Gorsuch, R.
     The definition and measurement of national morale and
     morality.   JOURNAL OF SOCIAL PSYCHOLOGY 67:77-96, 1965.

321 Chadwick, Richard W.
     An inductive, empirical analysis of intra- and international
     behavior, aimed at a partial extension of inter-nation
     simulation theory. JOURNAL OF PEACE RESEARCH No. 3:193-214,
     1969.

322 Chichilnisky, G.
     Development patterns and the international order.   JOURNAL
     OF INTERNATIONAL AFFAIRS 31, No. 2, 1977.

323 Choucri, N. and North, R.
     Dynamics of international conflict: some policy implications
     of population, resources and technology.   WORLD POLITICS
     24:80-122, 1972.

324 Choucri, N. and Bennett, J.
     Population, resources and technology: political implications
     of the environmental crisis.   INTERNATIONAL ORGANIZATION
     26, No. 1:175-212, 1972.

325 Choucri, Nazli
     The perceptual base of nonalignment.   JOURNAL OF CONFLICT
     RESOLUTION 13, No. 1:57-74, March 1969.

326 Conrath, David W.
     Experience as a factor in experimental gaming behavior.
     JOURNAL OF CONFLICT RESOLUTION 14, No. 2:195-202, June 1970.

327 Coser, Lewis, ed.
     Collective violence and civil conflict.   JOURNAL OF SOCIAL
     ISSUES (Special issue) 28, No. 1, 1972.

328 Denton, F. and Phillips, W.
     Some patterns in the history of violence. JOURNAL OF CONFLICT
     RESOLUTION 12, No. 2:182-95, 1968.

329 Deutsch, K, and Senghaas, D.
     The steps to war: a survey of system levels, decision stages
     and research results. SAGE INTERNATIONAL YEARBOOK OF FOREIGN
     POLICY STUDIES 1:275-329.

330 Dolbear, F. T.; Lave, L. B.; Bowman, G.; Lieberman, A.;
     Prescott, E.; Rueter, F. and Sherman, R.
     Collusion in the Prisoner's Dilemma: number of strategies.
     JOURNAL OF CONFLICT RESOLUTION 13, No. 2:252-61, June 1969.

331 Dowty, A.
     Foreign-linked factionalism as a historical pattern. JOURNAL
     OF CONFLICT RESOLUTION 15:429-42, 1971.

332 Druckman, Daniel
     The influence of the situation in interparty conflict. JOURNAL
     OF CONFLICT RESOLUTION 15, No. 4:523-54, Dec. 1971.

333 Eckhardt, W. and Azar, E.
     Major world conflicts and interventions, 1945-75.
     INTERNATIONAL INTERACTIONS 5, No. 1:75-110, 1978.

334 Eckhardt, W. and Azar, E.
     Major military conflicts and interventions, 1945-79. JOURNAL
     OF PEACE RESEARCH 11, No. 4:201-08, 1979.

335 Eide, Asbjorn
     Dialogue and confrontation in Europe. JOURNAL OF CONFLICT
     RESOLUTION 16, No. 4:511-522, Dec. 1972.

336 Everts, Philip P.
     Developments and trends in peace and conflict research,
     1965-71: a survey of institutions. JOURNAL OF CONFLICT
     RESOLUTION 16, No. 4:477-510, Dec. 1972.

337 Falk, Richard A.
     Arms control, foreign policy and global reform. DAEDALUS
     104, No. 3, Summer 1975.

338 Falk, Richard A.
     The Sherrill hypothesis--international law and drastic reform:
     historical and futurist perspectives. YALE LAW JOURNAL
     84, No. 5, 1975.

339 Feierabend, I. and Feierabend, R.
     Aggressive behaviors within polities, 1948-62; a
     cross-national study. JOURNAL OF CONFLICT RESOLUTION 10,
     No. 3:249-71, 1966.

340 Feld, Bernard
     Making the world safe for Plutonium. BULLETIN OF THE ATOMIC
     SCIENTISTS 31, No. 5, May 1975.

341 Gallo, Philip S.
     Personality impression formation in a maximizing difference

game.   JOURNAL   OF   CONFLICT   RESOLUTION   13,   No.   1:118-22,
March 1969.

342 Galtung, Johan
     A structural theory of imperialism.   JOURNAL OF PEACE RESEARCH
     8, No. 2, 1971.

343 Galtung, Johan
     Limits   to   growth   and   class   politics.   JOURNAL   OF   PEACE
     RESEARCH Nos. 1/2, 1973.

344 Galtung, Johan
     Europe--bipolar,   bicentric,   cooperative?   JOURNAL   OF   PEACE
     RESEARCH No. 1:1-26, 1972.

345 Galtung, Johan
     Japan and future world politics.   JOURNAL OF PEACE RESEARCH
     No. 4:355-85, 1973.

346 Galtung, Johan
     The Middle East and the theory of conflict.   JOURNAL OF
     PEACE RESEARCH Nos. 3/4:173-206, 1971.

347 Galtung, Johan
     Violence, peace and peace research.   JOURNAL OF PEACE RESEARCH
     No. 3:167-92, 1969.

348 Galtung, J.
     A structural theory of aggression.   JOURNAL OF PEACE RESEARCH
     1:95-119, 1964.

349 Gantzel, Klaus Jurgen
     Dependency   structures   as   the   dominant   pattern   in   world
     society. JOURNAL OF PEACE RESEARCH No. 3:203-16, 1973.

350 Glagolev, Igor and Goryainov, Makar
     Some   problems   of   disarmament   research.   JOURNAL   OF   PEACE
     RESEARCH No. 2:150-54, 1964.

351 Glenn, Edmund S.; Johnson, Robert H.; Kimmel, Paul R. and
     Wedge, Bryant
     A cognitive interaction model to analyze culture conflict
     in international relations.   JOURNAL OF CONFLICT RESOLUTION
     14, No. 1:35-48, March 1970.

352 Gift, Richard E.
     Trading in a threat system: the U.S.-Soviet case.   JOURNAL
     OF CONFLICT RESOLUTION 13, No. 4:418-37, Dec. 1969.

353 Goryainov, Makar and Glagolev, Igor
     Concerning research on peace and disarmament conducted in
     the USSR.   INTERNATIONAL SOCIAL SCIENCE JOURNAL 17, No.
     3:417-19, 1965.

354   Graber, Doris A.
      Perceptions of Middle East conflict in the UN: 1953-65.
      JOURNAL OF CONFLICT RESOLUTION 13, No. 4:454-84, Dec. 1969.

355   Grant, James P.
      Energy shock and the development prospect. INTERNATIONAL
      DEVELOPMENT REVIEW 16, No. 1, 1974.

356   Gruder, Charles L.
      Relationships with opponent and partner in mixed-motive
      bargaining. JOURNAL OF CONFLICT RESOLUTION 15, No. 3:403-16,
      Sept. 1971.

357   Gurr, T.
      The calculus of civil conflict. JOURNAL OF SOCIAL ISSUES
      28, No. 1:26-47, 1972.

358   Gurr, T.
      A causal model of civil strife: a comparative analysis
      using new indices. AMERICAN POLITICAL SCIENCE REVIEW 62,
      No. 4:1104-24, 1968.

359   Haas, Ernst B.
      On systems and international regimes. WORLD POLITICS 27,
      No. 2, Jan. 1975.

360   Haas, M.
      Societal approaches to the study of war. JOURNAL OF PEACE
      RESEARCH 2:307-24, 1965.

361   Hammond, Kenneth R.
      New directions in research on conflict resolution. JOURNAL
      OF SOCIAL ISSUES 21, No. 3, 1965.

362   Hanrieder, Wolfram F.
      The international system, bipolar or multibloc? JOURNAL
      OF CONFLICT RESOLUTION 9, No. 3:299-307, Sept. 1965.

363   Hardin, Garret
      Living on a lifeboat. BIOSCIENCE 24, Oct. 1974.

364   Harsanyi, J.
      International models for the genesis of war. WORLD POLITICS
      14, No. 4:687-99, 1962.

365   Horn, Klaus
      Approaches to social psychology relevant to peace research
      as developed in the Federal Republic of Germany. JOURNAL
      OF PEACE RESEARCH No. 3:305-16, 1973.

366   Horvath, W. and Foster, C.
      Stochastic models of war alliances. JOURNAL OF CONFLICT
      RESOLUTION 7, No. 2:110-16, 1963.

367 Horvath, W.
     A statistical model for the duration of wars and strikes.
     BEHAVIORAL SCIENCE 13:18-28, 1968.

368 Hueckel, Glenn
     A historical approach to future economic growth.   SCIENCE
     187:925-31, March 14, 1975.

369 Hveem, Helge
     The global dominance system.   JOURNAL OF PEACE RESEARCH
     No. 4:319-40, 1973.

370 Jahn, Egbert
     Civilian defense and civilian offensive.   JOURNAL OF PEACE
     RESEARCH No. 3:285-94, 1973.

371 Kegley, C.; Richardson, N. and Richter, G.
     Conflict at home and abroad: an empirical extension.   JOURNAL
     OF POLITICS 40, No. 3:743-52, 1978.

372 Kelsen, H.
     Law and peace in international relations.   Cambridge, MA:
     Harvard University Press, 1942.

373 Kende, I.
     Dynamics of wars, of arms trade and of military expenditure
     in the "third world", 1945-76.   INSTANT RESEARCH ON PEACE
     AND VIOLENCE 7, No. 2:59-67, 1977.

374 Kende, I.
     Twenty-five years of local wars.   JOURNAL OF PEACE RESEARCH
     8, No. 1:5-22, 1971.

375 Kende, I.
     Wars of ten years (1967-76).   JOURNAL OF PEACE RESEARCH 15,
     No. 3:227-41, 1978.

376 Kende, I.
     Wars from 1965 to 1978.   PEACE RESEARCH 11, No. 4:197-200,
     1979.

377 Kerr, Henry H., Jr.
     Changing attitudes through international participation:
     European parliamentarians and integration.   INTERNATIONAL
     ORGANIZATION 27, No. 2:45-83, Winter 1973.

378 Klingberg, F.
     Predicting the termination of wars: battle casualties and
     population losses.   JOURNAL OF CONFLICT RESOLUTION 10:129-71,
     1966.

379 Langholm, Sivert
     On the concepts of center and periphery.   JOURNAL OF PEACE
     RESEARCH Nos. 3/4:273-78, 1971.

380   Luschen, Gunther
      Cooperation, association, and contest. JOURNAL OF CONFLICT
      RESOLUTION 14, No. 1:21-34, March 1970.

381   Marks, S., et al.
      DISARMAMENT EDUCATION; Special issue of the Bulletin of
      Peace Proposals, Vol. 11, No. 3, 1980.

382   Meeker, Robert J. and Shure, Gerald H.
      Pacifist bargaining tactics: some "outsider" influence.
      JOURNAL OF CONFLICT RESOLUTION 13, No. 4:487-93, Dec. 1969.

383   Michelini, Ronald L.
      Effects of prior interaction, contact, strategy, and
      expectation of meeting on game behavior and sentiment.
      JOURNAL OF CONFLICT RESOLUTION 15, no. 1:97-103, March 1971.

384   Midlarsky, M.
      Power, uncertainty, and the onset of international violence.
      JOURNAL OF CONFLICT RESOLUTION 18, No. 3:395-431, 1974.

385   Mitchell, C. R.
      Conflict resolution and controlled communication. JOURNAL
      OF PEACE RESEARCH Nos. 1/2:123-32, 1973.

386   Mitchell, John D.
      Cross-cutting memberships, integration, and the international
      system. JOURNAL OF CONFLICT RESOLUTION 14, No. 1:49-55,
      March 1970.

387   Modelski, George
      The world's foreign ministers: a political elite. JOURNAL
      OF CONFLICT RESOLUTION 14, No. 2:135-75, June 1970.

388   Morrison, Bruce John; Enzle, Michael; Dunaway, Diana; Griffin,
      Michael; Kneisel, Kenneth and Gimperling, John
      The effect of electrical shock and warning on cooperation
      in a non-zero-sum game. JOURNAL OF CONFLICT RESOLUTION
      15, No. 1:105-08, March 1971.

389   Muney, Barbara F. and Deutsch, Morton
      The effects of role-reversal during the discussion of opposing
      viewpoints. JOURNAL OF CONFLICT RESOLUTION 12, No. 3:345-56,
      Sept. 1968.

390   Mytelka, Lynn K.
      The salience of gains in Third-World integrative systems.
      WORLD POLITICS 25, No. 2:236-50, Jan. 1973.

391   Newcombe, Hanna
      Alternative approaches to world government. PEACE RESEARCH
      REVIEWS 5, No. 3, Feb. 1974.

392   Newcombe, Alan G.
      Initiatives and responses in foreign policy. PEACE RESEARCH
      REVIEWS 3, No. 3, June 1969.

393   Newcombe, Alan G. and Newcombe, Hanna
      Approaches to peace research. ALTERNATIVE APPROACHES TO
      PEACE RESEARCH, PEACE RESEARCH REVIEWS 4, No. 4:1-23, Feb.
      1972.

394   Nieburg, H.
      Uses of violence. JOURNAL OF CONFLICT RESOLUTION 12, No.
      1:43-54, 1963.

395   Nitz, Lawrence H. and Philips, James L.
      The effects of divisibility of payoff on confederative
      behavior. JOURNAL OF CONFLICT RESOLUTION 13, No. 3:381-87,
      Sept. 1969.

396   North, R. and Choucri, N.
      Population, technology, and resources in the future of
      international system. JOURNAL OF INTERNATIONAL AFFAIRS
      25, No. 2:224-37, 1971.

397   Offshe, Richard
      The effectiveness of pacifist strategies: a theoretical
      approach. JOURNAL OF CONFLICT RESOLUTION 15, No. 2:261-69,
      June 1971.

398   Olson, M.
      Rapid growth as a destabilizing force. JOURNAL OF ECONOMIC
      HISTORY 23, No. 4:529-52, 1963.

399   Olson, Mancur
      Increasing the incentives for international cooperation.
      INTERNATIONAL ORGANIZATION 25, No. 4:845-65, Autumn 1971.

400   Orwant, Carol J. and Orwant, Jack E.
      A comparison of interpreted and abstract versions of
      mixed-motive games. JOURNAL OF CONFLICT RESOLUTION 14,
      No. 1:91-97, March 1970.

401   Patchen, Martin
      Models of cooperation and conflict: a critical review.
      JOURNAL OF CONFLICT RESOLUTION 14, No. 3:389-407, Sept.
      1970.

402   Peace research in transition: a symposium. JOURNAL OF
      CONFLICT RESOLUTION (special issue), Dec. 1972.

403   Podell, Jerome E. and Knapp, William M.
      The effect of mediation on the perceived firmness of the
      opponent. JOURNAL OF CONFLICT RESOLUTION 13, No. 4:511-20,
      Dec. 1969.

404   Rappoport, Leon
       Cognitive conflict as a function of socially induced cognitive
       differences. JOURNAL OF CONFLICT RESOLUTION 13, No. 1:143-48,
       March 1969.

405   Ridker, Ronald G.
       To grow or not to grow: that's not the relvant question.
       SCIENCE 192, Dec. 28, 1973.

406   Rittberger, V.
       International   organization   and   violence;   with   special
       reference to the performance of the UN system.   JOURNAL
       OF PEACE RESEARCH 3:217-27, 1973.

407   Rummel, R.
       Some dimensions in the foreign behavior of nations. JOURNAL
       OF PEACE RESEARCH 8:201-24, 1966.

408   Rummel, R.
       A field theory of social action with application to conflict
       within nations.   YEARBOOK   SOC.   GENERAL   SYSTEMS   RES.
       10:183-204, 1965.

409   Rummel, R.
       Dimensions of dyadic war, 1820-1952.   JOURNAL OF CONFLICT
       RESOLUTION 11, No. 2:176-83, 1967.

410   Russett, Bruce M. and Sullivan, John D.
       Collective   goods   and   international   organization.
       INTERNATIONAL ORGANIZATION 25, No. 4:845-65, Autumn 1971.

411   Saraydar, Edward
       A certainty-equivalent model of bargaining.   JOURNAL OF
       CONFLICT RESOLUTION 15, No. 3:281-97, Sept. 1971.

412   Shubik, Martin
       The dollar auction game: a paradox in non-cooperative
       behavior and escalation.   JOURNAL OF CONFLICT RESOLUTION
       15, No. 1:109-111, March 1971.

413   Shubik, Martin
       Game theory, behavior, and the paradox of the Prisoner's
       Dilemma: three solutions. JOURNAL OF CONFLICT RESOLUTION
       14, No. 2:181-93, June 1970.

414   Singer, J. David
       The correlates of war project. WORLD POLITICS 24, Jan. 1972.

415   Singer, J. D. and Wallace, M.
       Intergovernmental organization and the preservation of peace,
       1816-1964:   some   bivariate   relationships.   INTERNATIONAL
       ORGANIZATION 24, No. 3:20-47, 1970.

416   Singer, J. D. and Small, M.
      Formal alliances, 1816-1965: an extension of the basic
      data. JOURNAL OF PEACE RESEARCH 3:257-82, 1969.

417   Singer, J. David
      The correlates of war project: interim report and rationale.
      WORLD POLITICS 24, No. 2:243-70, Jan. 1972.

418   Siverson, Randolph M.
      International conflict and perceptions of injury: the case
      of the Suez crisis. INTERNATIONAL STUDIES QUARTERLY 14,
      No. 2:157-65, June 1970.

419   Siverson, Randolph M.
      Role and perception in international crises: the cases
      of Israeli and Egyptian decision makers in national capitals
      and the United Nations. INTERNATIONAL ORGANIZATION 27,
      No. 3:329-45, Summer 1973.

420   Small, Melvin and Singer, J. David
      Formal alliances, 1816-1965: an extension of the basic
      data. JOURNAL OF PEACE RESEARCH No. 3:257-82, 1969.

421   Small, Melvin and Singer, J. David
      The diplomatic importance of states, 1816-1970: an extension
      and refinement of the indicator. WORLD POLITICS 25, No.
      4:577-99, July 1973.

422   Sloan, T.
      Dyadic linkage politics in Lebanon. JOURNAL OF PEACE SCIENCE
      3, No. 2:147-58, 1978.

423   Sloan, T.
      The association between domestic and international conflict
      hypothesis revisited. INTERNATIONAL INTERACTIONS 4, No.
      1:3-32, 1977.

424   Smith, William P. and Emmons, Timothy D.
      Outcome information and competitiveness in interperson
      bargaining. JOURNAL OF CONFLICT RESOLUTION 13, No. 2:262-70,
      June 1969.

425   Smoker, Paul
      International relations simulations. PEACE RESEARCH REVIEWS
      3, No. 6, 1970.

426   Smoker, Paul
      A time series analysis of Sino-Indian relations. JOURNAL
      OF CONFLICT RESOLUTION 13, No. 2:172-91, June 1969.

427   Snyder, Glenn H.
      Prisoner's Dilemma and "chicken" models in international
      politics. INTERNATIONAL STUDIES QUARTERLY 15, No. 1:66-103,
      March 1971.

428 Stefflre, V.
     Long-term forecasting and the problem of large-scale wars.
     FUTURES, Aug. 1974, pp. 302-08.

429 Stein, A.
     Conflict and cohesion: a review of the literature. JOURNAL
     OF CONFLICT RESOLUTION 20, No. 1:143-72, 1976.

430 Stegenga, James A.
     Peacekeeping: post-mortems   or   previews?   INTERNATIONAL
     ORGANIZATION 27, No. 3:373-85, Summer 1973.

431 Stohl, M.
     War and domestic political violence: the case of the United
     States 1890-1970. JOURNAL OF CONFLICT RESOLUTION 19, No.
     3:379-416, 1975.

432 Sunkel, Osvaldo
     Big business and "dependencia": a Latin American view.
     FOREIGN AFFAIRS 50, No. 3:517-31, April 1972.

433 Tanter, R.
     Dimensions of conflict behavior within and between nations,
     1958-60. JOURNAL OF CONFLICT RESOLUTION 10, No. 1:41-64,
     1966.

434 Tanter, Raymond
     The policy relevance of models in world politics. JOURNAL
     OF CONFLICT RESOLUTION 16, No. 4:555-83, Dec. 1972.

435 Teitelbaum, Michael S.
     Population and development: is a consensus possible? FOREIGN
     AFFAIRS 52, No. 4, 1974.

436 Terhune, Kenneth W. and Firestone, Joseph M.
     Global war, limited war and peace: hypotheses from three
     experimental worlds. INTERNATIONAL STUDIES QUARTERLY 14,
     No. 2:195-218, June 1970.

437 Terrell, Louis M.
     Societal stress, political instability, and levels of military
     efforts. JOURNAL OF CONFLICT RESOLUTION 15, No. 3:329-46,
     Sept. 1971.

438 Thompson, William R.
     The regional subsystem: a conceptual explication and a
     propositional inventory. INTERNATIONAL STUDIES QUARTERLY
     17, No. 1:89-117, March 1973.

439 Underdal, Arild
     Multinational negotiation parties: the case of the European
     community. COOPERATION AND CONFLICT 8, Nos. 3/4:173-82,
     1973.

440 van Benthem van den Berg, Gottfried
     Theory or taxonomy? Some critical notes on Johan Galtung's
     "A structural theory of imperialism." JOURNAL OF PEACE
     RESEARCH No. 1:77-86, 1972.

441 Vasquez, J.
     Statistical findings in international politics: a data-based
     assessment. INTERNATIONAL STUDIES QUARTERLY 20, No.
     2:171-218, 1976.

442 Vincent, Jack E. and Schwerin, Edward W.
     Ratios of force and escalation in a game situation. JOURNAL
     OF CONFLICT RESOLUTION 15, No. 4:489-511, Dec. 1971.

443 Voevodski, J.
     Quantitative analysis of nations at war. PEACE RESEARCH
     REVIEWS 3, No. 5:1-63, 1969.

444 Voevodski, J.
     Quantitative behavior of warring nations. JOURNAL OF
     PSYCHOLOGY 72:269-92, 1968.

445 Voevodski, J.
     Crises waves: the growth and decline of war-related
     behavioral events. JOURNAL OF PSYCHOLOGY, March 1972, p.
     289-308.

446 Wallace, Donnel and Rothaus, Paul
     Communication, group loyalty, and trust in the PD game.
     JOURNAL OF CONFLICT RESOLUTION 13, No. 3:370-80, Sept. 1969.

447 Wallace, M.
     Power, status and international war. JOURNAL OF PEACE
     RESEARCH 8, No. 1:23-35, 1971.

448 Wallace, Michael
     The radical critique of peace research: an interpretation
     and evaluation. PEACE RESEARCH REVIEWS 4, 1972.

449 Warren, Roland
     The conflict intersystem and the change agent. JOURNAL
     OF CONFLICT RESOLUTION 8, No. 3, Sept. 1964.

450 Wehr, Paul, ed.
     Peace research and study in North America. INTERNATIONAL
     PEACE RESEARCH NEWSLETTER 11, No. 3, 1973.

451 Weston, B. H., ed.
     Peace education, Special issue of the BULLETIN OF PEACE
     PROPOSALS 10, No. 4, 1979.

452 Wilkenfeld, J.
     Some further findings regarding the domestic and foreign
     conflict behavior of nations. JOURNAL OF PEACE RESEARCH
     6, No. 2:147-56, 1969.

453   Wilkenfeld, J.
Domestic and foreign conflict behavior of nations. JOURNAL
OF PEACE RESEARCH 5, No. 1:56-69, 1968.

454   Williams, R.
Conflict and social order: a research strategy for complex
propositions. JOURNAL OF SOCIAL ISSUES 28, No. 1:11-26,
1972.

455   Wilson, Warner
Cooperation and the cooperativeness of the other player.
JOURNAL OF CONFLICT RESOLUTION 13, No. 1:110-17, March 1969.

456   Wilson, Warner
Reciprocation and other techniques for inducing cooperation
in the Prisoner's Dilemma game. JOURNAL OF CONFLICT
RESOLUTION 15, No. 2:167-96, June 1971.

457   Wolf, Peter
International organization and attitude change: a
re-examination of the functionalist approach. INTERNATIONAL
ORGANIZATION 27, No. 3:347-71, Summer 1973.

458   Wright, Q.
The escalation of international conflicts. JOURNAL OF
CONFLICT RESOLUTION 9:434-49, 1965.

459   Yalem, Ronald J.
Controlled communication and conflict resolution. JOURNAL
OF PEACE RESEARCH Nos. 3/4:263-72, 1971.

III. BIBLIOGRAPHIC SUBJECT INDEX

PART IV
DIRECTORY OF
INFORMATION
SOURCES

I. UNITED NATIONS INFORMATION SOURCES

AUDIO MATERIALS LIBRARY
United Nations, Department of Public Information, Radio and Visual
Services Division, United Nations Plaza, New York, NY 10017.

DAG HAMMARSKJOLD LIBRARY
United Nations, Department of Conference Services, United Nations
Plaza, New York, NY 10017.

UNITED NATIONS BIBLIOGRAPHIC INFORMATION SYSTEM
United Nations, Department of Conference Services, Dag Hammarskjold
Library, United Nations Plaza, New York, NY 10017.

UNBIS DATA BASE
United Nations, Department of Conference Services, Dag Hammarskjold
Library, United Nations Plaza, New York, NY 10017.

DEVELOPMENT INFORMATION SYSTEM
United Nations, Department of International Economic and Social
Affairs, Information Systems Unit, Room DC 594, New York, NY
10017.

DEVELOPMENT INFORMATION SYSTEM DATA BASE
United Nations, Department of International Economic and Social
Affairs, Information Systems Unit, Room DC 594, New York, NY
10017.

UNITED NATIONS CENTRE FOR DISARMAMENT INFORMATION SYSTEM
United Nations, Department of Political and Security Council
Affairs, United Nations Centre for Disarmament, New York, NY
10017.

UNITED NATIONS PHOTO LIBRARY
United Nations, Department of Public Information, Radio and Visual
Services Division, United Nations Plaza, New York, NY 10017.

UNITED NATIONS VISUAL MATERIALS LIBRARY
United Nations, Department of Public Information, Radio and Visual Services Division, United Nations Plaza, New York, NY 10017.

RESEARCH AND REFERENCE COLLECTION
United Nations Office at Geneva, Geneva Unit of the Centre for Disarmament, 8-14 avenue de la Paix, Palais des Nations, 1211 Geneva 10, Switzerland.

UNITED NATIONS LIBRARY AT GENEVA
United Nations Office at Geneva, 8-14 avenue de la Paix, Palais des Nations, 1211 Geneva 10, Switzerland.

UNITAR LIBRARY
United Nations Institute for Training and Research, 801 United Nations Plaza, New York, NY 10017.

II. BIBLIOGRAPHY OF BIBLIOGRAPHIES

ANNOTATED BIBLIOGRAPHY OF COUNTRY SERIALS is a listing of periodicals, annuals and other serials containing information of economic, business or trade interest. The listing is organized on a regional and country basis. Copies are available from the Documentation Service, International Trade Centre UNCTAD/GATT, 1211 Geneva 10, Switzerland.

BASIC-NEEDS APPROACH: A SURVEY OF ITS LITERATURE, edited by M. Rutjes, contains a brief analysis of the concept of basic needs, its targets, its strategy and implications, followed by a concise bibliography related to the topic. Copies may be obtained from the Centre for the Study of Education in Developing Countries, Badhuisweg 251, The Hague, The Netherlands.

DEVELOPMENT PLANS AND PLANNING - BIBLIOGRAPHIC AND COMPUTER AIDS TO RESEARCH, by August Schumacher, is arranged in three parts. The first contains more than 100 selected bibliographies on development plans and planning, the second is concerned with a new source of empirical materials for the development planner - the automated documentation centre, and the third analyzes recent work on computer aids for the research library. The publication is available from Seminar Press Ltd., 24-28 Oval Road, London NW1, England.

BIBLIOGRAPHY ON DEVELOPMENT EDUCATION lists books, manuals, resource materials, magazines, and articles in the field of development education. The listing was prepared by the Dutch Central Bureau of Catholic Education. Copies are available from the Central Bureau of Catholic Education, G. Verstijnen, Secretary Foreign Department, Bezuidenhoutseweg 275, The Hague, Netherlands.

BIBLIOGRAPHY OF GERMAN RESEARCH ON DEVELOPING COUNTRIES, prepared by the German Foundation for International Development, is divided into two sections: Part A contains an index of research institutes, author index, subject-matter index, and a geographical index. Part B contains specific information on each of the studies listed. The text is in German with explanatory notes in German, English, French and Spanish. Copies may be obtained from the Deutsche Stiftung fur Internationale Entwicklung (DSE), Endenicher Strasse 41, 53 Bonn, Federal Republic of Germany.

BIBLIOGRAPHY OF SELECTED LATIN AMERICAN PUBLICATIONS ON DEVELOPMENT is a listing of over 200 titles in Latin American development literature, including subject and author indexes. The document was prepared by the Institute of Development Studies Library. Copies are available from the Librarian, Institute of Development Studies, University of Sussex, Brighton BN1 9RE, England.

CANADIAN DEVELOPMENT ASSISTANCE: A SELECTED BIBLIOGRAPHY 1950-70, compiled by Shirley B. Seward and Helen Janssen, covers Canada's foreign aid programs and policies from 1950 to 1970. Copies are available from the Distribution Unit, International Development Research Centre, P.O. Box 8500, Ottawa, Canada KIG 3H9.

DEVINDEX CANADA is a bibliography of literature on social and economic development in Third World countries, which originated in Canada in 1975. Copies may be obtained from the International Development Research Centre, Box 8500, Ottawa, Canada KIG 3H9.

The UNESCO Division of Scientific Research and Higher Education has compiled **A DIRECTORY AND BIBLIOGRAPHY ON THE THEME "RESEARCH AND HUMAN NEEDS"**, listing organizations, journals, newsletters, reports and papers, information services and data banks. The bibliographical section includes headings such as food and nutrition, health, housing and sanitation, environment, energy, technology. For copies contact "Research and Human Needs", Division of Scientific Research and Higher Education, UNESCO, Place de Fontenoy, 75007 Paris, France.

GUIDE TO CURRENT DEVELOPMENT LITERATURE ON ASIA AND THE PACIFIC is published every two months by the Library and Documentation Centre of the Asia Pacific Development Information Service. For more information write to the Centre, United Nations Asian and Pacific Development Institute, P.O. Box 2-136, Sri Ayudhya Road, Bangkok, Thailand.

Hald, Marjorie W.
A SELECTED BIBLIOGRAPHY ON ECONOMIC DEVELOPMENT AND FOREIGN AID, rev. ed., Santa Monica, CA: The Rand Corporation, 1958.

Hazelwood, Arthur
THE ECONOMICS OF "UNDERDEVELOPED" AREAS: AN ANNOTATED READING LIST OF BOOKS, ARTICLES, AND OFFICIAL PUBLICATIONS. London: Oxford University Press for the Institute of Colonial Studies, 1954. 623 titles.

THE ECONOMICS OF DEVELOPMENT: AN ANNOTATED LIST OF BOOKS AND ARTICLES PUBLISHED 1958-1962. London: Oxford University Press, for the Institute of Commonwealth Studies, 1964.

INTERNATIONAL BIBLIOGRAPHY, INFORMATION DOCUMENTATION (IBID) provides bibliographic details and annotations necessary to identify the full range of publications prepared by the United Nations and its related agencies, plus those of ten organizations outside the UN system. IBID is published quarterly by Unipub. Available from Unipub, Box 433, Murray Hill Station, New York, New York 10016, USA.

THE 1978/79 PUBLICATIONS LIST OF THIRD WORLD PUBLICATIONS contains over 300 titles of pamphlets, books and teaching materials about the Third World. The listing is available from Third World Publications, Ltd., 151 Stratford Road, Birmingham B11 1RD, England.

A list of 200 books on **NORTH-SOUTH WORLD RELATIONS** has been compiled by the Developing Country Courier. The listing is organized by subject and region. For copies write to the Courier, P.O. Box 239, McLean, Virginia 22101, USA.

United States Agency for International Development
A PRACTICAL BIBLIOGRAPHY FOR DEVELOPING AREAS. Washington, D.C., 1966. 2 vols. (Vol. 1 - A selective, annotated and graded list of United States publications in the social sciences. 202 pp.) (Vol. 2 - A selective, annotated and graded list of United States publications in the physical and applied sciences. 332 pp.)

PUBLIC ADMINISTRATION--A SELECT BIBLIOGRAPHY, prepared by the British Ministry of Overseas Development Library is the second supplement to the 1973 revised edition. Copies may be obtained from Eland House, Stag Place, London SW1E 5DH, England.

PUBLIC ADMINISTRATION--A SELECT BIBLIOGRAPHY, prepared by the Library of the British Ministry of Overseas Development, is a supplement to the revised edition which appeared in 1973. It includes material published in the period 1972-1975 with 1,600 references. Copies may be obtained from the Library, British Ministry of Overseas Development, Eland House, Stag Place, London SW1E 5DH, England.

The OECD Development Centre has gathered together in the catalog **PUBLICATION AND DOCUMENT, 1962-1979** all the books and documents it has published since its establishment in 1962 up to August 1979. Copies available from OECD Development Centre, 94 rue Chardon Lagache, 75016 Paris, France.

REGISTER OF RESEARCH PROJECTS IN PROGRESS IN DEVELOPMENT STUDIES IN SELECTED EUROPEAN COUNTRIES was prepared by the Centre for Development Studies of the University of Antwerp at the request of the European Association of Development Research and Training Institutes. Copies are available from the Centre, St. Ignatius

Faculties, University of Antwerp, 13 Prinsstraat, 2000 Antwerp, Belgium.

Re Qua, Eloise and Statham, Jane
THE DEVELOPING NATIONS: A GUIDE TO INFORMATION SOURCES CONCERNING THEIR ECONOMIC, POLITICAL, TECHNICAL AND SOCIAL PROBLEMS. Detroit: Gale Research Company, 1965.

The East African Academy has published two new bibliographies. **SCIENCE AND TECHNOLOGY IN EAST AFRICA** contains more than 5,000 titles about research in the agriculture, medical technological, and related fields in East Africa, with short summaries on the problems and progress of research in these areas. **TANZANIA EDUCATION SINCE UHURU: A BIBLIOGRAPHY--1961-1971** was compiled by Dr. George A. Auger of the University of Dar es Salaam. Both publications are available from the East African Academy, RIPS, P.O. Box 47288, Nairobi, Kenya.

SELECTIVE ANNOTATED BIBLIOGRAPHY ON BRAZILIAN DEVELOPMENT has been prepared by the SID Sao Paulo Chapter. This first issue contains only references that have appeared in 1975. Copies are available from the Society for International Development, Sao Paulo Chapter, Caixa Postal 20.270-Vila Clementino, 04023-Sao Paulo-S.P. Brazil.

A SELECTED ANNOTATED BIBLIOGRAPHY: INDIGENOUS TECHNICAL KNOWLEDGE IN DEVELOPMENT, compiled by Liz O'Keefe and Michael Howes, is contained in the January 1979 IDS BULLETIN. This issue of the BULLETIN is devoted to the importance of indigenous technical knowledge in rural areas. Single copies of the BULLETIN are from the Communications Office, Institute of Development Studies, University of Sussex, Brighton N1 9RE, United Kingdom.

SELECTED BIBLIOGRAPHY OF RECENT ECONOMIC DEVELOPMENT PUBLICATIONS covers a period of one year, from July 1977 to June 1978 and contains two main sections, one for general and theoretical works, the other for literature related to regions and countries. For copies write to the Graduate Program in Economic Development, Vanderbilt University, Nashville, Tennessee 37235, USA.

International Bank for Reconstruction and Development; Economic Development Institute
SELECTED READINGS AND SOURCE MATERIALS ON ECONOMIC DEVELOPMENT. A list of books, articles, and reports included in a small library assembled by the Economic Development Institute, Washington, D.C., 1961.

SOCIAL AND ECONOMIC DEVELOPMENT PLANS - MICROFICHE PROJECT is a cumulative catalogue listing the holdings of Inter Documentation Company AG on social and economic development plans around the world. About 1400 plans from over 180 countries are included. Copies of the catalogue and other catalogues of IDC's microfiche projects are free on request from Inter Documentation Company AG, Poststrasse 14, 6300 Zug-Switzerland.

Powelson, John
A SELECT BIBLIOGRAPHY ON ECONOMIC DEVELOPMENT.   Boulder, Colorado:
Westview Press, 1979.

THIRD WORLD BIBLIOGRAPHY AND RESOURCE GUIDE features a wide range
of material on Third World issues.   It is designed for students
and general readers.   Copies may be obtained from the Development
Education Library Project, c/o OSFAM/Ontario, 175 Carlton Street,
Toronto, Canada.

The United Nations Asian and Pacific Development Institute has
prepared a **SPECIAL BIBLIOGRAPHY ON ALTERNATIVE STRATEGIES FOR
DEVELOPMENT WITH FOCUS ON LOCAL LEVEL PLANNING AND DEVELOPMENT**
in connection with a UNAPDI meeting, held in Bangkok, October
31 - November 4, 1978.   Copies are available from the APDI Library
and Documentation Centre.   UNAPDI, P.O. Box 2-136, Sri Ayudhya
Road, Bangkok, Thailand.

Vente, Role and Dieter Seul
MACRO-ECONOMIC   PLANNING: A   BIBLIOGRAPHY.   Nomos
Verlagsgesellshaft, Baden-Baden, 1970.

Volunteers in Technical Assistance (VITA) has published its 1979
CATALOGUE OF BOOKS, BULLETINS AND MANUALS.   The listing contains
VITA documents related to appropriate technology, as well as
materials published by other development organizations around
the world.   Copies are available from VITA, 2706 Rhode Island
Avenue, Mt. Ranier, Maryland   20822, USA.

DEVELOPMENT--A BIBLIOGRAPHY, was compiled by Vaptistis-Titos
Patrikios (Rome: FAO, 1974) and updates the first edition,
published in 1970, to cover the 1970/73 period.   Contains eight
sections relating to development: theories and problems;
perspectives of the Third World countries; population and food
production; aid, trade and international cooperation; agriculture;
manpower and employment; education; and environment.   A ninth
section lists bibliographies.

III. DIRECTORY OF PERIODICALS

ACTUEL DEVELOPPEMENT, English Digest Edition, Paris.

AFRICA, London, Africa Journal, Ltd.

AFRICA INSTITUTE, Pretoria, Africa Institute.

AFRICA QUARTERLY, New Delhi, India Council for Africa.

AFRICA RESEARCH BULLETIN, Exeter, Eng. Africa Research, Ltd.

AFRICA, SOUTH OF THE SAHARA, London, Europa Publications.

AFRICA TODAY, New York, American Committee on Africa.

AFRICAN AFFAIRS, London, Journal of the Royal African Society.

AFRICAN DEVELOPMENT, London.

AFRICAN DEVELOPMENT BANK, Annual Report, Ibadan.

AFRICAN ENVIRONMENT, Dakar, United Nations Environmental Program.

AFRICAN STATISTICAL YEARBOOK, Addis Ababa, Economic Commission for Africa.

AFRICAN STUDIES REVIEW, Stanford, Boston, East Lansing, African Studies Association.

AFRICAN URBAN STUDIES, East Lansing, Mich., African Studies Center.

AGENDA, Washington, D.C., U.S. Agency for International Development.

APPROPRIATE TECHNOLOGY, London, Intermediate Technology Publications, Ltd.

APPROTECH, Ann Arbor, Mich., International Association for the Advancement of Appropriate Technology for Developing Countries.

ARTHA VIJNANA, Poona, Gokhale Institute of Politics and Economics.

ASIA AND THE WORLD MONOGRAPHS, Taipei, Asia and the World Forum.

ASIA YEARBOOK, Hong Kong, Far Eastern Economic Review.

ASIAN AFFAIRS, London, Royal Central Asian Society.

ASIAN DEVELOPMENT BANK, Annual Report, Manila.

ASIAN REGIONAL CONFERENCE OF THE INTERNATIONAL LABOR ORGANIZATION, Proceedings, Geneva, ILO.

ASIAN SURVEY, Berkeley, Institute of International Studies.

BANGLADESH DEVELOPMENT STUDIES, Dhaka, Bangladesh Institute of Development Studies.

BANGLADESH ECONOMIC REVIEW, Dhaka, Bangladesh Institute of Development Economics.

BULLETIN OF INDONESIAN ECONOMIC STUDIES, Canberra, Dept. of Economics, Australian National University.

CEPAL REVIEW, Santiago, Chile.

CANADIAN JOURNAL OF AFRICAN STUDIES, Montreal, Loyola College.

COMMUNITY DEVELOPMENT JOURNAL, Manchester, U.K., Oxford University Press.

DEVELOPING ECONOMIES, Tokyo, The Institute of Asian Economic Affairs.

DEVELOPMENT, Rome, Society for International Development.

DEVELOPMENT CENTER STUDIES, OECD, Paris.

DEVELOPMENT AND CHANGE, Beverly Hills, Calif.: Sage Publications.

DEVELOPMENT CO-OPERATION, Paris, OECD.

DEVELOPMENT DIGEST, Washington, D.C., U.S. Agency for International Development.

DEVELOPMENT DIALOGUE, Uppsala, Sweden, Dag Hammarskjold Foundation.

EASTERN AFRICA ECONOMIC REVIEW, Nairobi, Oxford University Press.

ECONOMIC DEVELOPMENT AND CULTURAL CHANGE, Chicago, University of Chicago Press.

ETHIOPIAN JOURNAL OF DEVELOPMENT RESEARCH, Addis Ababa, Institute of Development Research.

FAR EASTERN ECONOMIC REVIEW, Hong Kong.

FINANCE AND DEVELOPMENT, Washington, D.C.

IDS BULLETIN, Institute of Development Studies, University of Sussex, U.K.

IMPACT OF SCIENCE ON SOCIETY, Paris, UNESCO.

INDIAN JOURNAL OF INDUSTRIAL RELATIONS, New Delhi, India.

INDUSTRY AND DEVELOPMENT, Vienna, UNIDO.

INTERNATIONAL DEVELOPMENT REVIEW, Rome, Society for International Development.

INTERNATIONAL LABOR REVIEW, Geneva, ILO.

INTERNATIONAL STUDIES QUARTERLY, San Francisco.

JOURNAL OF AFRICAN STUDIES, Los Angeles, UCLA African Studies Center.

JOURNAL OF DEVELOPING AREAS, Macomb, IL, Western Illinois Univ.

JOURNAL OF DEVELOPMENT ECONOMICS, Amsterdam, North Holland Publishing Co.

JOURNAL OF DEVELOPMENT STUDIES, London, U.K.

JOURNAL OF ECONOMIC DEVELOPMENT, JOURNAL OF INTERNATIONAL AFFAIRS, New York, Columbia University.

JOURNAL OF MODERN AFRICAN STUDIES, New York, Cambridge University Press.

LATIN AMERICAN RESEARCH REVIEW, Chapel Hill, North Carolina.

MODERN ASIAN STUDIES, New York, Cambridge University Press.

MONOGRAPH, DEVELOPMENT STUDIES CENTER, AUSTRALIAN NATIONAL UNIVERSITY.

MONOGRAPH, OVERSEAS DEVELOPMENT COUNCIL, Washington, D.C.

ODI REVIEW, Overseas Development Institute, London, U.K.

OXFORD ECONOMIC PAPERS, Oxford, U.K.

PAKISTAN DEVELOPMENT REVIEW, Karachi, Pakistan.

PUBLIC ADMINISTRATION AND DEVELOPMENT, Sussex, U.K., Royal Institute of Public Administration.

THIRD WORLD QUARTERLY, London, Third World Foundation for Social and Economic Studies.

WORLD BANK STAFF WORKING PAPER, IBRD, Washington, D.C.

WORLD DEVELOPMENT, Pergamon Press, N.Y.

NOTE:

For more information on relevant periodicals please consult:

1. **DIRECTORY OF UNITED NATIONS INFORMATION SYSTEMS**

2. **REGISTER OF UNITED NATIONS SERIAL PUBLICATIONS**

Public by **Inter-Organization Board for Information Systems,** IOB Secretariat, Palais des Nations, CH-1211 Geneva 10, Switzerland.

IV. RESEARCH INSTITUTIONS

INTERNATIONAL

AFRICAN INSTITUTE FOR ECONOMIC DEVELOPMENT AND PLANNING
United Nations, Economic Commission for Africa. B. P. 3186
Dakar, Senegal.

ASPAC CULTURAL AND SOCIAL CENTER
ASPAC, Pension Building, P. O. Box 3129. Yongdungpo. Seoul,
Korea.

ASSOCIATION MONDIALE POUR L'ECOLE COMME INSTRUMENT DE PAIX
27, rue des Eaux-Vivas. 1207-Geneva, Switzerland.

ATLANTIC INSTITUTE FOR INTERNATIONAL AFFAIRS
120 rue de Longchamp. 75016 Paris, France.

CHRISTIAN PEACE CONFERENCE
Jungmannova 9. 11121 Prague 1, Czechoslovakia.

CLUB OF ROME
Via Giorgione 163. 00147 Rome, Italy.

COMMISSION OF THE CHURCHES ON INTERNATIONAL AFFAIRS
Central Office: 150 Route de Ferney. 1211 Geneva, Switzerland.

COMMITTEE ON SOCIETY, DEVELOPMENT AND PEACE
Ecumenical Centre. 150 Route de Ferney. 1211 Geneva 20,
Switzerland.

CONSEJO LATINOAMERICANO DE INVESTIGACION PARA LA PAZ
Apartado Postal 20-105. Mexico D. F., Mexico.

COUNCIL FOR THE DEVELOPMENT OF ECONOMIC AND SOCIAL RESEARCH IN
AFRICA
B. P. 3304. Dakar, Senegal.

EUROPEAN ASSOCIATION OF DEVELOPMENT RESEARCH AND TRAINING
INSTITUTES
Karntnerstrasse 25/6. A-1010 Vienna, Austria.

EUROPEAN CO-ORDINATION CENTRE FOR RESEARCH AND DOCUMENTATION
IN SOCIAL SCIENCES
Grunangergasse 2. P.O. Box 974. A 1011, Vienna, Austria.

FACULTAD LATINOAMERICANA DE CIENCIAS SOCIALES
Casilla 249o/c. Central. Buenos Aires, Argentina.

FEDERACION DE UNIVERSIDADES DE AMERICA CENTRAL Y PANAMA
12 Calle 2-04. Zona 9, Edificio Plaza del Sol. 50 Nivel Oficina
408, Guatemala.

INSTITUTE OF INTERNATIONAL LAW
82 Avenue du Castel. 1200 Brussels, Belgium.

INSTITUTE ON MAN AND SCIENCE/INTERNATIONAL
Rensselaerville. New York 12147, U.S.A.

INSTITUTO LATINOAMERICANO DE ESTUDIOS TRANSNACIONALES
Apartado Postal 85-025. Mexico 20, D.F., Mexico.

INTERNATIONAL ASSOCIATION OF EDUCATORS FOR WORLD PEACE
P.O. Box 3282. Blue Springs Station. Huntsville, Alabama 35810.

INTERNATIONAL CONFEDERATION FOR DISARMAMENT AND PEACE
6 Endsleigh Street. London, W.C. 1, United Kingdom.

INTERNATIONAL FELLOWSHIP OF RECONCILIATION
Hof van Sonoy. Veerstraat 1. 1811 LD Alkmaar, Netherlands.

INTERNATIONAL FOUNDATION FOR DEVELOPMENT ALTERNATIVES
2 place du Marche. 1260 Nyon, Switzerland.

INTERNATIONAL INSTITUTE FOR PEACE
Mollwaldplatz 5. A-1040 Vienna, Austria.

INTERNATIONAL INSTITUTE FOR STRATEGIC STUDIES
18 Adam Street. London WC2N 6AL, United Kingdom.

INTERNATIONAL PEACE ACADEMY
777 United Nations Plaza, New York, N.Y. 10017.

INTERNATIONAL PEACE BUREAU
41 rue de Zurich, 1201 Geneva, Switzerland.

INTERNATIONAL PEACE RESEARCH ASSOCIATION
c/o Tampere Peace Research Institute. Tammelanpuistokatu 58
BV KR, P.O. Box 70, 33101 Tampere 10, Finland.

NORDIC COOPERATION COMMITTEE FOR INTERNATIONAL POLITICS, INCLUDING
CONFLICT AND PEACE RESEARCH

Swedish Institute of International Affairs. Lilla Nygatan 23, S-111 28 Stockholm, Sweden.

PAX CHRISTI-INTERNATIONAL CATHOLIC MOVEMENT FOR PEACE
International-Secretary, Celebesstraat 60, B.P. 85627.   The Hague 2011, Netherlands.

PEACE RESEARCH INSTITUTE-DUNDAS
25 Dundana Ave., Dundas, Ontario L9H 4E5, Canada.

PEACE SCIENCE SOCIETY-INTERNATIONAL
c/o Graduate Group in Peace Science, Mcneill Building, 3718 Locust Street, University of Pennsylvania, Philadelphia, Pennsylvania 19174, U.S.A.

SOCIETE EUROPEENNE DE CULTURE
San Marco 2516, 30124 Venice, Italy.

STOCKHOLM INTERNATIONAL PEACE RESEARCH INSTITUTE
Sveavagen 156, S-11345 Stockholm, Sweden.

TRANSNATIONAL INSTITUTE
Paulus Potterstraat 20, 1971 DA Amsterdam, Netherlands.

UNITED NATIONS DISARMAMENT CENTER
UN Building, 325 Third Avenue, New York, New York, 10022, U.S.A.

UNITED NATIONS EDUCATIONAL , SCIENTIFIC AND CULTURAL ORGANIZATION.
DIVISION OF HUMAN RIGHTS AND PEACE
7 Place de Fontenoy, 75700 Paris, France.

UNITED NATIONS INSTITUTE FOR TRAINING AND RESEARCH
801 United Nations Plaza, New York, N.Y., U.S.A.

UNIVERSITIES AND THE QUEST FOR PEACE
State University of New York at Binghamton, Binghamton, New York 13901, U.S.A.

VIENNA INSTITUTE FOR DEVELOPMENT
Karntner Strasse 25, A-1010 Vienna, Austria.

WAR RESISTERS' INTERNATIONAL
3 Caledonian Road, London, N. 1, United Kingdom.

WOMEN'S INTERNATIONAL LEAGUE FOR PEACE AND FREEDOM
Rue de Varembe, 1211 Geneve 20, Switzerland.

WORLD FUTURE STUDIES FEDERATION
Casella Postale 6203, Rome Prati, Italy.

WORLD PEACE COUNCIL
Lonnrotinkatu 25 A 6 Krs.   00180 Helsinki 18, Finland.

WORLD PEACE THROUGH LAW CENTER

400 Hill Building, Washington D.C., 20006, U.S.A.

ALGERIA

CENTRE DE RECHERCHES EN ECONOMIE APPLIQUEE D'ALGER
20, rue Chahid Khalef Moustapha, Ben Aknoun, Algiers, Algeria.

ARGENTINA

CENTRO DE INVESTIGACIONES EN CIENCIAS SOCIALES
Entre Rios 101-6 B. Buenos Aires, Argentina.

INSTITUTO FORCUATO DI TELLA
11 de Septiembre 2133, Buenos Aires, Argentian.

AUSTRALIA

STRATEGIC AND DEFENCE STUDIES CENTRE
Research School of Pacific Studies, Australian National University.
P.O. Box 4, Canberra, Australia.

AUSTRIA

ARBEITSGEMEINSCHAFT OSTERREICHISCHER FRIEDENSVEREINE
Wilhelm-Exner Gasse 34, 1090 Vienna IX, Austria.

OSTERREICHISCHE GESELLSCHAFT FUR AUSSENPOLITIK UND INTERNATIONALE
BEZIEHUNGEN
Josefsplatz 6, 1010 Vienna, Austria.

UNIVERSITATSZENTRUM FUR FRIEDENSFORSCHUNG
Schottenring 21, A 1010 Vienna, Austria.

BELGIUM

CENTER FOR DEVELOPMENT STUDIES
University of Antwerp, Department of Economics, Prinsstraat 13.
B-2000 Antwerp, Belgium.

CENTRE DE RECHERCHE SUR LA PAIX
Place Montesquieu 1, Louvain-la-Neuve, B-1348, Belgium.

CENTRE DE SOCIOLOGIE DE LA GUERRE
Institut de Sociologie, Universite Libre de Bruxelles, 44, Avenue
Jeanne, Brussels 1050, Belgium.

CENTRE D'ETUDE DES ORGANISATIONS
Institut de Sociologie, Universite Libre de Bruxelles, 44, Avenue
Jeanne, Brussels 5, Belgium.

CENTRUM VOOR POLEMOLOGIE VAN VRIJE UNIVERISTEIT BRUSEL
Pleinlaan 2, 1050 Brussels, Belgium.

COLLEGE VOOR DE ONTWIKKELINGSLANDEN, RIJKSUNIVERSITAIR CENTRUM
ANTWERPEN

424 Directory of Information Sources

A. Goemarerelei 52, B-2020 Antwerp, Belgium.

INSTITUUT VOOR CONFLICTSTUDIE
Handelsbeurs, Twaalfmaandenstraat, Antwerpen, Belgium.

BRAZIL

CENTRO BRASILEIRO DE ANALISE ET PLANEJAMENTO
Alameda Campinas, 463/138 Andar, CEP 0104, Brazil.

DEPARTAMENTO DE CIENCIA POLITICA-FACULDADE DE FILOSOFIA E CIENCIAS
HUMANAS DE UNIVERSIDADE FEDERAL DE MINAS GERAIS
Ura Carangola, 288-3 anda, 30.000 Belo Horizonte, Minas, Brazil.

INSTITUTO DE ESTUDOS BRASILEIROS
Universidade de Sao Paulo, C.P. 11.154, 01000 Sao Paulo, Brazil.

BULGARIA

RESEARCH INSTITUTE FOR FOREIGN POLICY
21 Moskovska, Sofia, Bulgaria.

CANADA

CANADIAN INSTITUTE OF INTERNATIONAL AFFAIRS
15 King's College Circle, Toronto, Ontario M5S 2V9, Canada.

CANADIAN PEACE RESEARCH AND EDUCATION ASSOCIATION
25 Dundana Avenue, Dundas, Ontario L9H 4E5, Canada.

CANADIAN PEACE RESEARCH INSTITUTE
119 Thomas Street, Oakville, Ontario L6J 3AJ, Canada.

CENTRE QUEBECOIS DE RELATIONS INTERNATIONALES
Universite Laval, Faculte des Sciences Sociales, Quebec G1K 7P4,
Canada.

CONRAD GREBEL COLLEGE INSTITUTE FOR PEACE AND CONFLICT STUDIES
University of Waterloo, Waterloo, Ontario, Canada.

INSTITUT DE RECHERCHES POLITIQUES
3535 Chemin Queen Mary, Bureau 514, Montreal, Quebec H3V 1HS,
Canada.

INSTITUTE OF INTERNATIONAL RELATIONS
University of British Columbia, Vancouver 8, Canada.

LATIN AMERICAN RESEARCH UNIT
P.O. Box 673, Adelaide St., Toronto 1, Canada.

CHILE

INSTITUTO DE ESTUDIOS INTERNACIONALES
University of Chile, Avda, Condell 249, Santiago, Casilla 14187,
Correo 21, Chile.

COLOMBIA

CORPORACION INTEGRAL PARA EL DESARROLLO CULTURAL Y SOCIAL
Carrera 21 no. 56-33, Apartado aereo 20439, Bogota, Colombia.

INSTITUTO DE INVESTIGACIONES DE LA UNIVERSIDAD LA GRAN COLOMBIA
Cra. 6a. NO. 13-40, Oficina 207, Bogota, D.E., Colombia.

CZECHOSLOVAKIA

USTAV MEZINARODNICH VZTAHU
Nerudova 3, Mala Strana, Prague 1, Czechoslovakia.

DENMARK

CENTER FOR UDVIKLINGSFORSKNING
Ewaldsgade 7-9, DK-2200 Copenhagen N, Denmark.

DANISH PEACE RESEARCH GROUP
Roanebaervej 90 A., 2840 Holte, Denmark.

KOBENHAVNS UNIVERSITETS INSTITUT FOR SAMFUNDSFAG
Rosenborggade 15, 1130 Copenhagen K, Denmark.

FINLAND

DEPARTMENT OF JOURNALISM AND MASS COMMUNICATIION, UNIVERSITY
OF TAMPERE
P.O. Box 507, 33101 Tampere 10, Finland.

DEPARTMENT OF POLITICAL SCIENCE, UNIVERSITY OF TAMPERE
P.O. Box 607, SF-33101, Tampere 10, Finland.

FINNISH PEACE RESEARCH ASSOCIATION
c/o Rurku Peace Research Group, P.O. Box 229, SF-20101, Turku
AO, Finland.

HELSINGIN YLIIOPISTO KEHITYSMAAINSTITUUTTI
Unioninkatu 10 B, SF-20170, Helsinki 17, Finland.

HELSINGIN YLIOPISTON YLEISEN VALTO-OPIN LAITOS
Hallituskatu 11-13, SF-00100 Helsinki 10, Finland.

RAUHAN-JA KONFLINKTINTURKIMUSLAITOS
Tammelanpuistokatu 58 B, 33100 Tampere 10, Finland.

TURKU PEACE RESEARCH GROUP
P.O. Box 229, SF-20101, Turku 10, Finland.

ULKOPOLIITTINEN INSTITUUTTI UTRIKESPOLITISKA INSTITUTET
Museokatu 18 a 9, SF-00100 Helsinki 10, Finland.

FRANCE

ASSOCIATION FRANCAISE POUR LA PAIX UNIVERSELLE
12, Rue Dohis, 94300 Vincennes, France.

CENTRE DE RECHERCHE D'ETUDES SUR LES SOCIETES
Faculte de Droit, Avenue Robert-Schuman, 13621 Aix-en-Provence, France.

CENTRE D'ETUDE DES RELATIONS INTERNATIONALES
Fondation Nationale des Sciences Politiques, 27, rue Saint Guillaume, 75007 Paris, France.

CENTRE D'ETUDES DE POLITIQUE ETRANGERE
6, rue Ferrus, 75014 Paris, France.

GROUPE DE SOCIOLOGIE DE LA DEFENSE DE L'ECOLE DES HAUTES ETUDES EN SCIENCE SOCIALE
Ecole des Hautes Etudes en Sciences Sociales, 54, Bd. Raspail, 75006 Paris, France.

INSTITUT DE RECHERCHE ECONOMIQUE ET DE PLANIFICATION
BP 47 X, 38020 Grenoble Cedex, France.

INSTITUT DU DROIT DE LA PAIX ET DU DEVELOPPEMENT
Universite de Nice, 34 Avenue R. Schuman, 06000 Nice, France.

INSTITUT FRANCCAIS DE POLEMOLOGIE
Hotel National des Invalides, (Escalier M. 4e etage, Bureau 10). 129 rue de Grenelle, 75007 Paris, France.

MOUVEMENT CONTRE LE RACISME, L'ANTISEMITISME ET POUR LA PAIX
120 rue Saint-Denis, 75002 Paris, France.

GERMAN DR

INSTITUT FUR INTERNATIONALE BEZIEHUNGEN
August-Bebel Strasse 89, 1502 Potsdam Babelsberg, Germany (Democratic Republic).

GERMANY FR

ANTIMILITARISMUS INFORMATION
Leibnizstr, 80, D-1000 Berlin 12, Germany (Federal Republic).

ARBEITSGEMEINSCHAFT FRIEDENSFORSCHUNG, INSTITUT FUR POLITIKWISSENSCHAFT, UNIVERSITAT TUBINGEN
Brunnenstrasse 30, D-7400 Tubingen 1, Germany (Federal Republic).

ARBEITSGEMEINSCHAFT FUR FRIEDENS-UND KONFLIKTFORSCHUNG E.V.
Konigstrasse 47, 53 Bonn, Germany (Federal Republic).

ARBEITSGEMEINSCHAFT FUR KONFLIKT-UND FRIEDENSFORSCHUNG AM INSTITUT FUR POLITISCHE WISSENSCHAFT
Universitat Heidelberg, Hauptstrasse 52, D-69 Heidelberg, Germany (Federal Republic).

GERMAN PEACE SOCIETY
Rellinghauser   Street,   214,   D-4300   Essen,   Germany   (Federal
Republic).

INDIA

CENTER FOR STUDIES IN PEACE AND NON-VIOLENCE
Sri Venkateswara University, Tirupati-517502, India.

CENTRE FOR THE STUDY OF DEVELOPING SOCIETIES
29 Rajpur Road, Delhi 110054, India.

DEPARTMENT OF SOCIOLOGY, UNIVERSITY OF RAJASTHAN
Jaipur-4, Rajasthan, India.

GANDHI PEACE FOUNDATION
221/223 Deen Dayal Upadhyaya Marg, New Delhi-110001, India.

GANDHIAN INSTITUTE OF STUDIES
P.O. Box 116, Rajghat, Varanasi-1, India.

INDIAN COUNCIL OF PEACE RESEARCH
223 Deen Dayal Upadhyaya Marg, New Delhi, India.

INDIAN COUNCIL OF WORLD AFFAIRS
Sapru House, Barakhamba Road, New Delhi 110001, India.

INDIAN SCHOOL OF INTERNATIONAL STUDIES
35 Ferozeshah Road, New Delhi 1, India.

INSTITUTE OF CULTURAL RELATIONS AND DEVELOPMENT STUDIES
63 F Block, Sujan Singh Park, New Delhi-3, India.

INSTITUTE OF GANDHIAN THOUGHT AND PEACE STUDIES
University of Allanhabad, Allahabad, Uttar Pradesh, India.

PEACE RESEARCH CENTER
Gujarat Vidyapith, Ahmedabad 380014, India.

ISRAEL

CENTER FOR STRATEGIC STUDIES
Tel-Aviv University, Tel-Aviv, Israel.

DAVID HOROWITZ INSTITUTE FOR THE RESEARCH OF DEVELOPING COUNTRIES
Tel-Aviv University, Ramat-Aviv, Israel.

INSTITUTE FOR SOCIO-PSYCHOLOGOCAL RESEARCH
P.O. Box 104, Givatayim, Israel.

ISRAELI INSTITUTE OF INTERNATIONAL AFFAIRS
P.O. Box 17027, Tel-Aviv 61170, Israel.

LEONARD DAVIS INSTITUTE FOR INTERNATIONAL RELATIONS
Hebrew University, Givat Ram. Jerusalem, Israel.

MIDDLE EAST PEACE INSTITUTE
ZP.O. Box 1777, Tel-Aviv, Israel.

ITALY

INTERNATIONAL SCHOOL ON DISARMAMENT AND RESEARCH ON CONFLICTS
c/o C. Schaerf, Istituto di Fisica, Universita Degli Studi,
Piazzele Delle Scienze, 5, 00100 Rome, Italy.

ITALIAN PEACE RESEARCH INSTITUTE
c/o Centro Comunitario Materdei, Largo S. Gennaro a Materdei
3a, Naples 80136, Italy.

JAMAICA

PEACE, ACTION, DEVELOPMENT AND FRIENDSHIP CENTRE
12c Pouyatt St., Jones Town, Kingston 12, Jamaica.

JAPAN

DEPARTMENT OF INTERNATIONAL RELATIONS, UNIVERSITY OF TOKYO
3-8-1 Komaba, Meguro-ku, Tokyo 153, Japan.

INSTITUTE FOR WORLD AFFAIRS, KYOTO SANGYO UNIVERSITY
Room 201 Noguchi Hideyo Kinenkaikan, 26 Daikyo-cho, Shinjuku-ku,
Tokyo 160, Japan.

INSTITUTE OF INTERNATIONAL RELATIONS FOR ADVANCED STUDIES OF
PEACE AND DEVELOPMENT IN ASIA
Sophia University, 7 Kioi-cho, Chiyoda-ku, Tokyo 102, Japan.

JAPAN INSTITUTE OF INTERNATIONAL AFFAIRS
19th Mori Bodg., 40-2 Shiba-Kotohira-cho, Minato-ku, Tokyo, Japan.

PEACE STUDIES ASSOCIATION OF JAPAN
Department of Political Science and Economics, Waseda University,
1-6-1 Nishi-Shinjuku, Tokyo 160, Japan.

MALTA

JOHN XXIII PEACE LABORATORY
Hal Far Malta, Malta.

NETHERLANDS

DEVELOPMENT RESEARCH INSTITUTE
Hogeschoollan 225, Tilburg, Netherlands.

FOUNDATION RESHAPING THE INTERNATIONAL ORDER
P.O. Box 299, NL-3003 AG Rotterdam, Netherlands.

JOHN F. KENNEDY INSTITUTE
Center for International Studies, Hogeschoollaan 225, Tilburg,
Netherlands.

NEW ZEALAND

NEW ZEALAND FOUNDATION FOR PEACE STUDIES
CPO Box 4110, Auckland 1, New Zealand.

NEW ZEALAND INSTITUTE OF INTERNATIONAL AFFAIRS
P.O. Box 195, Wellington, New Zealand.

NIGERIA

NIGERIAN INSTITUTE OF INTERNATIONAL AFFAIRS
Kofo Abayomi Road, Victoria Island, G.P.O. Box 1727, Lagos,
Nigeria.

PEACE RESEARCH INSTITUTE OF NIGERIA
c/o Department of Political Science, University of Nigeria, Nsukka,
Nigeria.

NORWAY

CHRISTIAN MICHELSEN INSTITUTE - DEVELOPMENT RESEARCH AND ACTION
PROGRAMME
Fantoftv, 38, N-5036 Fantoft, Norway.

PAKISTAN

DEPARTMENT OF INTERNATIONAL RELATIONS
University of Karachi, Karachi 32, Pakistan.

SRI LANKA

MARGA INSTITUTE
61, Isipathasa Mawatha, (P.O. Box 601), Colombo 5, Sri Lanka.

SWEDEN

DEPARTMENT OF PEACE AND CONFLICT RESEARCH, UNIVERSITY OF GOTHENBURG
Viktoriagatan 30, 41135 Gothenburg, Sweden.

RESEARCH POLICY PROGRAM
University of Lund, Magistratsvagen 55N III, S-222 44 Lund, Sweden.

TRINIDAD AND TOBAGO

TRINIDAD AND TOBAGO INSTITUTE OF INTERNATIONAL AFFAIRS
14 St. Vincent Street, Port-of-Spain, Trinidad and Tobago.

UK

CENTRE FOR THE ANALYSIS OF CONFLICT
University College of London, 4 Endsleigh Gardens, London WCI,
United Kingdom.

CONFLICT RESEARCH UNIT, LONDON SCHOOL OF ECONOMICS AND POLITICAL
SCIENCE

13 Endsleigh Street, London WCI, United Kingdom.

INSTITUTE OF DEVELOPMENT STUDIES
University of Sussex, Falmer, Brighton BNI 9RE, Sussex, United Kingdom.

J. D. BERNAL PEACE LIBRARY
70 Great Russel Street, London WCI B 3BN, United Kingdom.

LENTZ FOUNDATION
c/o The Programme of Peace and Conflict Research. The University of Lancaster, Bailrigg, Lancaster, United Kingdom.

NATIONAL PEACE COUNCIL
29 Great James St., London WCIN 3ES, United Kingdom.

OVERSEAS DEVELOPMENT GROUP
University of East Anglia, Norwich NR4 7TJ, United Kingdom.

PEACE AND CONFLICT RESEARCH PROGRAMME
University of Lancaster, Lancaster, United Kingdom.

PUGWASH CONFERENCES ON SCIENCE AND WORLD AFFAIRS
9 St. Russell Mansions, 60 Gt. Russell St., London WCIB 3BE, United Kingdom.

RICHARDSON INSTITUTE FOR CONFLICT AND PEACE RESEARCH
Department of Politics, University of Lancaster, Fylde College, Bailrigg, Lancaster LAI 4YF, United Kingdom.

ROYAL INSTITUTE OF INTERNATIONAL AFFAIRS
Chatham House, 19 St. James's Square, London SW1Y 4LE, United Kingdom.

SCHOOL OF PEACE STUDIES
University of Bradford, Bradford, Yorkshire, BD7 1DP, United Kingdom.

SCIENCE POLICY RESEARCH UNIT
University of Sussex, Mantell Building, Brighton BNI 9RF, United Kingdom.

USA

AD HOC COMMITTEE FOR PEACE STUDIES
Horace Mann School, Riverdale, New York 10471, U.S.A.

ALTERNATIVES, INC.
1924 E. Third, Bloomington, Indiana 47401, U.S.A.

AMERICAN ETHICAL UNION
2 West 64th Street, New York, N.Y. 10023, U.S.A.

AMERICAN FRIENDS SERVICE COMMITTEE PEACE STUDIES PROGRAM
980 N. Fair Oaks Ave., Pasadena, California 91103, U.S.A.

AMERICAN UNIVERSITIES FIELDSTAFF, INC.
P.O. Box 150, Hanover, New Hampshire 03755, U.S.A.

ARMS CONTROL ASSOCIATION
11 Dupont Circle, Washington, D.C., 20036, U.S.A.

ASSEMBLY OF BEHAVIORAL AND SOCIAL SCIENCES
2101 Constitution Avenue, Washington D.C. 20418, U.S.A.

AVILA COLLEGE PEACE INSTITUTE
11901 Wornall Road, Kansas City, Missouri 64145, U.S.A.

BROOKINGS INSTITUTION
1775 Massachusetts Ave., N.W., Washington, D.C. 20036, U.S.A.

BUREAU OF SOCIAL SCIENCE RESEARCH
1990 M Street, N.W. Washington, D.C. 20036, U.S.A.

CALIFORNIA SEMINAR ON ARMS CONTROL AND FOREIGN POLICY
P.O. Box 925, Santa Monica, California 90406, U.S.A.

CARNEGIE ENDOWMENT FOR INTERNATIONAL PEACE
United Nations Plaza at 46th Street, New York, N.Y. 10017, U.S.A.

CENTER FOR CONFLICT RESOLUTION
University of Wisconsin, 731 State Street, Madison, Wisconsin
53703, U.S.A.

CENTER FOR DEFENSE INFORMATION
122 Maryland Ave., NE. Washington, D.C. 20002, U.S.A.

CENTER FOR INTERNATIONAL AFFAIRS
Harvard University, 6 Divinity Ave., Cambridge, Massachusetts
02138, U.S.A.

CENTER FOR INTERNATIONAL STUDIES
Massachusetts Institute of Technology, 30 Waisworth Street,
Cambridge, Massachusetts 02139, U.S.A.

CENTER FOR INTERNATIONAL STUDIES, NEW YORK UNIVERSITY
New York University School of Law, Room 4400, 40 Washington Square
South, New York, N.Y. 10003, U.S.A.

CENTER FOR NONVIOLENT CONFLICT RESOLUTION
Haverford College, Haverford, Pennsylvania 19041, U.S.A.

CENTER FOR PEACE AND CONFLICT STUDIES
Wayne State University, Detroit, Michigan, U.S.A.

CENTER FOR PEACE STUDIES, GEORGETOWN UNIVERSITY
No. 2 O'Gara, Georgetown University, Washington, D.C. 20057,
U.S.A.

CENTER FOR PEACE STUDIES, UNIVERSITY OF AKRON
University of Akron, Akron, Ohio 44325, U.S.A.

CENTER FOR PEACEFUL CHANGE
Kent State University, Stopher Hall, Kent, Ohio 44242, U.S.A.

CENTER FOR THE STUDY OF ARMAMENT AND DISARMAMENT
California State College, 5151 State College Drive, Los Angeles,
California 90032, U.S.A.

CENTER FOR THE STUDY OF POWER AND PEACE
110 Maryland Avenue N.E., Washington D.C. 20002, U.S.A.

CENTER FOR WAR/PEACE STUDIES
218 East 18th Street, New York, N.Y. 10003, U.S.A.

CENTER OF INTERNATIONAL STUDIES, PRINCETON UNIVERSITY
Princeton University, 118 Corwin Hall, Princeton, New Jersey
08540, U.S.A.

COALITION FOR A NEW FOREIGN AND MILITARY POLICY
120 Maryland Ave. NE. Washington, D.C. 20002, U.S.A.

COMMITTEE ON CONFLICT STUDIES
Graduate University of Washington, 268 Condon Hall, Seattle,
Washington 98105, U.S.A.

CONFERENCE ON PEACE RESEARCH IN HISTORY
Dept. of History, University of Toledo, 2801 W. Bancroft Street,
Toledo, Ohio 43606, U.S.A.

CONSORTIUM ON PEACE RESEARCH, EDUCATION AND DEVELOPMENT
Bethel College, North Newton, Kansas 67117, U.S.A.

CORRELATES OF WAR PROJECT
Mental Health Research Institute, University of Michigan, Ann
Arbor, Michigan 48109, U.S.A.

COUNCIL ON FOREIGN RELATIONS
Harold Pratt House, 58 East 68th Street, New York, N.Y. 10021,
U.S.A.

COUNCIL ON INTERNATIONAL AND PUBLIC AFFAIRS, INC.
60 East 42nd Street, New York, N.Y. 10017, U.S.A.

DEPARTMENT OF POLITICAL SCIENCE, YALE UNIVERSITY
3532 Yale Station, New Haven Connecticut 06520, U.S.A.

DIMENSIONALITY OF NATIONS PROJECT
University of Hawaii, 2500 Campus Road, Honolulu, Hawaii 96822,
U.S.A.

EAST-WEST CENTER
1777 East-West Road, Honolulu, Hawaii 96848, U.S.A.

FOREIGN POLICY RESEARCH INSTITUTE
3508 Market Street, Suite 350, Philadelphia, Pennsylvania 19104,
U.S.A.

FUND FOR PEACE
1865 Broadway, New York, N.Y. 10023, U.S.A.

GLOBAL EDUCATION ASSOCIATES
552 Park Avenue, East Orange, New Jersey 07017, U.S.A.

HAROLD SCOTT QUIGLEY CENTER OF INTERNATIONAL STUDIES
University of Minnesota, 1246 Social Sciences Building, 267 19th
Avenue South, Minneapolis, Minnesota 55455, U.S.A.

HOOVER INSTITUTION ON WAR, REVOLUTION AND PEACE
Stanford University, Stanford, California 94305, U.S.A.

HUDSON INSTITUTE
Quaker Ridge Road, Croton-on-Hudson, N.Y. 10520, U.S.A.

INSTITUTE FOR EDUCATION IN PEACE AND JUSTICE
3700 West Pine, St. Louis, Missouri 63108, U.S.A.

INSTITUTE FOR FOOD AND DEVELOPMENT POLICY
2588 Mission Street, San Francisco, California 94110, U.S.A.

INSTITUTE FOR POLICY STUDIES
1901 Q Street, N.W., Washington, D.C. 20009, U.S.A.

INSTITUTE FOR WORLD ORDER
1140, Avenue of the Americas, New York, N.Y. 10036, U.S.A.

INSTITUTE OF BEHAVIORAL SCIENCES
University of Colorado, Boulder, Colorado 80302, U.S.A.

INSTITUTE OF COMMUNICATIONS RESEARCH
University of Illinois, 1207 West Oregon, Urbana, Illinois 61801,
U.S.A.

INSTITUTE OF INTERNATIONAL STUDIES (UNIVERSITY OF CALIFORNIA)
University of California, 2538 Channing Way, Berkeley, California
94720, U.S.A.

INSTITUTE OF WAR AND PEACE STUDIES
Columbia University, 420 West 118 Street, New York, N.Y. 10027,
U.S.A.

INTERNATIONAL AFFAIRS CENTER
Indiana University, 703 E 7th Street, Bloomington, Indiana 47401,
U.S.A.

INTERNATIONAL ORGANIZATION FOR THE STUDY OF GROUP TENSIONS INC.
7 West 96th Street, Room 170, New York, N.Y. 10025, U.S.A.

INTERNATIONAL STUDIES
211 Longfellow Hall, Harvard University, Cambridge, Massachusetts, 02138, U.S.A.

INTERNATIONAL STUDIES ASSOCIATION
University Center for International Studies, University of Pittsburgh, Pittsburgh, Pennsylvania 15260, U.S.A.

INTER-UNIVERSITY SEMINAR ON ARMED FORCES AND SOCIETY
University of Chicago, Box 46, 1126 East 59th Street, Chicago, Illinois 60637, U.S.A.

JANE ADDAMS PEACE ASSOCIATION
345 East 45 Street, New York, N.Y. 10017, U.S.A.

MERSHON CENTER
199 West 10th Avenue, Columbus, Ohio 43201, U.S.A.

MISSOURI PEACE STUDY INSTITUTE
Ecumenical Center, 813 Maryland Avenue, Columbia, Missouri 65201, U.S.A.

NATIONAL ACTION/RESEARCH ON THE MILITARY INDUSTRIAL COMPLEX
c/o American Friends Service Committee, 1501 Cheany St., Philadelphia, Pennsylvania 19102, U.S.A.

NORTH AMERICAN CONFERENCE ON LATIN AMERICA
P.O. Box 57, Cathedral Station, New York, N.Y. 10025, U.S.A.

PATH INSTITUTE OF RESEARCH ON INTERNATIONAL PROBLEMS
46-393 Holopu Place, Kaneohe, Hawaii 96744, U.S.A.

PEACE AND CONFLICT STUDIES PROGRAM, EARLHAM COLLEGE
Earlham College, Richmond, Indiana 47374, U.S.A.

PEACE AND WORLD ORDER STUDIES
Colgate University, Hamilton, N.Y. 13346, U.S.A.

PEACE RESEARCH LABORATORY
438 North Skinker, St. Louis, Missouri 63130, U.S.A.

PEACE RESEARCH ORGANIZATION FUND
First National Bank Building, Denver, Colorado 80202, U.S.A.

PEACE SCIENCE UNIT, UNIVERSITY OF PENNSYLVANIA
University of Pennsylvania, Philadelphia, Pennsylvania 19174, U.S.A.

PEACE STUDIES INSITUTE AND PROGRAM IN CONFLICT RESOLUTION
Manchester College, North Manchester, Indiana 46962, U.S.A.

PEACE STUDIES INSTITUTE, MANHATTAN COLLEGE
Manhattan College PKWY. Bronx, New York, N.Y. 10471, U.S.A.

PEACE STUDIES PROGRAM
Cornell University, Uris Hall, Ithaca, New York 14850, U.S.A.

PEACE STUDIES PROGRAM, BETHEL COLLEGE
N. Newton, Kansas 67117, U.S.A.

PROGRAM IN NONVIOLENT CONFLICT AND CHANGE
Syracuse University, 249 Physics Building, Syracuse, N.Y. 13210,
U.S.A.

RULE OF LAW RESEARCH CENTER
Law School at Duke University, Durham, North Carolina 27706,
U.S.A.

SOCIETY FOR SOCIAL RESPONSIBILITY IN SCIENCE
221 Rockhill Road, Bala-Cynwyd, Pennsylvania 19004, U.S.A.

SOCIETY FOR THE STUDY OF SOCIAL PROBLEMS
208 Rockwell Hall, State University College, 1300 Elmwood Ave.,
Buffalo, N.Y. 14222, U.S.A.

STANLEY FOUNDATION
Stanley Building, Muscatine, Iowa 52761, U.S.A.

UNITED STATES ARMS CONTROL AND DISARMAMENT AGENCY
320 21st Street, N.W., Washington D.C. 20451, U.S.A.

WASHINGTON CENTER OF FOREIGN POLICY RESEARCH
John Hopkins University, 1740 Masachusetts Ave., N.W. Washington
D.C. 20036, U.S.A.

WORLD PEACE FOUNDATION
40 Mt. Vernon Street, Boston, Massachusetts 02108, U.S.A.

USSR

COMMISSION ON SCIENTIFIC ASPECTS OF DISARMAMENT OF THE PRAESIDIUM
OF THE ACADEMY OF SCIENCES OF THE USSR
Leninski Prospekt 14, Moscow, U.S.S.R.

DISARMAMENT COMMISSION OF THE SOVIET PEACE COMMITTEE
Ulitsa Kropotkina 10, Moscow, U.S.S.R.

ECONOMIC COMMISSION OF THE SOVIET PEACE COMMITTEE
Ulitsa Kropotkina 10, Moscow, U.S.S.R.

INSTITUTE OF STATE AND LAW OF THE ACADEMY OF SCIENCES OF THE
USSR
Frunze 10, Moscow, U.S.S.R.

INSTITUTE OF WORLD ECONOMICS AND INTERNATIONAL RELATIONS OF THE
ACADEMY OF SCIENCES OF THE USSR
Jaroslavskaja ul, 13, Moscow, U.S.S.R.

SCIENTIFIC COUNCIL OF THE ACADEMY OF SCIENCES OF THE U.S.S.R.
ON ECONOMIC COMPETITION OF THE TWO SYSTEMS
13 Yaroslavskaya Street, Moscow I-243, U.S.S.R.

YUGOSLAVIA

INTER-UNIVERSITY CENTRE OF POSTGRADUATE STUDIES, DUBROVNIK
Frana Bulica 4, YU-50000 Dubrovnik, Yugoslavia.

Appendix

INDUSTRIALIZED COUNTRIES

Australia
Austria
Belgium
Canada
Denmark
Finland
France
Germany, Fed. Rep. of
Iceland
Ireland
Italy
Japan
Luxembourg
Netherlands
New Zealand
Norway
South Africa
Sweden
Switzerland
United Kingdom
United States

DEVELOPING COUNTRIES BY INCOME GROUP
(Excluding Capital Surplus Oil Exporters)

High Income (over $2500)

American Samoa
Bahamas
Bermuda
Brunei
Canal Zone
Channel Islands
Faeroe Islands
French Polynesia
Gabon
Gibraltar
Greece
Greenland
Guam
Israel
Martinique
New Caledonia
Oman
Singapore
Spain
Venezuela
Virgin Islands (U.S.)

Upper Middle Income ($1136-2500)

Argentina
Bahrain
Barbados
Brazil
Cyprus
Djibouti
Fiji

French Guiana
Guadeloupe
Hong Kong
Iran
Iraq
Isle of Man
Lebanon
Malta
Netherlands Antilles
Panama
Portugal
Puerto Rico
Reunion
Romania
Surinam
Trinidad & Tobago
Uruguay
Yugoslavia

Intermediate Middle Income ($551-1135)

Algeria
Antigua
Belize
Chile
China, Rep. of
Colombia
Costa Rica
Dominica
Dominican Republic
Ecuador
Ghana
Gilbert Islands
Guatemala
Ivory Coast
Jamaica
Jordan
Korea, Rep. of
Macao
Malaysia
Mauritius
Mexico
Namibia
Nicaragua
Paraguay
Peru
Seychelles
St. Kitts-Nevis
St. Lucia
Syrian Arab Rep.
Trust Territory of the Pacific
   Islands
Tunisia
Turkey

Lower Middle Income ($281-550)

Angola
Bolivia
Botswana
Cameroon
Cape Verde
Congo, P.R.
El Salvador
Equatorial Guinea
Grenada
Guyana
Honduras
Liberia
Mauritania
Morocco
New Hebrides
Nigeria
Papua New Guinea
Philippines
Rhodesia
Sao Tome & Principe
Senegal
St. Vincent
Sudan
Swaziland
Thailand
Tonga
Western Samoa
Zambia

Low Income ($280 or less)

Afghanistan
Bangladesh
Benin
Bhutan
Burma
Burundi
Cambodia
Central African Empire
Chad
Comoros
Egypt
Ethiopia
Gambia, The
Guinea
Guinea-Bissau
Haiti
India
Indonesia
Kenya
Lesotho
Madagascar
Malawi

Maldives
Mali
Mozambique
Nepal
Niger
Pakistan
Rwanda
Sierra Leone
Solomon Islands
Somalia
Sri Lanka
Tanzania
Togo
Uganda
Upper Volta
Viet Nam
Yemen Arab Rep.
Yemen P.D.R.
Zaire

**CAPITAL SURPLUS OIL EXPORTING
DEVELOPING COUNTRIES**

Kuwait
Libya
Qatar
Saudi Arabia
United Arab Emirates

CENTRALLY PLANNED COUNTRIES

Albania
Bulgaria
China, People's Rep. of
Cuba
Czechoslovakia
German Dem. Rep.
Hungary
Korea, Dem. Rep. of
Lao People's Dem. Rep.
Mongolia
Poland
U.S.S.R.

Index

About the Editor

Pradip K. Ghosh is President of the World Academy of Development and Cooperation, Washington, D.C. and Adjunct Associate Professor and Visiting Fellow at the Center for International Development at the University of Maryland, College Park. He is the author of *Thinking Sociology* and *Land Use Planning,* and editor of the International Development Resource Books series for Greenwood Press.